voices of revolution

voices of revolution
rebels and rhetoric

thomas e hachey
ralph e weber

marquette university

The Dryden Press Inc.
Hinsdale, Illinois

Library of Congress Catalog Card Number: 72-90705
ISBN: 0-03-089173-6
Printed in the United States of America
2345 090 987654321

For Jane and Rosemarie

preface

So often in historical accounts, great revolutionary leaders and writers appear without their works and rhetoric. Rather, these men and occasional women are briefly described in their historical setting, and a perfunctory summary is given of their contribution. Aware of this, we have sought out the ideas, speeches, and writings of the major world revolutionaries over the last two hundred years. The selections which follow contain their evaluation of society and their visions of the world which should be. Many of the selections also reveal the deep anger and frustration which these revolutionaries experienced.

Those interested in the course of revolution, those curious about the rhetorical approach to major protest, those in the disciplines of history, political science, sociology, and English may find in this book the outstanding figures whose ideas, ideals, and visions helped to change a ruler, or a society, or a civilization, or, finally, the world.

The vagaries of spelling and punctuation have been retained for the most part in order to preserve the style of the era or original manuscript. Obvious spelling errors in the original have been corrected.

We wish to acknowledge with deep appreciation the generous and prompt assistance given by many persons in preparing this book. All of the following helped in the preparation and research of this book: William Knowles, History Editor of the Dryden Press; Herman J. Viola, Editor, *Journal of the National*

Archives, and Thomas Gedosch at the National Archives; John McDonough, Waldon Moore, and James Roberts at the Library of Congress; and the following persons at the Marquette University Memorial Library: Elizabeth Devine, the Reverend John Philip Talmage, Harry Onufrock, and James Hansen. Through the work of the following, the manuscript was prepared for publication: Jane Hachey; Mary, Elizabeth, and Ralph A. Weber; Carol Kuechler, Carol Bergmann, Kathleen Connelly, Julie McMahon, Professor Roman Gawkoski, and Mark Mulvaney. We are also grateful for the useful advice we received from Joseph Marcey and Steve Stein; and for the moral support offered by Rosemarie Weber, and Margaret and Leo Hachey, over the years in which this work was brought to completion.

The libraries at the following universities generously made available rare copies of their holdings: University of California-Berkeley, Cornell University, University of Idaho, University of Illinois-Urbana, University of Kansas, Northwestern University, University of Wisconsin-Madison, University of Wisconsin-Milwaukee, University of Chicago, Harvard University, University of Michigan; together with the Center for Research Libraries in Chicago, and the Milwaukee Public Library.

Thomas E. Hachey
Ralph E. Weber
Milwaukee, Wisconsin
July 1972

contents

introduction

If a man does not keep pace with his companions, perhaps it is because he hears a different drummer. Let him step to the music which he hears, however measured or far away.

Henry David Thoreau

Revolution is the narcotic of modern history. Under its compelling and hypnotic spell, men have altered destiny and entire nations have experienced delirious convulsions in transcending the spirit of their times. Frequently, revolution has left a people socially disoriented, emotionally traumatized, psychologically scarred, and spiritually disillusioned. Occasionally, it has liberated them psychically, physically, and politically.

It is difficult to distinguish illusion from reality in the revolutionary experience. Inspirational slogans often have generated myths which bear slight resemblance to the facts of history. "United we stand, divided we fall," "liberty, equality, and fraternity," "the proletarians have nothing to lose but their chains. They have a world to win. Working men of all countries, unite!" and "all power to the people," are a few of the watchwords which have mesmerized the multitudes. For some, the promise of the revolution became the reality, or at least partially so; for others, the dream became a nightmare.

Facile definitions of revolution have sometimes obscured the truth with idle generalizations and romantic incantations. "Revolutions are the festivals of the oppressed," or "revolutions are the locomotives of history," are two such examples from the literature of rebellion. Indeed, revolutions have toppled autocracies, broken the chains of tyranny, liberated the working classes, and more. But the American Protestant who rejoiced upon reading the Declaration of Independence may have wondered where the revolution was going when the United States made a treaty of alliance with Catholic France. Frenchmen who gleefully applauded the beheading of King Louis XVI, who for many symbolized the oppression of the *ancien régime*, probably reflected ruefully on the wisdom of their ecstasy during the frightening days of the "Reign of Terror." Russians who were enchanted by promises of "all land to the peasants" and "all factories for the workers" perhaps judged the privations of the past preferable to the forced regimentation and collectivization of Soviet life. Revolutions seldom, if ever, provide panaceas, and new grievances are sometimes substituted for old ones. The lesson of history is that revolutionary change has had both positive and negative features; that the radicalism of the revolutionary leadership opposed to the state frequently becomes reactionary when those leaders themselves control the state.

That the most crucial revolutionary processes are essentially political in nature is evidenced by the fact that their beginnings and their ends are themselves characteristically political: revolution begins with a political crisis and ends with a political settlement. Revolution is one of those emotion charged words which we invariably associate with "insurrection," "uprising," "rebellion," or "civil war." Almost always the word connotes violence or the use of armed force. And, indeed, most of the great revolutions of the past two centuries, the American, French, Russian, Chinese, and Cuban Revolutions, have been accompanied by much bloodshed. Yet the use of force or the resort to violence is not indigenous to revolutions in either political theory or in historic fact. A revolution may involve action in defiance of the law and yet be conducted without violence on the part of participants, as in the instance of the rebellion which Gandhi led in India by the method of civil disobedience.

All revolutions do have one common denominator: protest against prevailing authority. This authority may be the state, church, an economic system such as capitalism, a social institution such as the family, or an individual king, president, or dictator. Moreover, all revolutions introduce a fever, often called freedom, into the political affairs of empires, nations, or states; or into the social, cultural, or economic institutions of a given society, which may range from public morals or mores to racial rebellion, or from educational innovation to prison reform. Indeed, revolutions may serve as catalysts of change within the system or, alternately, may seek the complete overthrow of the system for reasons which may pertain to race, nationality, religion, economic status, or sex.

Revolutions can and do vary quite considerably in their nature and purpose. Romantic nationalism and middle class revolutions between 1789 ard 1900 have been succeeded by ideological and proletarian revolutions in the twentieth century. In the former, the slogans and rhetoric reflected egalitarian objectives which in practice were seldom fulfilled after the middle class had achieved its own ends. In the latter, the orientation has been toward either a completely "classless" society, or one in which the working class predominates. While political revolutions have frequently sought the reform of existing socio-economic, cultural, or religious institutions, their primary objective has been the redistribution of political power.

An objective which is therefore sought in every revolution is change from the *status quo,* although the manner of such change will differ according to the period. Revolutions in an earlier age were usually preceded by demands for the overthrow of oppressive monarchs, or for the national unification of a race or people. The twentieth century is the first to speak of "the revolution of rising expectations," or of a "war on poverty." The revolutionary protest against authority extends even to the dictionary itself.

Almost two hundred years ago, the American Revolution officially began with the Declaration of Independence. The most important characteristics of that Revolution included the idea that "consent of the governed" was crucial to good government. It should be noted that consent was not sought from women, Indians, slaves, and many unpropertied persons. Thus the reality of consent differed from the theory. The Revolution did, however, bring into practice some of the principles developed by John Locke and other early eighteenth century philosophers: that men have inalienable rights such as life, liberty, and the pursuit of happiness.

When American revolutionaries spoke of liberty, they meant it in political terms and did not, with one or two exceptions, apply it to the institution of slavery. In addition, the American Revolution did nothing to change the institution of private property. As the Revolution led to the Constitution, states retained the power over suffrage; too often that right extended only to those with property. Therefore, seen in the perspective of the last 200 years, the American Revolution, radical and daring for its time, was extremely moderate in both its aims and in its execution.

Revolution took a different turn in 1789. The French Revolution, like the American, was inspired by the tenets of the Enlightenment: rationalism, deism, and the idea of progress. But it was markedly different in its ideological tone. Both revolutions included internecine civil wars. In the American experience, however, monarchism versus republicanism was the central issue between loyalists and patriots, and opposing sides were not determined along strict socio-economic lines. By contrast, the French Revolution aligned the peasantry, the proletariat, and the bourgeoisie against the aristocracy. Moreover, the atrocities and terror of the French experience were much more intense than the American, fundamentally because it was a vicious class war in addition to being a political struggle.

Nineteenth century European revolutions were largely the product of continued class struggle and the growth of cultural and political nationalism. Some of the rebellions of the 1830's and 1840's derived from efforts to enfranchise a larger part of the bourgeois class; other revolutions of that century proceeded from the campaigns for national unification. It was during this period that Germany and Italy overcame their more stubborn disunity and emerged as nation-states. Formerly in the West, there had always been narrower allegiances—to municipality, guild, feudal lord, or the like—to compete with and divide the national loyalty of the individual. And there had also been wider allegiances—to the Holy Roman Empire, to a universal church, to the solidarity of an international aristocracy. By the third quarter of the nineteenth century, these older political loyalties were either dead or in decay. Nationalism became a religion for men like Louis Kossuth, Giuseppe Garibaldi, and Apolinario Mabini, and salvation for them took the form of revolution and the liberation of their homelands.

In many respects, industrialization had a greater influence in shaping the modern world than either the Enlightenment or the political revolutions. Industrialization depersonalized and, in some instances, dehumanized man. He lost his identity and his independence in the factory. The exploitation and abuses of capitalism gave rise to a reaction: socialism. In contradistinction to the bourgeois or nationalist revolutionaries of an earlier period, the socialist revolutionaries supported the rule of the working classes and control over the means and modes of production. Their expressed aim was not the abolition of private property, but rather the equitable distribution of it. Moderate socialists like William Morris, Pierre Proudhon, and Eugene V. Debs, anarchists like Mikhail Bakunin and Emma Goldman, and militant socialists like Karl Marx and Mao Tse-tung, each had his or her view of how this goal might best be achieved.

Although the first major revolution of the twentieth century erupted in Russia, subsequent revolutions have taken place in non-European worlds. Latin America, Asia, and Africa have been the scenes of violent protest against economic and/or political imperialism. These contemporary heartlands of revolution are seething with all of the volatile ingredients of emergent nationalism which once convulsed Europe; and they are being simultaneously subjected to the more recent revolutionary phenomenon of socialism.

A characteristic common to European, American, and Third World revolutionaries has been their determination either to free the oppressed or to secure the rights of minorities. Twentieth century proletarian and socialist revolutions were not the first to be concerned with the rights of women, or with those of minorities. But they did champion these causes more zealously than earlier revolutionaries, and often extended their appeal beyond the working classes to the poor and nonwhite races of the world. Final judgment on the achievements and consequences of these peculiarly different revolutionary experiences must await the further passage of time.

Revolutionary theorists and leaders included in this book, with one or two exceptions, wrote and published their ideas on revolution. Some were literary stylists, like Thomas Jefferson, William Morris, and Leo Tolstoy, while others were polemicists, like Leon Trotsky and Ernesto Che Guevara. Many of them gained their fame in history from their books, articles, resolutions, and newspaper accounts. Others are more memorable for their careers as revolutionary activists. All the revolutionaries viewed themselves as personally charged with a mission to effect change.

Revolutions too often have involved only surface changes, such as the transfer of power from one personality to another, or the replacement of one form of tyranny by another. But a vital or genuine revolution must be concerned with the triumph of human values and human rights. While there may be no common agreement on the means of achieving these ends among the revolutionaries included in this volume, all of them spoke and wrote about the essential needs of man and were exceedingly sensitive to the inequities surrounding them. Truly they marched to a "different drummer."

part one europe

maximilien robespierre
louis kossuth
giuseppe mazzini
giuseppe garibaldi
pierre proudhon
mikhail bakunin
karl marx
leo tolstoy
william morris
peter kropotkin
georges sorel
emmeline pankhurst
lenin
james connolly
leon trotsky

maximilien robespierre

Robespierre, a key figure during the period of the French Revolution and a leading member of both the Jacobin Club and the Committee of Public Safety, is most frequently associated with the "Reign of Terror" (1793-94) in France. Born at Arras on May 6, 1758, he was descended from a modest bourgeois family. His mother died when he was four years of age and shortly thereafter his father, an advocate who had gone bankrupt, deserted the family. Raised by grandparents, Robespierre attended a school conducted by the Oratorian order in Arras and later earned a scholarship to the College of Louis-le-Grand in Paris. A brilliant student, he matriculated in 1780, took a master's degree in law in 1781, and registered as an advocate at the Arras bar. He won admiration for his abilities, but his austerity and dedication isolated him from close companionships with either sex. Robespierre rapidly established a respected legal reputation and was appointed a judge in the Salle Épiscopale, a court with jurisdiction over the provostship of the diocese.

In the period following his return to Arras, Robespierre came under the influence of Rousseau's theories of democracy and deism. Already known as the advocate of the poor, he chastised the privileged classes, inveighed against royal absolutism, and decried arbitrary justice. Elected to the States-General of 1789, he labored for a time in obscurity but his influence in the Jacobin Club grew steadily and he soon became its president. Upon election to the Constituent

Assembly, Robespierre unsucessfully championed democratic elections and successfully backed a law which made members of the Constituent Assembly ineligible to the Legislative Assembly. Despite a weak voice and frail appearance (he was a slight man who stood only 5 feet 3 inches tall), Robespierre's biting rhetoric made him a forceful spokesman for his cause. He fought tenaciously for universal suffrage, for unrestricted entry to public offices and commissions, and for the right to petition. He opposed the veto, religious and racial discrimination and also defended actors, Jews, and blacks.

During the first two years of the French Revolution, Robespierre remained adamantly opposed to spreading revolution beyond the borders of France. He denounced the secret intrigues of the Court and of the royalists, their collusion with Austria, and the unpreparedness of the army. He violently attacked the marquis de Lafayette, the commander of the French Army, whom he suspected of wanting to establish a military dictatorship, but failed to obtain his dismissal and arrest. France's declaration of war against Austria and Prussia in April 1792 resulted in prompt military reverses for the French. A civil insurrection resulted which led to the formation of a new French assembly, the National Convention.

From the inception of the Convention in the latter part of September 1792, Robespierre, who was an elected representative of the Insurrectional Commune of Paris, condemned the majority Girondists for their inept direction of the war; the Girondists in turn accused Robespierre of seeking a personal dictatorship. The trial of King Louis XVI, which opened in December, heightened the conflict. Robespierre intervened eleven times during the course of the debates and his speech of December 3 (excerpts from this address follow) succeeded in rallying those who had been hesitant to kill the King.

But the execution of the King on January 21, 1793, did not resolve the struggle between the Girondins and the Jacobins; it only heightened passions on both sides. The treason of Girondist General Charles Dumouriez, who defected to the Austrian side in April, gave Robespierre the needed leverage to have the Convention suppress other Girondists during May and June, 1793. He was elected to a second Committee of Public Safety in July where his powers and prestige grew. The dangers of foreign invasion and the urgent need to maintain order and unity led the committee to inaugurate the "Reign of Terror." Although this was a collective effort, Robespierre's name is always most prominently associated with it. In order to clothe executive decrees with legitimacy, Robespierre, in what was also a tribute to the heroism of the soldiers in the French Army, asked the Convention in October 1793 to proclaim the Government of the Republic as the bona fide revolutionary government until peace was restored (excerpts from this speech follow).

Robespierre opposed both the extreme left, under Hébert, and the moderates led by Danton and Desmoulins, as evidenced by his address to the Convention on February 5, 1794 (excerpts from this speech also follow). The latter two had once been Robespierre's close comrades and it was with considerable reluctance that he ultimately supported their convictions and executions. Now faced by divisions within the Committee of Public Safety and no longer commanding the support of the independents who were a majority in the Convention, Robespierre found his position precarious. Perhaps most serious was the fact that he began to lose the support of the French people generally, whose hardships continued despite the recent French victories. It was precisely because the external threat from France's enemies no longer seemed as perilous that French people began to question the continued need for repressive measures at home.

Robespierre's motives and character have long been the subject of much debate. Some have considered him a ruthless dictator; others have judged him an idealistic champion of social revolution. It is now generally recognized that he did not make the Terror an instrument of personal ambition. To him, it was an expedient which was required for ruling in extraordinary circumstances. His courage, integrity, and devoted republicanism would seem to be above reproach.

Robespierre's address delivered before the Convention of July 26, 1794, was interpreted as presaging further purges and, on the following day, the forces of the right joined the independents in a dramatic rising which resulted in the arrest of Robespierre, his brother Augustin, and three close friends. On July 28, the Convention declared Robespierre to be an outlaw and ordered his execution. He was guillotined on the same evening on the Place de la Revolution (now the Place de la Concorde). Revolution was beginning to give way to reaction; and it had begun to devour its own children.

Asking the Death Penalty For Louis XVI

CITIZENS! Without its knowledge, the Constituent Assembly has been turned aside from its proper task. The point is not merely that of trying the King. Louis is not the accused. You are not the judges! You are—you cannot be other than statesmen, the representatives of the nation. You have not to give a judgment for

From "Speeches of Maximilien Robespierre," as reprinted in *Voices of Revolt*, International Publishers, New York, 1927, I, 46-47, 51. The trial of the King was opened by the Constituent Assembly (the Convention). In December 3, 1792, Robespierre delivered his first address on this subject.

or against an individual; on the contrary, you must adopt a measure of public welfare, achieve an act of national wisdom. In a republic, a dethroned king is a source of danger; he will either endanger the safety of the state and attempt to destroy liberty, or he will take steps to consolidate both.

... Our object should be to engrave deep in the hearts of men a contempt for royalty, and to terrify all the King's supporters.

... Louis was King and the Republic was founded. The question before you is disposed of by these few words alone. Louis was dethroned by his crimes. Louis denounced the French people as counter-revolutionaries; to conquer them he summoned the armies of the tyrants, his brothers. The victory and the masses have decided that it was he who was the rebel. Louis cannot be judged. He is already condemned, or we have no republic. To propose now that we begin to try Louis XVI would be equivalent to retracing our steps to royal or constitutional despotism. This is a counter-revolutionary idea, for it means nothing more nor less than to indict the Revolution itself. In fact, if it is still possible to make Louis the object of a trial, it is also possible he may be acquitted. He may be not guilty, nay, even more: it may be assumed, before the sentence is pronounced, that he has committed no crime. But if Louis may be declared guiltless, if Louis may go free of punishment, what will then become of the Revolution?

... Louis must die in order that the nation may live. In more peaceful times, once we have secured respect and have consolidated ourselves within and without, it might be possible for us to consider generous proposals. But to-day, when we are refused our freedom; to-day, when, after so many bloody struggles, the severity of the law as yet assails only the unhappy; to-day, when it is still possible for the crimes of tyranny to be made a subject of discussion; on such a day there can be no thought of mercy; at such a moment the people cry for vengeance. I request you to come to a decision at once concerning the fate of Louis. ... Louis XVI must at once be proclaimed by the National Assembly a traitor to the nation, a criminal against mankind, and the judgment must be carried out on the same square on which the great martyrs of freedom died on August 10.

Report on the Principles of a Revolutionary Government

CITIZENS, members of the Convention! Success induces the weak to sleep, but fills the strong with even more powers of resistance.

Let us leave to Europe and to history the task of lauding the marvels of Toulon, and let us arm for new victories of liberty!

The defenders of the Republic will be guided by Caesar's maxim, and believe that nothing has been accomplished so long as anything remains to be accomplished.

To judge by the power and the will of our republican soldiers, it will be easy to defeat the English and the traitors. But we have another task of no less importance, but unfortunately of greater difficulty. This task is the task of frustrating, by an uninterrupted excess of energy, the eternal intrigues of all enemies of freedom within the country, and of paving the way for the victory of the principles on which the general weal depends.

... The theory of the revolutionary government is as new as the Revolution itself, from which this government was born. This theory may not be found in the books of the political writers who were unable to predict the Revolution, nor in the law books of the tyrants. The revolutionary government is the cause of the fear of the aristocracy, or the pretext for its calumnies. For the tyrants this government is a scandal, for most people it is a miracle. It must be explained to all, so that at least all good citizens may be rallied around the principles of the general weal. . . .

The goal of a constitutional government is the protection of the Republic; that of a revolutionary government is the establishment of the Republic.

The Revolution is the war waged by liberty against its foes—but the Constitution is the regime of victorious and peaceful freedom.

The Revolutionary Government will need to put forth extraordinary activity, because it is at war. It is subject to no constant laws, since the circumstances under which it prevails are those of a storm, and change with every moment. This government is obliged unceasingly to disclose new sources of energy to oppose the rapidly changing face of danger.

Under constitutional rule, it is sufficient to protect individuals against the encroachments of the state power. Under a revolutionary regime, the state power itself must protect itself against all that attack it.

From *Voices of Revolt,* I, 61-70. On 19 Vendemiaire (October 10, 1793), Saint-Just demanded, in the name of the Committee of Public Safety, that the Convention proclaim the Government of the Republic as the revolutionary government up to the conclusion of peace. Robespierre delivered this speech in motivation of this innovation, with which Robespierre was commissioned by the Committee of Public Safety. The speech was then posted publicly in all parishes by the Convention and by the Club of the Jacobins, and was brought to the attention of the Army of the Republic at home and at the front.

The revolutionary government owes a national protection to good citizens; to its foes it owes only death. . . .

Is the revolutionary government, by reason of the greater rapidity of its course and the greater freedom of its movements than are characteristic of an ordinary government, therefore less just and less legitimate? No, it is based on the most sacred of all laws, on the general weal and on the ironclad law of necessity!

This government has nothing in common with anarchy or with disorder; on the contrary, its goal requires the destruction of anarchy and disorder in order to realize a dominion of law. It has nothing in common with autocracy, for it is not inspired by personal passions.

The measure of its strength is the stubbornness and perfidy of its enemies; the more cruelly it proceeds against its enemies, the closer is its intimacy with the republicans; the greater the severities required from it by circumstances, the more must it recoil from unnecessary violations of private interests, unless the latter are demanded by the public necessity. . . .

If we were permitted a choice between an excess of patriotism and a base deficiency in public spirit, or even a morass of moderation, our choice should soon be made. A healthy body, tormented by an excess of strength, has better prospects than a corpse.

Let us beware of slaying patriotism in the delusion that we are healing and moderating it.

By its very nature, patriotism is energetic and enthusiastic. Who can love his country coldly and moderately? Patriotism is the quality of common men who are not always capable of measuring the consequences of all their acts, and where is the patriot to be found who is so enlightened as never to err? If we admit the existence of moderates and cowards who act in good faith, why should there not also exist patriots in good faith, who sometimes err by excess of zeal? If, therefore, we are to regard all those as criminals who have exceeded the limits of caution in the revolutionary movement, we should be obliged to condemn equally the bad citizens, the enemies of the republic, as well as its enthusiastic friends, and should thus destroy the stoutest props of the Republic. There could be no other outcome than that the emissaries of tyranny would be our public prosecutors.

. . . The establishment of the French Revolution was no child's play; it cannot be the work of caprice and carelessness, nor can it be the accidental product of the coalition of all the individual demands and of the revolutionary elements. Wisdom and power created the universe. In assigning to men from your own midst the terrible task of watching over the destinies of our country, you have placed at their disposal your abilities and your confidence. If the revolutionary government is not supported by the intelligence and the patriotism and by the

benevolence of all the representatives of the people, where else should it draw
the strength enabling it to face the efforts of a united Europe on an equal plane?
The authority of the Constituent Assembly must be respected by all Europe.
The tyrants are exhausting the resources of their politics, and sacrificing their
treasures, in order to degrade this authority and destroy it. The National
Assembly, however, prefers its government to the cabinets of London and all the
other courts of Europe. Either we shall rule, or the tyrants will rule us. What are
the resources of our enemies in this war of treachery and corruption waged by
them against the Republic? All the vices fight for them; the Republic has all the
virtues on its side. The virtues are simple, poor, often ignorant, sometimes
brutal. They are the heritage of the unhappy, the possession of the people. Vice
is surrounded by all the treasures, armed with all the charms of voluptuousness,
with all the enticements of perfidy; it is escorted by all the dangerous talents
that have placed their services at the disposal of crime.

Great skill is shown by the tyrants in turning against us—not to mention our
passions and our weaknesses—even our patriotism! No doubt the germs of dis-
union which they sow among us would be capable of rapid dissemination if we
should not hasten to stifle them.

By virtue of five years of treason, by virtue of feeble precautions, and by
virtue of our gullibility, Austria, England, Russia and Italy have had time to set
up, as it were, a secret government in France, a government that competes with
the French government.

. . . Foreign courts have for some time been spewing out on French soil their
well-paid criminals. Their agents still infect our armies, as even our victory at
Toulon will show. All the bravery of our soldiers, all the devotion of our generals, and all the heroism of the members of this Assembly had to be put forth
to defeat treason. These gentlemen still speak in our administrative bodies, in the
various sections; they secure admission to the clubs; they sometimes may be
found sitting among us; they lead the counter-revolution; they lurk about us,
they eavesdrop on our secrets; they flatter our passions and seek even to influence our opinions and to turn our own decisions against us. . . . Blood has
flowed all over the country on their account, but we need this blood in the
struggle against the tyrants of Europe. . . . We are surrounded by their hired
assassins and their spies. We know this, we witness it ourselves, and yet they live!
The perfidious emissaries who address us, who flatter us—these are the brothers,
the accomplices, the bodyguard of those who destroy our crops, who threaten
our cities, massacre our brothers, cut down our prisoners. They are all looking
for a leader, even among us. Their chief interest is to incite us to enmity among
ourselves. If they succeed in this, this will mean a new lease of life for the
aristocracy, the hour of the rebirth of the Federalist plans. . . . We shall continue

to make war, war against England, against the Austrians, against all their allies. Our only possible answer to their pamphlets and lies is to destroy them. And we shall know how to hate the enemies of our country.

It is not in the hearts of the poor and the patriots that the fear of terror must dwell, but there in the midst of the camp of the foreign brigands, who would bargain for our skin, who would drink the blood of the French people.

. . . The conspirators are very numerous. It is far less necessary to punish a hundred unknown, obscure wretches, than to seize and put to death a single leader of the conspirators.

. . . It is not enough to terrify the enemies of our country; we must also aid its defenders.

We ask that favorable conditions be created for the soldiers who are fighting and dying for liberty.

The French army is not only a terror to the tyrants, it is the glory of humanity and of the nation. In their march to victory, our victorious warriors shout, "Long live the Republic!" They die under the swords of the foe, with the shout, "Long live the Republic!" on their lips; their last words are paeans to liberty, their last gasps are exclamations of homage to their country. If the leaders of the army were as valiant as our soldiers, Europe would have been defeated long ago.

Any measure adopted in favor of the army is an act of national gratitude. . . .

Report on the Principles of Public Morality

. . . Having for some time been led often enough by accidents, the representatives of the French people are now beginning to aspire to a political consistency permeated with a strong revolutionary character. Thus far we have been led rather by the storms of circumstances, by our love of the good, by our feeling for the needs of the fatherland, than by any precise theory.

What is the purpose, what is the goal for which we strive? We wish a peaceful enjoyment of freedom and equality, the rule of that eternal justice whose laws are graven not in marble or in stone, but in the hearts of all men. We wish a social order that shall hold in check all base and cruel passions, which shall awaken to life all benevolent and noble impulses, that shall make the noblest ambition that of being useful to our country, that shall draw its honorable distinctions only from equality, in which the generality shall safeguard the wel-

From *Voices of Revolt*, I, 72-75, 77-81. Robespierre, on the instructions of the Committee of Public Safety, delivered this speech on February 5, 1794, in the Convention. It was an attack both on the Right and on the Left.

fare of the individual, and in which all hearts may be moved by any evidence of republican spirit. . . . We want morality in the place of egotism, principles in the place of mere habit, the rule of reason in the place of the slavery of tradition, contempt for vice in the place of contempt for misfortune, the love of glory in the place of avarice. Honest men instead of "good society," truth instead of empty show, manly greatness instead of the depravity of the great, a sublime, powerful, victorious and happy people!

The splendor of the goal pursued by our Revolution is simultaneously the source of our strength and our weakness. It is the source of our weakness, because it unites all the perfidious and vicious individuals, all the advocates of tyranny who think of plunder, who think to find in the Revolution a trade and in the Republic a booty. Thus we may explain the disaffection of many persons who began the struggle together with us, but who have left us when our path was but half accomplished, because they did not pursue the objects we were pursuing. . . .

You are surrounded beyond the boundaries; at home, all the friends of the tyrants conspire, and will continue to conspire, so long as treason still has a hope. We must stifle the domestic and foreign enemies of the Republic, or we must be destroyed with the Republic. And therefore, under the present circumstances, the principle of our Republic is this: to influence the people by the use of reason, to influence our enemies by the use of terror.

In times of peace, virtue is the source from which the government of the people takes it power. During the Revolution, the sources of this power are virtue and terror: virtue, without which terror will be a disaster; and terror, without which virtue is powerless. But terror is nothing more nor less than swift, severe and indomitable justice. . . .

It has been said that terror is the means by which a despotic government rules. Has your rule anything in common with such a government? Yes, indeed, but only in the sense that the sword in the hands of the protagonists of liberty resembles the sword in the hands of the champion of tyranny. When despots rule because their subjects are terrified, the despots are justified—as despots. You put down all the enemies of freedom by means of terror, and you are justified—as founders of the Republic. The government of the Revolution is the despotism of liberty against tyranny. Must might be used only in order to protect crime? . . .

If tyranny prevails for but a single day, all the patriots will have been wiped out by the next morning. And yet some persons dare declare that despotism is justice and that the justice of the people is despotism and rebellion. . . .

Either we or our enemies must succumb. "Show consideration for the Royalists!" shout some persons; "have compassion with the criminal!" "No, I tell you; have compassion with innocence, compassion with the weak, and compassion with humanity! . . ."

The whole task of protecting the Republic is for the advantage of the loyal citizen. In the Republic, only republicans may be citizens. The Royalists and conspirators are foreigners to us, enemies. Is not the terrible war in which we now are involved a single indissoluble struggle? Are the enemies within not the allies of those who attack us from without? The murderers who rend the flesh of their country at home; the intriguers who seek to purchase the conscience of the representatives of the people; the traitors who sell themselves; the pamphleteers who besmirch us and are preparing for a political counter-revolution by means of a moral counter-revolution;—are all these individuals any less dangerous than the tyrants whom they serve? All those who would intervene between these criminals and the sword of justice are like unto those who would throw themselves between the bayonets of our soldiers and the troops of the enemy, and the enthusiasm of their false feelings amounts in my eyes only to sighs directed toward England and Austria!

. . . The internal enemies of the nation have divided into two camps, the camp of the Moderates and the camp of the Counter-Revolutionaries. They are marching on "opposite" paths and under different colors, but they are aiming at the same goal. One of these factions would mislead us into weakness, the other into excess. The one would make of liberty a bacchante, the other a prostitute. The ones have been called "Moderates." The designation of "Ultra-Revolutionaries" perhaps is more brilliant than true. This designation, perhaps appropriate when used of men who, acting in good faith, and ignorant of the facts, have sometimes neglected to practice due caution in the revolutionary policy, is by no means applicable to those perfidious individuals who would compromise us, who would make the principles of the Revolution a plaything to trifle with. The poor revolutionary moves to and fro, straddles, sometimes on either side of the fence. To-day he is a moderate and to-morrow he becomes a fanatic, each time with as little reason. Whenever he discovers anything it is sure to be a plot unveiled long ago; he will tear the mask from the face of traitors who were unmasked long ago, but he will defend the living traitors. He is ever at an effort to adapt himself to the opinions of the moment and never undertakes to oppose them; he is always ready to adopt violent decisions, but he must always be assured in advance that these decisions cannot possibly be carried out; he calumniates those measures that might be fruitful of results, and even if he should approve of them, he will modify them with proposed amendments which would nullify any possible success in advance. Above all, he is very sparing in his use of the truth and resorts to it only as a means to enable him to lie the more shamelessly. High-sounding resolutions find him all fire and flame, but only so long as these resolutions have no real significance. Above all, he is indifferent on any subject that is of importance at the moment; he dotes on the forms of patriotism, the cult of patriotism, and he would rather wear out a hundred red caps than carry out a single revolutionary action.

What is the difference between these people and the Moderate? Both are servants of the same master, servants who maintain that they are hostile to each other, but only in order the better to conceal their misdeeds. Do not judge them by their different language; judge them by the identity of their results. Is he who attacks the Convention publicly in inflammatory speeches any different from him who seeks to deceive and compromise us? Are not these two persons acting in an understanding with each other? . . .

Even the aristocracy is now attempting to make itself popular. It conceals its counter-revolutionary pride, it hides its dagger under its rags and filth. Royalism is trying to overcome the victories of the Republic. The nobility, having learned from past experience, is ready to clasp liberty in a sweet embrace, in order to stifle it in the act. Tyranny strews flowers on the graves of the defenders of liberty. Their hearts have remained the same; only their masks have changed! How many traitors are attempting to ruin us by conducting our affairs?

But they should be put to the test. Instead of oaths and declamations, let us require them to deliver services and sacrifices!

Action is required—they talk. Deliberation is necessary—they declare we must act at once.

. . . It is in this way that these gentlemen serve the Revolution! They have found an excellent means of supporting the efforts of the Republican government: to disorganize us, degrade us, indeed, make war upon those who support us. If you are seeking means for provisioning the army, or if you are engaged in forcing from the hands of avarice and fear the foodstuffs necessary for our warriors—they will shed patriotic tears over the general woe and predict a sure famine. Their alleged desire to avoid the evil is always sufficient reason for them to increase the evil.

. . . It is impossible for you to conceive of all the devious ways pursued by all these sowers of discord, these spreaders of false rumors, who disseminate every possible kind of false report, which is not unprofitable in a country in which, as in ours, superstition is still so widespread . . . .

The domestic situation of our country demands your entire attention. Remember that it is our duty simultaneously to make war against the tyrants of all Europe, to keep fed and equipped an army of 1,200,000 men, and that the government is obliged ceaselessly to keep down with due energy and caution all our internal foes, as well as to repair all our defects. . . .

louis kossuth

Louis Kossuth was born in Monok, Hungary, on September 19, 1802 and was raised by Lutheran parents. He studied law but failed to obtain a post in the civil service and subsequently found employment as a legal agent, which had been his father's profession, for local landed magnates. It was in this capacity that he attended the Hungarian diets (parliaments) of 1825-27 and 1832-36. As a representative of the landed magnates, he was permitted to sit in the lower house but did not possess the right to speak. During the excited atmosphere of the latter session, the "long diet," Kossuth developed his social and political philosophy. His was one of extreme nationalism combined with advanced radicalism. He embraced many of the liberal reform ideas contemporary to his time, such as taxation of the nobles and the complete emancipation of the peasants, and he held to the belief that no political or social advance would be possible while Hungary remained subordinate to Austria. Intemperate toward those who did not agree with him, Kossuth was blind to the danger involved by too strong a challenge to Vienna, and he frequently treated objections from the Croats or non-Magyars of Hungary as either negligible or treasonable.

Kossuth was arrested in 1837 for his political activities, but popular pressure forced the Metternich regime to release him in 1840. A fiery orator and an accomplished polemicist, Louis Kossuth soon became a popular hero and the editor of a bi-weekly journal, *Pesti Hirlap*. His many articles on political and social subjects were brilliantly written, but they also alarmed the conservative authorities, and Kossuth was forced to resign as editor of the newspaper. Even though he was denied permission to start a journal of his own, Metternich offered him work with the government, an offer Kossuth promptly refused. His next enterprise was to found a society for promoting Hungarian industry, and while this effort realized rather modest economic results, it afforded him a further platform for agitation.

In 1847 the county of Pest sent Kossuth to the diet at Pozsony (Bratislava) where he at once assumed the leadership of the Reform Party. News of the outbreak of revolution in France, in February 1848, provided him with his long-awaited opportunity. On March 3 he delivered a memorable speech demanding the removal of the "dead hand" of Vienna as the only way to safeguard the liberties of Hungary. And when word of the Vienna revolution of March 13 reached Pozsony, he persuaded the Hungarian legislature to accept a program which included the appointment of a responsible ministry for Hungary, together with all of the social reforms favored by the liberals. Moreover, Kossuth accepted the invitation to serve as a member of the Hungarian deputation which carried these demands to Vienna, and much to his satisfaction he saw them all accepted by a panic-stricken Austrian Court.

Count Lajos Batthyany, the new Hungarian prime minister, appointed Kossuth minister of finance, and Kossuth promptly precipitated a crisis by forbidding the exportation of Hungarian revenues owed to the Austrian Crown. Louis Kossuth soon made himself the life and soul of the whole radical and extreme nationalist movement in Hungary. It was he who persuaded the Hungarian diet to refuse, except on political conditions unacceptable to Austria, the dispatch of 20,000 Hungarian troops to Italy. Instead, he called for a national force of 200,000 men to meet the danger of the invasion which he all but invited

When Austrian armies under the command of Joseph Jellachich invaded Hungary in September of 1848, the government resigned, and Kossuth became *de facto* dictator of Hungary by virtue of his presidency of the committee of national defense. In the absence of a regular government, the diet entrusted the conduct of affairs to this committee, and Kossuth was its dominant officer and personality. Perhaps no one but he could have given the Hungarian people the heart to face the overwhelming odds which faced them (his moving appeal to his countrymen, "Hear! patriots hear!" appears as the first selection which follows); but he also increased those odds by his intransigence and complicated Hungary's own difficulties by his jealousy and suspicion of his best general, Arthur Gorgey, and by his meddling in military affairs. Both his greatness and his lack of realism were manifest in the hours of crisis. It was Kossuth who prevailed upon the

Hungarian diet to refuse recognition of Austrian Emperor Ferdinand's abdication on December 2, 1848, after which he induced the diet to proclaim the dethronement of the Hapsburg dynasty in a declaration issued on April 14, 1849. The diet then proceeded to declare Hungary an independent republic and Kossuth became its president. Military victories in early battles with Austrian troops were cheering to Kossuth, but even he recognized the futility of his cause when the Russian armies entered into an alliance with the Austrians. Kossuth resigned his position in favor of General Gorgey and escaped to Turkey, where authorities kept him interned for two years. The Hungarian surrender at Vilagos marked the end of the republic.

Kossuth was an exile. Before he left Hungary and entered Turkey, he knelt for the last time on his native soil and gave a parting eulogy. His remarks on this occasion appear in the second of the selections from his speeches which follow.

After leaving Turkey, Kossuth travelled to the United States in 1851 where he was received with much popular enthusiasm. The public address which he delivered at the Plymouth Church in Brooklyn, New York (part of which appears as the third selection in the following excerpts from his speeches), was typical of the stirring rhetoric which he invoked during the many appearances of his American tour. Kossuth next travelled to England, where he continued his speaking engagements, always recalling the tragedy of the noble Hungarian cause. (His address at Birmingham, the last of the following selections, is representative of the memorializing speeches which became his hallmark.)

Kossuth never despaired of turning the international situation to Hungary's advantage, but there was little opportunity to do so. His plans for the creation of a Danubian confederation proved equally barren even though he had renounced much of his early chauvinism. In 1865 he moved to Italy where he continued to follow the national movement in Hungary, bitterly denouncing the Compromise of 1867 which established the Austro-Hungarian Monarchy. Kossuth always regarded the unequal status of Hungary, accorded by that Compromise, to be a betrayal of the nationalist cause. He spent his last years in relative seclusion at Turin, Italy, where he died on March 20, 1894. The government permitted his body to be brought back to Hungary and buried at Pest. Louis Kossuth had come home.

Hear! Patriots Hear!

...Hear! patriots hear!

The eternal God doth not manifest himself in passing wonders, but in ever-lasting laws.

It is an eternal law of God's that whosoever abandoneth himself will be of God forsaken.

It is an eternal law that whosoever assisteth himself him will the Lord assist.

It is a Divine law that swearing falsely is by its results selfchastised.

It is a law of God's that he who resorteth to perjury and injustice, prepareth his own shame and the triumph of the righteous cause.

In the name of that fatherland, betrayed so basely, I charge you to believe my prophecy, and it will be fulfilled.

In what consists Jellachich's power?

In a material force, seemingly mighty, of seventy thousand followers, but of which thirty thousand are furnished by the regulations of the military frontier.

But what is in the rear of this host? By what is it supported? There is nothing to support it!

Where is the population which cheers it with unfeigned enthusiasm? There is none.

Such a host may ravage our territories, but never can subdue us.

Batu-Chan deluged our country with his hundreds of thousands. He devastated, but he could not conquer.

Jellachich's host at worst will prove a locust-swarm, incessantly lessening in its progress till destroyed.

So far as he advances, so far will be diminished the number of his followers, never destined to behold the Drave again.

Let us—Hungarians—be resolved, and stones will suffice to destroy our enemy. This done, it will be time to speak of what further shall befall.

But every Hungarian would be unworthy the sun's light if his first morning thought, and his last thought at eve, did not recall the perjury and treason with which his very banishment from the realms of the living has been plotted.

Thus the Hungarian people has two duties to fulfill.

The first, to rise in masses, and crush the foe invading her paternal soil.

The second, to remember!

If the Hungarian should neglect these duties, he will prove himself dastardly and base. His name will be synonymous with shame and wickedness.

From P. C. Headley, *The Life of Louis Kossuth*, Derby and Miller, Auburn, New York, 1852, pp. 113-115.

So base and dastardly as to have himself disgraced the holy memory of his forefathers—so base, that even his Maker shall repent having created him to dwell upon this earth—so accursed that air shall refuse him its vivifying strength—that the corn-field, rich in blessings, shall grow into a desert beneath his hand—that the refreshing well-head shall dry up at his approach!—Then shall he wander homeless about the world, imploring in vain from compassion the dry bread of charity. The race of strangers for all alms will smite him on the face. Thus will do that stranger-race, which seeks in his own land to degrade him into the outcast, whom every ruffian with impunity may slay like the stray dog—which seeks to sink him into the likeness of the Indian Pariah, whom men pitilessly hound their dogs upon in sport to worry.

For the consolations of religion he shall sigh in vain.

The craven spirit by which Creation has been polluted will find no forgiveness in this world, no pardon in the next.

The maid to whom his eyes are raised shall spurn him from her door like a thing unclean; his wife shall spit contemptuously in his face; his own child shall lisp its first word out in curses on its father.

Terrible! terrible! but such the malediction, if the Hungarian race proves so cowardly as not to disperse the Croatian and Serbian invaders, 'as the wild wind disperses the unbinded sheaves by the way-side.'

But no, this will never be; and, therefore, I say the freedom of Hungary will be achieved by this invasion of Jellachich. Our duty is to triumph first, then to remember.

To arms! Every man to arms; and let the women dig a deep grave between Veszprem and Fehervar, in which to bury either the name, fame, and nationality of Hungary, or our enemy.

And either on this grave will rise a banner, on which shall be inscribed, in record of our shame, 'Thus God chastiseth cowardice;' or we will plant thereon the tree of freedom everlastingly green, and from out whose foliage shall be heard the voice of the Most High, saying, as from the fiery bush to Moses, 'The spot on which thou standest is holy ground.'

All hail! to Hungary, to her freedom, happiness, and fame.

He who has influence in a country, he who has credit in a village, let him raise his banner. Let there be heard upon our boundless plains no music but the solemn strains of the Rakoczy march. Let him collect ten, fifty, a hundred, a thousand followers—as many as he can gather, and marshal them to Veszprem.

Veszprem, where, on its march to meet the enemy, the whole Hungarian people shall assemble, as mankind will be assembled on the Judgment Day.

Farewell to the Father-Land

God be with thee, my beloved father-land! God be with thee, father-land of the Magyars! God be with thee, land of tortures! I shall not be able to behold the summits of thy mountains; no more shall I be able to call my father-land—the soil, where, on the mother's heart, I imbibed the milk of freedom and justice!

Pardon me, my father-land, me who am condemned to wander about far from thee, because I strove in thy welfare; pardon me, who no more can call any thing *free*, but the small place where I am now kneeling down with a few of thy sons. My looks fall upon thee, O, poor father-land! I see thee bent down with sufferings! I now turn them to futurity; thy future is nothing but a great grief! Thy plains are moistened with crimson gore, which will soon be blackened by unmerciful devastation and destruction, as if to mourn over the many conquests which thy sons have achieved over the accursed enemies of thy hallowed soil. How many grateful hearts lifted up their prayers to the throne of the Almighty! How many tears have flowed, which would even have moved hell to compassion! How many streams of blood have run, as proofs, how the Hungarian loves his father-land, and how he can *die* for it! and yet hast thou, beloved father-land, become a slave!

Thy beloved sons are chained and dragged away like slaves, destined to fetter again every thing that is holy; to become serviceable to all that is unholy! O Lord, if thou lovest thy people, whose heroic ancestors thou didst enable to conquer, under Arpad, amid so manifold dangers, I beseech Thee, and I implore Thee, O humble it not!

Behold, my dear father-land, thus speaks to thee thy son, in the whirlwind of troubles and despair, on thy utmost boundary!

Pardon me, if the great number of thy sons have shed their blood for my sake, or rather for thine, because I was their representative; because I protected thee, when on thy brow was written in letters of blood the word "DANGER!" because I, when it was called unto thee, "Be a slave!" took up the word for thee; because I girded on my sword when the enemy had the audacity to say, "Thou art no more a nation!" in the land of the Magyars!

With gigantic paces time rolled on—with black yellow letters FATE wrote on the pages of thy history "death!" and to stamp the seal upon it, it called the northern Colossus to assist. But the reddening morning dawn of the south will melt this seal!

From Henry W. De Puy, *Kossuth and His Generals,* Phinney & Co., Buffalo, 1852, pp. 284-288.

Behold, my dear father-land, for thee, who hast shed so much of thy blood, there is not even compassion, because on thy hills, which are towered up by the bones of thy sons, tyranny earns her bread.

O see, my dear father-land! the ungrateful, whom thou didst nourish from the fat of thy plenitude, has turned against thee, against thee has turned the traitor, to destroy thee from the head to the sole of thy foot! But thou, noble nation, hast endured all this; thou hast not cursed thy fate, because in thy bosom, over all suffering, HOPE is enshrined.

Magyars! turn your looks not from me; for even at this moment my tears flow only for you, and the soil, on which I am kneeling, yet bears your name!

...I love thee, Europe's truest nation! as I love the freedom for which thou fought so bravely! The God of liberty will never blot you out from His memory. Be blessed for evermore! My principles were those of Washington, though my deeds were not those of William Tell! I wish for a free nation, free as God only can create man—and thou art dead, because thy winter has arrived; but this will not last so long as thy fellow-sufferer, languishing under the sky of Siberia. No, fifteen nations have dug thy grave, the thousands of the sixteenth will arrive, to save thee!

...You may still be proud, for the lion of Europe had to be aroused to conquer the rebels! The whole civilized world has admired you as heroes, and the cause of the heroic nations will be supported by the freest of the free nations on earth!

Address at Plymouth Church, Brooklyn

... But I am told there are men of peace who say, after all it is very true—very fine, if you please, but they will have peace at any price. Now, I say, there are many things in the world which depend upon true definitions—and it is not true that they are men of peace who speak so—they are men who would conserve, at any price, the present condition of things. Is that present condition peace? Is the scaffold peace?—the scaffold, on which, in Lombardy, the blood of 3,742 patriots was spilled during three short years. Is that peace? Are the prisons of Austria filled with patriots, peace? Or is the blind murmur of discontent from all the nations, peace? I believe the Lord has not created the world to be in such a peaceful condition. I believe he has not created it to be the prison to humanity,

From P. C. Headley, *The Life of Louis Kossuth*, p. 273.

or to be the dominion of the Austrian jailer. No; the present condition of the world is not peace. It is a condition of oppression on the European continent, and because there is this condition of oppression there cannot be peace; for so long as men and nations are oppressed, and so long as men and nations are discontented, there cannot be peace—there can be tranquillity; but it will be the dangerous tranquillity of the volcano, boiling up constantly, and at the slightest opportunity breaking out again, and again, and sweeping away all the artificial props of tranquillity. Freedom is the condition of peace, and, therefore, I will not say that those who profess to be men of peace, and will not help the oppressed to obtain their liberty, are really so. Let them tell truly that they are not men of peace, but only desire to conserve the oppression of nations. With me and with my principles is peace, because I was always a faithful servant of the principles of liberty, and only on the principles of liberty, can nations be contented, and only with the contentment of nations, can there be peace on the earth. With me and with my principles there is peace—lasting peace—consistent peace; with the tyrants of the world there is oppression, struggles, and war.

Address at Birmingham, England

. . . Perhaps there might be some glory in inspiring such a nation, and to such a degree. But I cannot accept the praise. No; it is not I who inspired the Hungarian people—it was the Hungarian people who inspired me. Whatever I thought, and still think—whatever I felt, and still feel—is but a feeble pulsation of the heart which in the breast of my people beats. The glory of battles is ascribed to the leaders in history; theirs are the laurels of immortality. And yet on meeting the danger, they knew that, alive or dead, their name will upon the lips of the people forever live. How different, how much purer, is the light spread on the image of thousands of the people's sons, who, knowing that where they fall they will lay unknown, their names unhonored and unsung, but who, nevertheless, animated by the love of freedom and fatherland, went on calmly, singing national anthems, against the batteries, whose cross-fire vomited death and destruction on them, and took them without firing a shot—they who fell, falling with the shout, 'Hurrah for Hungary!' And so they died by thousands, THE UNNAMED DEMIGODS! Such is the people of Hungary.

With us, those who beheld the nameless victims of the love of country, lying

From P. C. Headley, *The Life of Louis Kossuth*, pp. 307-308.

on the death-field beneath Buda's walls, met but the impression of a smile on the frozen lips of the dead, and the dying answered those who would console but by the words, 'Never mind, Buda is ours. Hurrah for the fatherland!' So they spoke and died. He who witnessed such scenes, not as exception, but as a constant rule, of thousands of the people:s nameless sons; he who saw the adolescent weep when told he was yet too young to die for his land; he who saw the sacrifices of spontaneity; he who heard what a fury spread over the people on hearing of the catastrophe; he who marked his behavior towards the victors after all was lost; he who knows what sort of curse is mixed in the prayers of the Magyar, and knows what sort of sentiment is burning alike in the breast of the old and of the child, of the strong man and of the tender wife, and ever will be burning on, till the hour of national resurrection strikes; he who is aware of all this, will surely bow before this people with respect, and will acknowledge, with me, that such a people wants not to be inspired, but that it is an everlasting source of inspiration itself.

giuseppe mazzini

Italian patriot and the guiding revolutionary spirit of the Risorgimento (resurgence), Giuseppe Mazzini was born and raised in Genoa, a city then under French rule. His father was a successful physician who extended his practice to many charity patients; his mother was a public-spirited woman who instilled Mazzini with his republican instincts. A sickly and studious boy, Mazzini obtained his early education under priests with Jansenist leanings, and he became strongly religious yet anticlerical. He attended Genoa University where he studied law, philosophy, medicine, and literature; the latter was his first love. Mazzini graduated in 1827 and in the same year he won acclaim for his essay "Patriotism of Dante," in which he hailed Dante as the prophet of Italian unity.

As a youth Mazzini joined the Carbonari, an illegal Italian revolutionary movement, but soon lost interest in its aimless ritualism. His association with the organization, however, earned him a three-month jail sentence from the Piedmont-Sardinia government in 1831. It was during this confinement that Mazzini completely rejected the Carbonari and formulated his lifetime objective: a united Italy with Rome as its capital. Upon his release, he went into exile and settled for a time in Marseilles. Believing that the future lay in the hands of youth, Mazzini organized *Giovini Italia* (Young Italy), and founded a journal of the same name which was soon printed on secret presses and sold in North and Central Italy. At the prodding of Piedmont authorities, France expelled Mazzini in 1833, and Switzerland did likewise in 1836. In the meantime, Mazzini continued his revolutionary writings and activities (the following selection "Interests and Principles" dates from this period) and he eventually found refuge in 1837 in London, where he spent the greater part of his life.

Doubtlessly Mazzini's influence inspired the many insurrections which finally made Italian nationalism a dynamic force. His chief function in the Risorgimento, in which cause many of his friends were killed in uprisings which occurred between 1833 and 1857, was to venerate the executed as martyrs and to help make nationalism virtually a religion. The Italian insurrections of 1848 brought Mazzini to Italy in April. When the Austrians recaptured Milan, he organized and directed the defense of Rome against French forces seeking to return the exiled Pope Pius IX to his lost throne. Rome was forced to surrender at the end of June, and Mazzini succeeded in escaping to London with the assistance of the United States consul. But the defense of Rome compared so favorably with the humiliating defeat of the Piedmontese army in the north that Mazzini won much respect among Italian nationalists.

After 1849, however, he was less successful. His support of the disastrous revolutions at Mantua in 1852 and at Milan in 1853, weakened his influence. But in London, far from the Italian scene, Mazzini failed to recognize that ordinary people in Italy were not totally committed to nationalism or republicanism. Obstinately refusing to accept any compromise of these goals, he was deserted by Garibaldi and many of his other friends. His letter to Daniele Manin, dated June 8, 1856, and republished here in part, is an example of both this growing alienation and Mazzini's passionate, fervent, and quasi-religious nationalism.

Mazzini rejected socialism because it was too materialistic, too much concerned with rights instead of duties. He aimed for the support of the Italian working class, but he was far too religious and mystical to understand them and was painfully frustrated by their preference for Bakunin's anarchism or Marx's socialism. His relations with Cavour were strained despite their common goal of Italian unification. Cavour relied for help on a foreign power, France, and Mazzini believed in revolution and war based on direct popular action. In 1861 Italy had officially become a nation, but Mazzini was still in exile. Even after the death sentence passed upon him by the Cavour government was removed in 1866, Mazzini could not bring himself to approve Italian unity under the pragmatic Piedmont political leadership. Messina elected him to parliament, but he was prevented from taking his seat because the rulers of the new state did not wish to provoke further controversies. Indeed, Mazzini remained unreconciled even after the capture of Rome in 1870, which, under different circumstances, would have been the climax of his life's dream.

In 1870, he set out for Sicily, but a former associate informed the police and

Mazzini was arrested and imprisoned for several months in Gaeta. He died at Pisa on March 10, 1872, disguised as a Dr. Brown, a fugitive even in his own country.

Interests and Principles

... Every revolution is the work of a principle which has been accepted as a basis of faith. Whether it invoke nationality, liberty, equality, or religion, it always fulfills itself in the name of a principle, that is to say, of a great truth, which, being recognized and approved by the majority of the inhabitants of a country, constitutes a common belief, and sets before the masses a new aim, while authority misrepresents or rejects it. A revolution, violent or peaceful, includes a negation and an affirmation: the negation of an existing order of things, the affirmation of a new order to be substituted for it. A revolution proclaims that the state is rotten; that its machinery no longer meets the needs of the greatest number of the citizens; that its institutions are powerless to direct the general movement; that popular and social thought has passed beyond the vital principle of those institutions; that the new phase in the development of the national faculties finds neither expression nor representation in the official constitution of the country, and that it must therefore create one for itself. This the revolution does create. Since its task is to increase, and not diminish the nation's patrimony, it violates neither the truths that the majority possess, nor the rights they hold sacred; but it reorganizes everything on a new basis; it gathers and harmonizes round the new principle all the elements and forces of the country; it gives a unity of direction toward the new aim, to all those tendencies which before were scattered in the pursuit of different aims. Then the revolution has done its work.

We recognize no other meaning in revolution. If a revolution did not imply a general reorganization by virtue of a social principle; if it did not remove a discord in the elements of a state, and place harmony in its stead; if it did not secure a moral unity; so far from declaring ourselves revolutionists, we should believe it our duty to oppose the revolutionary movement with all our power.

Without the purpose hinted at above, there may be riots, and at times victorious insurrections, but no revolutions. You will have changes of men and administration; one caste succeeding to another; one dynastic branch ousting the other.

From "Interests and Principles, (January 6, 1836)," translated by Thomas Okey, in *The Literature of Italy, 1265-1907*, VI, edited by Rossiter Johnson and Dora K. Ranous, The National Alumni, New York, 1907, pp. 296-300, 303, 305.

This necessitates retreat; a slow reconstruction of the past, which the insurrection had suddenly destroyed; the gradual re-establishment, under new names, of the old order of things, which the people had risen to destroy. Societies have such need of unity that if they miss it in insurrection they turn back to a restoration. Then there is a new discontent, a new struggle, a new explosion. France has proven it abundantly. In 1830 she performed miracles of daring and valor for a negation. She rose to destroy, without positive beliefs, without any definite organic purpose, and thought she had won her end when she canceled the old principle of legitimacy. She descended into that abyss which insurrection alone can never fill; and because she did not recognize how needful is some principle of reconstruction, she finds herself today, six years after the July Revolution, five years after the days of November, two years after the days of April, well on her way to a thorough restoration.

We cite the case of France because she is expected to give political lessons, hopes, and sympathies; and because France is the modern nation in which theories of pure reaction founded on suspicion, on individual right, on liberty alone, are most militant, therefore the practical consequences of her mistakes are shown most convincingly. But twenty other instances might be cited. For fifty years, every movement which, in its turn, was successful as an insurrection, but failed as a revolution, has proven how everything depends on the presence or absence of a principle of reconstruction.

Wherever, in fact, individual rights are exercised without the influence of some great thought that is common to all; wherever individual interests are not harmonized by some organization that is directed by a positive ruling principle, and by the consciousness of a common aim, there must be a tendency for some to usurp others' rights. In a society like ours, where a division into classes, call them what you will, still exists in full strength, every right is bound to clash with another right, envious and mistrustful of it; every interest naturally conflicts with an opposing interest: the landlord's with the peasant's; the manufacturer's or capitalist's with the workman's. All through Europe—since equality, however accepted in theory, has been rejected in practice, and the sum of social wealth has accumulated in the hands of a small number of men, while the masses gain but a mere pittance by their relentless toil—it is a cruel irony, it gives inequality a new lease of life, if you establish unrestricted liberty, and tell men they are free, and bid them use their rights.

A social sphere must have its center; a center to the individualities that jostle with each other inside it; a center to all the scattered rays that diffuse and waste their light and heat. The theory that bases the social structure on individual interests cannot supply this center. The absence of a center, or the selection among opposing interests of that which has the most vigorous life, means either anarchy or privilege—that is, either barren strife or the germ of aristocracy, under whatever name it disguises itself: this is the parting of the ways, which it is impossible to avoid.

Is this what we want when we invoke a revolution, since a revolution is indispensable to reorganize our nationality?

... We are therefore driven to the sphere of principles. We must revive belief in them; we must fulfill a work of faith. The logic of things demands it.

Principles alone are constructive. Ideals are never translated into facts without the general recognition of some strong belief. Great things are never done except by the rejection of individualism and a constant sacrifice of self to the common progress. Self-sacrifice is the sense of duty in action. . . . The individual is sacred; his interests, his rights are inviolable. But to make them the only foundation of the political structure, and tell each individual to win his future with his own unaided strength, is to surrender society and progress to the accidents of chance and the vicissitudes of a never-ending struggle; to neglect the great fact of man's nature, his social instinct; to plant egotism in the soul; and in the long run impose the dominion of the strong over the weak, of those who have over those who have not. The many futile attempts of the past forty years prove this.

... If by dint of example you can root in a nation's heart the principle that the French Revolution proclaimed but never carried out, that the State owes every member the means of existence or the chance to work for it, and add a fair definition of existence, you have prepared the triumph of right over privilege; the end of the monopoly of one class over another, and the end of pauperism; for which at present there are only palliatives . . . Christian charity, or cold and brutal maxims like those of the English school of political economists.

When you have raised men's minds to believe in the other principle—that society is an association of laborers—and can, thanks to that belief, deduce both in theory and practice all its consequences; you will have no more castes, no more aristocracies, or civil wars, or crises. You will have a People.

To Daniele Manin (June 8, 1856)

Daniele Manin was an Italian patriot and statesman. He became head of the Venetian Republic in 1848 but resigned the same year when Venice voted in

From *Mazzini's Letters*, translated by Alice De Rosen Jervis, J.M. Dent and Sons, Ltd., London, 1930, pp. 152, 154-163.

favor of union with the kingdom of Sardinia. In 1849, Manin again became head of a provisional government and after the Sardinian rout at Novara he was given dictatorial powers and organized a heroic resistance of Venice to its Austrian besiegers. Famine and disease forced Venice to surrender in August, 1849, whereupon Manin went into exile at Paris. He subsequently supported the leadership of Sardinia in the movement for Italian unification.

... One of your last letters, under the pretext of a moral lesson, has brought such an accusation against the party, that to leave it unrefuted would appear like indifference or agreement. Therefore I am writing to you.

In that letter you assert that the party will never succeed in its patriotic enterprise, unless it formally abjures the *theory of the dagger.*

...I have been told by some that, in denouncing the *theory of the dagger,* you pointed indirectly at me, without mentioning my name, at me and the men who are associated with me in the idea of action. I do not believe that you have a mean mind, and I reject the suspicion. But how was it that the affection owed to him, who has been fighting for the Italian cause for more than twenty-five years, did not suggest to you that others might interpret your words in this sense? How was it that you did not remember that the governments and journals of the *moderate* party in Piedmont and Lombardy, and *The Times,* depositary of your thoughts, had vied with each other in spreading this cowardly accusation against me, after the 6th February,1853? How was it that it did not occur to you that in haranguing against the *theory of the dagger* you were supporting—in discourteous forgetfulness—the calumnies of spies, credulous people, and unconscientious enemies, who imputed to me death-sentences, secret tribunals, and tendencies to illegal revenge?

And yet, it is not in my own name—it matters little to me now whether the opinion of others be good or bad, unless it is that of those whom I love—but in the name of a whole party, that I ask you solemnly: when was the *theory of the dagger* sanctioned in Italy? Who spread it? Who supported it by word or deed?

If by *theory of the dagger* you mean the language of him who cries to a subjugated people, without a country, without a banner to spread over its sons in the cradle or the grave: "Rise up: slay or die: you are not men, but tools employed at pleasure by the foreigner; you are not a people, but a disinherited race of slaves, despised all the more when you whine; you are not Italians, but Israelites, Pariahs, the Helots of Europe; you have no name, no national baptism, but are merely a number; you are represented by a cipher, and the Emperor Francis I brutally used one to describe some of our finest men sighing, tortured and crushed, in the secret cells of the Spielberg. Your one and only duty is to become men and citizens; all education begins with this: no progress can start except from what already exists; *rise up* then and *exist;* rise up mightily against all who by brute force impede you from following the way taught you by Providence; rise up, in sublime fury. If your oppressors have disarmed you, create arms with which to fight them; let your weapons of war be the iron of your crosses, the nails from your workshops, the pebbles of your streets, the daggers with which a file can furnish you. Conquer by artifice and surprise the arms with which the foreigner deprives you of honour, substance, liberty, rights, and life. From the dagger of the Vespers to the stone of Balilla, and the knife of Palafox, blessed by everything which can destroy the enemy and emancipate you."—This language is mine, and ought to be yours.

. . . But if by *theory of the dagger* you mean the language of him who would say to our fellow-citizens: "Strike, not to begin an insurrection, but with the sole intent of striking, and because you do not wish or are not able to rise in insurrection; strike in the dark; strike isolated individuals, whose life is not an obstacle to the Country nor their death a deliverance for it; substitute revenge, which dishonours, for the conspiracy, which emancipates; form yourselves into a tribunal before being citizens, and before being able to concede to the victim time for repentance or justification." Who has held such language? Who has spread such an atrocious theory in Italy? It is your duty to say this, or to retract the accusation.

. . . The theory of the dagger subsists in this: in the insane, incessant, and cruel persecution of thought, and of the smallest acts which give rise to suspicion in those who are guilty, or believed to be guilty, of affection for their Country, their substance being forfeited and their lives threatened—in flogging taking the place of law in Italy—in the perpetual insolence of the foreign rulers—in the feverish irritation caused by the orders given out and by the shameful espionage—in the hatreds aroused by paid denunciations—in the overbearing deeds perpetrated (under cover of a Government abhorred like the Papal Government), by tyrannical underlings known to everyone in our small cities—in the unavoidable scorn for every existing institution—in the impossibility of obtaining justice against the extortions of the oppressors—in the contempt of life (an inevitable consequence of the uncertainty of the future)—in a condition of things which depends solely upon the despotism of those in power—in the culpable indifference of the Governments of Europe to our idea of a common Country, this immense aspiration of ours, nourished and repressed for half a century.

The party, collectively, has always rejected the great temptation that our oppressors place before us. If a few individuals, acting only upon their own initiative, now and then succumb, the fact is a result of the causes which I have pointed out, and it will not cease except with their cessation. You ought to have said this. You ought to have reminded Europe how, in every part of Italy, our people has been sublime in pardon and oblivion, whenever it had a ray of freedom. You ought to have reminded her how, only yesterday, an English minister, contradicting himself, declared in the House of Commons, concerning Rome, that our cities were never so well governed or so free from crime and violence as when a banner of the Country floated over their towers. You ought to have re-evoked the picture of our wretched conditions, and to have cried: *"The Austrian Government, which, against the unanimous vote of the population, persists in keeping what does not belong to it; the French Government, which deprived Rome of every means of amelioration; the Protestant English Government, which declared in its dispatches that it desired the return of the Pope; the Governments of all Europe, which forbid Italy to be a Nation—are responsible before God and man for the daggers that flash through the darkness of our land. They all conspire to prevent our free development, and to maintain a great injustice upon our soil: let them blame themselves if an abnormal and violent protest should sometimes issue from an enslaved and uneducated people, who are abandoned by all."*

It seems to me that this should have been your part. To cry to the men who are agonizing unjustly under the knife of the executioner: *"do not use the knife which falls into your hands,"* is the same as crying to one who is dying in a vitiated atmosphere: *"let the blood circulate freely through your veins, and you will be cured."* It is the same error as that of the worthy men who wait to initiate the republican institution, till those born and bred under monarchical despotism develop republican virtues.

The *theory of the dagger* has never existed in Italy; the *fact* of the dagger will disappear when Italy has her own life, recognized rights, and justice.

To-day, I do not approve, I deplore; but I have not the heart to condemn. When a man, Vandoni, at Milan, cunningly persuades one of his old friends to accept from him a ticket in the National Loan, and then hastens to denounce him to the foreign police, if a man of the people rises the next day and stabs the Judas at noon in the public thoroughfare, I have not the courage to cast a stone at this man who makes himself a representative of social justice, hated by tyranny.

I abhor a single drop of blood being shed, when not imperatively required for the triumph or the consecration of a sacred principle. I believe the death-sentence to be a crime when applied by a society which can defend itself, and it is my earnest desire that the first decree of the triumphant republic may be the abolition of the gallows. I sigh over individual acts of vengeance, even when against iniquitous persons, and even when every means of legal justice is wanting where they are committed. Braving the accusation of weakness, I refused to append my signature to a sentence of death pronounced by a tribunal of war against a guilty soldier. Therefore I do not fear a wrong interpretation being put upon my words by honest people, if I add that there are exceptional moments, both in life and in the history of nations, to which normal human justice cannot adapt itself, and when men can only act as their conscience and God inspire them.

The sword in Judith's hand which destroyed Holophernes was sacred; the dagger of Brutus, the stiletto of the Sicilian who started the Vespers, and the arrow of Tell, were sacred. Where all Justice is dead, and a tyrant denies and destroys by terrorism the conscience of a nation towards God who willed it to be free—and a man, without hatred or base passion, but actuated only by devotion to his Country and the eternal right which he embodies, arises to confront the tyrant, crying: *thou tormentest millions of my brothers; thou deprivest them of that which was given them by God; thou slayest their bodies and corruptest their souls; thou condemnest my countrymen to live in agony day after day; in thee is embodied the whole edifice of servitude, dishonour, and guilt: therefore I destroy this edifice in slaying thee*—I recognize the finger of God in that manifestation of tremendous equality between the ruler of millions and a single individual. Most men feel as I do in their hearts, but I acknowledge it.

Therefore I will not cry anathema, like you, Manin, on these assailants; I will not say to them, with evident injustice: *you are cowards*; I will not say to the party, which never encourages these deeds: *you will fail in your object, if you do not stop them;* but I will say: "Why do you strike, wretched men? What do you hope for? If ever man has a right to take the life of another, I know that death is deserved by the spy and the traitor, and by the vile Italian who in return for money from the foreign oppressor accepts the infamous mission of torturing at the gallows his brothers who were intolerant of the Country's servitude; but what is the use of slaying them, and can you slay them all? And can you, unaided, be judges of what is stirring in the conscience of your victim? Do you know whether he will not repent and be better to-morrow? Anyway, do you wish to be as bad as he is? To conquer, we must be better; to deserve the victory, we must drive anger, ferocity, and vengeance, out of our hearts. We are the apostles of the future Country, and wish to found a Nation. In this sacred idea, and in the duty of making it triumph, lies the source of our rights. Now can you found a Nation and conquer a Country in this way?

"It is your business to slay, not a few satellites of your tyrants, but tyranny itself. As long as tyranny exists, as long as there are corrupt rulers, foreign bayonets, and the gallows, there will also be corrupt and servile people, cowardly traitors, torturers, and executioners. And they will always spring up afresh, because your dagger flashes rarely and uncertainly, whilst the bayonet of the oppressors shines steadily before everyone's eyes, inexorable and omnipotent. Concentrate your energy, then, in an idea of collective insurrection, which may free your soil at one blow from the causes that create vile and cowardly men. In concord amongst yourselves, turn your weapons against the foreign invaders, instead of assuming the solemn office of judges—without allowing examination of defence—and using them against men who are merely tools of the tyranny which rules over you. When once you are free, you need not fear or punish traitors or iniquitous judges. The right of conquering your Country for your-selves is a right given you by God; that which you derogate to yourselves against individuals who are the blind agents of despotism sways between justice and crime."

These men might allow me to use this language to them, because I cry: *Rise up!* and point out the only simple and rational way of doing so, making it possible as far as I can, accepting and invoking the fraternal co-operation of everyone, and summoning all Italians to unite and to work in concord, with a programme which no one can refuse without intolerance or treachery to the common Country: *Let the Nation deliver the Nation: Let the Nation, free and united, decide its destiny.* But you?

Place your hand on your heart, and answer me: if one of those men upon whom you call down anathema were to rise up and say: "Daniele Manin, you, amongst others, preached hatred of the foreign rule, national unity, and abhor-rence of the Italians who deny our faith. You, amongst others, put the fever for our Country into our souls. Why do you not join with the others to guide us to the conquest of that ideal? Why do you leave us alone? Why, instead of turning to us, your brothers, do you turn to diplomacy, to foreign courts, and to a monarchy which does not wish and is not able to save us? There are millions of us; we have proved in 1848 and 1849 that we are capable of emancipating our soil; we are stronger now than we were then, and the very facts which you blame show it you; why do you not help us in the work of common redemption, which we shall certainly undertake? Why do not you and the others whom we hailed as our leaders, and whom we are still ready to hail as such, unite with those who are working for us? You do not like our daggers: why do you not give us muskets? You could do so; if you and a dozen others whose names are dear to all were to join in saying openly and boldly: "the hour has arrived"; were to join in asking wealthy people to give part of their substance to help us, who place our lives in the balance, you would succeed in convincing and in inducing to make sacrifices those who are now wavering irresolutely amidst the disorder of the party. Why do you not do this? Why do you draw us on from one illusion to another, until we are overwhelmed by despair? Do you expect the European Powers to come to be slain for our sake? Do you wish the emancipation of Italy to be accomplished by foreign forces? No; join us openly and frankly. Join your intellect to our strong arms. Then only will you have the right to advise us." What answer could you make to such language?

giuseppe garibaldi

Italian patriot and guerrilla leader of the Risorgimento (resurgence), Garibaldi was a republican who by his conquest of Sicily and Naples greatly contributed to the achievement of Italian unity under the royal house of Savoy. Born on July 4, 1807, at Nice, then a French town but from 1815 to 1860 included in the kingdom of Sardinia-Piedmont, Garibaldi entered the Sardinian navy in 1833. After meeting Giuseppe Mazzini, the pre-eminent Italian nationalist of that day, he joined *Giovini Italia* (Young Italy). In 1834, he became involved in an unsuccessful republican plot in Piedmont and was forced to flee to South America the following year. There he gained his first experience in irregular warfare. He fought primarily at sea on behalf of partisans in Brazil, and on behalf of Uruguay against Argentina. In 1843, however, he helped form an Italian legion, the first "Redshirts," with whom he gained much of his experience of guerrilla warfare. It was in Uruguay that he met Anna Maria Ribeiro da Silva, known as Anita, whom he married in 1842. She accompanied him on his expeditions and became a figure only less legendary than Garibaldi himself.

When revolution swept over Europe in 1848, Garibaldi found a new theatre of action. Although a convinced republican, he offered his services to King Charles Albert of Sardinia in the war against Austria but received no encouragement. After the Sardinian defeat at Custozza, Garibaldi led a small guerrilla band and harassed the Austrians in the area around lakes Maggiore and Varese. From there he travelled to Rome in 1849 and, at the head of some improvised forces, fought for Mazzini's short-lived Roman republic against the French forces intervening for Pope Pius IX. The bravery and tenacity of the defenders at Rome, at a time when other revolutionaries were offering but feeble resistance to the return of the old regimes, proved to the world that Italians could and would fight for national freedom. During Garibaldi's spectacular retreat across central Italy, Anita died. Garibaldi was refused asylum by the king of Sardinia and came to the United States where he resumed his seafaring life.

Permitted to return to Sardinia in 1854, Garibaldi bought part of the island of Paprera, lying between Corsica and Sardinia, with the intention of retiring. By this date he had renounced the dream of an Italian republic and gave his support to the pragmatic policies of Cavour, publicly declaring that the monarchy as represented by Sardinian King Victor Emmanuel II should be the basis of Italian unity. Garibaldi's popularity won many of Mazzini's republican followers for the monarchist cause. Indeed, Garibaldi was made a major general in the Sardinian army and was placed in charge of a brigade of "volunteers" in the war of 1859 against Austria. After the Treaty of Villafranca di Verona he violently attacked Cavour and denounced the cession of Savoy and his native Nice to France.

The greatest exploit of his life was the expedition to Sicily and Naples (May-November, 1860), which he undertook with the connivance of Victor Emmanuel. He set sail from the Genoese coast on May 6, with the object of assisting a revolt in Sicily. His force consisted then of just more than 1,000 volunteers and is therefore known as "the Thousand." Insofar as they had a uniform, it was the red shirt. On May 11 they reached Marsala, and Garibaldi was proclaimed dictator of Sicily in the name of King Victor Emmanuel. The campaign in Sicily was astonishingly successful, and, after the capitulation of the Neapolitan forces garrisoned in Sicily, Garibaldi crossed the strait of Messina on the night of August 18, 1860. On September 7 he entered Naples as the Sardinian army marched south against the Papal States. Garibaldi held the line against powerful Neapolitan forces along the Volturno River until the Sardinians arrived on October 26. When King Victor Emmanuel II made his triumphal entry into Naples on November 7, Garibaldi was with him. But two days later he returned to Caprera, refusing any reward.

Only a part of the Papal States remained outside the new kingdom, and Garibaldi decided to liberate the area without reference to Victor Emmanuel. Garibaldi expected to be able to complete the unification of Italy in the same unconventional fashion in which he had begun, but the King, fearing international intervention, sent an Italian army which defeated Garibaldi at Aspromonte. Wounded and then captured, he was quickly freed. During his convalescence Garibaldi paid a visit to London, in April 1864, where he received an unparalleled welcome. In the war of 1866 he was allowed a subsidiary role in the effort against the Austrians, which he performed well. Then in 1867 he embarked on another expedition to Rome. He was arrested and sent back to Caprera, which the Italian navy proceeded to blockade. He eluded his guard, however, and made a final attempt to seize Rome in 1867. On November 2, his forces were defeated at Mentana by French and papal troops. Recrossing the Italian frontier, he was again arrested and taken back to his island.

In 1870 Garibaldi formed a fresh volunteer corps, this time to assist France against Prussia. For this service he was rewarded by his election to the Bordeaux national assembly. But parliamentary life was ill-suited to his temperament, and he soon resigned. He lived most of the rest of his life in retirement and died at Caprera on June 2, 1882.

Garibaldi was not without serious shortcomings for all of his accomplishments. He was not intellectually oriented: he did not think and argue; he believed and declaimed. In some ways he presaged the twentieth century dictators. He distrusted parliaments because he did not understand politics and so usually made a fool of himself when he participated in the national assembly. Yet he was no bad ruler. It is arguable that he provided better government with his simple minded radicalism when he was dictator of Sicily and Naples than the Kingdom of Italy was to provide with its subtle conservatism. He was, however, a soldier, and there was perhaps no greater master of guerrilla warfare in the nineteenth century.

Garibaldi never lacked admirers. During his lifetime he attracted an almost fanatical devotion that extended well beyond the borders of Italy to a world which worshipped romance and heroism. In America and England, just as in Italy, the working classes identified with him and hailed his career as a promise of a better world to come. His simple eloquence, evidenced in the edited selections which follow, impressed Gandhi and suggested to Jawaharlal Nehru how an idealistic and unselfish patriotism might triumph over seemingly impossible difficulties and bring a new nation to birth. Garibaldi gave the world a Latin heart.

The Sicilian Campaign, May 1860

SICILY! a filial and well-merited affection makes me consecrate these first words of a glorious period to thee, the land of marvels and of marvellous men. The mother of Archimedes, thy glorious history bears the impress of two achievements paralleled in that of no other nation on earth, however great—two achievements of valour and genius, the first of which proves that there is no tyranny, however firmly constituted, which may not be overthrown in the dust, crushed into nothingness by the dash, the heroism, of a people like thine, intolerant of outrages.

... Once more, Sicily, it was thine to awaken sleepers, to drag them from the lethargy in which the stupefying poison of diplomatists and doctrinaires had sunk them—slumberers who, clad in armour not their own, confided to others the safety of their country, thus keeping her dependent and degraded.

Austria is powerful, her armies are numerous; several formidable neighbours are opposed, on account of petty dynastic aims, to the resurrection of Italy. The Bourbon has a hundred thousand soldiers. Yet what matter? The heart of twenty-five millions throbs and trembles with the love of their country! Sicily, coming forward as champion and representative of these millions, impatient of servitude, has thrown down the gauntlet to tyranny, and defies it everywhere, combating it alike within convent walls and on the peaks of her ever-active volcanoes. But her heroes are few, while the ranks of the tyrant are numerous; and the patriots are scattered, driven from the capital, and forced to take to the mountains. But are not the mountains the refuge, the sanctuary, of the liberty of nations? The Americans, the Swiss, the Greeks, held the mountains when overpowered by the ordered cohorts of their oppressors. "Liberty never escapes those who truly desire to win her." Well has this been proved true by those resolute islanders, who, driven from the cities, kept up the sacred fire in the mountains. Weariness, hardships, sacrifices—what do they matter, when men are fighting for the sacred cause of their country, of humanity?

O noble Thousand! in these days of shame and misery. I love to remember you! Turning to you, the mind feels itself rise above this mephitic atmosphere of robbery and intrigue, relieved to remember that, though the majority of your gallant band have scattered their bones over the battle-fields of liberty, there yet remain enough to represent you, ever ready to prove to your insolent detractors that all are not traitors and cowards—all are not shameless self-seekers, in this land of tyrants and slaves! "Where any of our brothers are fighting for liberty,

From *Autobiography of Giuseppe Garibaldi*, II, translated by A. Werner, Walter Smith and Innes, London, 1889, pp. 143-147.

thither all Italians must hasten!"—such was your motto, and you hastened to the spot without asking whether your foes were few or many, whether the number of true men was sufficient, whether you had the means for the arduous enterprise. You hastened, defying the elements, despising difficulties and dangers and the obstacles thrown in your way by enemies and self-styled friends. In vain did the numerous cruisers of the Bourbon armament surround as with a circle of iron the island about to shake off their yoke; in vain they ploughed the Tyrrhene seas in all directions, to overwhelm you in their abysses—in vain! Sail on, sail on, argonauts of Liberty!

. . . Yet sail on, sail on fearlessly, *Piemonte* and *Lombardo*, [The two steamers which carried the Thousand to Marsala], noble vessels manned by the noblest of crews; history will remember your illustrious names in despite of calumny. And when the survivors of the Thousand, the last spared by the scythe of time, sitting by their own fireside, shall tell their grandchildren of the expedition—mythical as it will seem in those days—in which they were found worthy to share, they will recall to the astonished youth the glorious names of the vessels which composed it.

Sail on! sail on! Ye bear the Thousand, who in later days will become a million—in the day when the blindfolded masses shall understand that the priest is an impostor, and tyrannies a monster anachronism. How glorious were thy Thousand, O Italy, fighting against the plumed and gilded agents of despotism, and driving them before them like sheep!—glorious in their motley array, just as they came from their offices and workshops, at the trupet-call of duty—in the student's coat and hat, or the more modest garb of the mason, the carpenter, or the smith.

Address to the People of Palermo

People of Palermo!—Your aspirations are those of the whole peninsula. Let all Italians be unanimous in one will—the unity of the country. But let us have no words; let us have deeds and protests—not in writing—the protests of a brave people determined to free their brethren still groaning in fetters. The master of France, the traitor of the 2nd of December, under the pretence of screening from harm the person of the Pope, of protecting religion, Catholicism, occupies Rome. It is a false pretence—or lie. . . . He is actuated by covetousness, by a

From *The Times* (London), July 17, 1862, p. 12.

robber's lust, by an infamous thirst for empire; he is the first supporter of brigandage! the chief of Southern assassins!

People of the Vespers! people of 1860! Napoleon must depart from Rome. If it be necessary, we must resort to a new rehearsal of the Vespers. Let every citizen who cares for the emancipation of the country have a weapon in readiness (*un ferro* a sword or dagger). Strong and compact, we shall be able to overcome the greatest power.

. . . The Pope-King, or the King-Pope, is a negation of Italy. Our Government is not strong enough to shake off the yoke of France. The people must strengthen them by its compactness and energy. Let us throw our well-sharpened weapons into the scales of diplomacy, and diplomacy will respect our rights; she will give us Rome and Venice.

The programme with which we crossed the Ticino and landed at Marsala must still be 'Italy and Victor Emmanuel.' The same programme will lead us to Rome and Venice.

I will rouse Italy from the sloth in which she is lying. I will come with you; I will be your companion, in this last struggle. Once more I recommend concord; we must avoid intestine war. All of us have committed errors, but all of us wish for the emancipation of Italy. If we disagree in some things, it matters not so we are all brethren.

Proclamation to the Volunteers at Bois Fienzi

My young fellow soldiers,—Again to-day the holy cause of our country reunites us. Again to-day, without asking whither going, what to do, with what hope of reward to our labours, with a smile on your lips and joy in your hearts, you hastened to fight our overbearing dominators, throwing a spark of comfort to our enslaved brethren. I only ask of Providence to strengthen your good trust in me and make me worthy of it. Such is and ever was the desire of my whole life. I can only promise you toils, hardships, and perils; but I rely on your self-denial. I know you, ye brave young men, crippled in glorious combat. It is idle to beg you to display valour in fight. What I ask is discipline, for without that no army can exist. The Romans were disciplined, and they mastered the world. Endeavour to conciliate the good will of the population we are about to visit, as you did in 1860, and no less to win the esteem of our valiant army, in order, thus gaited

From *The Times* (London), August 6, 1862, p. 9.

with that army, to bring about the longed-for unity of the country. This time, again, the brave Sicilians will be the forerunners of the great destinies which are in store for our country.

Appeal to the Hungarians

Hungarians!—What is Hungary about? Is that noble nation, which already the victorious Turk has seen rise suddenly armed in the defence of the civilization of Europe—that nation before which the proud Emperors of Hapsburg have bent as supplicants, asking aid and mercy—is it gone to sleep for ever?

Brothers of Hungary! Revolution is on your threshold. Sharpen your glance, and you will see the flag of liberty floating on the towers of Belgrade. Listen attentively, and you will hear the rattle of Servian rifles, who, up and armed in defence of their rights, are fighting against the abhorred system.

And you,—what are you about? You, a strong people, who have not had the misfortune, which Italy once suffered, of being divided between seven tyrants— you, a people of warriors, what are you waiting for? Have you broken your swords? Have you forgotten your martyrs, renounced your vows of vengeance, or do you rely on the perfidious promises of your oppressors? Do you put faith in those who advise you to accept the insidious offers of Austria, who seems inclined now to grant you your rights, but who is already preparing to betray you, and to take from you by force or fraud what she reluctantly gives you?

... You also are oppressed under a ferocious despotism; you also have Austria like a rock on your chest, stopping your breath—Austria, whose empire you have saved more than once—Austria, who, as a reward for having lent her many a time the bulwark of your powerful breasts, has violated your laws, annihilated your statutes, attempted to abolish your language, exiled your best citizens, and erected gallows in your cities! Do you despair of your own strength and valour! Do not forget that in 1848 you had only to push on your triumphal road to Vienna to destroy for ever the old sanguinary throne of the Hapsburgs.

The present moment is more propitious. Russia will not now offer a helping hand to Austria to thwart your efforts; she has been paid with too much ingratitude; and Prussia, the ancient rival of the Empire, will not defend her against your attacks.

Woe to Hungary!—woe to every oppressed people—if you obey fallacious and

From *The Times* (London), August 27, 1862, p. 9.

cowardly counsels, if you think any other pact between you and Austria possible except hatred and war! Oh, brothers! do not miss this propitious opportunity.

. . . And you. . . you want liberty. You. . . oppressed and outraged, you have the right—more than the right—the duty of reasserting the rank earned by your glorious deeds, your virtues, and the services which you have rendered to civilization.

. . . Courage! You have sufficient strength if you have sufficient daring. Hearken not to those who counsel patience and an ignominious servility, but listen to the voice of your conscience, which says, 'Up! follow the example of Servia and of Montenegro; imitate those who are ready to apply the torch of revolution on other points of Europe.'

Italy, who loves you as brothers, who has promised to repay you the price of blood which your brave sons have shed for her on many battle-fields—Italy,. . . calls upon you to share her new battles and her new victories over despotism; she invokes you, in the name of the holy fraternity of peoples, in the name of the welfare of all.

. . Will you fail to join the rendezvous of nations when they meet to do battle against despotism? Certainly liberty abandoned by you would run great risks; but your fame would be lost for ever.

. . . Oh! I know you! I do not doubt you. Hungary, too long deceived by perfidious friends, will awaken to the cry of liberty, which to-day reaches it across the Danube, and will to-morrow resound from Italy. And when the solemn hour of nations strikes I shall, I am sure, meet your invincible phalanxes on that field where a death-struggle will be fought between liberty and tyranny, between barbarism and civilization.

Palermo, July 26, 1862

To the English Nation

Suffering under repeated blows, both moral and physical, a man can more exquisitely feel both good and ill, hurl a malediction at the authors of evil, and consecrate to his benefactors unlimited gratitude and affection.

And I owe you gratitude, O English nation! and I feel it as much as my soul is capable of feeling it. You were my friend in my good fortune, and you will

From *The Times* (London), October 3, 1862, p. 7.

continue your precious friendship to me in my adversity. May God bless you. My gratitude is all the more intense, O kind nation! that it rises high above all individual feeling, and becomes sublime in the universal sentiment towards nations of which you represent the progress. Yes, you deserve the gratitude of the world, because you offer a safe shelter to the unfortunate from whatever side they may come, and you identify yourself with the misfortunes of others you pity and help. The French or Neapolitan exile.finds refuge in your bosom against tyranny. He finds sympathy and aid because he is an exile, because he is unfortunate. The Haynaus, the iron executioners of autocrats, will not be supported by the soil of your free country; they will fly from the tyrannicidal anger of your generous sons.

And what should we be in Europe without your dignified behaviour! Autocracy can strike her exiled ones in other countries where only a bastard freedom is enjoyed—where freedom is but a lie. But let one seek for it on the sacred ground of Albion. I, like so many others, seeing the cause of justice oppressed in so many parts of the world, despair of all human progress. But when I turn my thoughts to you, I find tranquillity from your steady and fearless advancement towards that end to which the human race seems to be called by Providence.

Follow your path undisturbed, O unconquered nation! and be not backward in calling sister nations on the road of human progress. Call the French nation to co-operate with you. You are both worthy to walk hand in hand in the front rank of human improvement. But call her! In all your meetings let the words of concord of the two great sisters rebound. Call her! Call her in every way with your own voices, and with that of her great exiles—with that of her Victor Hugo, the hierophant of sacred brotherhood. Tell her that conquests are to-day an aberration, the emanation of insane minds. And why should we conquer foreign lands when we must all be brothers? Call her, and do not care if she is for the moment under the dominion of the Spirit of Evil. She will answer in due time, if not to-day,to-morrow, and, if not to-morrow, she will later answer to the sound of your generous and regenerating words. Call, and at once, Helvetia's strong sons and clasp them for ever to your heart. The warrior sons of the Alps—the Vestals of the sacred fire of freedom in the European Continent, they will be yours! And what allies! Call the great American Republic. She is, after all, your daughter, risen from your bosom; and, however she may go to work, she is struggling to-day for the abolition of slavery so generously proclaimed by you. Aid her to come out from the terrible struggle in which she is involved by the traffickers in human flesh. Help her, and then make her sit by your side, in the great assembly of nations, the final work of human reason. Call unto you such nations as possess free will, and do not delay a day. The initiative that to-day belongs to you might not be yours to-morrow. May God avert this! Who more bravely took the initiative than France in 1789. She who in that solemn moment gave to the world the goddess Reason, levelled tyranny to the dust, and consecrated free brotherhood between nations. After almost a century she is reduced to combat the liberty of nations, to protect tyranny, and to direct her efforts to steady, on the ruins of the temple of Reason, that hideous, immoral monstrosity—the Papacy. Rise, therefore, O Britannia! and lose no time. Rise with uplifted brow and point out to other nations the road to follow. War would no longer be possible where a world's Congress would judge of the differences arisen between nations. No more standing armies, with which freedom is incompatible! Away with shells and iron plating! Let spades and reaping machines come forth; let the millards [billions] spent in destructive implements be employed to encourage industry and to diminish the sum of human misery. Begin, O English people! for the love of God begin the great era of the human compact, and benefit present generations with so great a gift.

Besides Switzerland, Belgium, and others that will rise at your call, you will see other nations, urged on by the good sense of their populations, rush to your embrace and unite in one. Let London be at the present time the seat of the Congress, in due course to be chosen by mutual understanding and general consent. I repeat to you, may God bless you, and may He amply repay you for the benefits you have showered upon me.

Varignano, Sept. 28, [1862]

Proclamation to the Italian People

Before the hypocritical intrigues of diplomacy, which now denying and now caressing the most sacred cause and the most solemn rights, makes a mask of them to cover the shame of its object selfishness, what remains there for Italians to do?

Betrayed in their aspirations, and their generous initiative misrepresented, the Treasury overladen with debts, dishonest or incapable men in power, a warlike enemy fortifying himself in the north, with enemies not warlike, but no less iniquitous, who seek to force us to ally ourselves with their frauds or become slaves to their influence, what remains there for Italians to do?

Let them unite; but no longer in support of men whose antecedents of tor-

From *The Times* (London), January 5, 1864, p. 9.

tuous policy promise nought save hatred, discord, renewal of party violence, and fatal disenchantment.

Let them unite; but not in the spirit which by incapacity and malignity has spent the vital forces of the nation in fratricidal conflict.

Let them unite; but in the name of him in whose loyalty alone we confide with filial truth in a supreme crisis—in Victor Emmanuel II.

He alone never failed in his given word. The insidious acts of diplomacy will shiver, as they have ever done, against his truth and honesty. The country may confide in him in the approaching struggle, because he who was ever the bulwark of the destinies of Italy, and who risked his crown in the unequal struggle on the field of battle, will never descend to compromise, but will conduct us gloriously to Rome and Venice.

Let us, then, unite in the name and with the honesty of Victor Emmanuel. Let him be promptly invested with the Dictature of the entire kingdom. Let the Parliament be closed. Let the lists for the conscription open before the arrival of spring for the speedy formation of columns of volunteers, who will form the vanguard of the regular army. Let squadrons of National Guards be formed as a reserve, and let us march without loss of time on the Mincio.

In the name of Italy and Victor Emmanuel Dictator all parties will unite; the brigandage will come which infests the fairest jewel of the Italian crown; the ramparts of Austria will yield; the people of Venice and Myria will rise in insurrection; Italy will regain her own influence, and mistress of her own destinies, will be in a position to seize her capital.

pierre proudhon

French moralist and advocate of social reform, Pierre Proudhon was born on January 15, 1809, at Besançon, in the Jura mountain district of France. His mother worked as a cook, and his father, who failed in a variety of menial jobs, fought a constant and losing battle against poverty. Although a promising scholar in his youth, Proudhon was forced to leave school in 1827 because of his financial circumstances and he apprenticed himself to a printer; later, as a proof-reader, he acquired knowledge of theology from reading the galley proofs of books and he also taught himself Greek and Hebrew. The revolution of 1830 resulted in economic upheavals, and Proudhon lost his job. He remained un-employed until 1833, when he returned to the printing shop in Besançon. As a recipient of a three year scholarship sponsored by his local municipality to encourage promising young writers, Proudhon was able to attend university lectures in Paris. By 1840 his interests had turned to economics and politics; in that year he published his sensational book *What Is Property?* and answered this question with the resounding reply, "Property is theft."

Proudhon's thinking has been often misrepresented as a socialist attack on private property. Actually his was a defense of property, in that he believed in its equal division among all workers, rather than an attack on the concept of private individual ownership. But the incendiary slogan, appearing as it did when many nations were in the throes of revolution and radical change, brought

Proudhon a kind of notoriety he very likely did not desire. In 1842 his pension was revoked, and he was placed on trial for "offending against religion and morals" but was subsequently acquitted. In 1842 Karl Marx wrote an enthusiastic review of Proudhon's work, but the latter's later publications led Marx bitterly and permanently to break with him. The founder of modern Communism argued that finance capitalism, which Proudhon sought to abolish, and industrial capitalism, which Proudhon wished to strengthen, were inextricably intertwined. This controversy, which was manifest in Proudhon's writing, *The Philosophy of Misery* and in Marx's reply, *The Misery of Philosophy*, is of current interest. It illustrates the roots of the continuing conflict between middle class reformers and the would-be transformers of capitalism.

Proudhon's philosophy is rife with apparent inconsistencies. It is difficult to reconcile his revolutionary sympathies with his sturdy defense of bourgeois family life and his opposition to Italian unification; his egalitarianism with his antifeminism; and his democratic concepts with his opposition to universal suffrage. Although he was a revolutionary, he could not align himself with any revolutionary party. Trotsky called him "the Robinson Crusoe of Socialism." The revolutionary figure with whom Proudhon had the greatest affinity was Bakunin; the aim of revolution, Proudhon insisted, is not a new government, but ultimately no government. He believed that the goal of free society should be anarchy, and that the highest perfection of social organization was that which made the state expendable.

In the revolution of 1848, Proudhon enjoyed an influential position as a recognized leader of radical socialist thought. During June of that year he was elected to the Constituent Assembly, but he soon alienated himself from most of his political allies. His editorial attacks upon the government of Louis Napoleon led to his arrest and trial for sedition in 1849. He was sentenced to three years imprisonment but was permitted to continue editing and writing, and to receive visits from his wife.

Proudhon had married Euphrasie Piegard, a girl from a working class family, while on parole from prison in 1849. Four daughters were born of this union. Upon his release in 1852, Proudhon lived quietly on the outskirts of Paris until 1858 when he published a book which focused upon the fundamental incompatibility of the teaching of the Church and the teaching of the Revolution. The book caused a sensation, particularly in clerical circles, and Proudhon was tried again and sentenced to another three-year term in prison. Before being taken into custody, however, he fled to Belgium and settled in Brussels where he wrote his last important work *La guerre et la paix* (Tolstoy knew the book and may have taken his title for *War and Peace* from it), a peculiar book which both justifies and glorifies war. Proudhon returned to France in 1862 and worked incessantly to support his family by writing. He died at his house at Passy on January 19, 1865, probably of heart failure brought on by asthma. His funeral was attended by a crowd of several thousand.

Much of Proudhon's untrained philosophy is merely perceptive journalism, particularly his treatises on national and international political affairs. But the bulk of his writings had an undeniable impact upon the shaping of French syndicalism. He never surrendered the belief that man's ethical progress would eventually make government unnecessary; and he remained convinced that the abuses of private property were responsible for the most serious injustices in society. Much of his later career was spent in poverty, and the convictions which he expressed in his 1840 study *What Is Property?* did not change in the last twenty-five years of his life. For many, they continue to hold real meaning.

What Is Property?

If I were asked to answer the following question: *What is slavery?* and I should answer in one word, *It is murder,* my meaning would be understood at once. No extended argument would be required to show that the power to take from a man his thought, his will, his personality, is a power of life and death; and that to enslave a man is to kill him. Why, then, to this other question: *What is property?* may I not likewise answer, *It is robbery* without the certainty of being misunderstood; the second proposition being no other than a transformation of the first?

... Such an author teaches that property is a civil right, born of occupation and sanctioned by law; another maintains that it is a natural right, originating in labor,—and both of these doctrines, totally opposed as they may seem, are encouraged and applauded. I contend that neither labor, nor occupation, nor law, can create property; that it is an effect without a cause: am I censurable?

But murmurs arise!

Property is robbery! That is the war-cry of 1793! That is the signal of revolutions!

Reader, calm yourself: I am no agent of discord, no firebrand of sedition. I anticipate history by a few days; I disclose a truth whose development we may try in vain to arrest; I write the preamble of our future constitution. This proposition which seems to you blasphemous—*property is robbery*—would, if

From *What Is Property?* The Humboldt Publishing Co., New York, 1890; pp. 11-14, 268-272, 277-282, 284-288.

our prejudices allowed us to consider it, be recognized as the lightning-rod to shield us from the coming thunderbolt; but too many interests stand in the way!...Alas! philosophy will not change the course of events: destiny will fulfill itself regardless of prophecy. Besides, must not justice be done and our education be finished?

Property is robbery!...What a revolution in human ideas! *Proprietor* and *robbery* have been at all times expressions as contradictory as the beings whom they designate are hostile; all languages have perpetuated this opposition. On what authority, then do you venture to attack universal consent, and give the lie to the human race? Who are you, that you should question the judgment of the nations and the ages?

Of what consequence to you, reader, is my obscure individuality? I live, like you, in a century in which reason submits only to fact and to evidence. My name, like yours, is TRUTH-SEEKER. My mission is written in these words of the law: *Speak without hatred and without fear; tell that which thou knowest!* The work of our race is to build the temple of science, and this science includes man and Nature. Now, truth reveals itself to all; to-day to Newton and Pascal, to-morrow to the herdsman in the valley and the journeyman in the shop. Each one contributes his stone to the edifice; and, his task accomplished, disappears. Eternity precedes us, eternity follows us; between two infinites, of what account is one poor mortal that the century should inquire about him?

Disregard then, reader, my title and my character, and attend only to my arguments.

...I build no system. I ask an end to privilege, the abolition of slavery, equality of rights, and the reign of law. Justice, nothing else; that is the alpha and omega of my argument: to others I leave the business of governing the world.

One day I asked myself: Why is there so much sorrow and misery in society? Must man always be wretched? And not satisfied with the explanations given by the reformers,—these attributing the general distress to governmental cowardice and incapacity, those to conspirators and *emeutes,* still others to ignorance and general corruption,—and weary of the interminable quarrels of the tribune and the press, I sought to fathom the matter myself....In this laborious work, I have collected many interesting facts which I shall share with my friends and the public as soon as I have leisure. But I must say that I recognized at once that we had never understood the meaning of these words, so common and yet so sacred: *Justice, equity, liberty;* that concerning each of these principles our ideas have been utterly obscure; and, in fact, that this ignorance was the sole cause both of the poverty that devours us, and of all the calamities that have ever afflicted the human race.

... Justice. .. commences as the right of the strongest. In a society which is trying to organize itself, inequality of faculties calls up the idea of merit; *equit* suggests the plan of proportioning not only esteem, but also material comforts, to personal merit; and since the highest and almost the only merit then recognized is physical strength, the strongest. .. and consequently the best. .. is entitled to the largest share; and if it is refused him, he very naturally takes it by force. From this to the assumption of the right of property in all things, it is but one step.

... From the right of the strongest springs the exploitation of man by man, or bondage; usury, or the tribute levied upon the conquered by the conqueror; and the whole numerous family of taxes, duties, monarchical prerogatives, house-rents, farm-rents, etc.; in one word,–property.

Force was followed by artifice.

... From artifice sprang the profits of manufactures, commerce, and banking, mercantile frauds, and pretensions which are honored with the beautiful names of *talent* and *genius,* but which ought to be regarded as the last degree of knavery and deception; and, finally, all sorts of social inequalities.

In those forms of robbery which are prohibited by law, force and artifice are employed alone and undisguised; in the authorized forms, they conceal themselves within a useful product, which they use as a tool to plunder their victim.

The direct use of violence and strategem was early and universally condemned; but no nation has yet got rid of that kind of robbery which acts through talent, labor, and possession, and which is the source of all the dilemmas of casuistry and the innumerable contradictions of jurisprudence.

The right of force and the right of artifice. .. inspired the legislation of the Greeks and Romans, from which they passed into our morals and codes. Christianity has not changed at all. The Gospel should not be blamed, because the priests, as stupid as the legists, have been unable either to expound or to understand it. The ignorance of councils and popes upon all questions of morality is equal to that of the market-place and the money-changers; and it is this utter ignorance of right, justice, and society, which is killing the Church, and discrediting its teachings for ever. The infidelity of the Roman church and other Christian churches is flagrant; all have disregarded the precept of Jesus; all have erred in moral and doctrinal points; all are guilty of teaching false and absurd dogmas, which lead straight to wickedness and murder. Let it ask pardon of God and men,–this church which called itself infallible, and which has grown so corrupt in morals; let its reformed sisters humble themselves ... and the people, undeceived, but still religious and merciful, will begin to think.

... The second effect of property is despotism. Now, since despotism is in-

separably connected with the idea of legitimate authority, in explaining the
natural causes of the first, the principle of the second will appear.

What is to be the form of government in the future? I hear some of my
younger readers reply: "Why, how can you ask such a question? You are a
republican." "A republican! Yes; but that word specifies nothing. *Res publica;*
that is, the public thing. Now, whoever is interested in public affairs—no matter
under what form of government—may call himself a republican. Even kings are
republicans."—"Well! you are a democrat?"—"No."—"What! you would have a
monarchy."—"No."—"A constitutionalist?"—"God forbid!"—"You are then an
aristocrat?"—"Not at all."—"You want a mixed government?"—"Still less."—
"What are you, then?"—"I am an anarchist."

"Oh! I understand you; you speak satirically. This is a hit at the government."—"By no means. I have just given you my serious and well-considered
profession of faith. Although a firm friend of order, I am (in the full force of the
term) an anarchist."

. . . in a given society, the authority of man over man is inversely proportional
to the stage of intellectual development which that society has reached; and the
probable duration of that authority can be calculated from the more or less
general desire for a true government,—that is, for a scientific government. And
just as the right of force and the right of artifice retreat before the steady
advance of justice, and must finally be extinguished in equality, so the sovereignty of the will yields to the sovereignty of the reason, and must at last be lost
in scientific socialism. Property and royalty have been crumbling to pieces ever
since the world began. As man seeks justice in equality, so society seeks order in
anarchy.

Anarchy,—the absence of a master, of a sovereign,—such is the form of government to which we are every day approximating, and which our accustomed habit
of taking man for our rule, and his will for law, leads us to regard as the height
of disorder and the expression of chaos. The story is told, that a citizen of Paris
in the seventeenth century having heard it said that in Venice there was no king,
the good man could not recover from his astonishment, and nearly died from
laughter at the mere mention of so ridiculous a thing. So strong is our prejudice.
As long as we live, we want a chief or chiefs; . . . The most advanced among us
are those who wish the greatest possible number of sovereigns,—their most
ardent wish is for the royalty of the National Guard. Soon, undoubtedly, some
one, jealous of the citizen militia, will say, "Everybody is king." But, when he
has spoken, I will say, in my turn, "Nobody is king; we are, whether we will or
no, associated." Every question of domestic politics must be decided by depart-
mental statistics; every question of foreign politics is an affair of international

statistics. The science of government rightly belongs to one of the sections of the Academy of Sciences, whose permanent secretary is necessarily prime minister; and, since every citizen may address a memoir to the Academy, every citizen is a legislator. But, as the opinion of no one is of any value until its truth has been proven, no one can substitute his will for reason,—nobody is king.

. . . I do not see how the liberty of citizens would be endangered by entrusting to their hands, instead of the pen of the legislator, the sword of the law. The executive power, belonging properly to the will, cannot be confided to too many proxies. That is the true sovereignty of the nation.

The proprietor, the robber, the hero, the sovereign—for all these titles are synonymous—imposes his will as law, and suffers neither contradiction nor control; that is, he pretends to be the legislative and the executive power at once. Accordingly, the substitution of the scientific and true law for the royal will is accomplished only by a terrible struggle; and this constant substitution is, after property, the most potent element in history, the most prolific source of political disturbances.

. . . Now, property necessarily engenders despotism,—the government of caprice, the reign of libidinous pleasure. That is so clearly the essence of property that, to be convinced of it, one need but remember what it is, and observe what happens around him. Property is the right to *use* and *abuse*. If, then, government is economy,—if its object is production and consumption, and the distribution of labor and products,—how is government possible while property exists? And if goods are property, why should not the proprietors be kings, and despotic kings. . . . And if each proprietor is sovereign lord within the sphere of his property, absolute king throughout his own domain, how could a government of proprietors be any thing but chaos and confusion?

. . . Then, no government, no public economy, no administration, is possible, which is based upon property.

Communism seeks *equality* and *law*. Property, born of the sovereignty of the reason, and the sense of personal merit, wishes above all things *independence* and *proportionality*.

But communism, mistaking uniformity for law, and levelism for equality, becomes tyrannical and unjust. Property, by its despotism and encroachments, soon proves itself oppressive and anti-social.

The objects of communism and property are good—their results are bad. And why? Because both are exclusive, and each disregards two elements of society. Communism rejects independence and proportionality; property does not satisfy equality and law.

Now, if we imagine a society based upon these four principles,—equality, law, independence, and proportionality,—we find:—

1. That *equality*, consisting only in *equality of condition*, that is, *of means*, and not in *equality of comfort,*—which it is the business of the laborers to achieve for themselves, when provided with equal means,—in no way violates justice and *equit.*

2. That *law,* resulting from the knowledge of facts, and consequently based upon necessity itself, never clashes with independence.

3. That individual *independence,* or the autonomy of the private reason, originating in the difference in talents and capacities, can exist without danger within the limits of the law.

4. That *proportionality,* being admitted only in the sphere of intelligence and sentiment, and not as regards material objects, may be observed without violating justice or social equality.

This third form of society, the synthesis of communism and property, we will call *liberty.*

. . . Liberty is equality, because liberty exists only in society; and in the absence of equality there is no society.

Liberty is anarchy, because it does not admit the government of the will, but only the authority of the law; that is, of necessity.

Liberty is infinite variety, because it respects all wills within the limits of the law.

Liberty is proportionality, because it allows the utmost latitude to the ambition for merit, and the emulation of glory.

. . . Liberty is essentially an organizing force. To insure equality between men and peace among nations, agriculture and industry, and the centres of education, business, and storage, must be distributed according to the climate and the geographical position of the country, the nature of the products, the character and natural talents of the inhabitants, etc., in proportions so just, so wise, so harmonious, that in no place shall there ever be either an excess or a lack of population, consumption, and products. There commences the science of public and private right, the true political economy. It is for the writers on jurisprudence, henceforth unembarrassed by the false principle of property, to describe the new laws, and bring peace upon earth. Knowledge and genius they do not lack; the foundation is now laid for them.

I have accomplished my task; property is conquered, never again to arise. Wherever this work is read and discussed, there will be deposited the germ of death to property; there, sooner or later, privilege and servitude will disappear, and the despotism of will will give place to the reign of reason.

. . . The old civilization has run its race; a new sun is rising, and will soon renew the face of the earth. Let the present generation perish, let the old prevaricators die in the desert! the holy earth shall not cover their bones. Young man, exasperated by the corruption of the age, and absorbed in your zeal for justice!—if your country is dear to you, and if you have the interests of humanity at heart, have the courage to espouse the cause of liberty! Cast off your old selfishness, and plunge into the rising flood of popular equality! There your regenerate soul will acquire new life and vigor; your enervated genius will recover unconquerable energy; and your heart, perhaps already withered, will be rejuvenated! Every thing will wear a different look to your illuminated vision; new sentiments will engender new ideas within you; religion, morality, poetry, art, language will appear before you in nobler and fairer forms; and thenceforth, sure of your faith, and thoughtfully enthusiastic, you will hail the dawn of universal regeneration!

And you, sad victims of an odious law!—you, whom a jesting world despoils and outrages!—you, whose labor has always been fruitless, and whose rest has been without hope,—take courage! your tears are numbered! The fathers have sown in affliction, the children shall reap in rejoicings!

O God of liberty! God of equality! Thou who didst place in my heart the sentiment of justice, before my reason could comprehend it, hear my ardent prayer! Thou hast dictated all that I have written; Thou hast shaped my thought; Thou hast directed my studies; Thou hast weaned my mind from curiosity and my heart from attachment, that I might publish Thy truth to the master and the slave. I have spoken with what force and talent Thou hast given me: it is Thine to finish the work. Thou knowest whether I seek my welfare or Thy glory, O God of liberty! Ah! perish my memory, and let humanity be free! Let me see from my obscurity the people at last instructed; let noble teachers enlighten them; let generous spirits guide them! Abridge, if possible, the time of our trial; stifle pride and avarice in equality; annihilate this love of glory which enslaves us; teach these poor children that in the bosom of liberty there are neither heroes nor great men! Inspire the powerful man, the rich man, him whose name my lips shall never pronounce in Thy presence, with a horror of his crimes; let him be the first to apply for admission to the redeemed society; let the promptness of his repentance be the ground of his forgiveness! Then, great and small, wise and foolish, rich and poor, will unite in an ineffable fraternity; and, singing in unison a new hymn, will rebuild Thy altar, O God of liberty and equality!

mikhail bakunin

A Russian revolutionary and the most prominent figure among nineteenth century anarchists, Mikhail Bakunin was the eldest son of a retired diplomat and prosperous landowner. Commissioned in 1832, he served for two years with an artillery regiment in eastern Poland before resigning from the military in order to study philosophy. Bakunin left army life because it was dull and regimented, and his interests took him to Berlin university where, for a year and a half, he read Hegel. But Bakunin also rebelled against Hegelian uniformity and concluded that the only true philosophy was the negation of all philosophy; that real religion lay in "political action and the social struggle."

Mikhail Bakunin was by this time a militant atheist whose goals were to spread the religion of revolution and to command personally an international anarchist army. In Paris, he met Karl Marx, whom he criticized for intellectualizing the working classes and thus corrupting their fundamental honesty. He had some contact with the French anarchist Pierre Proudhon, and the latter quite probably influenced his thesis regarding the rise of federal republics, the consequent end of all sovereign states, and the end of the wars endemic to this process. At times he imagined a vast Slavonic federation which would replace the Austrian and Russian empires.

Bakunin played an active role in the Paris rebellion of 1848 and in the Dresden uprising of 1849. Arrested in Dresden on May 10, he was condemned to death.

The sentence was not executed, however, and in 1851 he was turned over to the custody of the Russian government. While serving time in Petropavlovsk prison, Bakunin wrote a formal apologia and confessed to political misdeeds and to fits of madness. Transferred to a penal settlement in eastern Siberia, in 1857, he escaped four years later. By way of Japan and the United States, he reached London, where he began writing for the Russian journal *Kolokol* ("The Bell").

The failure of the Polish rising in 1863 convinced Bakunin to begin in earnest his campaign for universal anarchy. In 1865 he devised a scheme for a global organization, a so-called International Brotherhood of national families secretly manipulated by an international group of coordinators. He condemned the state socialism of Marx as "official democracy and red bureaucracy," and after 1868 he struggled with Marx for control over the First International. Bakunin lost that contest and he later bitterly condemned the Marxists as despots who sought to establish their particular school of thought as the sole source and guide of living. He was also reluctant to place blind faith in the wisdom of the proletariat. Bakunin noted that former manual workers, once they had become rulers and representatives, tended to despise the so-called working class.

When a short-lived commune developed following a rebellion at Lyons in the wake of the Franco-German War of 1870-71, Bakunin rushed to join the insurgents. The revolt failed, as had so many previous efforts in which Bakunin had participated, and he seems ultimately to have lost his old faith in spontaneous popular insurrection as the only sure means of destroying state governments. His influence, nevertheless, remained considerable, and Bakunist "cells" spread from Europe into his native Russia. His followers preached the violent overthrow of the state and embraced Bakunin's view that complete freedom could be achieved through "anarchism, collectivism, and atheism." When he died at Berne, Switzerland, on July 1, 1876, Mikhail Bakunin's anarchist revolution seemed an unlikely prospect.

Bakunin's best known work, *God and the State*, was posthumously published in 1882. In his pamphlets and other writings, edited in an English edition by G. P. Maximoff, Bakunin provides his own definitions of the nature and scope of his particular form of social revolution. Like Mao, who warned guerrilla fighters never to alienate the peasants, Bakunin advises the urban proletariat to be cautious in dealing with the rural peasantry. Indeed, he reminds his city followers that a revolution which is imposed upon any class of people is not a revolution at all but rather a form of reactionism. These and other of his considered judgments on revolution follow.

Scientific Anarchism

Revolutions are not child's play, nor are they academic debates in which only, vanities are hurt in furious clashes, nor literary jousts wherein only ink is spilled profusely. Revolution means war, and that implies the destruction of men and things. Of course it is a pity that humanity has not yet invented a more peaceful means of progress, but until now every forward step in history has been achieved only after it has been baptized in blood. For that matter, reaction can hardly reproach revolution on this point; it has always shed more blood than the latter.

Revolution is overthrow of the State.

...Every political revolution which does not have economic equality as its *immediate* and *direct* aim is, from the point of view of popular interests and rights, only a hypocritical and disguised reaction.

According to the almost unanimous opinion of the German Socialists, *a political revolution has to precede a social revolution*—which, in my opinion, is a grave and fatal error, because every political revolution which takes place prior to and consequently apart from a social revolution, necessarily will be a bourgeois revolution, and a bourgeois revolution can only further bourgeois Socialism; that is, it will necessarily end in new exploitation of the proletariat by the bourgeoisie—exploitation perhaps more skilful and hypocritical, but certainly no less oppressive.

...Either the bourgeois-educated world will subdue and then enslave the rebellious, elemental forces of the people in order, through the power of the knout and bayonets (consecrated, of course, by some sort of divinity and rationalized by science), to force the working masses to toil as they have been doing, which leads directly to re-establishment of the State in its most natural form, that is, the form of a military dictatorship or rule by an Emperor—or the working masses will throw off the hateful, age-long yoke, and will destroy to its very roots bourgeois exploitation and bourgeois civilization based upon that exploitation; and that would mean the triumph of the Social Revolution, the uprooting of all that is represented by the State.

Thus the State, on the one hand, and social revolution, on the other hand, are the two opposite poles, the antagonism which constitutes the very essence of the genuine social life of the whole continent of Europe.

...The Social Revolution must put an end to the old system of organization based upon violence, giving full liberty to the masses, groups, communes, and associations, and likewise to individuals themselves, and destroying once and for all the historic cause of all violences, the power and the very existence of the

From *The Political Philosophy of Bakunin: Scientific Anarchism*, edited by G. P. Maximoff, The Free Press, Glencoe, Illinois, 1953, pp. 372-379, 397-404, 407-408, 413-415.

State, the downfall of which will carry down with it all the iniquities of juridical right, and all the falsehoods of the diverse religious cults—that right and those cults being simply the complaisant consecration (ideal as well as real) of all the violences represented, guaranteed, and furthered by the State.

Within the depths of the proletariat itself—at first within the French and Austrian proletariat, and then in that of the rest of Europe—there began to crystallize and finally took shape an altogether new tendency which aims directly at sweeping away every form of exploitation and every kind of political and juridical as well as governmental oppression—that is, at the abolition of all classes by means of economic equality and the abolition of their last bulwark, the State.

Such is the program of the Social Revolution.

Thus at present there exists in all the civilized countries in the world only one universal problem—the fullest and final emancipation of the proletariat from economic exploitation and State oppression. It is clear then that this question cannot be solved without a terrible and bloody struggle, and that in view of that situation the right and the importance of every nation will depend upon the direction, character, and degree of its participation in this struggle.

. . . But social revolution cannot be confined to a single people: it is international in its very essence.

Under the historic, juridical, religious, and social organization of most civilized countries, the economic emancipation of the workers is a sheer impossibility— and consequently, in order to attain and fully carry out that emancipation, it is necessary to destroy all modern institutions: the State, Church, Courts, University, Army, and Police, all of which are ramparts erected by the privileged classes against the proletariat. And it is not enough to have them overthrown in one country only: it is essential to have them destroyed in all countries, for since the emergence of modern States—in the seventeenth and eighteenth centuries— there has existed among those countries and those institutions an ever-growing international solidarity and powerful international alliances.

. . . Revolutions are not improvised. They are not made at will by individuals, and not even by the most powerful associations. They come about through force of circumstances, and are independent of any deliberate will or conspiracy. They can be foreseen. . . but never can their explosion be accelerated.

. . . The time of great political personalities is over. When it was a question of waging political revolutions, those individuals were in their place. Politics has for its object the foundation and preservation of the States; but he who says "the State" says domination on one hand and subjection on the other. Great dominant individuals are absolutely necessary in a political revolution; in a social revolution they are not only useless, they are positively harmful and are incompatible with the foremost aim of that revolution, the emancipation of the masses. At present, in revolutionary action as in modern labor, the collective must supplant the individual.

In a social revolution, which is diametrically opposed in every way to a political revolution, the actions of individuals are virtually null while the spontaneous action of the masses should be everything. All that individuals can do is to elaborate, clarify, and propagate ideas corresponding to the popular instinct and contribute their incessant efforts to the revolutionary organization of the natural power of the masses, but nothing over and above that; the rest can and should be done by the masses themselves.

. . . As to organization, it is necessary in order that when the Revolution, brought about through the force of circumstances, breaks out in full power, there be a real force in the field, one that knows what should be done and by virtue thereof capable of taking hold of the Revolution and giving it a direction salutary for the people: a serious international organization of workers' associations in all countries, capable of replacing the departing political world of the States and the bourgeoisie.

Universal public and private bankruptcy is the first condition for a social-economic revolution.

. . . But States do not crumble by themselves; they are overthrown by a universal international social organization. And organizing popular forces to carry out that revolution—such is the only task of those who sincerely aim at emancipation.

. . . The initiative in the new movement will belong to the people . . . in Western Europe, to the city and factory workers—in Russia, Poland, and most of the Slavic countries, to the peasants.

But in order that the peasants rise up, it is absolutely necessary that the initiative in this revolutionary movement be taken by the city workers, for it is the latter who combine in themselves the instincts, ideas, and conscious will of the Social Revolution. Consequently, the whole danger threatening the existence of the States is focused in the city proletariat.

. . . The social transformation to which we wholeheartedly aspire is the great act of justice, finding its basis in the rational organization of society with equal rights for all.

. . . Even profound historians and jurists have not understood the simple truth, the explanation and confirmation of which they could have read on every page of history, namely: that in order to render harmless any political force whatever, to pacify and subdue it, only one way is possible, and that is to proceed with its destruction. Philosophers have not understood that against political forces there can be no other guarantees but complete destruction; that in politics, as in the arena of mutually struggling forces and facts, words, promises, and vows mean nothing—and that is so because every political force, while it remains an actual force, even apart from and contrary to the will of the kings and other authorities who direct it, must steadfastly tend toward the realization of its own aims; this by virtue of its essential nature and because of the danger of self-destruction.

... And be on guard—a question reduced to terms of force remains a doubtful question.

But if force cannot obtain justice for the proletariat, what is capable of obtaining it? A miracle? We do not believe in miracles, and those who speak to the proletariat of such miracles are liars and corrupters. Moral propaganda? The moral conversion of the bourgeoisie under the influence of Mazzini's sermons? But it is utterly wrong on the part of Mazzini, who certainly should know history, to speak of such a conversion and to lull the proletariat with those ridiculous illusions. Was there ever, at any period, or in any country, a single example of a privileged and dominant class which granted concessions freely, spontaneously, and without being driven to it by force or fear?

... The awareness of the justice of its own cause is no doubt vital to the proletariat in order to organize its own members into a power capable of attaining a triumph. And the proletariat now does not lack this awareness. Where such awareness is still lacking it is our duty to build it up among the workers; that justice has become incontestable even in the eyes of our adversaries. But the mere consciousness of such justice is not sufficient. It is necessary that the proletariat add to it the organization of its own forces, for the time is passed when the walls of Jericho would crumble at the blowing of trumpets; now force is necessary to vanquish and repulse other force.

... We say to the workers: The justice of your cause is certain; only scoundrels can deny it. What you lack, however, is the organization of your own forces. Organize those forces and overthrow that which stands in the way of the realization of your justice. Begin by striking down all those who oppress you. And then after having assured your victory and having destroyed the power of your enemies, show yourselves humane toward the unfortunate stricken-down foes, henceforth disarmed and harmless; recognize them as your brothers and invite them to live and work alongside of you upon the unshakable foundation of social equality.

... Fortunately the proletariat of the cities, not excepting those who swear by the names of Mazzini and Garibaldi, never could let itself be completely converted to the ideas and cause of Mazzini and Garibaldi. And the workers could not do it for the simple reason that the proletariat—that is, the oppressed, despoiled, maltreated, miserable, starved mass of workers—necessarily possess the logic inherent in the historic role of labor.

Workers may accept the programs of Mazzini and Garibaldi; but deep down in their bellies, in the livid pallor of their children and their companions in poverty and suffering, in their everyday actual slavery, there is something which calls for a social revolution. They are all Socialists in spite of themselves, with the exception of a few individuals—perhaps one out of thousands—who, owing to a certain cleverness, to chance or knavery on their part, have entered, or hope to enter, the ranks of the bourgeoisie. All others—and I am referring to the masses of workers who follow Mazzini and Garibaldi—are such only in their imagination, and in reality they can be only revolutionary Socialists.

... If you will organize yourselves for this purpose throughout Italy, harmoniously, fraternally, without recognizing any leaders but your own young collective, I vow to you that within the year there will be no more Mazzinist or Garibaldist workers; they all will be revolutionary Socialists, and patriots, too, but in a very human sense of that word. That is, they will simultaneously be both patriots and internationalists. Thus you will create an unshakable foundation for the future of the Social Revolution.

... Organize the city proletariat in the name of revolutionary Socialism, and in doing this, unite it into one preparatory organization together with the peasantry. An uprising by the proletariat alone would not be enough; with that we would have only a political revolution which would necessarily produce a natural and legitimate reaction on the part of the peasants, and that reaction, or merely the indifference of the peasants, would strangle the revolution of the cities, as it happened recently in France.

Only a wide-sweeping revolution embracing both the city workers and peasants would be sufficiently strong to overthrow and break the organized power of the State, backed as it is by all the resources of the possessing classes. But an all-embracing revolution, that is, a social revolution, is a simultaneous revolution of the people of the cities and of the peasantry. It is this kind of revolution that must be organized—for without a preparatory organization, the most powerful elements are insignificant and impotent. ...

The principal reason why all the revolutionary authorities in the world have accomplished so little toward the Revolution *is that they always wanted to create the Revolution themselves, by their own authority and by their own power,* a circumstance which never failed to produce two results:

In the first place, it greatly narrowed down revolutionary activity, for it is impossible even for the most intelligent, most energetic, most candid revolutionary authority to encompass at once the great number of questions and interests stirred up by the Revolution. For every dictatorship (individual as well as collective, in so far as it is made up of several official persons) is necessarily very circumscribed, very blind, and is incapable of either penetrating the depths or comprehending the scope of the people's lives, just as it is impossible for the largest and most powerful sea-going vessel to measure the depth and expanse of the ocean. Second, every act of official authority, legally imposed, necessarily awakens within the masses a rebellious feeling, a legitimate counter-reaction.

What should revolutionary authorities—and let us try to have as few of them as possible—do in order to organize the Revolution? *They must not do it them-selves, by revolutionary decrees, by imposing this task upon the masses; rather their aim should be that of provoking the masses to action. They must not try to impose upon the masses any organization whatever, but rather should induce the people to set up autonomous organizations. This can be done by gaining in-fluence over the most intelligent and advanced individuals of high standing in each locality*, so that these organizations will conform as much as possible to our principles. Therein lies the whole secret of our triumph.

... There is no need to grumble nor to scorn or disparage the peasants. *It is necessary to lay down a line of revolutionary conduct which will obviate the difficulty of proselytizing the peasants and which will not only prevent the individualism of the peasants from pushing them into the camp of reaction but, on the contrary, will make it instrumental in the triumph of the Revolution.*

Remember, my dear friends, and keep repeating to yourselves a hundred, a thousand times a day, that upon the establishment of this line of conduct depends the outcome of the Revolution: victory or defeat.

... I do not believe that even under the most favorable circumstances the city workers will have sufficient power to impose Communism or collectivism upon the peasants; and I have never wanted this way of realizing Socialism, because I hate every system imposed by force, and because I sincerely and passionately love freedom. This false idea and this hope are destructive of liberty and they constitute the basic delusion of authoritarian Communism, which, because it needs the regularly organized violence of the State, and thus needs the State, necessarily leads to the re-establishment of the principle of authority and of a privileged class of the State.

Collectivism can be imposed only upon slaves—and then collectivism becomes the negation of humanity. Among a free people collectivism can come about only in the natural course of things, by force of circumstances, not by imposing it from above, but by a spontaneous movement from below, which springs forth freely and necessarily when the conditions of privileged individualism—State politics, the codes of civil and criminal law, the juridical family and inheritance rights—have been swept away by the Revolution.

... One must be mad, I have said, to impose anything upon the peasants under present conditions: it would surely make enemies out of them and surely would ruin the Revolution. What are the principal grievances of the peasants, the main causes of their sullen and deep hatred for the cities?

1. The peasants feel that the cities despise them, and that contempt is felt directly, even by the children, and is never forgiven.

2. The peasants imagine, *not without plenty of reasons,* although lacking sufficient historic proofs and experiences to back up those assumptions, that the cities want to dominate and govern them, that they frequently want to exploit them, and that they always want to impose upon the peasants a political order which is very little to the liking of the latter.

3. In addition, the peasants consider the city workers *partisans of dividing up property,* and they fear that the Socialists will confiscate their land, which they love above everything else.

. . . Then what should the city workers do in order to overcome this distrust and enmity of the peasants toward themselves? In the first place, they must cease displaying their contempt, stop despising the peasants. This is necessary for the salvation of the Revolution and of the workers themselves, for the hatred of the peasants constitutes an immense danger. Had it not been for this distrust and hatred, the Revolution would long ago have become an accomplished fact, for it is this animosity, which unfortunately the peasants have been showing toward the cities, that in all countries serves as the basis and the principal force of reaction. In the interest of the revolution which is to emancipate the industrial workers, the latter must get rid of their supercilious attitude toward the peasants. They also should do this for the sake of justice, for in reality they have no reason to despise or detest the peasants. The peasants are not idling parasites, they are rugged workers like the city proletariat. Only they toil under different conditions. In the presence of bourgeois exploitation, the city workers should feel themselves brothers of the peasants.

. . . The peasants will join cause with the city workers as soon as they become convinced that the latter do not pretend to impose upon them their will or some political and social order invented by the cities for the greater happiness of the villages; they will join cause as soon as they are assured that the industrial workers will not take their lands away.

It is altogether necessary at the present moment that the city workers really renounce this claim and this intention, and that they renounce it in such a manner that the peasants get to know and become convinced of it. Those workers must renounce it, for even when that claim and that intention seemed to lie within the bounds of realization, they were *highly unjust and reactionary,* and now when that realization becomes impossible, it would be no less than criminal folly to attempt it.

By what right would the city workers impose upon the peasants any form of government or economic organization whatever? By the right of revolution, we are told. But the Revolution ceases to be a revolution when it acts despotically, when, instead of promoting freedom among the masses, it promotes reaction. The means and condition, if not the principal aim of the Revolution, is the annihilation of the principle of authority in all of its possible manifestations—the abolition, the utter destruction, and, if necessary, the violent destruction of the State. For the State, the lesser brother of the Church, as Proudhon has proven it, is the historic consecration of all despotisms, of all privileges, the political reason for all economic and social enslavement, the very essence and focal point of all reaction. Therefore, whenever a State is built up in the name of the Revolution, it is reaction and despotism that are being furthered and not freedom, it is the establishment of privilege versus equality that comes as a result thereof.

... This is as clear as daylight. But the Socialist workers of France, brought up in the political traditions of Jacobinism, have never wanted to understand it. Now they will be compelled to understand it, which is fortunate for the Revolution and for themselves. Whence this ridiculous as well as arrogant, unjust as well as baneful, claim on their part to impose their political and social ideal upon ten million peasants who do not want it? Manifestly this is one more bourgeois legacy, a political bequest of bourgeois revolutionism. What is the basis, the explanation, the underlying theory of this claim? It is the pretended or real superiority of intelligence, of education—in a word, of workers' civilization over that of the rural population.

But do you realize that with this principle one could easily justify any kind of conquest and oppression? The bourgeoisie have always fallen back upon that principle to prove their mission and their right to *govern* or, what amounts to the same thing, to exploit the world of labor. In conflicts between nations as well as between classes this fatal principle, which is simply the principle of authority, explains and poses as a right all invasions and conquests. Did not the Germans always put forth this principle by way of justifying their attempts upon the liberty and independence of the Slavic peoples and of legitimizing the violent and forcible Germanization of the latter? That, they say, is the victory of civilization over barbarism.

Beware, the Germans already are remarking that the German Protestant civilization is much superior to the Catholic civilization of the peoples of the Latin race in general, and of the French civilization in particular. Beware lest the Germans soon imagine that their mission is to civilize you and to make you happy, just as you now imagine that it is your mission to civilize and forcibly free your compatriots, your brothers, the peasants of France. To me both claims are equally hateful, and I declare to you that in international relations, as well as in the relations of one class to another, I will be on the side of those who are to be civilized in this manner. Together with them I will revolt against all those arrogant civilizers—whether they call themselves Germans or workers—and in rebelling against them I shall serve the cause of revolution against reaction.

... But if this is the case, I shall be asked, must we then abandon the ignorant and superstitious peasants to all kinds of influences and intrigues, on the part of reaction? Not at all! Reaction must be destroyed in the villages just as it has to be destroyed in the cities. But in order to attain this goal, it is not enough to say: We want to destroy reaction; it must be destroyed and torn out by its roots, which can be done only by decrees. On the contrary—and I can prove it by citing history—decrees, and in general all acts of authority extirpate nothing; they perpetuate that which they set out to destroy.

What follows? Since revolution cannot be *imposed* upon the villages, *it must be generated right there, by promoting a revolutionary movement among the peasants themselves, leading them on to destroy through their own efforts the public order, all the political and civil institutions, and to establish and organize anarchy in the villages.*

But what is to be done? There is only one way—and that is, to revolutionize the villages as much as the cities. But who can do it? The only class which is now the real outspoken agent of the Revolution is the working class of the cities.

... It is necessary to send free detachments into the villages as propagandists for the Revolution.

There is a general rule to the effect that those who want to spread the Revolution by means of propaganda must be revolutionists themselves. One must have the Devil within himself in order to be able to arouse the masses; otherwise there can be only abortive speeches and empty clamor, but not revolutionary acts. Therefore, above all else the propagandistic free detachments have to be inspired and organized along revolutionary lines. They must carry the Revolution within themselves in order to be able to provoke and arouse it in their listeners. And then they have to draw up a plan, a line of conduct conforming to the aim which they have set for themselves.

What is this aim? It is not to impose the Revolution upon the peasants, but to provoke and arouse it among them. A revolution that is imposed upon people—whether by official decree or by force of arms—is not a revolution, but its opposite, for it necessarily provokes reaction.

... Civil war, so baneful for the power of the States, is on the contrary and by virtue of this very cause, always favorable to the awakening of popular initiative and the intellectual, moral, and even material development of the people. The reason thereof is quite simple: civil war upsets and disturbs in the masses the sheepish state so beloved of all governments, a state turning the people into herds to be tended and to be shorn at will by their shepherds. Civil war breaks up the brutalizing monotony of their daily existence, a mechanical existence devoid of thought, and compels them to reflect upon the claims of the various princes or parties contending for the right to oppress and exploit the masses of people. And it often leads them to the realization—if not conscious at least instinctive realization—of the profound truth that neither one of the contending parties has any claim upon them, and that both are equally bad.

Besides, from the moment that the people's collective mind, which is usually kept in a state of torpor, wakes up at one point, it necessarily asserts itself in other directions. It becomes stirred up, it breaks away from its worldly inertia, and, transcending the confines of a mechanical faith, shaking off the yoke of traditional and petrified representations which have served it in the place of genuine thoughts, it subjects all its idols of yesterday to a passionate and severe criticism, one that is guided by its own sound sense and upright conscience, which often are of greater value than science.

It is thus that the people's mind awakens. And with the awakening of that mind comes the sacred instinct, the essentially human instinct of revolt, the source of all emancipation; and simultaneously there develop within the people morality and material prosperity—those twin children of freedom. This freedom, so beneficial to the people, finds its support, guarantee, and encouragement in the civil war itself, which, by dividing the forces of the people's oppressors, exploiters, tutors, and masters, necessarily undermines the baneful power of one and the other.

... All the other classes [except the city and rural proletariat] must vanish from the face of the earth; they must vanish not as individuals but as classes. Socialism is not cruel; it is a thousand times more humane than Jacobinism, that is, than the political revolution. It is not directed against individuals, not even against the most nefarious among them, since it realizes only too well that all individuals, good or bad, are the inevitable product of the social status created for them by society and history. True, Socialists will not be able to prevent the people in the early days of the Revolution from giving vent to their fury by doing away with a few hundreds of the most odious, the most rabid and dangerous enemies. But once that hurricane passes, the Socialists will oppose with all their might hypocritical—in a political and juridical sense—butchery perpetrated in cold blood.

... As soon as the Revolution begins to take on a Socialist character, it will cease to be cruel and sanguinary. The people are not at all cruel; it is the ruling classes that have shown themselves to be cruel. At times the people rise up, raging against all the deceits, vexations, oppressions, and tortures, of which they are victims, and then they break forth like an enraged bull, seeing nothing ahead of them and demolishing everything in their way. But those are very rare and very brief moments. Ordinarily the people are good and humane. They suffer too much themselves not to sympathize with the sufferings of others.

But alas! too often have they served as instruments of the systematic fury of the privileged classes. All the national, political, and religious ideas, for the sake of which the people have shed their own blood and the blood of their brothers, the blood of foreign peoples, all these ideas have always served only the interests of those classes, ever turning into means of new oppression and exploitation of the people. In all the furious scenes in the history of all the countries wherein the masses of the people, enraged to the point of madness, have turned their energies to mutual destruction, you will invariably find that behind those masses are agitators and leaders belonging to the privileged classes: Army officers, noblemen, priests, and bourgeois. It is not among the people that one should look for cruelty and concentrated and systematically organized cold fury, but in the instincts, the passions, and the political and religious institutions of the privileged classes: in the Church and in the State, in their laws, and in the ruthless and iniquitous application of those laws.

. . . It inevitably comes about that after killing many people, the revolutionaries see themselves driven to the melancholy conviction that nothing has been gained and that not a single step has been made toward the realization of their cause, but that, on the contrary, they did an ill turn to the Revolution by employing those methods, and that they prepared with their own hands the triumph of reaction. And that is so for two reasons: first, that the causes of the reaction having been left intact, the reaction is given a chance to reproduce and multiply itself in new forms; and second, that ere long all those bloody butcheries and massacres must arouse against them everything that is human in man.

The [French] revolution . . . whatever one may say about it, was neither Socialist nor materialist, nor, using the pretentious expression of M. Gambetta, was it by any means a *positivist* revolution. It was essentially bourgeois, Jacobin, metaphysical, political, and idealist. Generous and sweeping in its aspirations, it reached out for an impossible thing: establishment of an ideal equality in the midst of material inequality. While preserving as *sacred foundations* all the conditions of economic inequality, it believed that it could unite and envelop all men in a sweeping sentiment of brotherly, humane, intellectual, moral, political, and social equality. That was its dream, its religion, manifested by the enthusiasm, by the grandly heroic acts of its best and greatest representatives. But the realization of that dream was impossible because it ran contrary to all natural and social laws.

karl marx

Karl Marx, German political philosopher and the most important figure in the history of socialist thinking, was born in Trier, the son of an enlightened and successful lawyer. Although both his father and his Dutch mother were descendants of Jewish rabbinical families, Marx's father had converted to Lutheranism and all members of the family were baptized Protestants. Consequently, Marx never held any particular racial, religious, or national allegiance but always considered himself a European.

During his student days at the universities of Bonn and Berlin, young Karl distinguished himself as an excellent student in law, political science, philosophy, and history. After receiving his doctoral degree in philosophy in 1842 from the University of Jena, Marx's liberal political views led him to consider journalism as a career. In 1842 he became editor of the *Rheinische Zeitung*, a liberal newspaper in Cologne.

Marx married Jenny von Westphalen in 1843. Also the product of a bourgeois background, Jenny was the daughter of a high government official and had been a close friend from the days of Karl's boyhood. Their marriage was a happy one, although the tribulations of subsequent years occasionally contributed to some severe strain. Six children were born of this union; only three survived childhood. When Marx's newspaper was suppressed by the government in 1843, he and Jenny moved to Paris where they met a wealthy manufacturer's son, Friedrich Engels, who became a lifelong friend, collaborator, and supporter.

In 1847, at a new place of exile in Brussels, Marx wrote a reply to Pierre Proudhon's book *The Philosophy of Misery* and entitled it *The Misery of Philosophy*. In this work he developed the fundamental propositions of his economic interpretation of history. His opposition to utopian socialists like Proudhon derived from his distrust of any scheme which sought the morally most desirable order. Marx's early Hegelian training had rendered him a determinist, and he believed that the system which soon would replace capitalism would by necessity emerge from the inevitable operation of historical forces. It was also during his stay in Brussels that Marx, who was gaining increasing prominence in socialist circles, was commissioned by the London Center of the Communist League to compose a definite statement of its aims and beliefs. This work appeared as *Manifest der Kommunistischen Partei* ("Manifesto of the Communist Party"). Published in 1848, it is a historic document of tremendous force, succinctness, and clarity which has achieved worldwide significance.

The revolutionary atmosphere in Germany in 1848 enabled Marx to return to Cologne and revive his newspaper under the title of *Neue Rheinische Zeitung,* but in 1849 he was expelled. This time he settled in London, where he spent the rest of his life in poverty. The generosity of his friend and benefactor Engels, and the income earned from commissioned writings for such newspapers as the *New York Tribune,* then under the editorship of a utopian socialist, spared Marx from starvation. Several of Marx's children died, among them Edgar, the only son from his marriage. He also had an illegitimate son, Frederic, about whom little is known. Of Marx's three daughters who reached adulthood, two married French socialists; the third committed suicide after an unhappy association with British Marxist Edward Aveling. Marx died on March 14, 1883, fifteen months after the death of his wife. He was buried at Highgate cemetery in London.

Despite poverty and persistent illness, Marx was a prolific writer. He published numerous articles and books, but his most famous work was *Das Kapital.* The first volume appeared in 1867; the second and third volumes, published posthumously in 1885 and 1894, were edited by Engels. Collectively, these volumes provide a thorough exposition of Marxism and they became the foundation of international socialism. As Marx's reputation spread, so did public fear of him. He had insisted on authoritarian sway within the International, and finally, after controversy with Bakunin, virtually destroyed the International rather than risk losing control over its direction.

Marx was primarily a revolutionist who was interested in ideas only as a means of influencing the course of events. Convinced of the righteousness of his cause, he was intolerant of criticism and contradiction. His was a powerful, incisive, unsentimental, and thoroughly practical mind. Marx's method was developed according to practical intellectual principles which considered the feasibility of achievement. He termed himself a "scientific" socialist in contradistinction to the utopian socialists. Regarding Czarist Russia as the greatest enemy of freedom in all Europe, Marx wished to see British imperial power bolstered as a counterweight. He also hated the autocratic rule of Napoleon III and Bismarck. Occasionally he was capable of sharing national feelings, exemplified in his passionate interest in the American Civil War and championing of the North. Since Marx treasured the liberal-humanitarian tradition from which the socialist movement had sprung, he very probably would abhor the antihumanitarian practices of some contemporary Communist regimes.

Marx's purpose was to provide a social philosophy for the rising proletariat. Although he regarded the course of history as proceeding from timeless economic laws toward the predetermined goal of socialism, he felt a mission to accelerate this inevitable historical process. To Marx, private ownership was the source of all evil in society; it produced class distinctions, class interests, and ultimately, class struggle. As he stated in his *Manifesto of the Communist Party* (selections from which follow), "The history of all hitherto existing society is the history of class struggles." The importance of his dialectical method and of his theories extends far beyond their immense political influence. Estimates of Marx vary greatly. Communists look to him as their messiah; countless scholars consider him the founder of economic history and sociology; some regard him as an unscrupulous, bloodthirsty destroyer of society. In general, however, Marx should be viewed against the background of the early industrial society whose injustices he so effectively attacked. In his book entitled *Karl Marx,* Isaiah Berlin states: "No thinker in the nineteenth century has had so direct, deliberate and powerful an influence upon mankind as Karl Marx." Only the future will tell whether his legacy will have equal import for this and subsequent centuries.

Manifesto of the Communist Party

... The history of all hitherto existing society is the history of class struggles.

Freeman and slave, patrician and plebeian, lord and serf, guild-master and journeyman, in a word, oppressor and oppressed, stood in constant opposition

From *Karl Marx and Friedrich Engels: Selected Works,* I, Foreign Languages Publishing House, Moscow, 1955, pp. 34-49, 51-54, 64-65.

to one another, carried on an uninterrupted, now hidden, now open fight, a fight that each time ended, either in a revolutionary re-constitution of society at large, or in the common ruin of the contending classes.

... The modern bourgeois society that has sprouted from the ruins of feudal society has not done away with class antagonisms. It has but established new classes, new conditions of oppression, new forms of struggle in place of the old ones.

Our epoch, the epoch of the bourgeoisie, possesse, however, this distinctive feature: it has simplified the class antagonisms. Society as a whole is more and more splitting up into two great hostile camps, into two great classes directly facing each other: Bourgeoisie and Proletariat.

... The bourgeoisie, historically, has played a most revolutionary part.

The bourgeoisie, wherever it has got the upper hand, has put an end to all feudal, patriarchal, idyllic relations. It has pitilessly torn asunder the motley feudal ties that bound man to his "natural superiors," and has left remaining no other nexus between man and man than naked self-interest, then callous "cash payment." It has drowned the most heavenly ecstasies of religious fervour, of chivalrous enthusiasm, of philistine sentimentalism, in the icy water of egotistical calculation. It has resolved personal worth into exchange value, and in place of the numberless indefeasible chartered freedoms, has set up that single, unconscionable freedom—Free Trade. In one word, for exploitation, veiled by religious and political illusions, it has substituted naked, shameless, direct, brutal exploitation.

... The bourgeoisie has subjected the country to the rule of the towns. It has created enormous cities, has greatly increased the urban population as compared with the rural, and has thus rescued a considerable part of the population from the idiocy of rural life. Just as it has made the country dependent on the towns, so it has made barbarian and semi-barbarian countries dependent on the civilized ones, nations of peasants on nations of bourgeois, the East on the West.

The bourgeoisie keeps more and more doing away with the scattered state of the population, of the means of production, and of property. It has agglomerated population, centralized means of production, and has concentrated property in a few hands. The necessary consequence of this was political centralization. Independent, or but loosely connected provinces, with separate interests, laws, governments and systems of taxation, became lumped together into one nation, with one government, one code of laws, one national class-interest, one frontier and one customs-tariff.

... Modern bourgeois society with its relations of production, of exchange and of property, a society that has conjured up such gigantic means of production and of exchange, is like the sorcerer, who is no longer able to control the powers of the nether world whom he has called up by his spells. For many a decade past the history of industry and commerce is but the history of the revolt of modern productive forces against modern conditions of production, against the property relations that are the conditions for the existence of the bourgeoisie and of its rule. It is enough to mention the commercial crises that by their periodical return put on its trial, each time more threateningly, the existence of the entire bourgeois society. In these crises a great part not only of the existing products, but also of the previously created productive forces, are periodically destroyed. In these crises there breaks out an epidemic that, in all earlier epochs, would have seemed an absurdity—the epidemic of overproduction. Society suddenly finds itself put back into a state of momentary barbarism; it appears as if a famine, a universal war of devastation had cut off the supply of every means of subsistence; industry and commerce seem to be destroyed: and why? Because there is too much civilisation, too much means of subsistence, too much industry, too much commerce. The productive forces at the disposal of society no longer tend to further the development of the conditions of bourgeois property; on the contrary, they have become too powerful for these conditions, by which they are fettered, and so soon as they overcome these fetters, they bring disorder into the whole of bourgeois society, endanger the existence of bourgeois property. The conditions of bourgeois society are too narrow to comprise the wealth created by them. And how does the bourgeoisie get over these crises? On the one hand by enforced destruction of a mass of productive forces; on the other, by the conquest of new markets, and by the more thorough exploitation of the old ones. That is to say, by paving the way for more extensive and more destructive crises, and by diminishing the means whereby crises are prevented.

The weapons with which the bourgeoisie felled feudalism to the ground are now turned against the bourgeoisie itself.

But not only has the bourgeoisie forged the weapons that bring death to itself; it has also called into existence the men who are to wield those weapons—the modern working class—the proletarians.

In proportion as the bourgeoisie, i.e., capital, is developed, in the same proportion is the proletariat, the modern working class, developed—a class of labourers, who live only so long as they find work, and who find work only so long as their labour increases capital. These labourers, who must sell themselves piecemeal, are a commodity, like every other article of commerce, and are consequently exposed to all the vicissitudes of competition, to all the fluctuations of the market.

... Modern industry has converted the little workshop of the patriarchal master into the great factory of the industrial capitalist. Masses of labourers, crowded into the factory, are organised like soldiers. As privates of the industrial army they are placed under the command of a perfect hierarchy of officers and sergeants. Not only are they slaves of the bourgeois class, and of the bourgeois State; they are daily and hourly enslaved by the machine, by the over-looker, and, above all, by the individual bourgeois manufacturer himself. The more openly this despotism proclaims gain to be its end and aim, the more petty, the more hateful and the more embittering it is.

. . . with the development of industry the proletariat not only increases in number; it becomes concentrated in greater masses, its strength grows, and it feels that strength more. The various interests and conditions of life within the ranks of the proletariat are more and more equalised, in proportion as machinery obliterates all distinctions of labour, and nearly everywhere reduces wages to the same low level. The growing competition among the bourgeois, and the resulting commercial crises, make the wages of the workers ever more fluctuating. The unceasing improvement of machinery, ever more rapidly developing, makes their livelihood more and more precarious; the collisions between individual workmen and individual bourgeois take more and more the character of collisions between two classes. Thereupon the workers begin to form combinations (Trades' Unions) against the bourgeois; they club together in order to keep up the rate of wages; they found permanent associations in order to make provision beforehand for these occasional revolts. Here and there the contest breaks out into riots.

. . . .This organization of the proletarians into a class, and consequently into a political party, is continually being upset again by the competition between the workers themselves. But it ever rises up again, stronger, firmer, mightier. It compels legislative recognition of particular interests of the workers, by taking advantage of the divisions among the bourgeoisie itself.

. . . .Of all the classes that stand face to face with the bourgeoisie today, the proletariat alone is a really revolutionary class. The other classes decay and finally disappear in the face of modern industry; the proletariat is its special and essential product.

. . . .The proletarians cannot become masters of the productive forces of society, except by abolishing their own previous mode of appropriation, and thereby also every other previous mode of appropriation. They have nothing of their own to secure and to fortify; their mission is to destroy all previous securities for, and insurances of, individual property.

All previous historical movements were movements of minorities, or in the interest of minorities. The proletarian movement is the self-conscious, independent movement of the immense majority, in the interests of the immense majority. The proletariat, the lowest stratum of our present society, cannot stir, cannot raise itself up, without the whole superincumbent strata of official society being sprung into the air.

Though not in substance, yet in form, the struggle of the proletariat with the bourgeoisie is at first a national struggle. The proletariat of each country must, of course, first of all settle matters with its own bourgeoisie.

In depicting the most general phases of the development of the proletariat, we traced the more or less veiled civil war, raging within existing society, up to the point where that war breaks out into open revolution, and where the violent overthrow of the bourgeoisie lays the foundation for the sway of the proletariat.

....The essential condition for the existence, and for the sway of the bourgeois class, is the formation and augmentation of capital; the condition for capital is wage-labour. Wage-labour rests exclusively on competition between the labourers. The advance of industry, whose involuntary promoter is the bourgeoisie, replaces the isolation of the labourers, due to competition, by their revolutionary combination, due to association. The development of Modern Industry, therefore, cuts from under its feet the very foundation on which the bourgeoisie produces and appropriates products. What the bourgeoisie, therefore, produces, above all, is its own grave-diggers. Its fall and the victory of the proletariat are equally inevitable.

In what relation do the Communists stand to the proletarians as a whole?

The Communists do not form a separate party opposed to other working-class parties.

They have no interests separate and apart from those of the proletariat as a whole.

They do not set up any sectarian principles of their own, by which to shape and mould the proletarian movement.

The Communists are distinguished from the other working-class parties by this only: 1. In the national struggles of the proletarians of the different countries, they point out and bring to the front the common interests of the entire proletariat, independently of all nationality. 2. In the various stages of development which the struggle of the working class against the bourgeoisie has to pass through, they always and everywhere represent the interests of the movement as a whole.

The Communists, therefore, are on the one hand, practically, the most advanced and resolute section of the working-class parties of every country, that section which pushes forward all others; on the other hand, theoretically, they have over the great mass of the proletariat the advantage of clearly understanding the line of march, the conditions, and the ultimate general results of the proletarian movement.

The immediate aim of the Communists is the same as that of all the other proletarian parties: formation of the proletariat into a class, overthrow of the bourgeois supremacy, conquest of political power by the proletariat.

. . . .The distinguishing feature of Communism is not the abolition of property generally, but the abolition of bourgeois property. But modern bourgeois private property is the final and most complete expression of the system of producing and appropriating products, that is based on class antagonisms, on the exploitation of the many by the few.

In this sense, the theory of the Communists may be summed up in the single sentence: Abolition of private property.

We Communists have been reproached with the desire of abolishing the right of personally acquiring property as the fruit of a man's own labour, which property is alledged to be the groundwork of all personal freedom, activity and independence.

Hard-won, self-acquired, self-earned property! Do you mean the property of the petty artisan and of the small peasant, a form of property that preceded the bourgeois form? There is no need to abolish that; the development of industry has to a great extent already destroyed it, and is still destroying it daily.

Or do you mean modern bourgeois private property?

But does wage-labour create any property for the labourer? Not a bit. It creates capital, i.e., that kind of property which exploits wage-labour, and which cannot increase except upon condition of begetting a new supply of wage-labour for fresh exploitation. Property, in its present form, is based on the antagonism of capital and wage-labour. Let us examine both sides of this antagonism.

To be a capitalist, is to have not only a purely personal, but a social *status* in production. Capital is a collective product, and only by the united action of many members, nay, in the last resort, only by the united action of all members of society, can it be set in motion

Capital is, therefore, not a personal, it is a social power.

When, therefore, capital is converted into common property, into the property of all members of society, personal property is not thereby transformed into social property. It is only the social character of the property that is changed. It loses its class-character.

Let us now take wage-labour.

The average price of wage-labour is the minimum wage, i.e., the quantum of the means of subsistence, which is absolutely requisite to keep the labourer in bare existence as a labourer. What, therefore, the wage-labourer appropriates by means of his labour, merely suffices to prolong and reproduce a bare existence. We by no means intend to abolish this personal appropriation of the products of labour, an appropriation that is made for the maintenance and reproduction of human life, and that leaves no surplus wherewith to command the labour of others. All that we want to do away with, is the miserable character of this appropriation, under which the labourer lives merely to increase capital, and is allowed to live only in so far as the interest of the ruling class requires it.

In bourgeois society, living labour is but a means to increase accumulated labour. In Communist society, accumulated labour is but a means to widen, to enrich, to promote the existence of the labourer.

In bourgeois society, therefore, the past dominates the present; in Communist society, the present dominates the past. In bourgeois society capital is independent and has individuality, while the living person is dependent and has no individuality.

And the abolition of this state of things is called by the bourgeois, abolition of individuality and freedom! And rightly so. The abolition of bourgeois individuality, bourgeois independence, and bourgeois freedom is undoubtedly aimed at.

. . . .You are horrified at our intending to do away with private property. But in your existing society, private property is already done away with for nine-tenths of the population; its existence for the few is solely due to its non-existence in the hands of those nine-tenths. You reproach, us, therefore, with intending to do away with a form of property, the necessary condition for whose existence is, the non-existence of any property for the immense majority of society.

In one word, you reproach us with intending to do away with your property. Precisely so; that is just what we intend.

From the moment when labour can no longer be converted into capital, money, or rent, into a social power capable of being monopolised, i.e., from the moment when individual property can no longer be transformed into bourgeois property, into capital, from that moment, you say, individuality vanishes.

You must, therefore, confess that by "individual" you mean no other person than the middle-class owner of property. This person must, indeed, be swept out of the way, and made impossible.

Communism deprives no man of the power to appropriate the products of society; all that it does is to deprive him of the power to subjugate the labour of others by means of such appropriation.

. . . .The Communists are further reproached with desiring to abolish countries and nationality.

The working men have no country. We cannot take from them what they have not got. Since the proletariat must first of all acquire political supremacy, must rise to be the leading class of the nation, must constitute itself *the* nation, it is, so far, itself national, though not in the bourgeois sense of the word.

National differences and antagonisms between peoples are daily more and more vanishing, owing to the development of the bourgeoisie, to freedom of commerce, to the world-market, to uniformity in the mode of production and in the conditions of life corresponding thereto.

The supremacy of the proletariat will cause them to vanish still faster. United action, of the leading civilised countries at least, is one of the first conditions for the emancipation of the proletariat.

In proportion as the exploitation of one individual by another is put an end to, the exploitation of one nation by another will also be put an end to. In proportion as the antagonism between classes within the nation vanishes, the hostility of one nation to another will come to an end.

The charges against Communism made from a religious, a philosophical, and, generally, from an ideological standpoint, are not deserving of serious examination.

...The Communist revolution is the most radical rupture with traditional property relations; no wonder that its development involves the most radical rupture with traditional ideas.

But let us have done with the bourgeois objections to Communism.

...The first step in the revolution by the working class is to raise the proletariat to the position of ruling class, to win the battle of democracy.

The proletariat will use its political supremacy to wrest, by degrees, all capital from the bourgeoisie, to centralise all instruments of production in the hands of the State, i.e., of the proletariat organised as the ruling class; and to increase the total of productive forces as rapidly as possible.

Of course, in the beginning, this cannot be effected except by means of despotic inroads on the rights of property, and on the conditions of bourgeois production; by means of measures, therefore, which appear economically insufficient and untenable, but which, in the course of the movement, outstrip themselves, necessitate further inroads upon the old social order, and are unavoidable as a means of entirely revolutionising the mode of production.

These measures will of course be different in different countries.

Nevertheless in the most advanced countries, the following will be pretty generally applicable.

1. Abolition of property in land and application of all rents of land to public purposes.

2. A heavy progressive or graduated income tax.

3. Abolition of all right of inheritance.

4. Confiscation of the property of all emigrants and rebels.

5. Centralisation of credit in the hands of the State, by means of a national bank with State capital and an exclusive monopoly.

6. Centralisation of the means of communication and transport in the hands of the State.

7. Extension of factories and instruments of production owned by the State; the bringing into cultivation of waste-lands, and the improvement of the soil generally in accordance with a common plan.

8. Equal liability of all to labour. Establishment of industrial armies, especially for agriculture.

9. Combination of agriculture with manufacturing industries; gradual abolition of the distinction between town and country, by a more equable distribution of the population over the country.

10. Free education for all children in public schools. Abolition of children's factory labour in its present form. Combination of education with industrial production, etc., etc.

When, in the course of development, class distinctions have disappeared, and all production has been concentrated in the hands of a vast association of the whole nation, the public power will lose its political character. Political power, properly so called, is merely the organized power of one class for oppressing another. If the proletariat during its contest with the bourgeoisie is compelled, by the force of circumstances, to organize itself as a class, if, by means of a revolution, it makes itself ruling class, and, as such, sweeps away by force the old conditions of production, then it will, along with these conditions, have swept away the conditions for the existence of class antagonisms and of classes generally, and will thereby have abolished its own supremacy as a class.

In place of the old bourgeois society, with its classes and class antagonisms, we shall have an association, in which the free development of each is the condition for the free development of all.

. . .The Communists fight for the attainment of the immediate aims, for the enforcement of the momentary interests of the working class; but in the movement of the present, they also represent and take care of the future of that movement.

. . .the Communists everywhere support every revolutionary movement against the existing social and political order of things.

In all these movements they bring to the front, as the leading question in each, the property question, no matter what its degree of development at the time.

Finally, they labour everywhere for the union and agreement of the democratic parties of all countries.

The Communists disdain to conceal their views and aims. They openly declare that their ends can be attained only by the forcible overthrow of all existing social conditions. Let the ruling classes tremble at a Communistic revolution. The proletarians have nothing to lose but their chains. They have a world to win.

WORKING MEN OF ALL COUNTRIES, UNITE!

leo tolstoy

Russian author, reformer, moral thinker and one of the world's greatest novelists, Leo Tolstoy was born on September 9, 1828, on the family estate at Yasnaya Polyana, about a hundred miles south of Moscow. Orphaned at nine, he was brought up by aunts and tutored in a fashion common to children of the Russian nobility. At the age of sixteen he entered the University of Kazan, but, disappointed with the instruction there, he returned to Yasnaya Polyana in 1847 to manage his estate and conduct his own education. His attempt at establishing a school for peasants on the family estate proved less than successful, and Tolstoy spent the next few years leading a wasteful life amidst the social circles of Moscow and St. Petersburg.

Disgusted with his shiftless existence, Tolstoy joined his soldier-brother Nikolai in the Caucasus in 1851; and in the following year, he joined the army himself and performed bravely in several engagements against the hill tribes. Much of his leisure time he spent in writing, completing his first published work, *Childhood,* in 1852. Transferred to the Danube front in 1854, Tolstoy participated in the siege of Sevastopol during the Crimean War. In notes kept during the next two years, he contrasted the simple heroism of the common soldier with the false heroics of his fellow officers. Some of these writings were published in a journal, *Contemporary,* and foreshadowed his later views on war. *War and Peace,* in which he gave even more eloquent form to these ideas, also grew out of his experiences at Sevastopol. At the end of the fighting in 1856, he left the army and went to St. Petersburg, where he became the idol of rival literary groups which sought his endorsement of their respective social and aesthetic views. Tolstoy by this date had become a pronounced individualist and, rather than pander to either party, he rebuffed both and left for the family estate at Yasnaya Polyana.

Tolstoy traveled abroad in 1857, visiting France, Switzerland, and Germany. His diary for this period reveals the remorseful soul-searching which he underwent as he began to question the bases of modern civilization. A renewed concern for the education of the poor prompted him once again to open a school for peasant children at the family estate. The success of his original teaching methods, which anticipated modern progressive education, drew him deeper into pedagogical studies. In 1860-61 he traveled to other parts of Western Europe, where he investigated educational theory and practice, and his subsequent texts and other publications in the field made him a renowned authority in the discipline.

Leo Tolstoy married Sophia Andreyevna Bers in 1862. Thereafter he dropped his educational activities and for the next fifteen years devoted himself to his marriage and to his family, which ultimately included thirteen children. During this period he wrote, among other things, *The Cossacks, War and Peace,* and *Anna Karenina,* all of which illustrate the author's view of history as a force proceeding inexorably toward its own end and depicts man as a helpless and accidental instrument.

A constant probing into the purpose of life, which had troubled him since his youth, eventually drove Tolstoy into a state of spiritual crisis. In or around 1876, he embraced the doctrine of Christian love and accepted the principle of nonresistance to evil. For the remainder of his life, Tolstoy preached his peculiar faith of non-violence and the simplistic, non-material life in books such as *What I Believe In* (1882). His new convictions took a form of Christian anarchism which led him to disavow immortality and reject the authority of the church. By 1901, the Russian Orthodox Church had become sufficiently provoked by his writings and teachings that it excommunicated him.

Following his "conversion," Tolstoy strove to live the life he preached. He gave up smoking and drinking, became a vegetarian, and frequently dressed in common peasant clothes. Since he also condemned private property, he would have preferred to donate his entire estate to the needs of the poor, but his family took legal action to prevent such a move. Believing that no one should exist on the labors of others, Tolstoy became as self-sufficient as possible, cleaning his own room, working in the fields, and making some of his own clothes. His asceticism extended to his sexual relations with his wife, who by this time was almost totally estranged from him anyway. She, and all of the children except the youngest daughter Alexandra, resented the strange types of people who became Tolstoy's adherents and who frequently sought him out at his home. Many of his followers set up communes in order to live together according to their "Leader's" precepts. But Tolstoy distrusted such organized efforts and kept insisting that the truth that brings happiness can only be achieved by individuals who honestly look within themselves.

All of the excerpts which follow were written in this latter part of Tolstoy's life, and they keenly reflect his moral and social concepts. The first selection reveals Tolstoy's reaction to the establishment of the Nobel Peace Prize and his judgement that the Dukhobors would make deserving recipients of such an award. The Dukhobors were a pacifist sect persecuted by the Russian government. Indeed, while nearly all monies earned from his many publications went to the family following Tolstoy's voluntary transfer of his legacy to them, he did retain the income from his last long novel, *Resurrection* (1899), and he promptly donated it to the Dukhobors.

A second selection, "Letter to a Corporal" (1899), is a scathing attack against all forms of military service, which his own experience had taught him to hate so intensely. Whatever the merits of his arguments, they certainly embody as much relevance today as they did at the time in which they were written.

The final selection, "Patriotism and Government," was published only six months before his death and contains a preface by Ernest Belfort Bax. Ernest Bax (1854-1926) was a co-founder, with William Morris, of the Socialist League in Britain in 1885; Bax's own socialist beliefs tended toward anarchism. Tolstoy's theme in this particular essay is the folly of patriotism, particularly the more perverse forms of jingoistic and chauvinistic patriotism. His remarks, written in 1910, seem no less suitable for the world of the 1970s.

The aging Tolstoy was profoundly troubled in the last days of his life by the embarrassing and painful contradiction between the simplistic life he preached, and the life of ease and creature comforts which surrounded him at the family estate. Finally, with domestic relations progressively deteriorating, he left home stealthily one night, accompanied by his youngest daughter, Alexandra, in search of a place where he could rest quietly and come closer to God. A few days later, on November 20, 1910, he died of pneumonia at the remote railway junction of Astapovo, in the province of Ryazan. The forlorn home in which he was to die was less than a hundred miles from the home in which he could not live.

Nobel's Bequest

I read in some Swedish papers that by Nobel's will a certain sum of money is bequeathed to him who shall most serve the cause of peace.

I assume that the men who served the cause of peace did so only because they served God; and every monetary reward can only be disagreeable to them, in that it gives a selfish character to their service of God. For this reason it would seem that this condition of Nobel's will can hardly be executed correctly. Indeed, it cannot be correctly executed in relation to the men themselves who have all the time served the cause of peace; but, I presume, it will be quite correctly executed, if the money shall be distributed among the families of those men who have served the cause of peace and in consequence of this service are in a most difficult and wretched condition. I am speaking of the families of the Dukhobors of the Caucasus, who, to the number of four thousand people, have been suffering these three years from the Russian government's severe treatment of them, because their husbands, sons, and fathers refuse to do active or reserve military service.

Thirty-two of those who have refused have, after having stayed in the disciplinary battalion, where two of them died, been sent to the worst parts of Siberia, and about three hundred men are pining away in the prisons of the Caucasus and of Russia.

The incompatibility of military service with the profession of Christianity has always been clear for all true Christians, and has many times been expressed by them; but the church sophists, who are in the service of the authorities, have always known how to drown these voices, so that simple people have not seen this incompatibility and, continuing to call themselves Christians, have entered military service and have obeyed the authorities, which practised them in acts of murder, but the contradiction between the profession of Christianity and the participation in military matters has become more obvious with every day, and finally, in our day, when, on the one hand, the amicable communion and unity of the Christian nations is growing more and more intimate and, on the other, these same nations are more and more burdened with terrible armaments for mutually hostile purposes, it has reached the utmost degree of tension. Everybody speaks of peace, and peace is preached by the preachers and pastors in their churches, by the peace societies in their gatherings, by writers in newspapers and books, by representatives of the government—in their speeches, toasts, and all kinds of demonstrations. Everybody speaks and writes about peace, but nobody believes in it and nobody can believe in it, because these same

From Count Leo N. Tolstoy, "Miscellaneous Letters and Essays," translated and edited by Leo Wiener, in *The Complete Works of Count Tolstoy*, XXIII, Colonial Press Company, New York, 1905, pp. 332-337. This essay is dated August 29, 1897.

preachers and pastors, who to-day preach against war, to-morrow bless the flags and cannon and, extolling the commanders, welcome their armies; the members of the peace societies, their orators and writers against war, as soon as their turns come, calmly enter the military caste and prepare themselves for murder; the emperors and kings, who yesterday solemnly assured all men that they are concerned only about peace, the next day exercise their troops for murder and boast to one another of their well-prepared multitudes armed for murder, and so the voices, raised amidst this universal lie, by men who actually want peace, and show not only in words, but also in their acts, that they really want it, cannot help but be heard. These people say: "We are Christians, and so we cannot agree to being murderers. You may kill and torture us, but we will still refuse to be murderers, because that is contrary to that same Christianity which you profess."

...These words again point out to the world that simple, indubitable, and only means for the establishment of actual peace which was long ago pointed out by Christ, but which has been so forgotten by men that they on all sides search for means for the establishment of peace, and have no recourse to the one, long familiar method, which is so simple that for its application nothing new has to be undertaken, but we need only stop doing what we always and for everybody consider to be bad and disgraceful,—if we stop being submissive slaves of those who prepare men for murder. Not only is this method simple,—it is also indubitable. Any other method for the establishment of peace may be doubtful, but not this one, with which men who profess Christianity recognize, what no one has ever doubted, that a Christian cannot be a murderer. And Christians need only recognize what they cannot help recognizing, and there will be eternal inviolable peace among all Christians. Not only is the method simple and indubitable,—it is also the only method for the establishment of peace among Christians. It is the only one, because, so long as Christians will recognize the possibility of their taking part in military service, so long will the armies be in the power of the governments; and so long as they shall be in the power of the governments, there will be wars.

...The Dukhobors look upon their ruin, their want, imprisonment, and deportations as the work of serving God, and do this service with pride and joy, concealing nothing and fearing nothing, because nothing worse can be done to them unless they be put to death, which they do not fear.

But not such is the condition of the Russian government. If we, who are deceived by the government, do not see the whole significance of what the Dukhobors are doing, the government does see it; it not only sees the danger, but also the hopelessness of its position. It sees that as soon as people shall be freed from that spell under which they are now, and shall understand that a Christian cannot be a soldier,—and this they cannot help but understand,—and as soon as they hear what the Dukhobors did, the government will have inevitably to renounce, either Christianity,—and the governments rule in the name of Christianity—or its power. The government is in relation to the Dukhobors in a desperate state. They cannot be left alone, for all the rest will do likewise; nor is it possible to destroy them, to lock them up forever, as is done with individuals who interfere with the government—there are too many of them; the old men, wives, children, not only do not dissuade their fathers and husbands, but encourage them in their determination. What is to be done?

And so the government tries secretly, murderously, to destroy these men and to make them harmless, by keeping the men in solitary confinement, with the greatest secrecy, forbidding outsiders to commune with them, and by sending them to the most remote regions of Siberia, among the Yakuts; their families it deports among the Tartars and Georgians: it does not admit any one to them and forbids the printing of any information about the Dukhobors, and commands its accomplices to print all kinds of calumnies against them. But all these methods are inefficient. The light shineth in the dark. It is impossible at once to wipe off from the face of the earth a population of four thousand people who command the respect of all men; if they shall die out under the conditions in which they are placed, this extinction is slow, and extinction for the profession of the truth amidst other people is a most powerful sermon, and this sermon is being carried farther and farther. The government knows this and yet cannot help doing what it is doing; but we can already see on whose side is the victory.

It is this pointing out of the weakness of violence and of the power of truth which is in our time the great . . . [contribution] of the Dukhobors in the matter of the establishment of peace. For this reason I think that no one has more than they served the cause of peace, and the unfortunate conditions under which their families are living . . . are the reason why the money which Nobel wished should be given to those who more than any one else served the cause of peace could not be adjudged to any one with greater justice than to these very Dukhobor families.

Letter to a Corporal

You wonder how it is soldiers are taught that it is right to kill men in certain cases and in war, whereas in the Scripture, which is acknowledged to be sacred

From *The Complete Works of Count Tolstoy*, XXIII, pp. 449-456. The letter was written in 1889.

by those who teach this, there is nothing resembling such a permission, but there is the very opposite,—a prohibition to commit murder and even any insult against men, a prohibition to do to others what one does not wish to have done to oneself; you ask me whether this is not a deception, and if so, for whose advantage it is practised.

Yes, it is a deception, which is practised in favour of those who are accustomed to live by the sweat and blood of other people, and who for this purpose have been distorting Christ's teaching, which was given men for their good, but which now, in its distorted form, has become the chief source of all the calamities of men.

This happened in the following way:

The government and all those men of the upper classes who adhere to the government and live by the labours of others have to have means for controlling the labouring masses; the army is such a means. The defence against foreign enemies is only an excuse. The German government frightens its nation with the Russians and the French; the French frightens its nation with the Germans; the Russian frightens its nation with the Germans and the French, and so it is with all the nations; but neither the Germans, nor the Russians, nor the French wish to fight with their neighbours and with other nations; they prefer to live in peace with them and are afraid of war more than of anything in the world. But, to have an excuse in their control of the labouring masses, the governments and the upper idle classes act like a gypsy, who ships his horse around the corner and then pretends that he is not able to hold it back. They stir up their people and another government, and then pretend that for the good or for the defence of their nation they cannot help but declare war, which again is profitable for the generals, officers, officials, merchants, and, in general, for the wealthy classes. In reality, war is only an inevitable consequence of the existence of the armies; but the armies are needed by the governments merely for the purpose of controlling their own labouring masses.

...The masses are crushed, robbed, impoverished, ignorant,—they are dying out. Why? Because the land is in the hands of the rich; because the masses are enslaved in factories, in plants, in their daily occupations; because they are fleeced for the taxes, and the price for their labour is lowered, and the price for what they need is raised. How can they be freed? Shall the land again be taken away from the rich? But if that is done, the soldiers will come, will kill off the rioters, and will lock them up in prisons. Shall the factories, the plants, be taken away? The same will happen. Stick out in a strike? But that will never happen,—the rich can stick out longer than the labourers, and the armies will always be on the side of the capitalists. The masses will never get away from that want in which they are held, so long as the armies shall be in the power of the ruling classes.

But who are the armies, which hold the masses in this slavery? Who are those soldiers who will shoot at the peasants who have taken possession of the land, and at the strikers, if they do not disperse, and at the smugglers, who import wares without paying the revenue,—who will put into prisons and keep there those who refuse to pay the taxes? These soldiers are the same peasants whose land has been taken away, the same strikers, who want to raise their wages, the same payers of the taxes, who want to be freed from these payments.

Why do these men shoot at their brothers? Because it has been impressed upon them that the oath which they are compelled to take upon entering military service is obligatory for them, and that they may not kill men in general, but may kill them by command of the authorities, that is, the same deception which startled so much is practised upon them. But here arises the question,—how can people of sound mind, who frequently know the rudiments and are even educated, believe in such a palpable lie? No matter how little educated a man may be, he none the less cannot help knowing that Christ did not permit any murder, but taught meekness, humility, forgiveness of offences, love of enemies; he cannot help but see that on the basis of the Christian teaching he cannot make a promise in advance that he will kill all those whom he is commanded to kill.

The question is, how can people of sound mind believe, as all those who are now doing military service have believed, in such an obvious deception? The answer to the question is this, that people are not deceived by this one deception alone, but have been prepared for it from childhood by a whole series of deceptions, a whole system of deceptions, which is called the Orthodox Church, and which is nothing but the coarsest kind of idolatry.

...Only a man who is completely stupified by that false faith, called Orthodox, which is given out to him as being Christian, is able to believe that it is no sin for a Christian to enter the army, promising blindly to obey any man who will consider himself higher in rank, and, at the command of another man, to learn to kill and to commit this most terrible crime, which is prohibited by all the laws.

... By making use of the power which it has, the government produces and maintains the deception, and the deception maintains its power.

And so the only means for freeing men from all the calamities consists in freeing them from that false faith which is inculcated upon them by the government, and in impressing upon them the true Christian teaching, which is concealed from them by this false doctrine.

... It is impossible to fill a vessel with what is important if it is already filled with what is useless. It is necessary first to pour out what is useless. Even so it is with the acquisition of the true Christian teaching. We must first understand that all the stories about how God created the world six thousand years ago, and how

Adam sinned, and how the human race fell, and how the son of God and God Himself, born of a virgin, came into the world and redeemed it, and all the fables of the Bible and of the Gospel, and all the lives of the saints, and the stories of miracles and relics, are nothing but a coarse mixing up of the superstitions of the Jewish nation with the deceptions of the clergy. Only for a man who is completely free from these deceptions can the simple and clear teaching of Christ, which demands no interpretations and is self-comprehensible, be accessible and comprehensible.

This teaching says nothing about the beginning or the end of the world, nor of God and His intentions, in general nothing about what we cannot know and need not know, but speaks only of what a man has to do in order to be saved, that is, in order in the best manner possible to pass the life into which he has come in this world, from his birth to his death. For this purpose we need only treat others as we wish to be treated. In this alone does the law and the prophets consist, as Christ has said. To do so, we need no images, no relics, no divine services, no priests, no sacred histories, no catechisms, no governments, but, on the contrary, a liberation from all that—because only the man who is free from those fables which the priests give out to him as the only truth, and who is not bound to other people by promises to act as they want him to act, can treat others as he wishes to be treated by them. Only in that case will a man be able to do, not his own will, nor that of others, but the will of God.

But the will of God consists, not in fighting and oppressing others, but in recognizing all men as brothers and serving one another.

Patriotism and Government

The time is fast approaching when to call a man a patriot will be the deepest insult you can offer him. Patriotism now means advocating plunder in the interests of the privileged classes of the particular State system into which we have happened to be born.

I have already several times expressed the thought that in our day the feeling of patriotism is an unnatural, irrational, and harmful feeling, and a cause of a great part of the ills from which mankind is suffering; and that, consequently, this

From Leo Tolstoy, *Essays and Letters*, translated by Aylmer Maude, Funk and Wagnalls Company, New York, 1904, pp. 238-240, 243-245, 251-253, 257-261. This essay is dated May 10, 1910.

feeling should not be cultivated, as is now being done, but should, on the contrary, be suppressed and eradicated by all means available to rational men. Yet, strange to say—though it is undeniable that the universal armaments and destructive wars which are ruining the peoples result from that one feeling—all my arguments showing the backwardness, anachronism, and harmfulness of patriotism have been met, and are still met, either by silence, by intentional misinterpretation, or by a strange unvarying reply to the effect that only bad patriotism (Jingoism, or Chauvinism) is evil, but that real good patriotism is a very elevated moral feeling, to condemn which is not only irrational but wicked.

What this real, good patriotism consists in, we are never told; or, if anything is said about it, instead of explanation we get declamatory, inflated phrases, or, finally, some other conception is substituted for patriotism—something which has nothing in common with the patriotism we all know, and from the results of which we all suffer so severely.

... the real patriotism, which we all know, by which most people to-day are swayed, and from which humanity suffers so severely, is not the wish for spiritual benefits for one's own people (it is impossible to desire spiritual benefits for one's own people only), but is a very definite feeling of preference for one's own people or State above all other peoples and States, and a consequent wish to get for that people or State the greatest advantages and power that can be got—things which are obtainable only at the expense of the advantages and power of other peoples or States.

It would, therefore, seem obvious that patriotism as a feeling is bad and harmful, and as a doctrine is stupid. For it is clear that if each people and each State considers itself the best of peoples and States, they all live in a gross and harmful delusion.

... Patriotism, as a feeling of exclusive love for one's own people, and as a doctrine of the virtue of sacrificing one's tranquillity, one's property, and even one's life, in defence of one's own people from slaughter and outrage by their enemies, was the highest idea of the period when each nation considered it feasible and just, for its own advantage, to subject to slaughter and outrage the people of other nations.

But, already some 2,000 years ago, humanity, in the person of the highest representatives of its wisdom, began to recognize the higher idea of a brotherhood of man; and that idea, penetrating man's consciousness more and more, has in our time attained most varied forms of realization. Thanks to improved means of communication, and to the unity of industry, of trade, of the arts, and of science, men are to-day so bound one to another that the danger of conquest, massacre, or outrage by a neighbouring people, has quite disappeared, and all peoples (the peoples, but not the Governments) live together in peaceful, mutually advantageous, and friendly commercial, industrial, artistic, and scientific relations, which they have no need and no desire to disturb. One would think, therefore, that the antiquated feeling of patriotism—being superfluous and incompatible with the consciousness we have reached of the existence of brotherhood among men of different nationalities—should dwindle more and more until it completely disappears. Yet the very opposite of this occurs: this harmful and antiquated feeling not only continues to exist, but burns more and more fiercely.

The peoples, without any reasonable ground, and contrary alike to their conception of right and to their own advantage, not only sympathize with Governments in their attacks on other nations, in their seizures of foreign possessions, and in defending by force what they have already stolen, but even themselves demand such attacks, seizures, and defences: are glad of them, and take pride in them. The small oppressed nationalities which have fallen under the power of the great States—the Poles, Irish, Bohemians, Finns, or Armenians—resenting the patriotism of their conquerors, which is the cause of their oppression, catch from them the infection of this feeling of patriotism—which has ceased to be necessary, and is now obsolete, unmeaning, and harmful—and catch it to such a degree that all their activity is concentrated upon it, and they, themselves suffering from the patriotism of the stronger nations, are ready, for the sake of patriotism, to perpetrate on other peoples the very same deeds that their oppressors have perpetrated and are perpetrating on them.

This occurs because the ruling classes (including not only the actual rulers with their officials, but all the classes who enjoy an exceptionally advantageous position: the capitalists, journalists, and most of the artists and scientists) can retain their position—exceptionally advantageous in comparison with that of the labouring masses—thanks only to the Government organization, which rests on patriotism. They have in their hands all the most powerful means of influencing the people, and always sedulously support patriotic feelings in themselves and in others, more especially as those feelings which uphold the Government's power are those that are always best rewarded by that power.

Every official prospers the more in his career, the more patriotic he is; so also the army man gets promotion in time of war—the war is produced by patriotism.

Patriotism and its result—wars—give an enormous revenue to the newspaper trade, and profits to many other trades. Every writer, teacher, and professor is more secure in his place the more he preaches patriotism. Every Emperor and King obtains the more fame the more he is addicted to patriotism.

The ruling classes have in their hand the army, money, the schools, the churches, and the press. In the schools they kindle patriotism in the children by means of histories describing their own people as the best of all peoples and always in the right. Among adults they kindle it by spectacles, jubilees, monuments, and by a lying patriotic press. Above all, they inflame patriotism in this way: perpetrating every kind of injustice and harshness against other nations, they provoke in them enmity towards their own people, and then in turn exploit that enmity to embitter their people against the foreigner.

The intensification of this terrible feeling of patriotism has gone on among the European peoples in a rapidly increasing progression, and in our time has reached the utmost limits, beyond which there is no room for it to extend.

... The Government, in the widest sense, including capitalists and the Press, is nothing else than an organization which places the greater part of the people in the power of a smaller part, who dominate them; that smaller part is subject to a yet smaller part, and that again to a yet smaller, and so on, reaching at last a few people, or one single man, who by means of military force has power over all the rest. So that all this organization resembles a cone, of which all the parts are completely in the power of those people, or of that one person, who happens to be at the apex.

The apex of the cone is seized by those who are more cunning, audacious, and unscrupulous than the rest, or by someone who happens to be the heir of those who were audacious and unscrupulous.

... And to such Governments is allowed full power, not only over property and lives, but even over the spiritual and moral development, the education, and the religious guidance of everybody.

People construct such a terrible machine of power, they allow anyone to seize it who can (and the chances always are that it will be seized by the most morally worthless)—they slavishly submit to him, and are then surprised, that evil comes of it. They are afraid of Anarchists' bombs, and are not afraid of this terrible organization which is always threatening them with the greatest calamities.

... To deliver men from the terrible and ever-increasing evils of armaments and wars, we want neither congresses nor conferences, nor treaties, nor courts of arbitration, but the destruction of those instruments of violence which are called Governments, and from which humanity's greatest evils flow.

To destroy Governmental *violence*, only one thing is needed: it is that people should understand that the feeling of patriotism, which alone supports that instrument of violence, is a rude, harmful, disgraceful, and bad feeling, and, above all, is immoral. It is a rude feeling, because it is one natural only to people standing on the lowest level of morality, and expecting from other nations such outrages as they themselves are ready to inflict; it is a harmful feeling, because it disturbs advantageous and joyous, peaceful relations with other peoples, and above all produces that Governmental organization under which power may fall, and does fall, into the hands of the worst men; it is a disgraceful feeling, because it turns man not merely into a slave, but into a fighting cock, a bull, or a gladiator, who wastes his strength and his life for objects which are not his own but his Governments'; and it is an immoral feeling, because, instead of confessing one's self a son of God (as Christianity teaches us) or even a free man guided by his own reason, each man under the influence of patriotism confesses himself the son of his fatherland and the slave of his Government, and commits actions contrary to his reason and his conscience.

It is only necessary that people should understand this, and the terrible bond, called Government, by which we are chained together, will fall to pieces of itself without struggle; and with it will cease the terrible and useless evils it produces.

... 'But' it is usually asked, 'what will there be instead of Governments?'

There will be nothing. Something that has long been useless and therefore superfluous and bad, will be abolished. An organ that, being unnecessary, has become harmful, will be abolished.

'But,' people generally say, 'if there is no Government, people will violate and kill each other.'

Why? Why should the abolition of the organization which arose in consequence of violence, and which has been handed down from generation to generation to do violence—why should the abolition of such an organization, now devoid of use, cause people to outrage and kill one another? On the contrary, the presumption is that the abolition of the organ of violence would result in people ceasing to violate and kill one another.

Now, some men are specially educated and trained to kill and to do violence to other people—there are men who are supposed to have a right to use violence, and who make use of an organization which exists for that purpose. Such deeds of violence and such killing are considered good and worthy deeds.

But then, people will not be so brought up, and no one will have a right to use violence to others, and there will be no organization to do violence, and—as is natural to people of our time—violence and murder will always be considered bad actions, no matter who commits them.

But should acts of violence continue to be committed even after the abolition of the Governments, such acts will certainly be fewer than are committed now, when an organization exists specially devised to commit acts of violence, and a state of things exists in which acts of violence and murders are considered good and useful deeds.

The abolition of Governments will merely rid us of an unnecessary organization which we have inherited from the past, an organization for the commission of violence and for its justification.

'But there will then be no laws, no property, no courts of justice, no police, no popular education,' say people who intentionally confuse the use of violence by Governments with various social activities.

The abolition of the organization of Government formed to do violence, does not at all involve the abolition of what is reasonable and good, and therefore not based on violence, in laws or law courts, or in property, or in police regulations, or in financial arrangements, or in popular education. On the contrary, the absence of the brutal power of Government, which is needed only for its own support, will facilitate a juster and more reasonable social organization, needing no violence. Courts of justice, and public affairs, and popular education, will all exist to the extent to which they are really needed by the people, but in a shape which will not involve the evils contained in the present form of Government. Only that will be destroyed which was evil and hindered the free expression of the people's will.

But even if we assume that with the absence of Governments there would be disturbances and civil strife, even then the position of the people would be better than it is at present. The position now is such that it is difficult to imagine anything worse. The people are ruined, and their ruin is becoming more and more complete. The men are all converted into warslaves, and have from day to day to expect orders to go to kill and to be killed. What more? Are the ruined peoples to die of hunger? Even that is already beginning in Russia, in Italy, and in India. Or are the women as well as the men to go to be soldiers? In the Transvaal even that has begun.

So that even if the absence of Government really meant Anarchy in the negative, disorderly sense of that word—which is far from being the case—even then no anarchical disorder could be worse than the position to which Governments have already led their peoples, and to which they are leading them.

And therefore emancipation from patriotism, and the destruction of the despotism of Government that rests upon it, cannot but be beneficial to mankind.

Men, recollect yourselves! For the sake of your well-being, physical and spiritual, for the sake of your brothers and sisters, pause, consider, and think of what you are doing!

Reflect, and you will understand that your foes are not the Boers, or the English, or the French, or the Germans, or the Finns, or the Russians, but that your foes—your only foes—are you yourselves, who by your patriotism maintain the Governments that oppress you and make you unhappy.

They have undertaken to protect you from danger, and they have brought that pseudo-protection to such a point that you have all become soldiers—slaves, and are all ruined, or are being ruined more and more, and at any moment may and should expect that the tight-stretched cord will snap, and a horrible slaughter of you and your children will commence.

And however great that slaughter may be, and however that conflict may end, the same state of things will continue. In the same way, and with yet greater intensity, the Governments will arm, and ruin, and pervert you and your children, and no one will help you to stop it or to prevent it, if you do not help yourselves.

And there is only one kind of help possible—it lies in the abolition of that terrible linking up into a cone of violence, which enables the person or persons who succeed in seizing the apex to have power over all the rest, and to hold that power the more firmly the more cruel and inhuman they are, as we see by the cases of the Napoleons, Nicholas I., Bismarck, Chamberlain, Rhodes, and our Russian Dictators who rule the people in the Tsar's name.

And there is only one way to destroy this binding together—it is by shaking off the hypnotism of patriotism.

Understand that all the evils from which you suffer, you yourselves cause by yielding to the suggestions by which Emperors, Kings, Members of Parliament, Governors, officers, capitalists, priests, authors, artists, and all who need this fraud of patriotism in order to live upon your labour, deceive you!

Whoever you may be—Frenchman, Russian, Pole, Englishman, Irishman, or Bohemian—understand that all your real human interests, whatever they may be—agricultural, industrial, commercial, artistic, or scientific—as well as your pleasures and joys, in no way run counter to the interests of other peoples or States; and that you are united, by mutual co-operation, by interchange of services, by the joy of wide brotherly intercourse, and by the interchange not merely of goods but also of thoughts and feelings, with the folk of other lands.

Understand that the question as to who manages to seize Wei-hai-wei, Port Arthur, or Cuba—your Government or another—does not affect you, or, rather, that every seizure made by your Government injures you, by inevitably bringing in its train all sorts of pressure on you by your government to force you to take part in the robbery and violence by which alone such seizures are made, or can be retained when made. Understand that your life can in no way be bettered by Alsace becoming German or French, and Ireland or Poland being free or enslaved—whoever holds them. You are free to live where you will, if even you be an Alsatian, an Irishman, or a Pole. Understand, too, that by stirring up patriotism you will only make the case worse, for the subjection in which your people are kept has resulted simply from the struggle between patriotisms, and every manifestation of patriotism in one nation provokes a corresponding reaction in another. Understand that salvation from your woes is only possible when you free yourself from the obsolete idea of patriotism and from the obedience to Governments that is based upon it, and when you boldly enter into the region of that higher idea, the brotherly union of the peoples, which has long since come to life, and from all sides is calling you to itself.

If people would but understand that they are not the sons of some fatherland or other, nor of Governments, but are sons of God, and can therefore neither be slaves nor enemies one to another—those insane, unnecessary, worn-out, pernicious organizations called Governments, and all the sufferings, violations, humiliations, and crimes which they occasion, would cease.

william morris

An English poet, artist, and printer, William Morris's interest in social reform was largely inspired by his hatred of the ugliness and soul-destroying effects which derived from the industrial revolution in nineteenth century Britain. Morris likened the capitalist system to a modern day form of slavery, equated the principle of competition with war, and proposed revolutionary social changes which he hoped could be accomplished without violence and destruction. Such an outcome would be possible, he thought, if the propertied classes recognized the futility of defending a thoroughly corrupt system, already in a state of decay, and consented gracefully to the changes required in providing equity and justice for everyone.

The eldest son of affluent parents, William Morris was born March 24, 1834, at Walthamstow, Essex, and was educated at Exeter College, Oxford. After graduation in 1855, Morris pursued his primary interest, architecture; he was also encouraged to paint and to write by Dante Gabriel Rossetti, the English poet and artist whose paintings of Morris's wife, Jane Burden, won wide acclaim. Morris's work as a decorator and designer revolutionized Victorian tastes; his reading of English critic and social theorist John Ruskin revolutionized his thought. Although neither politics nor writing interfered with his professional productivity as an artist, Morris devoted considerable energies to the Socialist cause.

Disillusioned with the Liberal Party's position on the Irish question and on a number of other serious domestic problems, Morris joined the Social Democratic federation in 1883. He became a leader of the Socialist League, formed the following year, as well as editor of its journal *The Commonweal*. Morris advocated socialist doctrines in his writings and lectures, and at meetings in industrial towns. He was arrested in 1885, and again in 1887 following a meeting in Trafalgar Square which was violently dispersed by London police on "Bloody Sunday" (November 13).

It was the Socialist League's increasing anarchist sympathies which prompted Morris to withdraw from the organization in 1890, but he remained committed to the Socialist cause and wrote and lectured widely on the relation of art to industry. His goal was a Socialist commonwealth where simplicity and happiness reigned. In his book *News from Nowhere,* Morris depicted his ideal society based upon the concept of joy in labor, with "useful work" replacing "useless toil." He believed in equality based upon a sense of mutual responsiblity between master and worker. The following selection is taken from a volume of his collected works and, like much of his writing, it reflects timeless moral lessons unmarred by active political propaganda.

William Morris spent his last years in Hammersmith, where he died on October 3, 1896. He was survived by his widow, Jane, and his two daughters, Jenny and May. The latter devoted herself to her father's memory and published his collected works in twenty-four volumes (1910-1915).

On the Coming of Socialism

The word Revolution, which we Socialists are so often forced to use, has a terrible sound in most people's ears, even when we have explained to them that it does not necessarily mean a change accompanied by riot and all kinds of violence, and cannot mean a change made mechanically and in the teeth of opinion by a group of men who have somehow managed to seize on the executive power for the moment. Even when we explain that we use the word revolution in its etymological sense, and mean by it a change in the basis of society, people are scared at the idea of such a vast change, and beg that you will speak of reform and not revolution. As, however, we Socialists do not at all mean by

From *The Collected Works of William Morris*, XXIII, Longmans Green and Company, London, 1915, pp. 3, 5, 7, 13-14, 20, 22-23, 26, 73-80.

our word revolution what these worthy people mean by their word reform, I can't help thinking that it would be a mistake to use it, whatever projects we might conceal beneath its harmless envelope. So we will stick to our word, which means a change of the basis of society; it may frighten people, but it will at least warn them that there is something to be frightened about, which will be no less dangerous for being ignored; and also it may encourage some people, and will mean to them at least not a fear, but a hope.

Fear and Hope—those are the names of the two great passions which rule the race of man, and with which revolutionists have to deal; to give hope to the many oppressed and fear to the few oppressors, that is our business; if we do the first and give hope to the many, the few *must* be frightened by their hope; otherwise we do not want to frighten them; it is not revenge we want for poor people, but happiness; indeed, what revenge can be taken for all the thousands of years of the sufferings of the poor?

... How do we live, then, under our present system? Let us look at it a little.

And first, please to understand that our present system of Society is based on a state of perpetual war. Do any of you think that this is as it should be? I know that you have often been told that the competition which is at present the rule of all production, is a good thing, and stimulates the progress of the race; but the people who tell you this should call competition by its shorter name of *war* if they wish to be honest, and you would then be free to consider whether or not war stimulates progress, otherwise than as a mad bull chasing you over your own garden may do. War, or competition, whichever you please to call it, means at the best pursuing your own advantage at the cost of some one else's loss, and in the process of it you must not be sparing of destruction even of your own possessions, or you will certainly come by the worse in the struggle. You understand that perfectly as to the kind of war in which people go out to kill and be killed; that sort of war in which ships are commissioned, for instance, "to sink, burn, and destroy;" but it appears that you are not so conscious of this waste of goods when you are only carrying on that other war called *commerce*; observe, however, that the waste is there all the same.

... Well, surely Socialism can offer you something in the place of all that. It can; it can offer you peace and friendship instead of war. We might live utterly without national rivalries, acknowledging that while it is best for those who feel that they naturally form a community under one name to govern themselves, yet that no community in civilization should feel that it had interests opposed to any other, their economical condition being at any rate similar; so that any citizen of one community could fall to work and live without disturbance of his life when he was in a foreign country, and would fit into his place quite naturally; so that all civilized nations would form one great community, agreeing together as to the kind and amount of production and distribution needed; working at such and such production where it could be best produced; avoiding waste by all means. Please to think of the amount of waste which they would avoid, how much such a revolution would add to the wealth of the world! What creature on earth would be harmed by such a revolution? Nay, would not everybody be the better for it?

... what Socialism offers you in place of ... artificial famines, with their so-called over-production is, once more, regulation of the markets, supply and demand commensurate; no gambling, and consequently (once more) no waste; not overwork and weariness for the worker one month, and the next no work and terror of starvation, but steady work and plenty of leisure every month; not cheap market wares, that is to say, adulterated wares with scarcely any *good* in them, mere scaffold-poles for building up profits; no labour would be spent on such things as these, which people would cease to want when they ceased to be slaves. Not these, but such goods as best fulfilled the real uses of the consumers would labour be set to make; for profit being abolished, people could have what they wanted, instead of what the profit-grinders at home and abroad forced them to take.

For what I want you to understand is this: that in every civilized country at least there is plenty for all—is, or at any rate might be. Even with labour so misdirected as it is at present, an equitable distribution of the wealth we have would make all people comparatively comfortable; but that is nothing to the wealth we might have if labour were not misdirected.

... even that share of work necessary to the existence of the simplest social life must, in the first place, whatever else it is, be reasonable work; that is, it must be such work as a good citizen can see the necessity for; as a member of the community, I must have agreed to do it.

To take two strong instances of the contrary, I won't submit to be dressed up in red and marched off to shoot at my French or German or Arab friend in a quarrel that I don't understand; I will rebel sooner than do that.

Nor will I submit to waste my time and energies in making some trifling toy which I know only a fool can desire: I will rebel sooner than do that.

However, you may be sure that in a state of social order I shall have no need to rebel against any such pieces of unreason; only I am forced to speak from the way we live to the way we might live.

... And once for all, there is nothing in our circumstances save the hunting of profit that drives us into it. It is profit which draws men into enormous unmanageable aggregations called towns, for instance; profit which crowds them up when they are there into quarters without gardens or open spaces; profit which won't take the most ordinary precautions against wrapping a whole district in a cloud of sulphurous smoke; which turns beautiful rivers into filthy sewers; which condemns all but the rich to live in houses idiotically cramped and confined at the best, and at the worst in houses for whose wretchedness there is no name.

I say it is almost incredible that we should bear such crass stupidity as this; nor should we if we could help it. We shall not bear it when the workers get out of their heads that they are but an appendage to profit-grinding, that the more profits that are made the more employment at high wages there will be for them, and that therefore all the incredible filth, disorder, and degradation of modern civilization are signs of their prosperity. So far from that, they are signs of their slavery. When they are no longer slaves they will claim as a matter of course that every man and every family should be generously lodged; that every child should be able to play in a garden close to the place his parents live in; that the houses should by their obvious decency and order be ornaments to Nature, not disfigurements of it; for the decency and order above-mentioned when carried to the due pitch would most assuredly lead to beauty in building. All this, of course, would mean the people—that is, all society—duly organized, having in its own hands the means of production, to be *owned* by no individual, but used by all as occasion called for its use, and can only be done on those terms; on any other terms people will be driven to accumulate private wealth for themselves, and thus, as we have seen, to waste the goods of the community and perpetuate the division into classes, which means continual war and waste.

... Hard as the work is, however, its reward is not doubtful. The mere fact that a body of men, however small, are banded together as Socialist missionaries shows that the change is going on. As the working-classes, the real organic part of society, take in these ideas, hope will arise in them, and they will claim changes in society, many of which doubtless will not tend directly towards their emancipation, because they will be claimed without due knowledge of the one thing necessary to claim, *equality of condition;* but which indirectly will help to break up our rotten sham society, while that claim for equality of condition will be made constantly and with growing loudness till it *must* be listened to, and then at last it will only be a step over the border, and the civilized world will be socialized; and, looking back on what has been, we shall be astonished to think of how long we submitted to live as we live now.

... There was no sign of revolutionary feeling in England twenty years ago: the middle class were so rich that they had no need to hope for anything—but a heaven which they did not believe in: the well-to-do working men did not hope, since they were not pinched and had no means of learning their degraded position: and lastly, the drudges of the proletariat had such hope as charity, the hospital, the workhouse, and kind death at last could offer them.

In this stock-jobbers' heaven let us leave our dear countrymen for a little, while I say a few words about the affairs of the people on the continent of Europe. Things were not quite so smooth for the fleecer there: Socialist thinkers and writers had arisen about the same time as Robert Owen; St. Simon, Proudhon, Fourier and his followers kept up the traditions of hope in the midst of a *bourgeois* world.

. . . Now, in all I have been saying, I have been wanting you to trace the fact that, ever since the establishment of commercialism on the ruins of feudality, there has been growing a steady feeling on the part of the workers that they are a class dealt with as a class, and in like manner to deal with others; and that as this class feeling has grown, so also has grown with it a consciousness of the antagonism between their class and the class which employs it, as the phrase goes; that is to say, which lives by means of its labour.

Now it is just this growing consciousness of the fact that as long as there exists in society a propertied class living on the labour of a propertyless one, there *must* be a struggle always going on between these two classes—it is just the dawning knowledge of this fact which should show us what civilization can hope for—namely, transformation into true society, in which there will no longer be classes with their necessary struggle for existence and superiority: for the antagonism of classes which began in all simplicity between the master and the chattel slave of ancient society, and was continued between the feudal lord and the serf of mediaeval society, has gradually become the contention between the capitalist developed from the workmen of the last-named period, and the wage-earner: . . . .

. . . Moreover, the capitalist or modern slave-owner has been forced by his very success, as we have seen, to organize his slaves, the wage-earners, into a co-operation for production so well arranged that it requires little but his own elimination to make it a foundation for communal life: in the teeth also of the experience of past ages, he has been compelled to allow a modicum of education to the propertyless, and has not even been able to deprive them wholly of political rights; his own advance in wealth and power has bred for him the very enemy who is doomed to make an end of him.

But will there be any new class to take the place of the present proletariat when that has triumphed, as it must do, over the present privileged class? We cannot foresee the future, but we may fairly hope not: at least we cannot see any signs of such a new class forming. It is impossible to see how destruction of privilege can stop short of absolute equality of condition; pure Communism is the logical deduction from the imperfect form of the new society, which is generally differentiated from it as Socialism.

Meantime, it is this simplicity and directness of the growing contest which above all things presents itself as a terror to the conservative instinct of the present day. Many among the middle class who are sincerely grieved and shocked at the condition of the proletariat which civilization has created, and even alarmed by the frightful inequalities which it fosters, do nevertheless shudder back from the idea of the class struggle, and strive to shut their eyes to the fact that it is going on. They try to think that peace is not only possible, but natural, between the two classes, the very essence of whose existence is that each can only thrive by what it manages to force the other to yield to it. They propose to themselves the impossible problem of raising the inferior or exploited classes into a position in which they will cease to struggle against the superior classes, while the latter will not cease to exploit them. This absurd position drives them into the concoction of schemes for bettering the condition of the working classes at their own expense, some of them futile, some merely fantastic; or they may be divided again into those which point out the advantages and pleasures of involuntary asceticism, and reactionary plans for importing the conditions of the production and life of the Middle Ages (wholly misunderstood by them, by the way) into the present system of the capitalist farmer, the great industries, and the universal world-market. Some see a solution of the social problem in sham co-operation, which is merely an improved form of joint-stockery: others preach thrift to (precarious) incomes of eighteen shillings a week, and industry to men killing themselves by inches in working overtime or to men whom the labour-market has rejected as not wanted: others beg the proletarians not to breed so fast; an injunction the compliance with which might be at first of advantage to the proletarians themselves in their present condition, but would certainly undo the capitalists, if it were carried to any lengths, and would lead through ruin and misery to the violent outbreak of the very revolution which these timid people are so anxious to forego.

...The greater part of these schemes aim, though seldom with the consciousness of their promoters, at the creation of a new middle-class out of the wage-earning class, and at their expense, just as the present middle-class was developed out of the serf-population of the early Middle Ages. It may be possible that such a *further* development of the middle-class lies before us, but it will not be brought about by any such artificial means as the above-mentioned schemes. If it comes at all, it must be produced by events, which at present we cannot foresee, acting on our commercial system, and reviving for a little time, maybe, that Capitalist Society which now seems sickening towards its end.

For what is visible before us in these days is the competitive commercial system killing itself by its own force: profits lessening, businesses growing bigger and bigger, the small employer of labour thrust out of his function, and the aggregation of capital increasing the numbers of the lower middle-class from above rather than from below, by driving the smaller manufacturer into the position of a mere servant to the bigger. The productivity of labour also increasing out of all proportion to the capacity of the capitalists to manage the market or deal with the labour supply: lack of employment therefore becoming chronic, and discontent therewithal.

All this on the one hand. On the other, the workman claiming everywhere political equality, which cannot long be denied; and education spreading, so that what between the improvement in the education of the working-class and the continued amazing fatuity of that of the upper classes, there is a distinct tendency to equalization here; and, as I have hinted above, all history shows us what a danger to society may be a class at once educated and socially degraded: though, indeed, no history has yet shown us—what is swiftly advancing upon us—a class which, though it shall have attained knowledge, shall lack utterly the refinement and self-respect which come from the union of knowledge with leisure and ease of life. The growth of such a class may well make the "cultured" people of to-day tremble.

Whatever, therefore, of unforeseen and unconceived-of may lie in the womb of the future, there is nothing visible before us but a decaying system, with no outlook but ever-increasing entanglement and blindness, and a new system, Socialism, the hope of which is ever growing clearer in men's minds—a system which not only sees how labour can be freed from its present fetters, and organized unwastefully, so as to produce the greatest possible amount of wealth for the community and for every member of it, but which bears with it its own ethics and religion and aesthetics· that is the hope and promise of a new and higher life in all ways. So that even if those unforeseen economical events above spoken of were to happen, and put off for a while the end of our Capitalist system, the latter would drag itself along as an anomaly cursed by all, a mere clog on the aspirations of humanity.

It is not likely that it will come to that: in all probability the logical outcome of the latter days of Capitalism will go step by step with its actual history: while all men, even its declared enemies, will be working to bring Socialism about, the aims of those who have learned to believe in the certainty and beneficence of its advent will become clearer, their methods for realizing it clearer also, and at last ready to hand. Then will come that open acknowledgment for the necessity of the change (an acknowledgment coming from the intelligence of civilization) which is commonly called Revolution. It is no use prophesying as to the events which will accompany that revolution, but to a reasonable man it seems unlikely to the last degree, or we will say impossible, that a moral sentiment will induce the proprietary classes—those who live by *owning* the means of production which the unprivileged classes must needs *use*—to yield up this privilege uncompelled; all one can hope is that they will see the implicit threat of compulsion in the events of the day, and so yield with a good grace to the terrible necessity of forming part of a world in which all, including themselves, will work honestly and live easily.

peter kropotkin

Prince Peter Kropotkin was a Russian geographer and revolutionary whose un-
worldly demeanor and cheerful endurance of hardships endeared him to leaders
of the anarchist movement which he supported. Born in Moscow, the son of
Prince Aleksei Petrovich Kropotkin, he was educated at the School of Pages in
St. Petersburg and was later appointed to the personal suite of Czar Alexander
II. The tedious formalities of court life not only disappointed his expectations
but also undermined his early impressions of the Czar who had emancipated
Russia's serfs. The intimacy of court life revealed the Czar to be a capricious and
vindictive man. Much to the dismay of his ambitious relatives, Kropotkin effected an escape from the Court by accepting a commission with the Amur
Kossack cavalry regiment. While serving five years with the regiment in Siberia,
during which time he lost all faith in government-imposed discipline, he developed his interest in wildlife and geological phenomena; he also made some
scientifically important discoveries about the structural lines of the main mountain ranges of eastern Asia.

Traveling to Switzerland in 1872, Kropotkin met the noted anarchist Mikhail
Bakunin and lived with the watchmakers of the Jura federation. The watchmakers' friendly, industrious, and efficient guilds made a significant impression
upon him, and Kropotkin concluded that they were a model of disciplined and
happy anarchy, a shining example of how the peoples of the world could achieve

practical social cooperation without oppressive state controls. Upon his return to Russia, he joined an activist group of social reformers, but in 1873 he was arrested and imprisoned for "seditious" propaganda. Kropotkin, whose desire to identify with the poor had led him to discontinue the use of his title, escaped two years later and made his way to France. When he was next arrested in that country, Georges Clemenceau and other friends secured him a pardon. He lived most of his remaining years in England, visiting the United States twice, where he gave addresses at Wellesley College and at Harvard University.

Viewing the nineteenth century nation-state as a repressive superstructure which had long since outgrown its original usefulness, Kropotkin expected that voluntary societies would gradually inherit and transform the system. He welcomed World War I because he believed that it would destroy, once and for all, the obsolete military powers which had provoked it. In 1917 he rejoiced at the March revolution in Russia and hastened back to his native land. Long idolized by the workers in France, and regarded with esteem in both Britain and America, Kropotkin did not find similar tolerance among some revolutionaries in his own country because his opposition to Bolshevism was fundamental and unconcealed. He called the followers of Lenin "aliens, enemies of Russia, gangsters," who had betrayed the revolution. He lamented that, instead of setting Russia on the path leading toward voluntary federation, the alleged Communists (who never practiced communism, but only national state socialism) would only succeed in making people hate their very name. Yet he vehemently denounced the western Allies' intervention in the Russian civil war.

Reduced to silent inactivity while the civil war was raging, Kropotkin died on February 8, 1921, at Dmitrov, forty miles from Moscow. The family, respecting his principles, declined the offer of a state funeral. The government chose to overlook the earlier criticisms of the popular Kropotkin; it made his birthplace a museum to contain his books and other suitable collections, and gave his name to a street in Moscow.

People who had remained unswayed by Bakunin's spell and resentful of the bomb-throwing that it inspired in earlier anarchists were fascinated by Kropotkin's personality, despite the naivete of some of his political ideas. He brought respectability to the anarchist movement, and his mellow humaneness and personal warmth had a strong appeal, especially in France and England. His major writings were produced between 1885 and 1904; one of his more significant works, *La conquête du pain* ("The Conquest of Bread"), appeared first in 1892 and perhaps best reveals the thinking and the humanity of this aristocrat of the people.

On Communistic Anarchy

... In our civilized societies we are rich. Why then are the many poor? Why this painful drudgery for the masses? Why, even to the best paid workman, this uncertainty for the morrow, in the midst of all the wealth inherited from the past, and in spite of the powerful means of production, which could ensure comfort to all, in return for a few hours of daily toil?

The Socialists have said it and repeated it unwearyingly. Daily they reiterate it, demonstrating it by arguments taken from all the sciences. It is because all that is necessary for production—the land, the mines, the highways, machinery, food, shelter, education, knowledge—all have been seized by the few in the course of that long story of robbery, enforced migration and wars, of ignorance and oppression, which has been the life of the human race before it had learned to subdue the forces of Nature. It is because, taking advantage of alleged rights acquired in the past, these few appropriate to-day two-thirds of the products of human labour, and then squander them in the most stupid and shameful way. It is because, having reduced the masses to a point at which they have not the means of subsistence for a month, or even for a week in advance, the few can allow the many to work, only on the condition of themselves receiving the lion's share. It is because these few prevent the remainder of men from producing the things they need, and force them to produce, not the necessaries of life for all, but whatever offers the greatest profits to the monopolists.

... Fine sermons have been preached on the text that those who have should share with those who have not, but he who would carry out this principle would be speedily informed that these beautiful sentiments are all very well in poetry, but not in practice. "To lie is to degrade and besmirch oneself," we say, and yet all civilized life becomes one huge lie. We accustom ourselves and our children to hypocrisy, to the practice of a double-faced morality. And since the brain is ill at ease among lies, we cheat ourselves with sophistry. Hypocrisy and sophistry become the second nature of the civilized man.

But a society cannot live thus; it must return to truth, or cease to exist.

Thus the consequences which spring from the original act of monopoly spread through the whole of social life. Under the pain of death, human societies are forced to return to first principles: the means of production being the collective work of humanity, the product should be the collective property of the race. Individual appropriation is neither just nor serviceable. All belongs to all. All things are for all men, since all men have need of them, since all men have

From Peter Kropotkin, *The Conquest of Bread*, Vanguard Press, New York, 1906, pp. 3, 10-11, 16-17, 19-23, 28-30, 32, 41-42, 44, 46, 49-50, 62-64, 167, 209-212.

worked in the measure of their strength to produce them, and since it is not possible to evaluate every one's part in the production of the world's wealth.

... All is for all! If the man and the woman bear their fair share of work, they have a right to their fair share of all that is produced by all, and that share is enough to secure them well-being. No more of such vague formulas as "The right to work," or "To each the whole result of his labour." What we proclaim is THE RIGHT TO WELL-BEING: WELL-BEING FOR ALL!

... But, if plenty for all is to become a reality, this immense capital—cities, houses, pastures, arable lands, factories, highways, education—must cease to be regarded as private property, for the monopolist to dispose of at his pleasure.

This rich endowment, painfully won, builded, fashioned or invented by our ancestors, must become common property so that the collective interests of men may gain from it the greatest good for all.

There must be EXPROPRIATION. The well-being of all—the end; expropriation—the means.

EXPROPRIATION, such then is the problem which History has put before the men of the twentieth century; the return to Communism in all that ministers to the well-being of man.

But this problem cannot be solved by means of legislation. No one imagines that. The poor, as well as the rich, understand that neither the existing Governments, nor any which might arise out of possible political changes, would be capable of finding such a solution. They feel the necessity of a social revolution; and both rich and poor recognize that this revolution is imminent, that it may break out in a few years.

... Whence will the revolution come? how will it announce its coming? No one can answer these questions. The future is hidden. But those who watch and think do not misinterpret the signs: workers and exploiters, Revolutionists and Conservatives, thinkers and men of action, all feel that a revolution is at our doors.

Well, then,—What are we going to do when the thunderbolt has fallen?

We have all been bent on studying the dramatic side of revolutions so much, and the practical work of revolutions so little, that we are apt to see only the stage effects, so to speak, of these great movements; the fight of the first days; the barricades. But this fight, this first skirmish, is soon ended, and it is only after the breakdown of the old system that the real work of revolution can be said to begin.

... All this may please those who like the stage, but it is not revolution. Nothing has been accomplished as yet.

And meanwhile the people suffer. The factories are idle, the workshops closed; trade is at a standstill. The worker does not even earn the meagre wage which was his before. Food goes up in price. With that heroic devotion which has always characterized them, and which in great crises reaches the sublime, the people will wait patiently.

... The people .... suffer and say: "How is a way out of these difficulties to be found?"

It seems to us that there is only one answer to this question: We must recognize, and loudly proclaim, that every one, whatever his grade in the old society, whether strong or weak, capable or incapable, has, before everything, THE RIGHT TO LIVE and that society is bound to share amongst all, without exception, the means of existence it has at its disposal. We must acknowledge this, and proclaim it aloud, and act up to it.

Affairs must be managed in such a way that from the first day of the revolution the worker shall know that a new era is opening before him; that henceforward none need crouch under the bridges, while palaces are hard by, none need fast in the midst of plenty, none need perish with cold near shops full of furs; that all is for all, in practice as well as in theory, and that at last, for the first time in history, a revolution has been accomplished which considers the NEEDS of the people before schooling them in their DUTIES.

This cannot be brought about by Acts of Parliament, but only by taking immediate and effective possession of all that is necessary to ensure the well-being of all; this is the only really scientific way of going to work, the only way which can be understood and desired by the mass of the people. We must take possession, in the name of the people, of the granaries, the shops full of clothing and the dwelling houses. Nothing must be wasted. We must organize without delay a way to feed the hungry, to satisfy all wants, to meet all needs, to produce not for the special benefit of this one or that one, but so as to ensure to society as a whole its life and further development.

Enough of ambiguous words like "the right to work," with which the people were misled in 1848, and which are still resorted to with the hope of misleading them. Let us have the courage to recognise that *Well-being for all,* henceforward possible, must be realized.

... The "right to well-being" means the possibility of living like human beings, and of bringing up children to be members of a society better than ours, whilst the "right to work" only means the right to be always a wage-slave, a drudge, ruled over and exploited by the middle class of the future. The right to well-being is the Social Revolution, the right to work means nothing but the Treadmill of Commercialism. It is high time for the worker to assert his right to the common inheritance, and to enter into possession of it.

Every society, on abolishing private property, will be forced, we maintain, to organize itself on the lines of Communistic Anarchy. Anarchy leads to Communism, and Communism to Anarchy, both alike being expressions of the predominant tendency in modern societies, the pursuit of equality.

... But ours is neither the Communism of Fourier ... nor of the German State Socialists. It is Anarchist Communism, Communism without government— the Communism of the Free. It is the synthesis of the two ideals pursued by humanity throughout the ages—Economic and Political Liberty.

In taking "Anarchy" for our ideal of political organization we are only giving expression to another marked tendency of human progress. Whenever European societies have developed up to a certain point, they have shaken off the yoke of authority and substituted a system founded more or less on the principles of individual liberty. And history shows us that these periods of partial or general revolution, when the old governments were overthrown, were also periods of sudden progress both in the economic and the intellectual field. So it was after the enfranchisement of the communes, whose monuments, produced by the free labour of the guilds, have never been surpassed; so it was after the great peasant uprising which brought about the Reformation and imperilled the papacy; and so it was again with the society, free for a brief space, which was created on the other side of the Atlantic by the malcontents from the Old World.

And, if we observe the present development of civilized nations, we see, most unmistakably, a movement ever more and more marked tending to limit the sphere of action of the Government, and to allow more and more liberty to the individual. This evolution is going on before our eyes, though cumbered by the ruins and rubbish of old institutions and old superstitions. Like all evolutions, it only waits a revolution to overthrow the old obstacles which block the way, that it may find free scope in a regenerated society.

After having striven long in vain to solve the insoluble problem—the problem of constructing a government "which will constrain the individual to obedience without itself ceasing to be the servant of society," men at last attempt to free themselves from every form of government and to satisfy their need for organization by free contacts between individuals and groups pursuing the same aim. The independence of each small territorial unit becomes a pressing need; mutual agreement replaces law in order to regulate individual interests in view of a common object—very often disregarding the frontiers of the present States.

All that was once looked on as a function of the Government is to-day called in question. Things are arranged more easily and more satisfactorily without the intervention of the State. And in studying the progress made in this direction, we are led to conclude that the tendency of the human race is to reduce Government interference to zero; in fact, to abolish the State, the personification of injustice, oppression, and monopoly.

We can already catch glimpses of a world in which the bonds which bind the individual are no longer laws, but social habits—the result of the need felt by each one of us to seek the support, the co-operation, the sympathy of his neighbours.

Assuredly the idea of a society without a State will give rise to at least as many objections as the political economy of a society without private capital. We have all been brought up from our childhood to regard the State as a sort of Providence; all our education, the Roman history we learned at school, the Byzantine code which we studied later under the name of Roman law, and the various sciences taught at the universities, accustom us to believe in Government and in the virtues of the State providential.

To maintain this superstition whole systems of philosophy have been elaborated and taught; all politics are based on this principle; and each politician, whatever his colours, comes forward and says to the people, "Give my party the power; we can and we will free you from the miseries which press so heavily upon you."

From the cradle to the grave all our actions are guided by this principle. Open any book on sociology or jurisprudence, and you will find there the Government, its organization, its acts, filling so large a place that we come to believe that there is nothing outside the Government and the world of statesmen.

. . . The history of the last fifty years furnishes a living proof that Representative Government is impotent to discharge all the functions we have sought to assign to it. In days to come the nineteenth century will be quoted as having witnessed the failure of parliamentarianism.

This impotence is becoming so evident to all; the faults of parliamentarianism, and the inherent vices of the representative principle, are so self-evident, that the few thinkers who have made a critical study of them (J. S. Mill, Leverdays), did but give literary form to the popular dissatisfaction. It is not difficult, indeed, to see the absurdity of naming a few men and saying to them, "Make laws regulating all our spheres of activity, although not one of you knows anything about them!"

We are beginning to see that government by majorities means abandoning all the affairs of the country to the tide-waiters who make up the majorities in the House and in election committees; to those, in a word, who have no opinion of their own.

. . . The ideas of Anarchism in general and of Expropriation in particular find much more sympathy than we are apt to imagine among men of independent character, and those for whom idleness is not the supreme ideal. "Still," our friends often warn us, "take care you do not go too far! Humanity cannot be changed in a day, so do not be in too great a hurry with your schemes of Expropriation and Anarchy, or you will be in danger of achieving no permanent result."

Now, what we fear with regard to Expropriation is exactly the contrary. We are afraid of not going far enough, of carrying out Expropriation on too small a scale to be lasting. We would not have the revolutionary impulse arrested in mid-career, to exhaust itself in half measures, which would content no one, and while producing a tremendous confusion in society, and stopping its customary activities, would have no vital power—would merely spread general discontent and inevitably prepare the way for the triumph of reaction.

. . . All is interdependent in a civilized society; it is impossible to reform any one thing without altering the whole. Therefore, on the day a nation will strike at private property, under any one of its forms, territorial or industrial, it will be obliged to attack them all. The very success of the Revolution will impose it.

Besides, even if it were desired, it would be impossible to confine the change to a partial expropriation. Once the principle of the "Divine Right of Property" is shaken, no amount of theorizing will prevent its overthrow, here by the slaves of the field, there by the slaves of the machine.

. . . Whether we like it or not, this is what the people mean by a revolution. As soon as they have made a clean sweep of the Government, they will seek first of all to ensure to themselves decent dwellings and sufficient food and clothes— free of capitalist rent.

And the people will be right. The methods of the people will be much more in accordance with science than those of the economists who draw so many distinctions between instruments of production and articles of consumption. The people understand that this is just the point where the Revolution ought to begin; and they will lay the foundations of the only economic science worthy the name—a science which might be called: *"The Study of the Needs of Humanity, and of the Economic Means to satisfy them."*

. . . "Bread, it is bread that the Revolution needs!"

Let others spend their time in issuing pompous proclamations, in decorating themselves lavishly with official gold lace, and in talking about political liberty! . . .

Be it ours to see, from the first day of the Revolution to the last, in all the provinces fighting for freedom, that there is not a single man who lacks bread, not a single woman compelled to stand with the wearied crowd outside the bakehousedoor, that haply a coarse loaf may be thrown to her in charity, not a single child pining for want of food.

... We have the temerity to declare that all have a right to bread, that there is bread enough for all, and that with this watchword of *Bread for All* the Revolution will triumph.

That we are Utopians is well known. So Utopian are we that we go the length of believing that the Revolution can and ought to assure shelter, food, and clothes to all—an idea extremely displeasing to middle-class citizens, whatever their party colour, for they are quite alive to the fact that it is not easy to keep the upper hand of a people whose hunger is satisfied.

All the same, we maintain our contention: bread must be found for the people of the Revolution, and the question of bread must take precedence of all other questions. If it is settled in the interests of the people, the Revolution will be on the right road; for in solving the question of Bread we must accept the principle of equality, which will force itself upon us to the exclusion of every other solution.

... If the entire nation, or, better still, if all Europe should accomplish the Social Revolution simultaneously, and start with thorough-going Communism, our procedure would be simplified; but if only a few communities in Europe make the attempt, other means will have to be chosen. The circumstances will dictate the measures.

We are thus led, before we proceed further, to glance at the State of Europe, and, without pretending to prophesy, we may try to foresee what course the Revolution will take, or at least what will be its essential features.

Certainly it would be very desirable that all Europe should rise at once, that expropriation should be general, and that communistic principles should inspire all and sundry. Such a universal rising would do much to simplify the task of our century.

But all the signs lead us to believe that it will not take place. That the Revolution will embrace Europe we do not doubt. ... But whether the Revolution would everywhere exhibit the same characteristics is highly doubtful.

It is more than probable that expropriation will be everywhere carried into effect on a larger scale, and that this policy carried out by any one of the great nations of Europe will influence all the rest; yet the beginnings of the Revolution will exhibit great local differences, and its course will vary in different countries.

... Will it therefore be necessary, as is sometimes suggested, that the nations in the vanguard of the movement should adapt their pace to those who lag behind? Must we wait till the Communist Revolution is ripe in all civilized countries? Clearly not! Even if it were a thing to be desired, it is not possible. History does not wait for the laggards.

... the day on which old institutions will fall under the proletarian axe, voices will cry out: "Bread, shelter, ease for all!" And those voices will be listened to; the people will say: "Let us begin by allaying our thirst for life, for happiness, for liberty, that we have never quenched. And when we shall have tasted of this joy, we will set to work to demolish the last vestiges of middle-class rule; its morality drawn from account books, its 'debit and credit' philosophy, its 'mine and your' institutions. 'In demolishing we shall build,' as Proudhon said; and we shall build in the name of Communism and Anarchy."

... We can easily perceive the new horizons opening before the social revolution.

... At what, then, should the hundreds of thousands of workers, who are asphyxiated to-day in small workshops and factories, be employed on the day they regain their liberty? Will they continue to shut themselves up in factories after the Revolution? Will they continue to make luxurious toys for export when they see their stock or corn getting exhausted, meat becoming scarce, and vegetables disappearing without being replaced?

Evidently not! They will leave the town and go into the fields! Aided by a machinery which will enable the weakest of us to put a shoulder to the wheel, they will carry revolution into previously enslaved culture as they will have carried it into institutions and ideas.

... And in two or three months the early crops will receive the most pressing wants, and provide food for a people who, after so many centuries of expectation, will at least be able to appease their hunger and eat according to their appetite.

... The only thing that may be wanting to the Revolution is the boldness of initiative.

With our minds already narrowed in our youth and enslaved by the past in our mature age, we hardly dare to think. If a new idea is mentioned—before venturing on an opinion of our own, we consult musty books a hundred years old, to know what ancient masters thought on the subject.

It is not food that will fail, if boldness of thought and initiative are not wanting to the revolution.

... it will ... be by the working in common of the soil that the enfranchised societies will find their unity and will obliterate the hatred and oppression which has hitherto divided them.

Henceforth, able to conceive solidarity—that immense power which increases man's energy and creative forces a hundredfold—the new society will march to the conquest of the future with all the vigour of youth.

Ceasing to produce for unknown buyers, and looking in its midst for needs and tastes to be satisfied, society will liberally assure the life and ease of each of its members, as well as the moral satisfaction which work gives when freely chosen and freely accomplished, and the joy of living without encroaching on the life of others.

Inspired by a new daring—born of the feeling of solidarity—all will march together to the conquest of the high joys of knowledge and artistic creation.

A society thus inspired will fear neither dissensions within nor enemies without. To the coalitions of the past it will oppose a new harmony, the initiative of each and all, the daring which springs from the awakening of a people's genius.

Before such an irresistible force "conspiring kings" will be powerless. Nothing will remain for them but to bow before it, and to harness themselves to the chariot of humanity, rolling towards new horizons opened up by the Social Revolution.

georges sorel

Georges Sorel was a civil engineer by profession, but his interests in contemporary social problems prompted him to resign his position and devote his energies to study and writing. Sorel, who was born in Cherbourg, France, on November 2, 1847, always retained a lively interest in the philosophies of science and technology as evidenced by his several publications on the subject. He is best remembered, however, as a French social philosopher and as an unorthodox commentator on Marxism.

Sorel was intensely critical of the French Third Republic in particular, and democracy in general, and he became increasingly interested in socialist thought. Finding in the political and social life of democracy the triumph of mediocrity, Sorel espoused various forms of socialism which led him gradually to syndicalism. The latter embraced a plan for reorganizing society and a strategy for revolutionary action for the overthrow of the state. Like anarchists, syndicalists believed that any form of state is an instrument of oppression and that all states should be abolished. They stressed the function of productive labor and regarded the trade union as the essential unit of production and of government. In motive, the work of the unions would be socialistic—for use, not for profit. The general strike, sabotage, slowdowns, and other means of disrupting ordinary production were advocated by some syndicalists as a means of assuming control of the manufacturing process, seen as essential to their aims.

Syndicalist doctrine was substantially influenced by the writings of Pierre Proudhon, with his attacks on property, and of Georges Sorel, who espoused violence. Syndicalism, like anarchism, flourished largely in Latin countries, especially in France, where trade unionism was for years strongly influenced by syndicalist programs. In the United States the chief organization of the syndicalist type was the Industrial Workers of the World, which flourished early in the twentieth century but was virtually extinguished after the First World War by government suppression and internal rifts.

After resigning as a civil engineer, Sorel devoted much of his time to writing articles for various French and Italian periodicals, but his writings were unsystematic and of uneven quality. Originally he had been a liberal conservative, as can be seen from his *Procès de Socrate* (1889), but in 1893 he discovered Marxism and began writing the analytical critiques that number among his most original and valuable achievements. He strongly opposed Karl Kautsky's determinist simplifications and viewed Marxism as a philosophy of freedom and action. By 1902 his thought had grown more extreme, and he enthusiastically supported revolutionary syndicalism, which focused upon the spontaneity of the class struggle. His most famous work *Ré flexions sur la violence* [Reflections on Violence] was published in 1908 and represents in many ways the high point in the development of his philosophical thinking.

After 1909 Sorel's thought took a less certain direction. Feeling obliged to revise his revolutionary syndicalism, he drifted, not without strong misgivings, toward the monarchist movement Action francaise. But he changed again in 1914, judging World War I to be a betrayal, and he eventually declared himself for Bolshevism in 1919—with the more enthusiasm because he truly believed it to be a lost cause. He died at Boulogne-sur-Seine on August 28, 1922.

Sorel is sometimes held to have inspired both Communist and Fascist dictatorships, but his influence on either is difficult to demonstrate. Lenin had only contempt for him since Sorel denounced everything that might subject socialist action to control by party leaders. Benito Mussolini, however, frequently professed himself to be a disciple of Sorel, whose theories of "myth" and of "violence" he took to glorify the blind motivation of the mob and to justify mere physical brutality—distortions which Sorel explicitly condemned.

Georges Sorel is receiving new attention today as both activists and political theorists explore classic writings on revolution and violence. One example of the renewed interest in Sorel is Irving Louis Horowitz's excellent study *Radicalism and the Revolt against Reason,* the 1968 edition of which examines the relation between the social theories of Georges Sorel and American thought in the 1960's.

The selection which follows was excerpted from Sorel's *Reflections on Vio-*

lence. In it he developed his notions of "force" and of "violence." Violence for Sorel was the revolutionary denial of the existing order; but in describing its creative historical role he opposed it to "force," that is, to the state's power of coercion, the abuse of which he consistently denounced. In the concluding appendix, here included, entitled "Apology for Violence," Sorel displays an intense bitterness toward Jean Juarès, the French socialist leader and historian. Juarès believed economic equality would come as the result of peaceful revolution, an idealism which was viewed as utopian by most socialists. Marxists, anarchists, and syndicalists like Sorel, who were apostles of force and violence, regarded such thinking with contempt.

On Violence and Revolutionary Syndicalism

...To examine the effects of violence it is necessary to start from its distant consequences and not from its immediate results. We should not ask whether it is more or less directly advantageous for contemporary workmen than adroit diplomacy would be, but we should inquire what will result from the introduction of violence into the relations of the proletariat with society. We are not comparing two kinds of reformism, but we are endeavouring to find out what contemporary violence is in relation to the future social revolution.

... the most decisive factor in social politics is the cowardice of the Government. This was shown in the plainest possible way in the recent discussions on the suppression of registry offices, and on the law which sent to the civil courts appeals against the decisions of the arbitrators in industrial disputes. Nearly all the Syndicalist leaders know how to make excellent use of this situation, and they teach the workers that it is not at all a question of demanding favours, but that they must profit by *middle-class cowardice* to impose the will of the proletariat. These tactics are supported by so many facts that they were bound to take root in the working class world.

One of the things which appear to me to have most astonished the workers during the last few years has been the timidity of the forces of law and order in the presence of a riot; magistrates who have the right to demand the services of soldiers dare not use their power to the utmost, and officers allow themselves to be abused and struck with a patience hitherto unknown in them. It is becoming

From Georges Sorel, *Reflections on Violence*, translated by T.E. Hulme, Peter Smith, New York, 1941, pp. 47-48, 69-73, 84-91, 98-99, 121-122, 186-187, 297-299.

more and more evident every day that working-class violence possesses an extraordinary efficacy in strikes: prefects, fearing that they may be obliged to use force against insurrectionary violence, bring pressure to bear on employers in order to compel them to give way; the safety of factories is now looked upon as a favour which the prefect may dispense as he pleases; consequently he arranges the use of his police so as to intimidate the two parties, and skilfully brings them to an agreement.

Trades union leaders have not been long in grasping the full bearing of this situation, and it must be admitted that they have used the weapon that has been put into their hands with great skill. They endeavour to intimidate the prefects by popular demonstrations which might lead to serious conflicts with the police, and they commend violence as the most efficacious means of obtaining concessions. At the end of a certain time and obsessed and frightened administration nearly always intervenes with the masters and forces an agreement upon them, which becomes an encouragement to the propagandists of violence.

Whether we approve or condemn what is called *the revolutionary and direct method,* it is evident that it is not on the point of disappearing; in a country as warlike as France there are profound reasons which would assure a considerable popularity for this method, even if its enormous efficacy had not been demonstrated by so many examples. This is the one great social fact of the present hour, and we must seek to understand its bearing.

I cannot refrain from noting down here a reflection made by Clemenceau with regard to our relations with Germany, which applies equally well to social conflicts when they take a violent aspect (which seems likely to become more and more general in proportion as a cowardly middle class continues to pursue the chimera of social peace): "There is no better means," he said (than the policy of perpetual concessions), "of making the opposite party ask for more and more. Every man or every power whose action consists solely in surrender can only finish by self-annihilation. Everything that lives resists; that which does not resist allows itself to be cut up piecemeal" (*Aurore,* August 15, 1905).

A social policy founded on middle-class cowardice, which consists in always surrendering before the threat of violence, cannot fail to engender the idea that the middle class is condemned to death, and that its disappearance is only a matter of time. Thus every conflict which gives rise to violence becomes a vanguard fight, and nobody can foresee what will arise from such engagements; although the great battle never comes to a head, yet each time they come to blows the strikers hope that it is the beginning of the great *Napoleonic battle* (that which will definitely crush the vanquished); in this way the practice of strikes engenders the notion of a catastrophic revolution.

A keen observer of the contemporary proletarian movement has expressed the same ideas: "They, like their ancestors (the French revolutionaries), are for struggle, for conquest; they desire to accomplish great works by force. Only, the war of conquest interests them no longer. Instead of thinking of battles, they now think of strikes; instead of setting up as their ideal a battle against the armies of Europe, they now set up the general strike in which the capitalist regime will be annihilated."

The theorists of social peace shut their eyes to these embarrassing facts; they are doubtless ashamed to admit their cowardice, just as the Government is ashamed to admit that its social politics are carried out under the threat of disturbances. It is curious that people who boast of having read Le Play have not observed that his conception of the conditions of social peace was quite different from that of his imbecile successors. He supposed the existence of a middle class of serious moral habits, imbued with the feelings of its own dignity, and having the energy necessary to govern the country without recourse to the old traditional bureaucracy. To those men, who held riches and power in their hands, he professed to teach their *social duty towards their subjects.* His system supposed an undisputed authority; it is well known that he deplored the licence of the press under Napoleon III as scandalous and dangerous; his reflections on this subject seem somewhat ludicrous to those who compare the newspaper of that time with those of to-day. Nobody in his time would have believed that a great country would accept peace at any price; his point of view in this matter did not differ greatly from that of Clemenceau. He would never have admitted that any one could be cowardly and hypocritical enough to decorate with the name of social duty the cowardice of a middle class incapable of defending itself.

Middle-class cowardice very much resembles the cowardice of the English Liberal party, which constantly proclaims its absolute confidence in arbitration between nations: arbitration nearly always gives disastrous results for England. But these *worthy progressives* prefer to pay, or even to compromise the future of their country, rather than face the horrors of war. The English Liberal party has the word *justice* always on its lips, absolutely like our middle class; we might very well wonder whether all the high morality of our great contemporary thinkers is not founded on a degradation of the sentiment of honour.

... According to Marx, capitalism, by reason of the innate laws of its own nature, is hurrying along a path which will lead the world of to-day, with the inevitability of the evolution of organic life, to the doors of the world of to-morrow. This movement comprises a long period of capitalistic construction, and it ends by a rapid destruction, which is the work of the proletariat. Capitalism creates the heritage which Socialism will receive, the men who will suppress the present regime, and the means of bringing about this destruction, at the same time that it preserves the results obtained in production. Capitalism begets new ways of working; it throws the working class into revolutionary organisations by the pressure it exercises on wages; it restricts its own political basis by competition, which is constantly eliminating industrial leaders. Thus, after having solved the great problem of the organisation of labour, to effect which Utopians have brought forward so many naive or stupid hypotheses, capitalism provokes the birth of the cause which will overthrow it, and thus renders useless everything that Utopians have written to induce enlightened people to make reforms; and it gradually ruins the traditional order, against which the critics of the idealists had proved themselves to be so deplorably incompetent.... Without any co-ordinated plan, without any directive ideas, without any ideal of a future world, it is the cause of an inevitable evolution; it draws from the present all that the present can give towards historical development; it performs in an almost mechanical manner all that is necessary, in order that a new era may appear, and that this new era may break every link with the idealism of the present times, while preserving the acquisitions of the capitalistic economic system.

Socialists should therefore abandon the attempt (initiated by the Utopians) to find a means of inducing the enlightened middle class to prepare the *transition to a more perfect system of legislation*; their sole function is that of explaining to the proletariat the greatness of the revolutionary part they are called upon to play. By ceaseless criticism, the proletariat must be brought to perfect their organisations; they must be shown how the embryonic forms which appear in their unions may be developed so that, finally, they may build up institutions without any parallel in the history of the middle class; that they may form ideas which depend solely on their position as producers in large industries, and which owe nothing to middle-class thought; and that they may acquire *habits of liberty* with which the middle class nowadays are no longer acquainted.

This doctrine will evidently be inapplicable if the middle class and the proletariat do not oppose each other implacably, with all the forces at their disposal; the more ardently capitalist the middle class is, the more the proletariat is full of a warlike spirit and confident of its revolutionary strength, the more certain will be the success of the proletarian movement.

The middle class with which Marx was familiar in England was still, as regards the immense majority, animated by their conquering, insatiable, and pitiless spirit, which had characterised at the beginning of modern times the creators of new industries and the adventurers launched on the discovery of unknown lands. When we are studying the modern industrial system we should always bear in mind this similarity between the capitalist type and the warrior type; it was for very good reasons that the men who directed gigantic enterprises were named *captains of industry.* This type is still found to-day in all its purity in the United States: there are found the indomitable energy, the audacity based on a just appreciation of its strength, the cold calculation of interests, which are the qualities of great generals and great capitalists. According to Paul de Rousiers, every American feels himself capable of "trying his luck" on the battlefield of business, so that the general spirit of the country is in complete harmony with that of the multimillionaires; our men of letters are exceedingly surprised to see these latter condemning themselves to lead to the end of their days a galley-slave existence, without ever thinking of leading a nobleman's life for themselves, as the Rothschilds do.

In a society so enfevered by the passion for the success which can be obtained in competition, all the actors walk straight before them like veritable automata, without taking any notice of the great ideas of the sociologists; they are subject to very simple forces, and not one of them dreams of escaping from the circumstances of his condition. Then only is the development of capitalism carried on with that inevitableness which struck Marx so much, and which seemed to him comparable to that of a natural law. If, on the contrary, the middle class, led astray by the *chatter* of the preachers of ethics and sociology, return to an *ideal of conservative mediocrity*, seek to correct the *abuses* of economics, and wish to break with the barbarism of their predecessors, then one part of the forces which were to further the development of capitalism is employed in hindering it, an arbitrary and irrational element is introduced, and the future of the world becomes completely indeterminate.

This indetermination grows still greater if the proletariat are converted to the ideas of social peace at the same time as their masters, or even if they simply consider everything from the corporative point of view; while Socialism gives to every economic contest a general and revolutionary colour.

Conservatives are not deceived when they see in the compromises which lead to collective contracts, and in corporative particularism, the means of avoiding the Marxian revolution; but they escape one danger only to fall into another, and they run the risk of being devoured by Parliamentary Socialism.

... It is often urged, in objection to the people who defend the Marxian conception, that it is impossible for them to stop the movement of degeneration which is dragging both the middle class and the proletariat far from the paths assigned to them by Marx's theory. They can doubtless influence the working classes, and it is hardly to be denied that strike violences do keep the revolutionary spirit alive; but how can they hope to give back to the middle class an ardour which is spent?

It is here that the role of violence in history appears to us as singularly great, for it can, in an indirect manner, so operate on the middle class as to awaken them to a sense of their own class sentiment. Attention has often been drawn to the danger of certain acts of violence which compromised *admirable social works,* disgusted employers who were disposed to arrange the happiness of their workmen, and developed egoism where the most noble sentiments formerly reigned.

To repay with *black ingratitude* the *benevolence* of those who would protect the workers, to meet with insults the homilies of the defenders of human fraternity, and to reply by blows to the advances of the propagators of social peace—all that is assuredly not in conformity with the rules of the fashionable Socialism . . . but it is a very practical way of indicating to the middle class that they must mind their own business and only that.

I believe also that it may be useful to thrash the orators of democracy and the representatives of the Government, for in this way you insure that none shall retain any illusions about the character of acts of violence. But these acts can have historical value only if they are the *clear and brutal expression of the class war:* the middle classes must not be allowed to imagine that, aided by cleverness, social science, or high-flown sentiments, they might find a better welcome at the hands of the proletariat.

The day on which employers perceive that they have nothing to gain by works which promote social peace, or by democracy, they will understand that they have been ill-advised by the people who persuaded them to abandon their trade of creators of productive forces for the noble profession of educators of the proletariat. Then there is some chance that they may get back a part of their energy, and that moderate or conservative economics may appear as absurd to them as they appeared to Marx. In any case, the separation of classes being more clearly accentuated, the proletarian movement will have some chance of developing with greater regularity than to-day

The two antagonistic classes therefore influence each other in a partly indirect but decisive manner. Capitalism drives the proletariat into revolt, because in daily life the employers use their force in a direction opposed to the desire of their workers; but the future of the proletariat is not entirely dependent on this revolt; the working classes are organised under the influence of other causes, and Socialism, inculcating in them the revolutionary idea, prepares them to suppress the hostile class. Capitalist force is at the base of all this process, and its action is automatic and inevitable. Marx supposed that the middle class had no need to be incited to employ force, but we are to-day faced with a new and very unforeseen fact-a middle class had no need to be incited its own strength. Must we believe that the Marxian conception is dead? By no means, for proletarian violence comes upon the scene just at the moment when the conception of social peace is being held up as a means of moderating disputes; proletarian violence confines employers to their role of producers, and tends to restore the separation of the classes, just when they seemed on the point of intermingling in the democratic marsh.

Proletarian violence not only makes the future revolution certain, but it seems also to be the only means by which the European nations—at present stupefied by humanitarianism—can recover their former energy. This kind of violence compels capitalism to restrict its attentions solely to its material role and tends to restore to it the warlike qualities which it formerly possessed. A growing and solidly organised working class can compel the capitalist class to remain firm in the industrial war; if a united and revolutionary proletariat confronts a rich middle class, eager for conquest, capitalist society will have reached its historical perfection.

Thus proletarian violence has become an essential factor of Marxism. Let us add once more that, if properly conducted, it will suppress the Parliamentary Socialists, who will no longer be able to pose as the leaders of the working classes and the guardians of order.

...The dangers which threaten the future of the world may be avoided, if the proletariat hold on with obstinacy to revolutionary ideas, so as to realise as much as possible Marx's conception. Everything may be saved, if the proletariat, by their use of violence, manage to re-establish the division into classes, and so restore to the middle class something of its former energy; that is the great aim towards which the whole thought of men—who are not hypnotised by the event of the day, but who think of the conditions of to-morrow—must be directed. Proletarian violence, carried on as a pure and simple manifestation of the sentiment of the class war, appears thus as a very fine and very heroic thing; it is at the service of the immemorial interests of civilisation; it is not perhaps the most appropriate method of obtaining immediate material advantages, but it may save the world from barbarism.

We have a very effective reply to those who accuse Syndicalists of being obtuse and ignorant people. We may ask them to consider the economic decadence for which they are working. Let us salute the revolutionaries as the Greek saluted the Spartan heroes who defended Thermopylae and helped to preserve the civilisation of the ancient world.

...I think that I have said sufficient to enable me to conclude that if by chance our Parliamentary Socialists get possession of the reins of Government, they will prove to be worthy successors of the Inquisition, of the Old Regime, and of Robespierre; political courts will be at work on a large scale, and we even suppose that the *unfortunate* law of 1848, which abolished the death penalty in political matters, will be repealed. Thanks to this *reform,* we might again see the State triumphing by the hand of the executioner.

Proletarian acts of violence have no resemblance to these proscriptions; they are purely and simply acts of war; they have the value of military demonstrations, and serve to mark the separation of classes. Everything in war is carried on without hatred and without the spirit of revenge: in war the vanquished are not killed; non-combatants are not made to bear the consequences of the disappointments which the armies may have experienced on the fields of battle; force is then displayed according to its own nature, without ever professing to borrow anything from the judicial proceedings which society sets up against criminals.

The more Syndicalism develops, by abandoning the old superstitions which come to it from the Old Regime and from the Church—through the men of letters, professors of philosophy, and historians of the Revolution,—the more will social conflicts assume the character of a simple struggle, similar to those of armies on campaign. We cannot censure too severely those who teach the people that they ought to carry out the highly idealistic decrees of a progressive justice. Their efforts will only result in the maintenance of those ideas about the State which provoked the bloody acts of 1793, whilst the idea of a class war, on the contrary, tends to refine the conception of violence.

... *The masses who are led* have a very vague and extremely simple idea of the means by which their lot can be improved; demagogues easily get them to believe that the best way is to utilise the power of the State to *pester* the rich. We pass thus from jealousy to vengeance, and it is well known that vengeance is a sentiment of extraordinary power, especially with the weak. The history of the Greek cities and of the Italian republics of the Middle Ages is full of instances of fiscal laws which were very oppressive on the rich, and which contributed not a little towards the ruin of governments ... If our contemporary social policy were examined closely, it would be seen that it also was steeped in ideas of jealousy and vengeance; many regulations have been framed more with the idea of pestering employers than of improving the situation of the workers. When the clericals are in a minority, they never fail to recommend severe regulations in order to be revenged on free-thinking free-mason employers.

The leaders obtain all sorts of advantages from these methods; they alarm the rich, and exploit them for their own personal profit; they cry louder than anybody against the privileges of fortune, and know how to obtain for themselves all the enjoyments which the latter procures; by making use of the evil instincts and the stupidity of their followers, they realise this curious paradox, that they get the people to applaud the inequality of conditions in the name of democratic equality. It would be impossible to understand the success of demagogues from the time of Athens to contemporary New York, if due account was not taken of the extraordinary power of the idea of vengeance in extinguishing reasonable reflection.

I believe that the only means by which this pernicious influence of the demagogues may be wiped out are those employed by Socialism in propagating the notion of the proletarian general strike; it awakens in the depths of the soul a sentiment of the sublime proportionate to the conditions of a gigantic struggle; it forces the desire to satisfy jealousy by malice into the background; it brings to the fore the pride of free men, and thus protects the worker from the quackery of ambitious leaders, hungering for the fleshpots.

... The study of the political strike leads us to a better understanding of a distinction we must always have in mind when we reflect on contemporary social questions. Sometimes the terms *force* and *violence* are used in speaking of acts of authority, sometimes in speaking of acts of revolt. It is obvious that the two cases give rise to very different consequences. I think it would be better to adopt a terminology which would give rise to no ambiguity, and that the term *violence* should be employed only for acts of revolt; we should say, therefore, that the object of force is to impose a certain social order in which the minority governs, while violence tends to the destruction of that order. The middle class have used force since the beginning of modern times, while the proletariat now reacts against the middle class and against the State by violence. . . .

Apology for Violence

Men who make revolutionary speeches to the people are bound to set before themselves a high standard of sincerity, because the workers understand their words in their exact and literal sense, and never indulge in any symbolic interpretation. When in 1905 I ventured to write in some detail on proletarian violence I understood perfectly the grave responsibility I assumed in trying to show the historic bearing of actions which our Parliamentary Socialists try to dissimulate, with so much skill. To-day I do not hesitate to assert that Socialism could not continue to exist without an apology for violence.

It is in strikes that the proletariat asserts its existence. I cannot agree with the view which sees in strikes merely something analogous to the temporary rupture of commercial relations which is brought about when a grocer and the wholesale dealer from whom he buys his dried plums cannot agree about the price. The strike is a phenomenon of war. It is thus a serious misrepresentation to say that violence is an accident doomed to disappear from the strikes of the future.

The social revolution is an extension of that war in which each great strike is an episode; this is the reason why Syndicalists speak of that revolution in the language of strikes; for them Socialism is reduced to the conception, the expectation of, and the preparation for the general strike, which, like the Napoleonic battle, is to completely annihilate a condemned *regime.*

Such a conception allows none of those subtle exegeses in which Jaures excels. It is a question here of an overthrow in the course of which both employers and the State would be set aside by the organised producers. Our Intellectuals, who hope to obtain the highest places from democracy, would be sent back to their literature; the Parliamentary Socialists, who find in the organisations created by the middle classes means of exercising a certain amount of power, would become useless.

The analogy which exists between strikes accompanied by violence and war is prolific of consequences. No one doubts . . . that it was war that provided the republics of antiquity with the ideas which form the ornament of our modern culture. The social war, for which the proletariat ceaselessly prepares itself in the syndicates, may engender the elements of a new civilisation suited to a people of producers. I continually call the attention of my young friends to the problems presented by Socialism considered from the point of view of a civilisation of producers; I assert that to-day a philosophy is being elaborated according to this plan, whose possibility even was hardly suspected a few years ago; this philosophy is closely bound up with the apology for violence.

I have never had that admiration for *creative hatred* which Juarès has devoted to it; I do not feel the same indulgence towards the guillotiners as he does; I have a horror of any measure which strikes the vanquished under a judicial disguise. War, carried on in broad daylight, without hypocritical attenuation, for the purpose of ruining an irreconcilable enemy, excludes all the abominations which dishonoured the middle-class revolution of the eighteenth century. The apology for violence in this case is particularly easy.

It would serve no purpose to explain to the poor that they ought not to feel sentiments of jealousy and vengeance against their masters; these feelings are too powerful to be suppressed by exhortations; it is on the widespread prevalence of these feelings that democracy chiefly founds its strength. Social war, by making an appeal to the honour which develops so naturally in all organised armies, can eliminate those evil feelings against which morality would remain powerless. If this were the only reason we had for attributing a high civilising value to revolutionary Syndicalism, this reason alone would, it seems to me, be decisive in favour of the apologists for violence.

The conception of the general strike, engendered by the practice of violent strikes, admits the conception of an irrevocable overthrow. There is something terrifying in this which will appear more and more terrifying as violence takes a greater place in the mind of the proletariat. But, in undertaking a serious, formidable, and sublime work, Socialists raise themselves above our frivolous society and make themselves worthy of pointing out new roads to the world.

Parliamentary Socialists may be compared to the officials whom Napoleon made into a nobility and who laboured to strengthen the State bequeathed by the Ancien Regime. Revolutionary Syndicalism corresponds well enough to the Napoleonic armies whose soldiers accomplished such heroic acts, knowing all the time that they would remain poor. What remains of the Empire? Nothing but the epic of the Grande Armée. What will remain of the present Socialist movement will be the epic of the strikes.

emmeline pankhurst

Women's liberation movements have assumed a variety of forms in modern history. Political, economic, social, and sexual equality have numbered among the demands made by advocates of female rights. One of the earliest feminist campaigns centered on the fight for political suffrage, and Mrs. Emmeline Pankhurst was one of the ablest and most courageous supporters of that cause. In many ways her task in England was more formidable than that of Susan B. Anthony in America, whose own distinctive achievements were well known to Mrs. Pankhurst because of the comparatively less emancipated status of women in the life and society of Victorian Britain.

Emmeline Pankhurst was born in Manchester, England, on July 14, 1858, the daughter of Robert Goulden, a prosperous calico painter. She received an excellent education and later attended finishing school in Paris, where she befriended the daughter of Henri Rochefort, the French radical. Emmeline married Richard Marsden Pankhurst, a barrister who, as a friend of John Stuart Mill, had drafted the first women's suffrage bill and the subsequent Married Women's Property Acts of 1870 and 1882. The Pankhursts had three daughters, including Christabel (1880-1958) and Sylvia (1882-1960), who were also prominent suffragettes, and two sons. Richard Pankhurst's death in 1898 left Emmeline as the breadwinner of the family, and she took employment as registrar of births and deaths for the city of Manchester.

Emmeline's abiding interest, however, was in the political emancipation of women. Disappointed by the apparent indifference of the Liberal Party, the Fabian Society, and the Independent Labour Party to this cause, she founded the Women's Social and Political Union (W.S.P.U.) in 1903 on nonparty lines. The movement first attracted public attention in 1905, when her daughter Christabel and a friend, Annie Kenny, were thrown out of a British Liberal Party meeting for demanding an answer from Sir Edward Grey about votes for women. Arrested on the charge of technical assault against the police, both girls refused to pay fines ordered by the court and were sent to prison.

In 1906 Mrs. Pankhurst moved to London, where she became increasingly involved in W.S.P.U. activities. With the support of her daughters, together with that of an increasing number of feminists, the W.S.P.U. grew rapidly in numbers, financial resources, and political significance. In 1910, the Liberal Government's sponsorship of suffrage legislation in the form of a "conciliation" bill prompted Mrs. Pankhurst to declare a truce, whereupon her followers obediently suspended their militant programs. But it soon became apparent that British Prime Minister Herbert Asquith's intention was merely to silence rather than to satisfy the suffragettes, particularly after he postponed action on the conciliation bill by virtue of his referral of it to the Committee of the whole House, where proposed legislation usually languished indefinitely.

Mrs. Pankhurst reacted angrily to the treachery of the Liberal Government. On November 18, 1910, the suffragettes conducted a march upon Parliament. In a confrontation with police in Parliament Square, remembered in suffragette history as "Black Friday," a virtual riot ensued for a period of six hours during which hundreds of women were repulsed by police, at first firmly and then violently, as suffragettes attempted to storm the Houses of Parliament. One hundred and fifteen women were arrested before the rioting was finally quelled. The attempt to physically occupy Parliament had failed, but the Government had been profoundly shaken by the horrible brutality which resulted from the suppression of the female militants.

Suffragettes became increasingly more violent, and in 1912 their tactics included the defacing or destruction of public and private buildings and similar targets. Attempts were also made to burn postal boxes, and the Government responded by ordering the arrest of W.S.P.U. leaders on the charge of conspiracy. Christabel received sufficient warning to permit her escape to Paris, where she continued to aid and direct militant suffragettes in London. Mrs. Pankhurst was arrested and sentenced to nine months in prison, but was released within three months following a hunger strike. In June 1913 she was arrested again and sentenced to three years' imprisonment. Her statement before the court on this occasion was an eloquent and forceful declaration of the suffragette position. In it she condemned the Prisoner's (Temporary Discharge for Ill Health) Act of 1913, known as the "Cat and Mouse"Act, whereby hunger-striking prisoners could be temporarily released and re-arrested. She also gave a reasoned argument for the justification of violence and civil disobedience when a political system provides no other alternatives for procuring fundamental human rights. Her testimony in the selection which follows contains lessons and principles which remain timely and are applicable in any number of circumstances in today's society.

Emmeline Pankhurst and her daughter Christabel called off the suffrage campaign at the outbreak of World War I, and the Government released all suffragette prisoners. Many of the same women who had displayed such zeal in seeking to destroy every symbol of British authority responded with equal fervor to the nationalist war effort; some worked in munitions factories while others served as nurses in the fields of Flanders or on the blood-stained beaches of Gallipoli. But Sylvia Pankhurst, the younger of Mrs. Pankhurst's suffragette daughters, continued to demand the vote and broke with her mother and sister by declaring that women should stand for peace, not bloodshed. In February, 1918, the Representation of the People Act gave the vote to a limited number of women. From 1919 to 1925 Mrs. Pankhurst lived in Canada and the United States. Upon her return to England she was selected as a prospective Conservative candidate for an East London constituency in 1926, but the strain of an active lifetime had sapped her vitality, and she died in London on June 14, 1928, a month before the passing of Stanley Baldwin's Representation of the People Act, which gave women full equality in the franchise.

The Struggle for Women's Suffrage

To account for the phenomenal growth of the Women's Social and Political Union after it was established in London, to explain why it made such an instant appeal to women hitherto indifferent, I shall have to point out exactly wherein our society differs from all other suffrage associations. In the first place, our members are absolutely single minded; they concentrate all their forces on one object, political equality with men. No member of the W.S.P.U. divides her attention between suffrage and other social reforms. We hold that both reason and justice dictate that women shall have a share in reforming the evils that

From Emmeline Pankhurst, *My Own Story*, Hearst's International Library Co., New York, 1914, pp. 57-62, 279-284, 292-299.

afflict society, especially those evils bearing directly on women themselves. Therefore, we demand, before any other legislation whatever, the elementary justice of votes for women.

There is not the slightest doubt that the women of Great Britain would have been enfranchised years ago had all the suffragists adopted this simple principle. They never did, and even to-day many English women refuse to adopt it. They are party members first and suffragists afterward; or they are suffragists part of the time and social theorists the rest of the time. We further differ from other suffrage associations, or from others existing in 1906, in that we clearly perceived the political situation that solidly interposed between us and our enfranchisement.

For seven years we had had a majority in the House of Commons pledged to vote favourably on a suffrage bill. The year before, they had voted favourably on one, yet that bill did not become law. Why? Because even an overwhelming majority of private members are powerless to enact law in the face of a hostile Government of eleven cabinet ministers. The private member of Parliament was once possessed of individual power and responsibility, but Parliamentary usage and a changed conception of statesmanship have gradually lessened the functions of members. At the present time their powers, for all practical purposes, are limited to helping to enact such measures as the Government introduces or, in rare instances, private measures approved by the Government. It is true that the House can revolt, can, by voting a lack of confidence in the Government, force them to resign. But that almost never happens, and it is less likely now than formerly to happen. Figureheads don't revolt.

This, then, was our situation: the Government all-powerful and consistently hostile; the rank and file of legislators impotent; the country apathetic; the women divided in their interests. The Women's Social and Political Union was established to meet this situation and to overcome it. Moreover we had a policy which, if persisted in long enough, could not possibly fail to overcome it. Do you wonder that we gained new members at every meeting we held?

There was little formality about joining the Union. Any woman could become a member by paying a shilling, but at the same time she was required to sign a declaration of loyal adherence to our policy and a pledge not to work for any political party until the women's vote was won. This is still our inflexible custom. Moreover, if at any time a member, or a group of members, loses faith in our policy; if any one begins to suggest that some other policy ought to be substituted, or if she tries to confuse the issue by adding other policies, she ceases at once to be a member. Autocratic? Quite so. But, you may object, a suffrage organisation ought to be democratic. Well the members of the W.S.P.U. do not agree with you. We do not believe in the effectiveness of the ordinary suffrage organisation. The W.S.P.U. is not hampered by a complexity of rules. We have no constitution and by-laws; nothing to be amended or tinkered with or quarrelled over at an annual meeting. In fact, we have no annual meeting, no business sessions, no elections of officers. The W.S.P.U. is simply a suffrage army in the field. It is purely a volunteer army, and no one is obliged to remain in it. Indeed we don't want anybody to remain in it who does not ardently believe in the policy of the army.

The foundation of our policy is opposition to a Government who refuse votes to women. To support by word or deed a Government hostile to woman suffrage is simply to invite them to go on being hostile. We oppose the Liberal party because it is in power. We would oppose a Unionist government if it were in power and were opposed to woman suffrage. We say to women that as long as they remain in the ranks of the Liberal party they give their tacit approval to the Government's anti-suffrage policy. We say to members of Parliament that as long as they support any of the Government's policies they give their tacit approval to the anti-suffrage policy. We call upon all sincere suffragists to leave the Liberal party until women are given votes on equal terms with men. We call upon all voters to vote against Liberal candidates until the Liberal Government does justice to women.

. . . The contention of the old-fashioned suffragists, and of the politicians as well, has always been that an educated public opinion will ultimately give votes to women without any great force being exerted in behalf of the reform. We agree that public opinion must be educated, but we contend that even an educated public opinion is useless unless it is vigorously utilised. The keenest weapon is powerless unless it is courageously wielded. In the year 1906 there was an immensely large public opinion in favour of woman suffrage. But what good did that do the cause? We called upon the public for a great deal more than sympathy. We called upon it to demand of the Government to yield to public opinion and give women votes. And we declared that we would wage war, not only on all anti-suffrage forces, but on all neutral and non-active forces. Every man with a vote was considered a foe to woman suffrage unless he was prepared to be actively a friend.

Not that we believed that the campaign of education ought to be given up. On the contrary, we knew that education must go on, and in much more vigorous fashion than ever before. The first thing we did was to enter upon a sensational campaign to arouse the public to the importance of woman suffrage, and to interest it in our plans for forcing the Government's hands. I think we can claim that our success in this regard was instant, and that it has proved permanent. From the very first, in those early London days, when we were few in numbers and very poor in purse, we made the public aware of the woman suffrage movement as it had never been before. We adopted Salvation Army methods and went out into the highways and the byways after converts. We threw away all our conventional notions of what was "ladylike" and "good form," and we applied to our methods the one test question, Will it help? Just as the Booths and their followers took religion to the street crowds in such fashion that the church people were horrified, so we took suffrage to the general public in a manner that amazed and scandalised the other suffragists.

    . . . It was at this time, February, 1913, less that two years ago as I write these words, that militancy, as it is now generally understood by the public began— militancy in the sense of continued, destructive, guerilla warfare against the Government through injury to private property. Some property had been destroyed before this time, but the attacks were sporadic, and were meant to be in the nature of a warning as to what might become a settled policy. Now we indeed lighted the torch, and we did it with the absolute conviction that no other course was open to us. We had tried every other measure, as I am sure that I have demonstrated to my readers, and our years of work and suffering and sacrifice had taught us that the Government would not yield to right and justice, what the majority of members of the House of Commons admitted was right and justice, but that the Government would, as other governments invariably do, yield to expediency. Now our task was to show the Government that it was expedient to yield to the women's just demands. In order to do that we had to make England and every department of English life insecure and unsafe. We had to make English law a failure and the courts farce comedy theatres; we had to discredit the Government and Parliament in the eyes of the world; we had to spoil English sports, hurt business, destroy valuable property, demoralise the world of society, shame the churches, upset the whole orderly conduct of life—

    That is, we had to do as much of this guerilla warfare as the people of England would tolerate. When they came to the point of saying to the Government: "Stop this, in the only way it can be stopped, by giving the women of England representation," then we should extinguish our torch.

    Americans of all people, ought to see the logic of our reasoning. There is one piece of American oratory, beloved of schoolboys, which has often been quoted from militant platforms. In a speech now included among the classics of the English language your great statesman, Patrick Henry, summed up the causes that led to the American Revolution. He said: "We have petitioned, we have remonstrated, we have supplicated, we have prostrated ourselves at the foot of the throne, and it has all been in vain. We must fight—I repeat it, sir, we must fight."

    Patrick Henry, remember, was advocating killing people, as well as destroying private property, as the proper means of securing the political freedom of men. The Suffragettes have not done that, and they never will. In fact the moving spirit of militancy is deep and abiding reverence for human life. In the latter course of our agitation I have been called upon to discuss our policies with many eminent men, politicians, literary men, barristers, scientists, clergymen. One of the last named, a high dignitary of the Church of England, told me that while he was a convinced suffragist, he found it impossible to justify our doing wrong that right might follow. I said to him: "We are not doing wrong—we are doing right in our use of revolutionary methods against private property. It is our work to restore thereby true values, to emphasise the value of human rights against property rights. You are well aware, sir, that property has assumed a value in the eyes of men, and in the eyes of the law, that it ought never to claim. It is placed above all human values. The lives and health and happiness, and even the virtue of women and children—that is to say, the race itself—are being ruthlessly sacrificed to the god of property every day of the world."

To this my reverend friend agreed, and I said: "If we women are wrong in destroying private property in order that human values may be restored, then I say, in all reverence, that it was wrong for the Founder of Christianity to destroy private property, as He did when He lashed the money changers out of the Temple and when He drove the Gaderene swine into the sea."

It was absolutely in this spirit that our women went forth to war. In the first month of guerilla warfare an enormous amount of property was damaged and destroyed. On January 31st a number of putting greens were burned with acids; on February 7th and 8th telegraph and telephone wires were cut in several places and for some hours all communications between London and Glasgow were suspended; a few days later windows in various of London's smartest clubs were broken, and the orchid houses at Kew were wrecked and many valuable blooms destroyed by cold. The jewel room at the Tower of London was invaded and a showcase broken. The residence of H.R.H. Prince Christian and Lambeth Palace, seat of the Archbishop of Canterbury, were visited and had windows broken. The refreshment house in Regents Park was burned to the ground on February 12th and on February 18th a country house which was being built at Walton-on-the-Hill for Mr. Lloyd-George was partially destroyed, a bomb having been exploded in the early morning before the arrival of the workmen. A hat pin and a hair pin picked up near the house—coupled with the fact that care had been taken not to endanger any lives—led the police to believe that the deed had been done by women enemies of Mr. Lloyd-George. Four days later I was arrested and brought up in Epsom police court, where I was charged with having "counselled and procured" the persons who did the damage. Admitted to bail for the night, I appeared next morning in court, where the case was fully reviewed.

. . . I heard that the authorities had arranged that my trial should take place on April 1st, instead of at the end of June, and at the Central Criminal Court, London, instead of the Guildford Court. I then gave the required undertaking and was immediately released on bail.

. . . After a hard fight to be allowed to tell the jury the reasons why women had lost respect for the law, and were making such a struggle in order to become law makers themselves, I closed my speech by saying:

"Over one thousand women have gone to prison in the course of this agitation, have suffered their imprisonment, have come out of prison injured in health, weakened in body, but not in spirit. I come to stand my trial from the bedside of one of my daughters, who has come out of Holloway Prison, sent there for two months' hard labour for participating with four other people in breaking a small pane of glass. She has hunger-struck in prison. She submitted herself for more than five weeks to the horrible ordeal of feeding by force, and she has come out of prison having lost nearly two stone in weight. She is so weak that she cannot get out of her bed. And I say to you, gentlemen, that is the kind of punishment you are inflicting upon me or any other woman who may be brought before you. I ask you if you are prepared to send an incalculable number of women to prison—I speak to you as representing others in the same position—if you are prepared to go on doing that kind of thing indefinitely, because that is what is going to happen. There is absolutely no doubt about it. I think you have seen enough even in this present case to convince you that we are not women who are notoriety hunters. We could get that, heaven knows, much more cheaply if we sought it. We are women, rightly or wrongly, convinced that this is the only way in which we can win power to alter what for us are intolerable conditions, absolutely intolerable conditions. A London clergyman only the other day said that 60 per cent of the married women in his parish were breadwinners, supporting their husbands as well as their children. When you think of the wages women earn, when you think of what this means to the future of the children of this country, I ask you to take this question very, very seriously. Only this morning I have had information brought to me which could be supported by sworn affidavits, that there is in this country, in this very city of London of ours, a regulated traffic, not only in women of full age, but in little children; that they are being purchased, that they are being entrapped, and that they are being trained to minister to the vicious pleasures of persons who ought to know better in their positions of life.

"Well, these are the things that have made us women determined to go on, determined to face everything, determined to see this thing out to the end, let it cost us what it may. And if you convict me, gentlemen, if you find me guilty, I tell you quite honestly and quite frankly, that whether the sentence is a long sentence, whether the sentence is a short sentence, I shall not submit to it. I shall, the moment I leave this court, if I am sent to prison, whether to penal servitude or to the lighter form of imprisonment—because I am not sufficiently versed in the law to know what his lordship may decide; but whatever my sentence is, from the moment I leave this court I shall quite deliberately refuse to eat food—I shall join the women who are already in Holloway on the hunger strike. I shall come out of prison, dead or alive, at the earliest possible moment; and once out again, as soon as I am physically fit I shall enter into this fight again. Life is very dear to all of us. I am not seeking, as was said by the Home Secretary, to commit suicide. I do not want to commit suicide. I want to see the women of this country enfranchised, and I want to live until that is done. Those are the feelings by which we are animated. We offer ourselves as sacrifices, just as your forefathers did in the past, in this cause, and I would ask you all to put this question to yourselves:—Have you the right, as human beings, to condemn another human being to death—because that is what it amounts to? Can you throw the first stone? Have you the right to judge women?

"You have not the right in human justice, not the right by the constitution of this country, if rightly interpreted, to judge me, because you are not my peers. You know, every one of you, that I should not be standing here, that I should not break one single law—if I had the rights that you possess, if I had a share in electing those who make the laws I have to obey; if I had a voice in controlling the taxes I am called upon to pay, I should not be standing here. And I say to you it is a very serious state of things. I say to you, my lord, it is a very serious situation, that women of upright life, women who have devoted the best of their years to the public weal, that women who are engaged in trying to undo some of the terrible mistakes that men in their government of the country have made, because after all, in the last resort, men are responsible for the present state of affairs—I put it to you that it is a very serious situation. You are not accustomed to deal with people like me in the ordinary discharge of your duties; but you are called upon to deal with people who break the law from selfish motives. I break the law from no selfish motive. I have no personal end to serve, neither have any of the other women who have gone through this court during the past few weeks, like sheep to the slaughter. Not one of these women would, if women were free, be law-breakers. They are women who seriously believe that this hard path that they are treading is the only path to their enfranchisement. They seriously believe that the welfare of humanity demands this sacrifice; they be-lieve that the horrible evils which are ravaging our civilisation will never be removed until women get the vote. They know that the very fount of life is being poisoned; they know that homes are being destroyed; that because of bad education, because of the unequal standard of morals, even the mothers and children are destroyed by one of the vilest and most horrible diseases that ravage humanity.

"There is only one way to put a stop to this agitation; there is only one way to break down this agitation. It is not by deporting us, it is not by locking us up in gaol; it is by doing us justice. And so I appeal to you gentlemen, in this case of mine, to give a verdict, not only on my case, but upon the whole of this agitation. I ask you to find me not guilty of malicious incitement to a breach of the law.

"These are my last words. My incitement is not malicious. If I had power to deal with these things, I would be in absolute obedience to the law. I would say to women, 'You have a constitutional means of getting redress for your grievances; use your votes, convince your fellow-voters of the righteousness of your demands. That is the way to obtain justice.' I am not guilty of malicious incitement, and I appeal to you, for the welfare of the country, for the welfare of the race, to return a verdict of not guilty in this case that you are called upon to try."

. . . I spoke once more to the Judge.

"The jury have found me guilty, with a strong recommendation to mercy, and I do not see, since motive is not taken into account in human laws, that they could do otherwise after your summing up. But since motive is not taken into account in human laws, and since I, whose motives are not ordinary motives, am about to be sentenced by you to the punishment which is accorded to people whose motives are selfish motives, I have only this to say: If it was impossible for a different verdict to be found; if it is your duty to sentence me, as it will be presently, then I want to say to you, as a private citizen, and to the jury as private citizens, that I, standing here, found guilty by the laws of my country, I say to you it is your duty, as private citizens, to do what you can to put an end to this intolerable state of affairs. I put that duty upon you. And I want to say, *whatever the sentence you pass upon me, I shall do what is humanly possible to terminate that sentence at the earliest possible moment. I have no sense of guilt. I feel I have done my duty. I look upon myself as a prisoner of war. I am under no moral obligation to conform to, or in any way accept, the sentence imposed upon me.* I shall take the desperate remedy that other women have taken. It is obvious to you that the struggle will be an unequal one, but I shall make it—I shall make it as long as I have an ounce of strength left in me, or any life left in me.

"I shall fight, I shall fight, I shall fight, from the moment I enter prison to struggle against overwhelming odds; I shall resist the doctors if they attempt to feed me. I was sentenced last May in this court to nine months' imprisonment. I remained in prison six weeks. There are people who have laughed at the ordeal of hunger-striking and forcible feeding. All I can say is, and the doctors can bear me out, that I was released because, had I remained there much longer, I should have been a dead woman.

"I know what it is because I have gone through it. My own daughter has only just left it. There are women there still facing that ordeal, facing it twice a day. Think of it, my lord, twice a day this fight is gone through. Twice a day a weak woman resisting overwhelming force, fights and fights as long as she has strength left; fights against women and even against men, resisting with her tongue, with her teeth, this ordeal. Last night in the House of Commons some alternative was discussed, or rather, some additional punishment. Is it not a strange thing, my lord, that laws which have sufficed to restrain men throughout the history of this country do not suffice now to restrain women—decent women, honourable women?

"Well, my lord, I do want you to realise it. I am not whining about my punishment. I invited it. I deliberately broke the law, not hysterically or emotionally, but of set serious purpose, because I honestly feel it is the only way. Now, I put the responsibility of what is to follow upon you, my lord, as a private citizen, and upon the gentlemen of the jury, as private citizens, and upon all the men in this court—what are you, with your political powers, going to do to end this intolerable situation?

"*To the women I have represented, to the women who, in response to my incitement, have faced these terrible consequences, have broken laws, to them I want to say I am not going to fail them, but to face it as they face it, to go through with it, and I know that they will go on with the fight whether I live or whether I die.*

"*This movement will go on and on until we have the rights of citizens in this country, as women have in our Colonies, as they will have throughout the civilised world before this woman's war is ended.*

"That is all I have to say."

lenin

Vladimir Ilyich Ulyanov, who assumed the pseudonym Lenin in 1901, was the greatest single driving force behind the Soviet revolution of November 1917. Born on April 22, 1870, at Simbirsk (later re-named Ulyanov) on the Volga, he was the son of a schoolmaster and the grandson of a physician. Lenin's elder brother, while a university student, was arrested and executed in 1887 for his part in a plot to assassinate Czar Alexander III. This is believed to have turned young Lenin's mind toward revolution; what is certain is that his interests turned toward Marxism and agitation. Expelled from Kazan University for participation in a student demonstration in 1887, he received a degree in law from St. Petersburg University four years later.

By 1895, Lenin was an authority on Marxism, and he travelled abroad during the summer of that year to learn first-hand about European socialism. Upon his return to St. Petersburg he was arrested for his political activities; after spending fourteen months in prison, Lenin was exiled to Siberia for three years in 1897. There he was joined by Nadezhda Krupskaya, whom he had first met at revolutionary functions in St. Petersburg. They were married in July 1898. It was during his exile that Lenin wrote *The Development of Capitalism in Russia*, published in 1899.

Having completed his political exile in 1900, Lenin settled for a time in Pskov (a town near St. Petersburg; the capital was still off-limits to him). There he addressed himself to a dual task: combating the growing influence of revisionist Marxists, like Eduard Bernstein and others in Germany, and building up a strong, strictly centralized party capable of taking complete control of the Marxist movement. In July of 1900 Lenin left Russia for five years, going first to Switzerland, then to Germany, London, Paris, and back to Switzerland. An important document of this period is Lenin's pamphlet *What Is to Be Done?*, composed in the winter of 1901-02, in which he warned that socialism was not natural to the worker and that a vigilant effort would be necessary to cultivate support for the Marxist cause. Another pamphlet, written in March and published in May 1903, which Lenin entitled *To the Rural Poor*, was intended as an explanation for the peasants of what the Social Democrats (Lenin's group) were seeking. It contains a section on political liberty, part of which is reproduced here among the edited selections of Lenin's writings, and provides an excellent illustration of the manner in which the intellectual of the proletariat sought to convert the rural peasant.

Indeed, a landmark in the history of Lenin's political strategy was the new emphasis which, after 1903, he placed upon the possible uses that might be made of the Russian peasantry in the interests of revolution. He came to appreciate how he could enroll the fundamentally conservative peasants on the side of revolution by promising them the property of the landlords. A radical revolution based upon the confiscation of those lands was calculated to appeal more to the peasants than the more limited goals of Russian social democratic reformers who sought the abolition of autocracy in favor of representative government. In another pamphlet published in 1905 and entitled *Two Tactics of Social-Democracy in the Democratic Revolution*, Lenin urged Marxists to remember that in the Social Democrats' war against the bourgeoisie the support of the peasants was essential for any complete victory. Karl Marx had distrusted the land-loving conservative peasants, and this pamphlet, which is included in part among the selections which follow, reveals that Lenin to some degree shared Marx's bias. Lenin bluntly stated that the peasants' allegiance could be won because radical agrarian reform was in their permanent interests. Nowhere did he credit the peasants with anything more than a subordinate role to the proletariat, which he believed to be genuinely committed to the Social Democratic revolution.

Lenin spent a substantial part of his energies after 1907 fighting with fellow socialists whose views on Marx he deemed heretical. Karl Kautsky, the German-Austrian socialist who disputed both Lenin's and Bernstein's revisionist interpretation of Marx, especially irritated Lenin. In addition, he had to combat not only the Mensheviks but also various deviations, philosophical as well as political, within the ranks of his own Bolsheviks.

When the revolution of February-March 1917 broke out in Russia, Lenin was in Switzerland. The German government assisted in his return to St. Petersburg since it knew Lenin to be more intent upon advancing social revolution in Russia than in seeing Germany defeated in World War I. After the Bolshevik-inspired disturbances of July 1917, the provisional Russian government ordered his arrest, but he went into hiding. Lenin continued to write and to guide his party until the provisional government headed by Alexander Kerensky was finally overthrown. Lenin emerged from seclusion on November 7 to become the chairman of the new Soviet government, an office to which he was elected by the revolutionary second congress of soviets. The Bolsheviks asserted that the November Revolution (October according to the old-style Russian calendar) had established a proletarian dictatorship. In fact, Lenin had set up a dictatorship of the Communist party, controlling the hierarchy of all local, regional, and central soviets (committees). Although he could justify dictatorship and the use of terror, as a ruler Lenin could not avoid compromises. He accepted the humiliating peace of Brest-Litovsk (March 1918) from the Germans, and, in the economic sphere, he retreated from orthodox Marxism with his "New Economic Policy." Lenin nevertheless eliminated all organized opposition to his government in a bloody civil war, and also silenced without mercy the hostile factions in his own party.

Russia's revolution of 1917 succeeded in overthrowing the oppressive czarist autocracy, but life in the newly emerged socialist state bore no resemblance to the constitution of the Russian democratic republic which Lenin had called for that same year (see the third selection of the edited entries on Lenin's writings which follow). In May 1922, Lenin suffered a stroke which seriously incapacitated him. On December 16 he had a second stroke and became paralyzed in the right arm and leg. He died on January 21, 1924, at Gorki near Moscow. His legacy is history. Today, more than a third of the world's population live under regimes which consider themselves in the Marxist-Leninist tradition.

To the Rural Poor

... What is political liberty?

To understand this the peasant should first compare his present state of

From *Lenin: Collected Works*, VI, edited by Clemens Dutt and Julius Katzer, Foreign Languages Publishing House, Moscow, 1961, pp. 367-371. This essay was written in April, 1903.

freedom with serfdom. Under the serf-owning system the peasant could not marry without the landlord's permission. Today the peasant is free to marry without anyone's permission. Under the serf-owning system the peasant had unfailingly to work for his landlord on days fixed by the latter's bailiff. Today the peasant is free to decide which employer to work for, on which days, and for what pay. Under the serf-owning system the peasant could not leave his village without the landlord's permission. Today the peasant is free to go wherever he pleases—if the *mir* [landlord] allows him to go, if he is not in arrears with his taxes, if he can get a passport, and if the governor or the police chief does not forbid his changing residence. Thus, even today the peasant is not quite free to go where he pleases; he does not enjoy complete freedom of movement; the peasant is still a semi-serf.

... Under the serf-owning system the peasant had no right to acquire property without the landlord's permission; he could not buy land. Today the peasant is free to acquire any kind of property (but even today he is not quite free to leave the *mir*; he is not quite free to dispose of his land as he pleases). Under the serf-owning system the peasant could be flogged by order of the landlord. Today the peasant cannot be flogged by order of the landlord, although he is still liable to corporal punishment.

This freedom is called *civil* liberty—freedom in family matters, in private matters, in matters concerning property. The peasant and the worker are free (although not quite) to arrange their family life and their private affairs, to dispose of their labour (choose their employer) and their property.

But neither the Russian workers nor the Russian people as a whole are yet free to arrange their *public* affairs. The people as a whole are the serfs of the government officials, just as the peasants were the serfs of the landlords. The Russian people have no right to choose their officials, no right to elect representatives to legislate for the whole country. The Russian people have not even the right to arrange meetings for the discussion of *state* affairs. We dare not even print newspapers or books, and dare not even speak to all and for all on matters concerning the whole state without permission from officials who have been put in authority over us without consent, just as the landlord used to appoint his bailiff without the consent of the peasants!

Just as the peasants were the slaves of the landlords, so the Russian people are still the slaves of the officials. Just as the peasants lacked civil freedom under the serf-owning system, so the Russian people still lack *political* liberty. Political liberty means the freedom of the people to arrange their public, state affairs. Political liberty means the right of the people to elect their representatives (deputies) to a State Duma (parliament). All laws should be discussed and passed, all taxes should be fixed only by such a State Duma (parliament) elected by the people themselves. Political liberty means the right of the people themselves to choose all their officials, arrange all kinds of meetings for the discussion of all state affairs, and publish whatever papers and books they please, without having to ask for permission.

All the other European peoples won political liberty for themselves long ago. Only in Turkey and in Russia are the people still politically enslaved by the sultan's government and by the tsarist autocratic government. Tsarist autocracy means the unlimited power of the tsar. The people have no voice in determining the structure of the state or in running it. All laws are made and all officials are appointed by the tsar alone, by his personal, unlimited, autocratic authority. But, of course, the tsar *cannot even know* all Russian laws and all Russian officials. The tsar cannot even know all that goes on in the country. The tsar simply endorses the will of a few score of the richest and most high-born officials. However much he may desire to, one man cannot govern a vast country like Russia. It is not the tsar who governs Russia—it is only a manner of speech to talk about autocratic, one-man rule! Russia is governed by a handful of the richest and most high-born officials. The tsar learns only what this handful are pleased to tell him. The tsar cannot in any way go against the will of this handful of high-ranking nobles: the tsar himself is a landlord and a member of the nobility; since his earliest childhood he has lived only among these high-born people; it was they who brought him up and educated him; he knows about the Russian people as a whole only that which is known to these noble gentry, these rich landlords, and the few very rich merchants who are received at the tsar's Court.

... We must clearly understand what a lie is being told the people by those who try to make out that tsarist government is the best form of government. In other countries—those people say—the government is elected; but it is the rich who are elected, and they govern unjustly and oppress the poor. In Russia the government is not elected; an autocratic tsar governs the whole country. The tsar stands above everyone, rich and poor. The tsar, they tell us, is just to everyone, to the poor and to the rich alike.

Such talk is sheer hypocrisy. Every Russian knows the kind of justice that is dispensed by our government. Everybody knows whether a plain worker or a farm labourer in our country can become a member of the State Council. In all other European countries, however, factory workers and farm-hands have been elected to the State Duma (parliament); they have been able to speak freely to all the people about the miserable condition of the workers, and call upon the workers to unite and fight for a better life. And no one has dared to stop these speeches of the people's representatives; no policeman has dared to lay a finger on them.

In Russia there is no elective government, and she is governed not merely by the rich and the high-born, but by the worst of these. She is governed by the most skillful intriguers at the tsar's Court, by the most artful tricksters, by those who carry lies and slanders to the tsar, and flatter and toady to him. They govern in secret; the people do not and cannot know what new laws are being drafted, what wars are being hatched, what new taxes are being introduced, which officials are being rewarded and for what services, and which are being dismissed. In no country is there such a multitude of officials as in Russia. These officials tower above the voiceless people like a dark forest—a mere worker can never make his way through this forest, can never obtain justice. Not a single complaint against bribery, robbery or abuse of power on the part of the officials is ever brought to light; every complaint is smothered in official red tape. The voice of the individual never reaches the whole people, but is lost in this dark jungle, stifled in the police torture chamber. An army of officials, who were never elected by the people and who are not responsible to the people, have woven a thick web, and men and women are struggling in this web like flies.

Tsarist autocracy is an autocracy of officials. Tsarist autocracy means the feudal dependence of the people upon the officials and especially upon the police. Tsarist autocracy is police autocracy.

That is why the workers come out into the streets with banners bearing the inscriptions: "Down with the autocracy!", "Long live political liberty!" That is why the tens of millions of the rural poor must also support and take up this battle-cry of the urban workers. Like them, undaunted by persecution, fearless of the enemy's threats and violence, and undeterred by the first reverses, the agricultural labourers and the poor peasants must come forward for a decisive struggle for the freedom of the whole of the Russian people and demand first of all the *convocation of the representatives of the people*. Let the people them selves all over Russia elect their representatives (deputies). Let those representatives form a supreme assembly, which will introduce elective government in Russia, free the people from feudal dependence upon the officials and the police, and secure for the people the right to meet freely, speak freely, and have a free press!

That is what the Social-Democrats want first and foremost. That is the meaning of their first demand: the *demand for political liberty*.

Two Tactics of Social Democracy in the Democratic Revolution

... The very position the bourgeoisie holds as a class in capitalist society inevitably leads to its inconsistency in a democratic revolution. The very position the proletariat holds as a class compels it to be consistently democratic. The bourgeoisie looks backward in fear of democratic progress which threatens to strengthen the proletariat. The proletariat has nothing to lose but its chains, but with the aid of democratism it has the whole world to win. That is why the more consistent the bourgeois revolution is in achieving its democratic transformations, the less will it limit itself to what is of advantage exclusively to the bourgeoisie. The more consistent the bourgois revolution, the more does it guarantee the proletariat and the peasantry the benefits accruing from the democratic revolution.

Marxism teaches the proletarian not to keep aloof from the bourgeois revolution, not to be indifferent to it, not to allow the leadership of the revolution to be assumed by the bourgeoisie but, on the contrary, to take a most energetic part in it, to fight most resolutely for consistent proletarian democratism, for the revolution to be carried to its conclusion. We cannot get out of the bourgeois-democratic boundaries of the Russian revolution, but we can vastly extend these boundaries, and within these boundaries we can and must fight for the interests of the proletariat, for its immediate needs and for conditions that will make it possible to prepare its forces for the future complete victory.

... A Social-Democrat must never for a moment forget that the proletariat will inevitably have to wage a class struggle for socialism even against the most democratic and republican bourgeoisie and petty bourgeoisie. This is beyond doubt. Hence, the absolute necessity of a separate, independent, strictly class party of Social-Democracy. Hence, the temporary nature of our tactics of "striking a joint blow" with the bourgeoisie and the duty of keeping a strict watch "over our ally, as over an enemy," etc. All this also leaves no room for doubt. However, it would be ridiculous and reactionary to deduce from this that we must forget, ignore, or neglect tasks which, although transient and temporary, are vital at the present time. The struggle against the autocracy is a temporary and transient task for socialists, but to ignore or neglect this task in any way amounts to betrayal of socialism and service to reaction. The revolutionary-democratic dictatorship of the proletariat and the peasantry is unques-

From *Lenin: Collected Works*, IX, edited by George Hanna, Foreign Languages Publishing House, Moscow, 1962, pp. 51-52, 85-86, 97-100, 108-109, 113. This essay was written in July 1905.

tionably only a transient, temporary socialist aim, but to ignore this aim in the period of a democratic revolution would be downright reactionary.

... Have you, gentlemen, ever given thought to real social forces that determine "the sweep of the revolution"? Let us disregard the foreign political forces, the international combinations, which have developed very favourably for us at the present time, but which we all leave out of the discussion, and rightly so, inasmuch as we are concerned with the question of Russia's internal forces. Examine these internal social forces. Aligned against the revolution are the autocracy, the imperial court, the police, the bureaucracy, the army, and a handful of the aristocracy. The deeper the indignation of the people grows, the less reliable the troops become, and the more the bureaucracy wavers. Moreover, the bourgeoisie, on the whole, is now in favour of revolution, zealously speechifying about liberty and holding forth more and more frequently in the name of the people and even in the name of the revolution. But we Marxists all know from theory and from daily and hourly observation of our liberals, Zemstvo people, and *Osvobozhdeniye* supporters, that the bourgeoisie is inconsistent, self-seeking, and cowardly in its support of the revolution. The bourgeoisie, in the mass, will inevitably turn towards counter-revolution, towards the autocracy, against the revolution, and against the people, as soon as its narrow, selfish interests are met, as soon as it "recoils" from consistent democracy (*and it is already recoiling from it*)! There remains the "people", that is, the proletariat and the peasantry: the proletariat alone can be relied on to march on to the end, for it goes far beyond the democratic revolution. That is why the proletariat fights in the forefront for a republic and contemptuously rejects stupid and unworthy advice to take into account the possibility of the bourgeoisie recoiling. The peasantry includes a great number of semi-proletarian as well as petty-bourgeois elements. This makes it also unstable, compelling the proletariat to rally in a strictly class party. However, the instability of the peasantry differs radically from that of the bourgeoisie, for at present the peasantry is interested not so much in the absolute preservation of private property as in the confiscation of the landed estates, one of the principal forms of private property. Without thereby becoming socialist, or ceasing to be petty-bourgeois, the peasantry is capable of becoming a wholehearted and most radical adherent of the democratic revolution. The peasantry will inevitably become such if only the course of revolutionary events, which brings it enlightenment, is not prematurely cut short by the treachery of the bourgeoisie and the defeat of the proletariat. Subject to this condition the peasantry will inevitably become a bulwark of the revolution and the republic, for only a completely victorious revolution can give the peasantry *everything* in the sphere of agrarian reforms—*everything* that the peasants desire, dream of, and truly need (not for the abolition of capitalism as the "Socialist-Revolutionaries" imagine, but) in order to emerge from the mire of semi-serfdom, from the gloom of oppression and servitude, in order to improve their living conditions, as much as they can be improved within the system of commodity production.

Moreover, it is not only by the prospect of radical agrarian reform that the peasantry is attached to the revolution, but by all its general and permanent interests as well. Even when fighting with the proletariat, the peasantry stands in need of democracy, for only a democratic system is capable of accurately expressing its interests and ensuring its predominance as a mass, as the majority. The more enlightened the peasantry becomes (and since the war with Japan it is becoming enlightened at a pace unsuspected by many who are accustomed to measure enlightenment with the school yardstick), the more consistently and resolutely will it stand for a thoroughgoing democratic revolution; for, unlike the bourgeoisie, it has nothing to fear from the people's supremacy, but on the contrary stands to gain by it. A democratic republic will become the peasantry's ideal as soon as it begins to throw off its naive monarchism, because the conscious monarchism of the bourgeois stock-jobbers (with an upper chamber, etc.) implies for the peasantry the same absence of rights and the same oppression and ignorance as it suffers today, only slightly polished over with the varnish of European constitutionalism.

That is why, as a class, the bourgeoisie naturally and inevitably tends to come under the wing of the liberal-monarchist party, while the peasantry, in the mass, tends to come under the leadership of the revolutionary and republican party. That is why the bourgeoisie is incapable of carrying through the democratic revolution to its consummation, while the peasantry is capable of doing so, and we must exert all our efforts to help it do so.

...*The proletariat must carry the democratic revolution to completion, allying to itself the mass of the peasantry in order to crush the autocracy's resistance by force and paralyse the bourgeoisie's instability. The proletariat must accomplish the socialist revolution, allying to itself the mass of the semi-proletarian elements of the population, so as to crush the bourgeoisie's resistance by force and paralyse the instability of the peasantry and the petty bourgeoisie.*

... Perhaps the most vivid expression of this rift between the intellectual opportunist wing and the proletarian revolutionary wing of the Party was the question: *durfen wir siegen?* "Dare we win?" Is it permissible for us to win? Would it not be dangerous for us to win? Ought we to win? This question, so strange at first sight, was however raised and had to be raised, because the opportunists were afraid of victory, were frightening the proletariat away from it, predicting that trouble would come of it and ridiculing slogans that straightforwardly called for it.

The same fundamental division into an intellectual-opportunist and proletarian-revolutionary trend exists among us too, with the very material difference, however, that here we are faced with the question of a democratic, not of a socialist revolution. The question "dare we win?" which seems so absurd at first sight, has been raised among us as well. It has been raised by Martynov in his *Two Dictatorships,* wherein he prophesies dire misfortune if we prepare well for an insurrection, and carry it out quite successfully.

... And although Kautsky, for instance, now tries to wax ironical and says that our dispute about a provisional revolutionary government is like sharing out the meat before the bear is killed, this irony only proves that even clever and revolutionary Social-Democrats are liable to put their foot in it when they talk about something they know of only by hearsay. German Social-Democracy is not yet so near to killing its bear (carrying out a socialist revolution), but the dispute as to whether we "dare" kill the bear has been of enormous importance from the point of view of principles and of practical politics. Russian Social-Democrats are not yet so close to being able to "kill their bear" (carry out a democratic revolution), but the question as to whether we "dare" kill it is of extreme importance to the whole future of Russia and that of Russian Social-Democracy. An army cannot be energetically and successfully mustered and led unless we are sure that we "dare" win.

... Revolutions are the locomotives of history, said Marx. Revolutions are festivals of the oppressed and the exploited. At no other time are the mass of the people in a position to come forward so actively as creators of a new social order, as at a time of revolution. At such times the people are capable of performing miracles, if judged by the limited, philistine yardstick of gradualist progress. But it is essential that leaders of the revolutionary parties, too, should advance their aims more comprehensively and boldly at such a time, so that their slogans shall always be in advance of the revolutionary initiative of the masses, serve as a beacon, reveal to them our democratic and socialist ideal in all its magnitude and splendour, and show them the shortest and most direct route to complete, absolute, and decisive victory.

Revision of the Party Program

. . . The constitution of the Russian democratic republic must ensure:

1. The sovereignty of the people; supreme power in the state must be vested entirely in the people's representatives, who shall be elected by the people and be subject to recall at any time, and who shall constitute a single popular assembly, a single chamber.

2. Universal, equal, and direct suffrage for all citizens, men and women, who have reached the age of twenty, in the elections to the legislative assembly and to the various bodies of local self-government; secret ballot; the right of every voter to be elected to any representative institution; biennial parliaments; salaries to be paid to the people's representatives; proportional representation to all elections; all delegates and elected officials, without exception, to be subject to recall at any time upon the decision of a majority of their electors.

3. Local self-government on a broad scale; regional self-government in localities where the composition of the population and living and social conditions are of a specific nature; the abolition of all state-appointed local and regional authorities.

4. Inviolability of person and domicile.

5. Unrestricted freedom of conscience, speech, the press, assembly, strikes, and association.

6. Freedom of movement and occupation.

7. Abolition of the social estates; equal rights for all citizens irrespective of sex, creed, race, or nationality.

8. The right of the population to receive instruction in their native tongue in schools to be established for the purpose at the expense of the state and local organs of self-government; the right of every citizen to use his native language at meetings; the native language to be used in all local public and state institutions; the obligatory official language to be abolished.

9. The right of all member nations of the state to freely secede and form independent states. The republic of the Russian nation must attract other nations or nationalities not by force, but exclusively by voluntary agreement on the question of forming a common state. The unity and fraternal alliance of the workers of all countries are incompatible with the use of force, direct or indirect, against other nationalities.

10. The right of all persons to sue any official in the regular way before a jury.

11. Judges and other officials, both civil and military, to be elected by the

From *Lenin: Collected Works*, XXIV, edited by Bernard Isaacs, Progress Publishers, Moscow, 1964, pp. 471-477. This essay was written in May 1917.

people with the right to recall any of them at any time by decision of a majority of their electors.

12. The police and standing army to be replaced by the universally armed people; workers and other employees to receive regular wages from the capitalists for the time devoted to public service in the people's militia.

13. Separation of the church from the state, and schools from the church; schools to be absolutely secular.

14. Free and compulsory general and polytechnical education (familiarising the student with the theoretical and practical aspects of the most important fields of production) for all children of both sexes up to the age of sixteen; training of children to be closely integrated with socially productive work.

15. All students to be provided with food, clothing, and school supplies at the cost of the state.

16. Public education to be administered by democratically elected organs of local self-government; the central government not to be allowed to interfere with the arrangement of the school curriculum, or with the selection of the teaching staffs; teachers to be elected directly by the population with the right of the latter to remove undesirable teachers.

As a basic condition for the democratisation of our country's national economy, the Russian Social-Democratic Labour Party demands the abolition of all indirect taxes and the establishment of a progressive tax on incomes and inheritances.

The high level of development of capitalism already achieved in banking and in the trustified branches of industry, on the one hand, and the economic disruption caused by the imperialist war, everywhere evoking a demand for state and public control of the production and distribution of all staple products, on the other, induce the party to demand the nationalisation of the banks, syndicates (trusts), etc.

To safeguard the working class from physical and moral deterioration, and develop its ability to carry on the struggle for emancipation, the Party demands:

1. An eight-hour working day for all wage-workers, including a break of not less than one hour for meals where work is continuous. In dangerous and unhealthy industries the working day to be reduced to from four to six hours.

2. A statutory weekly uninterrupted rest period of not less than forty-two hours for all wage-workers of both sexes in all branches of the national economy.

3. Complete prohibition of overtime work.

4. Prohibition of night-work (from 8 p.m. to 6 a.m.) in all branches of the national economy except in cases where it is absolutely necessary for technical reasons endorsed by the labour organisations—provided, however, that night-work does not exceed four hours.

5. Prohibition of the employment of children of *school* age (under sixteen), restriction of the working day of adolescents (from sixteen to twenty) to four hours, and prohibition of the employment of adolescents on night-work in unhealthy industries and mines.

6. Prohibition of female labour in all branches of industry injurious to women's health; prohibition of night work for women; women to be released from work eight weeks before and eight weeks after child-birth without loss of pay and with free medical and medicinal aid.

7. Establishment of nurseries for infants and young children and rooms for nursing mothers at all factories and other enterprises where women are employed; nursing mothers to be allowed recesses of at least half-hour duration at intervals of not more than three hours; such mothers to receive nursing benefit and their working day to be reduced to six hours.

8. Full social insurance of workers:

a) for all forms of wage-labour;

b) for all forms of disablement, namely, sickness, injury, infirmity, old age, occupational disease, childbirth, widowhood, orphanhood, and also unemployment, etc.

c) all insurance institutions to be administered entirely by the insured themselves;

d) the cost of insurance to be borne by the capitalists;

e) free medical and medicinal aid under the control of self-governing sick benefit societies, the management bodies of which are to be elected by the workers.

9. The establishment of a labour inspectorate elected by the workers' organisations and covering all enterprises employing hired labour, as well as domestic servants; women inspectors to be appointed in enterprises where female labour is employed.

10. Sanitary laws to be enacted for improving hygienic conditions and protecting the life and health of workers in all enterprises where hired labour is employed; questions of hygiene to be handled by the sanitary inspectorate elected by the workers' organisations.

11. Housing laws to be enacted and a housing inspectorate elected by the workers' organisations to be instituted for the purpose of sanitary inspection of dwelling houses. However, only by abolishing private property in land and building cheap and hygienic dwellings can the housing problem be solved.

12. Industrial courts to be established in all branches of the national economy.

13. Labour exchanges to be established for the proper organisation of work-finding facilities. These labour exchanges must be proletarian class organisations (organised on a non-parity basis), and must be closely associated with the trade

unions and other working-class organisations and financed by the communal self-governing bodies.

A Great Beginning

... And what does the "abolition of classes" mean? All those who call themselves socialists recognize this as the ultimate goal of socialism, but by no means all give thought to its significance. Classes are large groups of people differing from each other by the place they occupy in a historically determined system of social production, by their relation (in most cases fixed and formulated in law) to the means of production, by their role in the social organisation of labour, and, consequently, by the dimensions of the share of social wealth of which they dispose and the mode of acquiring it. Classes are groups of people one of which can appropriate the labour of another owing to the different places they occupy in a definite system of social economy.

Clearly, in order to abolish classes completely, it is not enough to overthrow the exploiters, the landowners and capitalists, not enough to abolish *their* rights of ownership; it is necessary also to abolish *all* private ownership of the means of production, it is necessary to abolish the distinction between town and country, as well as the distinction between manual workers and brain workers. This requires a very long period of time. In order to achieve this an enormous step forward must be taken in developing the productive forces; it is necessary to overcome the resistance (frequently passive, which is particularly stubborn and particularly difficult to overcome) of the numerous survivals of small-scale production; it is necessary to overcome the enormous force of habit and conservatism which are connected with these survivals.

The assumption that all "working people" are equally capable of doing this work would be an empty phrase, or the illusion of an antediluvian, pre-Marxist socialist; for this ability does not come of itself, but grows historically, and grows *only* out of the material conditions of large-scale capitalist production. This ability, at the beginning of the road from capitalism to socialism, is possessed by the proletariat *alone*.

... Notwithstanding all the laws emancipating woman, she continues to be a *domestic slave,* because *petty housework* crushes, strangles, stultifies and de-

From *Lenin: Collected Works*, XXIX, edited by George Hanna, Progress Publishers, Moscow, 1965, pp. 421, 429-430. This essay was written in July 1919.

grades her, chains her to the kitchen and the nursery, and she wastes her labour on barbarously unproductive, petty, nerve-racking, stultifying and crushing drudgery. The real *emancipation of women,* real communism, will begin only where and when an all-out struggle begins (led by the proletariat wielding the state power) against this petty housekeeping, or rather when its *wholesale transformation* into a large-scale socialist economy begins.

Do we in practice pay sufficient attention to this question, which in theory every Communist considers indisputable? Of course not. Do we take proper care of the *shoots* of communism which already exist in this sphere? Again the answer is *no* Public catering establishments, nurseries, kindergartens—here we have examples of these shoots, here we have the simple, everyday means, involving nothing pompous, grandiloquent or ceremonial, which can *really emancipate women,* really lessen and abolish their inequality with men as regards their role in social production and public life. These means are not new, they (like all the material prerequisites for socialism) were created by large-scale capitalism. But under capitalism they remained, first, a rarity, and secondly—which is particularly important—either *profit-making* enterprises, with all the worst features of speculation, profiteering, cheating and fraud, or "acrobatics of bourgeois charity," which the best workers rightly hated and despised.

There is no doubt that the number of these institutions in our country has increased enormously and that they are *beginning* to change in character. There is no doubt that we have far more *organising talent* among the working and peasant women than we are aware of, that we have far more people than we know of who can organise practical work, with the co-operation of large numbers of workers and of still larger numbers of consumers, without that abundance of talk, fuss, squabbling and chatter about plans, systems, etc., with which our big-headed "intellectuals" or half-baked "Communists" are "affected." But we *do not nurse* these shoots of the new as we should.

james connolly

James Connolly was a socialist and Irish Republican leader who played a decisive part in the Dublin Easter Uprising of 1916. Born near Clones, County Monaghan, Connolly was the son of a laborer, and from his earliest years he waged a struggle with poverty. When he was ten years old his family was forced, like countless others of their class, to seek work in Scotland. It was there that Connolly received his earliest experience with the socialist movement as a member of the Social Democratic Federation. He later spent seven years, from 1903 to 1910, in the United States, where he helped organize the Industrial Workers of the World. His sincerity and ability as a leader gained him the respect of organized workers. Upon his return from America, Connolly began promoting the socialist cause in Ireland. He championed the rights of the miserably underpaid women workers in Belfast and, in 1911, led demonstrations on behalf of the dock laborers in Dublin and other Irish ports. Connolly became James Larkin's chief assistant in organizing the Irish National Transport Union, which sought to enroll all Irish workers' support in every labor dispute. Reacting to a number of carefully staged "sympathetic strikes," Dublin employers joined to break Larkin's union in 1913 through a ruthless lockout.

It was partly as a response to the brutal dispersion of labor demonstrations by the authorities that Connolly formed the Citizen Army in 1913. Fundamentally a Marxist who was concerned with the exploitation of the working class in an industrial age, Connolly was not unaware of the importance of peasant support to the urban labor movement, or the fact that the peasants made up the vast majority of Ireland's population. Long before his theories were tested by the Russian Revolution of 1917, he was concerned with the "potential conflict" between town and country after the defeat of capitalism. Like Lenin, he realized the possible role of co-operatives in securing unity between the proletariat and the peasant, not only in the economic field, but also eventually in the political field.

Larkin was in the United States at the outbreak of World War I, and Connolly assumed charge of the Irish labor movement and committed it to opposing the Allied war effort; he insisted that peace could come only through the overthrow of all capitalist states. Because of his conviction that the triumph of Irish nationalism was a prerequisite for the success of Irish socialism, he joined the Easter Rebellion of 1916. Connolly's temporary military alliance with the Irish bourgeois nationalists did not prevent him from leveling scornful attacks at their leaders; he never ceased insisting that the ultimate freedom of the Irish people would be achieved only after they had seized control over the means and modes of production in Ireland. The bourgeois nationalist goal of political independence without sweeping social reform held no attraction for him. When the Dublin rising was suppressed after a week of fighting and considerable bloodshed, the wounded Connolly was executed along with other leaders of the insurrection.

With the exception of a few published works, the writings of James Connolly lie buried in museum files of obscure periodicals. His writings and achievements in Ireland have often been suppressed and distorted, and these distortions have served to bewilder that wider world audience which today stands in need of the lessons of his life and leadership. His non-sectarian support included members of both the Protestant and Catholic working class in Ulster. His eloquent condemnation of war, his vision of a free nation, and his concept of the socialist goal appear in the three essays which follow. His philosophy is perhaps best summarized in an excerpt from an editorial published in Connolly's labor newspaper, *The Worker's Republic*, on May 29, 1915:

In the long run the freedom of a nation is measured by the freedom of its lowest class; every upward step of that class to the possibility of possessing higher things raises the standard of the nation in the scale of civilization; every time that class is beaten back into the mire, the whole moral tone of the nation suffers. Condemned and despised though he may be, yet the rebellious docker is the sign and symbol that an imperfect civilization cannot last, for slavery cannot survive the awakened intelligence of the slave.

A War for Civilization

We are hearing and reading a lot just now about a war for civilization. In some vague, ill-defined manner we are led to believe that the great empires of Europe have suddenly been seized with a chivalrous desire to right the wrongs of mankind, and have sallied forth to war, giving their noblest blood and greatest treasures to the task of furthering the cause of civilization.

. . . This War for Civilization in the name of neutrality and small nationalities invades Persia and Greece, and in the name of the interests of commerce seizes the cargo of neutral ships, and flaunts its defiance of neutral flags.

In the name of freedom from militarism it establishes military rule in Ireland; battling for progress it abolishes trial by jury; and waging war for enlightened rule it tramples the freedom of the Press under the heel of a military despot.

Is it any wonder, then, that this particular War for Civilization arouses no enthusiasm in the ranks of the toiling masses of the Irish nation?

But there is another war for civilization in which these masses are interested. That war is being waged by the forces of organized Labour.

Civilization cannot be built upon slaves; civilization cannot be secured if the producers are sinking into misery; civilization is lost if they whose labour makes it possible share so little of its fruits that its fall can leave them no worse than its security.

The workers are at the bottom of civilized society. That civilization may endure they ought to push upward from their poverty and misery until they emerge into the full sunlight of freedom. When the fruits of civilization, created by all, are enjoyed in common by all then civilization is secure. Not till then.

Since this European war started, the workers as a whole have been sinking. It is not merely that they have lost in comfort—have lost a certain standard of food and clothing by reason of the increase of prices—but they have lost in a great measure, in England at least, all those hard-won rights of combination, of freedom of action, the possession of which was the foundation upon which they hoped to build the greater freedom of the future.

From being citizens with rights, the workers are being driven and betrayed into the position of slaves with duties. Some of them may have been well-paid slaves, but slavery is not measured by the amount of oats in the feeding trough to which the slave is tied; it is measured by his loss of control of the conditions under which he labours.

We here in Ireland, particularly those who follow the example of the Transport Union, have been battling to preserve those rights which others have sur-

From *The Workers' Republic*, October 30, 1915, pp. 51, 53-55.

rendered. We have fought to keep up our standards of life, to force up our wages, to better our conditions.

To that extent we have truly been engaged in a war for civilization. Every victory we have gained has gone to increase the security of life amongst our class, has gone to put bread on the tables, coals in the fires, clothes on the backs of those to whom food and warmth and clothing are things of ever-pressing moment.

Some of our class have fought in Flanders and the Dardanelles; the greatest achievement of them all combined will weigh but a feather in the balance for good compared with the achievements of those who stayed at home and fought to secure the rights of the working class against invasion.

The carnival of murder on the Continent will be remembered as a nightmare in the future, will not have the slightest effect in deciding for good the fate of our homes, our wages, our hours, our conditions. But the victories of Labour in Ireland will be as footholds, secure and firm, in the upward climb of our class to the fulness and enjoyment of all that Labour creates and organized society can provide.

Truly, Labour alone in these days is fighting the real WAR FOR CIVILIZATION.

What is a Free Nation?

We are moved to ask this question because of the extraordinary confusion of thought upon the subject which prevails in this country, due principally to the pernicious and misleading newspaper garbage upon which the Irish public has been fed for the past twenty-five years.

Our Irish daily newspapers have done all that human agencies could do to confuse the public mind upon the question of what the essentials of a free nation are, what a free nation must be, and what a nation cannot submit to lose without losing its title to be free.

It is because of this extraordinary newspaper-created ignorance that we find so many people enlisting in the British Army under the belief that Ireland has at long last attained to the status of a free nation, and that therefore the relations between Ireland and England have at last been placed upon the satisfactory basis of freedom. Ireland and England, they have been told, are now sister nations,

From *The Workers' Republic*, February 12, 1916, pp. 108, 110-114.

joined in the bond of Empire, but each enjoying equal liberties—the equal liberties of nations equally free.

How many recruits this idea sent into the British Army in the first flush of the war it would be difficult to estimate, but they were assuredly numbered by the thousand.

... Our Parliamentarians treat Ireland, their country, as an old prostitute selling her soul for the promise of favours *to come,* and in the spirit of that conception of their country they are conducting their political campaign.

... What is a free nation? A free nation is one which possesses absolute control over all its own internal resources and powers, and which has no restrictions upon its intercourse with all other nations similarly circumstanced except the restrictions placed upon it by nature. Is that the case of Ireland? If the Home Rule Bill were in operation would that be the case of Ireland? To both questions the answer is, No, most emphatically, NO!

A free nation must have complete control over its own harbours, to open them or close them at will, to shut out any commodity, or allow it to enter in, just as it seems best to suit the well-being of its own people, and in obedience to their wishes, and entirely free of the interference of any other nation, and in complete disregard of the wishes of any other nation. Short of that power no nation possesses the first essentials of freedom.

Does Ireland possess such control? No. Will the Home Rule Bill give such control over Irish harbours to Ireland? It will not. Ireland must open its harbours when it suits the interests of another nation, England, and must shut its harbours when it suits the interests of another nation, England, and the Home Rule Bill pledges Ireland to accept this loss of national control for ever.

How would you like to live in a house if the keys of all the doors of that house were in the pockets of a rival of yours who had often robbed you in the past? Would you be satisfied if he told you that he and you were going to be friends for ever more, but insisted upon you signing an agreement to leave him control of all your doors, and custody of all your keys?

That is the condition of Ireland to-day, and will be the condition of Ireland under Redmond and Devlin's precious Home Rule Bill.

That is worth dying for in Flanders, the Balkans, Egypt or India, is it not?

A free nation must have full power to nurse industries to health, either by Government encouragement, or by Government prohibition of the sale of goods of foreign rivals. It may be foolish to do either, but a nation is not free unless it has that power, as all free nations in the world have to-day.

Ireland has no such power, will have no such power under Home Rule. The nourishing of industries in Ireland hurts capitalists in England, therefore this power is expressly withheld from Ireland.

A free nation must have full power to alter, amend, or abolish or modify the laws under which the property of its citizens is held in obedience to the demand of its own citizens for any such alteration, amendment, abolition, or modification.

Every free nation has that power; Ireland does not have it, and is not allowed it by the Home Rule Bill.

It is recognized to-day that it is upon the wise treatment of economic power and resources, and upon the wise ordering of social activities that the future of nations depends. That nation will be the richest and happiest which has the foresight to most carefully marshal its natural resources to national ends. But Ireland is denied this power, and will be denied it under Home Rule. Ireland's rich natural resources, and the kindly genius of its children, are not to be allowed to combine for the satisfaction of Irish wants, save in so far as their combination can operate on lines approved of by the rulers of England.

Her postal service, her telegraphs, her wireless, her customs and excise, her coinage, her fighting forces, her relations with other nations, her merchant commerce, her property relations, her national activities, her legislative sovereignty—all, all the things that are essential to a nation's freedom are denied to Ireland now, and are denied to her under the provisions of the Home Rule Bill.

And Irish soldiers in the English Army are fighting in Flanders to win for Belgium, we are told, all those things which the British Empire, now as in the past, denies to Ireland.

... There is not a pacifist in England who would wish to end the war without Belgium being restored to full possession of all those national rights and powers which Ireland does not possess, and which the Home Rule Bill denies to her. But these same pacifists never mention Ireland when discussing or suggesting terms of settlement.

Why should they? Belgium is fighting for her independence, but Irishmen are fighting for the Empire that denies Ireland every right that Belgians think worth fighting for.

And yet Belgium as a nation is, so to speak, but a creation of yesterday—an artificial product of the schemes of statesmen; whereas the frontiers of Ireland, the ineffaceable marks of the separate existence of Ireland, are as old as Europe itself, the handiwork of the Almighty, not of politicians. And as the marks of Ireland's separate nationality were not made by politicians so they cannot be unmade by them.

... There can be no perfect Europe in which Ireland is denied even the least of its national rights; there can be no worthy Ireland whose children brook tamely such denial.

If such denial has been accepted by soulless slaves of politicians, then it must be repudiated by Irish men and women whose souls are still their own.

The peaceful progress of the future requires the possession by Ireland of all the national rights now denied to her. Only in such possession can the workers of Ireland see stability and security for the fruits of their toil and organization.

A destiny not of our fashioning has chosen this generation as the one called upon for the supreme act of self-sacrifice—to die if need be that our race might live in freedom.

Are we worthy of the choice? Only by our response to the call can that question be answered.

What Is Our Programme?

We are often asked the above question.

...The Labour movement is like no other movement. Its strength lies in being like no other movement. It is never so strong as when it stands alone. Other movements dread analysis and shun all attempts to define their objects. The Labour movement delights in analyzing and is perpetually defining and re-defining its principles and objects.

The man or woman who has caught the spirit of the Labour movement brings that spirit of analysis and definition into all public acts, and expects at all times to answer the call to define his or her position. They cannot live on illusions, nor thrive by them; even should their heads be in the clouds they will make no forward step until they are assured that their feet rest upon the solid earth.

...What is our programme? We at least, in conformity with the spirit of our movement, will try and tell it.

Our programme in time of peace was to gather into Irish hands in Irish Trade Unions the control of all the forces of production and distribution in Ireland. We never believed that freedom would be realized without fighting for it. From our earliest declaration of policy in Dublin in 1896 the editor of this paper has held to the dictum that our ends should be secured "peacefully if possible, forcibly if necessary." Believing so, we saw what the world outside Ireland is realizing to-day, that the destinies of the world and the fighting strength of armies are at the mercy of organized Labour as soon as that Labour becomes truly revolutionary. Thus we strove to make Labour in Ireland organized—and revolutionary.

•

From *The Workers' Republic*, January 22, 1916, pp. 120-125.

We saw that should it come to a test in Ireland (as we hoped and prayed it might come) between those who stood for the Irish nation and those who stood for the foreign rule, the greatest civil asset in the hand of the Irish nation for use in the struggle would be the control of Irish docks, shipping, railways and production by Unions who gave sole allegiance to Ireland.

We realized that the power of the enemy to hurl his forces upon the forces of Ireland would lie at the mercy of the men who controlled the transport system of Ireland; we saw that the hopes of Ireland as a nation rested upon the due recognition of the identity of interest between that ideal and the rising hopes of Labour.

. . . Have we a programme? We are the only people that had a programme—that understood the mechanical conditions of modern war, and the dependence of national power upon industrial control.

What is our programme now? At the grave risk of displeasing alike the per-fervid Irish patriot and the British "competent military authority," we shall tell it.

We believe that in times of peace we should work along the lines of peace to strengthen the nation, and we believe that whatever strengthens and elevates the working class strengthens the nation.

But we also believe that in times of war we should act as in war. We despise, entirely despise and loathe, all the mouthings and mouthers about war who infest Ireland in time of peace, just as we despise and loathe all the cantings about caution and restraint to which the same people treat us in times of war.

Mark well, then, our programme. While the war lasts and Ireland still is a subject nation we shall continue to urge her to fight for her freedom.

We shall continue, in season and out of season, to teach that the "far-flung battle line" of England is weakest at the point nearest its heart; that Ireland is in that position of tactical advantage; that a defeat of England in India, Egypt, the Balkans or Flanders would not be so dangerous to the British Empire as any conflict of armed forces in Ireland; that the time for Ireland's battle is NOW, the place for Ireland's battle is HERE; that a strong man may deal lusty blows with his fists against a host of surrounding foes, and conquer, but will succumb if a child sticks a pin in his heart.

But the moment peace is once admitted by the British Government as being a subject ripe for discussion, *that moment our policy will be for peace* and in direct opposition to all talk or preparation for armed revolution.

We will be no party to leading out Irish patriots to meet the might of an England at peace. The moment peace is in the air we shall strictly confine ourselves and lend all our influence to the work of turning the thought of labour in Ireland to the work of peaceful reconstruction.

That is our programme. You can now compare it with the programme of those who bid you hold your hand now, and thus put it in the power of the enemy to patch up a temporary peace, turn round and smash you at his leisure, and then go to war again with the Irish question settled—in the graves of Irish patriots.

We fear that is what is going to happen. It is to our mind inconceivable that the British public should allow conscription to be applied to England and not to Ireland. Nor does the British Government desire it. But that Government will use the cry of the necessities of war to force conscription upon the people of England, and will then make a temporary peace, and turn round to force Ireland to accept the same terms as have been forced upon England.

The English public will gladly see this done—misfortune likes company. The situation will then shape itself thus: The Irish Volunteers who are pledged to fight conscription will either need to swallow their pledge, and see the young men of Ireland conscripted, or will need to resent conscription, and engage the military force of England at a time when England is at peace.

This is what the diplomacy of England is working for, what the stupidity of some of our leaders . . . is making possible. It is our duty, it is the duty of all who wish to save Ireland from such shame or such slaughter, to strengthen the hand of those of the leaders who are for action as against those who are playing into the hands of the enemy.

We are neither rash nor cowardly. We know our opportunity when we see it, and we know when it has gone. We know that at the end of this war England will have an army of at least one million men, or *more than two soldiers for every adult male in Ireland,* and these soldiers veterans of the greatest war in history.

We shall not want to fight those men. We shall devote our attention to organizing their comrades who return to civil life, to organizing them into Trade Unions and Labour Parties to secure them their rights in civil life—unless we emigrate to some country where there are men.

leon trotsky

Leon Trotsky, a Russian revolutionist, an able theoretician of Marxism, an outstanding writer and orator, and the chief organizer of the primitive Red Army, was the offspring of Jewish parents who lived at Yanovka in the Ukraine; Trotsky's original name was Lev Davidovich Bronstein. His father, a prosperous farmer, sent him to Odessa in 1897 to study mathematics at the New Russia University. He left school the following year, however, and his populist inclinations led him into the Social Democratic (Marxist) circle in Odessa. Arrested for political activities in 1898 and banished to Siberia in 1900, he escaped in 1902, using a forged passport under the name of Trotsky, who was the head jailer of the Odessa prison in which he had been held.

After escaping from Russia, Trotsky traveled to London where he collaborated with Lenin on the revolutionary journal *Iskra* ("Spark"). Intimate contact with Lenin convinced him that Lenin's policies and methods would eventually result in a one-man dictatorship. When the Russian Social Democratic Labor Party split at its second congress in 1903, Trotsky emerged as a leading Menshevik and a forthright opponent of Lenin. It was in Munich during 1904-05 that Trotsky worked out his theory of "Permanent revolution," with the assistance of the Marxist A. I. (Parvus) Helfand. Returning to Russia at the time of the 1905 Revolution, he became chairman of the short-lived St. Petersburg soviet. Arrested and banished again to Siberia in 1907, Trotsky escaped en route, fled abroad once more, and settled in Vienna.

During his years in Vienna, Trotsky edited the pro-Menshevik newspaper *Pravda;* but he also made strenuous efforts to reconcile feuding Menshevik and Bolshevik factions within the Social Democratic movement. The attempt failed when Bolshevik leaders, and some Mensheviks, boycotted his 1912 "August Conference" in Vienna. At the outbreak of the First World War, Trotsky went to Switzerland and then to Paris, where he was active in pacifist and radical propaganda. On the war issue he assumed an "internationalist" position, though he opposed Lenin's advocacy of a defeat for Russia. In 1916 he was deported from France and moved to New York City where he edited, with Bukharin and Kollantai, the paper *Novy Mir* ("New World").

Trotsky returned to Russia in May 1917 following the overthrow of Czar Nicholas II. Upon his arrival in Petrograd (now Leningrad), he joined Lenin and took part in the unsuccessful Bolshevik uprising of July 1917. Trotsky was imprisoned by the Kerensky government, but was released in September and became one of the chief organizers of the October Revolution which brought the Bolsheviks to power.

As people's commissar for foreign affairs, Trotsky led the new Soviet Government's delegation which negotiated the humiliating peace of Brest-Litovsk with Germany. After March 1918, Trotsky was people's commissar for military and naval affairs. He devoted much of his energy to building up the Red Army, and its victory in the subsequent Civil War was in large measure due to him.

Intolerant, tactless, and never one to suffer fools, Trotsky made numerous enemies during the Civil War, most particularly the jealous and vengeful Stalin. After Lenin's death in 1924 Trotsky appeared as the obvious candidate for the leadership, but an alliance between Zinoviev, Kamenev (Trotsky's brother-in-law), and Stalin prevented him from succeeding to power. Although he remained a member of the party's Politburo, he lost his posts in government. Thereafter, until his final defeat in 1927, he was engaged in a continual struggle with his rivals on both political and personal grounds. Advocating world revolution, Trotsky came into increasing conflict with Stalin's plans for "socialism in one country." Trotsky had great prestige as a revolutionary leader and had followers in both the army and the government, but Stalin controlled the party machine. Zinoviev and Kamenev belatedly joined forces with Trotsky in 1926 in an effort to check Stalin's power.

Trotsky was expelled from the Politburo in 1926 and from the Communist Party in 1927. In the following January he was exiled to Siberia and then, in 1929, was ordered to leave the U.S.S.R. entirely. Refused admission by most countries, he was granted asylum by Turkey, where he lived on the Princes'

Islands near Istanbul. Deprived of his Soviet citizenship in 1932, Trotsky lived as an exile in Turkey (until 1933), France (1933-35), Norway (1935-36), and finally Mexico (from 1937). He continually denounced Stalin and acted as the theoretical leader of Trotskyites among foreign Communists. During the public treason trials held in Moscow during 1936-38, Trotsky was charged with heading a plot against the Stalinist regime. The accusations, which Trotsky bitterly denied, cloaked Stalin's real purpose of purging the party ranks of all who might prove disloyal to him. An international commission under the chairmanship of the U.S. philosopher John Dewey, set up to inquire into these allegations, rejected them in its report *Not Guilty* (1937). On August 20, 1940, Trotsky was mortally wounded by a Stalinist agent who had infiltrated the group of followers that met at Trotsky's home in the suburbs of Mexico City. He died on the following day.

Trotsky's prolific writings are reflective of his superlative intelligence—a fact unchallenged even by his enemies—his indomitable aggressiveness, and his incisive and polemical style. Together with his brilliant political works, Trotsky wrote on military theory and on problems of cultural life. He was more of a Marxian purist than most Bolsheviks and he insisted that the Communist Party should establish a completely classless society in which neither the proletarian nor any other class was accorded special consideration. He argued in his 1921 book *The Defense of Terrorism* (excerpts from the English edition *Terrorism and Communism* follow) that the revolutionary class must attain its end by all methods at its disposal—if necessary, by terrorism. He bitterly condemned Marxist Karl Kautsky for his objections to terror, brutality, and violence as appropriate means of consolidating the revolution. Trotsky lived by the creed of violence and, in 1940, he died by it.

Terrorism and Communism

... The scheme of the political situation on a world scale is quite clear. The bourgeoisie, which has brought the nations, exhausted and bleeding to death, to the brink of destruction—particularly the victorious bourgeoisie—has displayed its complete inability to bring them out of their terrible situation, and, thereby, its incompatibility with the future development of humanity. All the intermediate political groups, including here first and foremost the social-patriotic

From Leon Trotsky, *Terrorism and Communism*, The University of Michigan Press, Ann Arbor, Michigan, 1961, pp. 35-41, 54-55, 57-59.

parties, are rotting alive. The proletariat they have deceived is turning against them more and more every day, and is becoming strengthened in its revolutionary convictions as the only power that can save the peoples from savagery and destruction. However, history has not at all secured, just at this moment, a formal parliamentary majority on the side of the party of the social revolution. In other words, history has not transformed the nation into a debating society solemnly voting the transition to the social revolution by a majority of votes. On the contrary, the violent revolution has become a necessity precisely because the imminent requirements of history are helpless to find a road through the apparatus of parliamentary democracy. The capitalist bourgeois calculates: "while I have in my hands lands, factories, workshops, banks; while I possess newspapers, universities, schools; while—and this most important of all—I retain control of the army; the apparatus of democracy, however you reconstruct it, will remain obedient to my will. I subordinate to my interests spiritually the stupid, conservative, characterless lower middle class, just as it is subjected to me materially. I oppress, and will oppress, its imagination by the gigantic scale of my buildings, my transactions, my plans, and my crimes. For moments when it is dissatisfied and murmurs, I have created scores of safety-valves and lightning-conductors. At the right moment I will bring into existence opposition parties, which will disappear tomorrow, but which to-day accomplish their mission by affording the possibility of the lower middle class expressing their indignation without hurt therefrom for capitalism. I shall hold the masses of the people, under cover of compulsory general education, on the verge of complete ignorance, giving them no opportunity of rising above the level which my experts in spiritual slavery consider safe. I will corrupt, deceive, and terrorize the more privileged or the more backward of the proletariat itself. By means of these measures, I shall not allow the vanguard of the working class to gain the ear of the majority of the working class, while the necessary weapons of mastery and terrorism remain in my hands."

To this the revolutionary proletarian replies: "Consequently, the first condition of salvation is to tear the weapons of domination out of the hands of the bourgeoisie. It is hopeless to think of a peaceful arrival to power while the bourgeoisie retains in its hands all the apparatus of power. Three times over hopeless is the idea of coming to power by the path which the bourgeoisie itself indicates and, at the same time, barricades—the path of parliamentary democracy. There is only one way: to seize power, taking away from the bourgeoisie the material apparatus of government. Independently of the superficial balance of forces in parliament, I shall take over for social administration the chief forces and resources of production. I shall free the mind of the lower middle class from their capitalist hypnosis. I shall show them in practice what is the meaning of

Socialist production. Then even the most backward, the most ignorant, or most terrorized sections of the nation will support me, and willingly and intelligently will join in the work of social construction."

When the Russian Soviet Government dissolved the Constituent Assembly, that fact seemed to the leading Social-Democrats of Western Europe, if not the beginning of the end of the world, at all events a rude and arbitrary break with all the previous developments of Socialism. In reality, it was only the inevitable outcome of the new position resulting from imperialism and the war. If Russian Communism was the first to enter the path of casting up theoretical and practical accounts, this was due to the same historical reasons which forced the Russian proletariat to be the first to enter the path of the struggle for power.

All that has happened since then in Europe bears witness to the fact that we drew the right conclusions. To imagine that democracy can be restored in its general purity means that one is living in a pitiful, reactionary utopia.

... The doctrine of formal democracy is not scientific Socialism, but the theory of so-called natural law.

... If we look back to the historical sequence of world concepts, the theory of natural law will prove to be a paraphrase of Christian spiritualism freed from its crude mysticism. The Gospels proclaimed to the slave, that he had just the same soul as the slave-owner, and in this way established the equality of all men before the heavenly tribunal. In reality, the slave remained a slave, and obedience became for him a religious duty. In the teaching of Christianity, the slave found an expression for his own ignorant protest against his degraded condition. Side by side with the protest was also the consolation. Christianity told him:—"You have an immortal soul, although you resemble a pack-horse." Here sounded the note of indignation. But the same Christianity said:—"Although you are like a pack-horse, yet your immortal soul has in store for it an eternal reward." Here is the voice of consolation. These two notes were found in historical Christianity in different proportions at different periods and amongst different classes. But, as a whole, Christianity, like all other religions, became a method of deadening the consciousness of the oppressed masses.

Natural law, which developed into the theory of democracy, said to the worker: "all men are equal before the law, independently of their origin, their property, and their position; every man has an equal right in determining the fate of the people." This ideal criterion revolutionized the consciousness of the masses in so far as it was a condemnation of absolutism, aristocratic privileges, and the property qualification. But the longer it went on, the more it sent the consciousness to sleep, legalizing poverty, slavery and degradation: for how could one revolt against slavery when every man has an equal right in determining the fate of the nation?

. . . In the practical interests of the development of the working class, the Socialist Party took its stand at a certain period on the path of parliamentarism. But this did not mean in the slightest that it accepted in principle the metaphysical theory of democracy, based on extra-historical, super-class rights. The proletarian doctrines examined democracy as the instrument of bourgeois society entirely adapted to the problems and requirements of the ruling classes; but as bourgeois society lived by the labor of the proletariat and could not deny it the legalization of a certain part of its class struggle without destroying itself, this gave the Socialist Party the possibility of utilizing, at a certain period, and within certain limits, the mechanism of democracy, without taking an oath to do so as an unshakable principle.

The root problem of the party, at all periods of its struggle, was to create the conditions for real, economic, living equality for mankind as members of a united human commonwealth. It was just for this reason that the theoreticians of the proletariat had to expose the metaphysics of democracy as a philosophic mask for political mystification.

The democratic party at the period of its revolutionary enthusiasm, when exposing the enslaving and stupefying lie of church dogma, preached to the masses:—"You are lulled to sleep by promises of eternal bliss at the end of your life, while here you have no rights and you are bound with the chains of tyranny." The Socialist Party, a few decades later, said to the same masses with no less right:—"You are lulled to sleep with the fiction of civic equality and political rights, but you are deprived of the possibility of realizing those rights. Conditional and shadowy legal equality has been transformed into the convicts' chain with which each of you is fastened to the chariot of capitalism."

In the name of its fundamental task, the Socialist Party mobilized the masses on the parliamentary ground as well as on others; but nowhere and at no time did any party bind itself to bring the masses to Socialism only through the gates of democracy. In adapting ourselves to the parliamentary regime, we stopped at a theoretical exposure of democracy, because we were still too weak to overcome it in practice. But the path of Socialist ideas which is visible through all deviations, and even betrayals, foreshadows no other outcome but this: to throw democracy aside and replace it by the mechanism of the proletariat, at the moment when the latter is strong enough to carry out such a task.

. . . The problem of revolution, as of war, consists in breaking the will of the foe, forcing him to capitulate and to accept the conditions of the conqueror. The will, of course, is a fact of the physical world, but in contradistinction to a meeting, a dispute, or a congress, the revolution carries out its object by means of the employment of material resources—though to a less degree than war. The bourgeoisie itself conquered power by means of revolts, and consolidated it by the civil war. In the peaceful period, it retains power by means of a system of repression. As long as class society, founded on the most deep-rooted antagonisms, continues to exist, repression remains a necessary means of breaking the will of the opposing side.

Even if, in one country or another, the dictatorship of the proletariat grew up within the external framework of democracy, this would by no means avert the civil war. The question as to who is to rule the country, i.e., of the life or death of the bourgeoisie, will be decided on either side, not by references to the paragraphs of the constitution, but by the employment of all forms of violence.

... The degree of ferocity of the struggle depends on a series of internal and international circumstances. The more ferocious and dangerous is the resistance of the class enemy who have been overthrown, the more inevitably does the system of repression take the form of a system of terror.

... The Russian proletariat was the first to enter the path of the social revolution, and the Russian bourgeoisie, politically helpless, was emboldened to struggle against its political and economic expropriation only because it saw its elder sister in all countries still in power, and still maintaining economic, political, and, to a certain extent, military supremacy.

If our November revolution had taken place a few months, or even a few weeks, after the establishment of the rule of the proletariat in Germany, France, and England, there can be no doubt that our revolution would have been the most "peaceful," the most "bloodless" of all possible revolutions on this sinful earth. But this historical sequence—the most "natural" at the first glance, and, in any case, the most beneficial for the Russian working class—found itself infringed—not through our fault, but through the will of events. Instead of being the last, the Russian proletariat proved to be the first. It was just this circumstance, after the first period of confusion, that imparted desperation to the character of the resistance of the classes which had ruled in Russia previously, and forced the Russian proletariat, in a moment of the greatest peril, foreign attacks, and internal plots and insurrections, to have recourse to severe measures of State terror. No one will now say that those measures proved futile. But, perhaps, we are expected to consider them "intolerable"?

The working class, which seized power in battle, had as its object and its duty to establish that power unshakeably, to guarantee its own supremacy beyond question, to destroy its enemies' hankering for a new revolution, and thereby to make sure of carrying out Socialist reforms. Otherwise there would be no point in seizing power.

The revolution "logically" does not demand terrorism, just as "logically" it does not demand an armed insurrection. What a profound commonplace! But the revolution does require of the revolutionary class that it should attain its end by all methods at its disposal—if necessary, to an armed rising: if required, by terrorism. A revolutionary class which has conquered power with arms in its hands is bound to, and will, suppress, rifle in hand, all attempts to tear the power out of its hands. Where it has against it a hostile army, it will oppose to it its own army. Where it is confronted with armed conspiracy, attempt at murder, or rising, it will hurl at the heads of its enemies an unsparing penalty. Perhaps Kautsky has invented other methods? Or does he reduce the whole question to the *degree* of repression, and recommend in all circumstances imprisonment instead of execution?

The question of the form of repression, or of its degree, of course, is not one of "principle." It is a question of expediency. In a revolutionary period, the party, which has been thrown from power, which does not reconcile itself with the stability of the ruling class, and which proves this by its desperate struggle against the latter, cannot be terrorized by the threat of imprisonment, as it does not believe in its duration. It is just this simple but decisive fact that explains the widespread recourse to shooting in a civil war.

Or, perhaps, Kautsky wishes to say that execution is not expedient, that "classes cannot be cowed." This is untrue. Terror is helpless—and then only "in the long run"—if it is employed by reaction against a historically rising class. But terror can be very efficient against a reactionary class which does not want to leave the scene of operations. *Intimidation* is a powerful weapon of policy, both internationally and internally. War like revolution, is founded upon intimidation. A victorious war, generally speaking, destroys only an insignificant part of the conquered army, intimidating the remainder and breaking their will. The revolution works in the same way: it kills individuals, and intimidates thousands. In this sense, the Red Terror is not distinguishable from the armed insurrection, the direct continuation of which it represents. The State terror of a revolutionary class can be condemned "morally" only by a man who, as a principle, rejects (in words) every form of violence whatsoever—consequently, every war and every rising. For this one has to be merely and simply a hypocritical Quaker.

"But, in that case, in what do your tactics differ from the tactics of Tsarism?" we are asked, by the high priests of Liberalism and Kautskianism.

You do not understand this, holy men? We shall explain to you. The terror of Tsarism was directed against the proletariat. The gendarmerie of Tsarism throttled the workers who were fighting for the Socialist order. Our Extraordinary Commissions shoot landlords, capitalists, and generals who are striving to restore the capitalist order. Do you grasp this . . . distinction? Yes? For us Communists it is quite sufficient.

part two america

thomas paine

The morning of April 19, 1775, brought a radically new dimension to the tense struggle between the American colonies and Great Britain because armed violence erupted when the British army ordered American militia forces at Lexington to disband. A shooting war began, and the differences fostered by Massachusetts and Virginia leaders since 1763 turned into organized violence. From Lexington the raging fires of conflict spread to Concord, and finally Boston where militiamen and angry farmers attacked the red-coated British soldiers.

Moderate delegates led by John Dickinson of Pennsylvania prevented the Second Continental Congress, which began its meeting May 10 in Philadelphia, from declaring independence. As in the First Continental Congress in September 1774, the delegates appealed once again to the King for an end to the repressive legislation passed by Parliament which restricted American commerce and increased taxation. The King's reply came in the shape of further restrictions and additional troops. The conflict escalated during June 1775 as British troops destroyed militia forces on Breed's Hill overlooking Boston—an engagement often called the battle of Bunker Hill—and thereby retained control of the city. Hostilities extended subsequently to the other colonies during the summer and fall.

American observers during these tumultuous months viewed the fighting with uncertainty. Few believed in outright separation from Great Britain. Most

Americans viewed the appeal to arms as an attempt to gain recognition of American rights within the British Empire; indeed, most colonials earnestly hoped for reconciliation with the mother country. Though the colonies increasingly scorned Parliament, King George III still held the loyalty and respect of his subjects on the American continent. As frustrations mounted, however, and war ravaged the land, revolutionary talk became more common and attractive.

The focus on revolution sharpened when *Common Sense*, published anonymously as a fifteen-thousand-word pamphlet on January 10, 1776, came into the hands of Americans. Its author, Thomas Paine, then thirty-nine years old, had been born in England and attended school until the age of thirteen, when he became an apprentice in his father's trade of corset making. Later, he served briefly aboard a privateer and then, in succession, became an exciseman, teacher, and merchant. His first wife died less than a year after their wedding: his second marriage lasted three years before his wife sued for legal separation in 1774. Domestic troubles together with bankruptcy combined to increase his restlessness and frustrations.

Paine was acting as a lobbyist for excisemen when he first met Benjamin Franklin, who provided him with letters of introduction to friends in America. Paine arrived in Philadelphia in the fall of 1774 and supported himself by writing articles for the *Pennsylvania Magazine* on topics ranging from the abolition of Negro slavery to new inventions. After the confrontation between the colonial militia and British soldiers in Massachusetts, Paine prepared the pamphlet which would make his name synonymous with the spirit of the American Revolution. An estimated one-half million copies were sold and, just as importantly, colonial newspapers reprinted it and spread the fever of independence and the call for liberty throughout the colonies. Loyalty for King George III was replaced by revolutionary zeal. The Continental Congress translated that sentiment into action by adopting the Declaration of Independence, drafted by Thomas Jefferson and others, on July 4, 1776; by its terms America's separation from Great Britain was proclaimed.

Paine, after a brief stint in the army, continued publishing other pamphlets, and for a time served as secretary to the Congressional Committee on foreign affairs. When the Revolutionary War ended, he was awarded a confiscated Loyalist's farm in New Rochelle, New York; he also resided in New York City and in New Jersey before returning to Europe in 1787. Popular among liberals everywhere, he lived in both England and France. After the outbreak of the French Revolution in 1789, he wrote another defense of liberty, the *Rights of Man*. Explaining the measures taken in revolutionary France to establish a republic; he hoped the English would abolish hereditary distinctions based upon birth and rank and establish a republican form of government. While living in France, he was tried in his absence for treason in England and outlawed from his native land.

Awarded citizenship by the French Assembly in 1792, Paine served for a year as a representative in the revolutionary convention before a subsequent French government stripped him of his citizenship and imprisoned him as an English alien since England and France were at war. After almost a year of imprisonment, Paine won his freedom through the intervention of James Monroe, the American minister to France. In the next several years, Paine completed his deist study, *The Age of Reason*, which emphasizes the inconsistencies in the Bible and his belief in one God.

Returning to New York in 1802 he found himself, as a friend of President Thomas Jefferson, the target of Federalist attacks. Some Republicans were no less critical and proclaimed him an infidel. Besides such social alienation, poverty and ill health haunted Paine's last years before his death in 1809. Refused burial in consecrated cemetery grounds because of his religious beliefs, Paine was buried in a corner of his farm at New Rochelle.

Like many political theorists, Paine accumulated very little material wealth: *Common Sense* was a financial loss, and Paine donated the profits from *The Rights of Man* to a radical London society. Strongly opinionated, temperamental, and living most of his life on the edge of poverty, Paine remained through times of triumph and persecution hopeful for a better government and society. Though later judged a "filthy little atheist" by Theodore Roosevelt and others, Thomas Paine and his propaganda piece *Common Sense* served as a crucial catalyst in a revolutionary age.

On Monarchy and American Independence

... The cause of America is in a great measure the cause of all mankind. Many circumstances have, and will arise, which are not local, but universal, and through which the principles of all lovers of mankind are affected, and in the event of which, their affections are interested. The laying a country desolate with fire and sword, declaring war against the natural rights of all mankind, and extirpating the defenders thereof from the face of the earth, is the concern of

From Thomas Paine, *Common Sense*, R. Bell, Philadelphia, 1776, Intro., pp. 9-14, 20-38, 40-45, 47, 50-53, 57-60, 69-72, 79.

every man to whom nature hath given the power of feeling; of which class, regardless of party censure, is the AUTHOR.

... There is something exceedingly ridiculous in the composition of Monarchy; it first excludes a man from the means of information, yet empowers him to act in cases where the highest judgment is required. The state of a king shuts him from the World, yet the business of a king requires him to know it thoroughly; wherefore the different parts, by unnaturally opposing and destroying each other, prove the whole character to be absurd and useless.

Some writers have explained the English constitution thus; the King say they is one, the people another; the Peers are an house in behalf of the King; the commons in behalf of the people; but this hath all the distinctions of an house divided against itself, and though the expressions be pleasantly arranged, yet when examined they appear idle and ambiguous; and it will always happen that the nicest construction that words are capable of, when applied to the description of something which either cannot exist, or is too incomprehensible to be within the compass of description, will be words of sound only, and tho' they may amuse the ear, they cannot inform the mind: for this explanation includes a previous question, viz. *how came the king by a power which the people are afraid to trust and always obliged to check?* Such a power could not be the gift of a wise people, neither can any power, *which needs checking*, be from God, yet the provision, which the constitution makes, supposes such a power to exist.

But the provision is unequal to the task; the means either cannot, or will not accomplish the end, and the whole affair is a *Felo de se* [felony] : for as the greater weight will always carry up the less, and as all the wheels of a machine are put in motion by one, it only remains to know which power in the constitution has the most weight, for that will govern: and tho' the others, or a part of them, may clog, or, as the phrase is, check the rapidity of its motion, yet so long as they cannot stop it, their endeavours will be ineffectual: The first moving power will at last have its way, and what it wants in speed is supplied by time.

That the crown is this overbearing part in the English constitution needs not be mentioned, and that it derives its whole consequence merely from being the giver of places and pensions is self evident, wherefore, tho' we have been wise enough to shut and lock a door against Monarchy, we at the same time have been foolish enough to put the Crown in possession of the key.

The prejudice of Englishmen in favour of their own government by King, Lords and Commons, arises as much or more from national pride than reason. Individuals are undoubtedly safer in England than in some other countries: but the will of the King is as much the law of the land in Britain as in France, with this difference, that instead of proceeding directly from his mouth, it is handed to the people under the more formidable shape of an act of parliament. For the fate of Charles the First, hath only made kings more subtle – not more just.

... An enquiry into the *constitutional errors* in the English form of government, is at this time highly necessary; for as we are never in a proper condition of doing justice to others, while we continue under the influence of some leading partiality, so neither are we capable of doing it to ourselves while we remain fettered by any obstinate prejudice. And as a man who is attached to a prostitute is unfitted to choose or judge of a wife, so any prepossession in favour of a rotten constitution of government will disable us from discerning a good one.

Of MONARCHY and hereditary succession.

MANKIND being originally equals in the order of creation, the equality could only be destroyed by some subsequent circumstance: the distinctions of rich and poor may in a great measure be accounted for, and that without having recourse to the harsh ill-sounding names of oppression and avarice. Oppression is often the *consequence*, but seldom or never the *means* of riches: and tho' avarice will preserve a man from being necessitously poor, it generally makes him too timorous to be wealthy.

But there is another and greater distinction for which no truly natural or religious reason can be assigned, and that is, the distinction of men into KINGS and SUBJECTS. Male and female are the distinctions of nature, good and bad the distinctions of Heaven; but how a race of men came into the world so exalted above the rest, and distinguished like some new species, is worth enquiring into, and whether they are the means of happiness or of misery to mankind.

In the early ages of the world according to the scripture chronology there were no kings; the consequences of which was, there were no wars; it is the pride of kings which throws mankind into confusion. Holland without a king hath enjoyed more peace for this last century, than any of the monarchical governments in Europe. Antiquity favours the same remark; for the quiet and rural lives of the first Patriarchs hath a happy something in them, which vanishes away when we come to the history of Jewish royalty.

Government by kings was first introduced into the world by the Heathens, from whom the children of Israel copied the custom. It was the most prosperous invention the Devil ever set on foot for the promotion of idolatry. The Heathens paid divine honours to their deceased kings, and the Christian World hath improved on the plan by doing the same to their living ones. How impious is the title of sacred Majesty applied to a worm, who in the midst of his splendor is crumbling into dust.

. . . To the evil of monarchy we have added that of hereditary succession; and as the first is a degradation and lessening of ourselves, so the second, claimed as a matter of right, is an insult and an imposition on posterity. For all men being originally equals, no one by birth could have a right to set up his own family in perpetual preference to all others for ever, and tho' himself might deserve some decent degree of honours of his contemporaries, yet his descendants might be far too unworthy to inherit them. One of the strongest natural proofs of the folly of hereditary rights in kings, is, that nature disapproves it, otherwise she would not so frequently turn it into ridicule by giving mankind an *ass for a lion*.

Secondly, as no man at first could possess any other public honours than were bestowed upon him, so the givers of those honours could have no power to give away the right of posterity, and though they might say "we choose you for our head" they could not without manifest injustice to their children say "that your children and your children's children shall reign over ours forever." Because such an unwise, unjust, unnatural compact might (perhaps) in the next succession put them under the government of a rogue or a fool. Most wise men in their private sentiments have ever treated hereditary right with contempt; yet it is one of those evils, which when once established is not easily removed: many submit from fear, others from superstition, and the more powerful part shares with the king the plunder of the rest.

This is supposing the present race of kings in the world to have had an honorable origin: whereas it is more than probable, that could we take off the dark covering of antiquity and trace them to their first rise, that we should find the first of them nothing better than the principal ruffian of some restless gang, whose savage manners or preeminence in subtilty obtained him the title of chief among plunderers: and who by increasing in power and extending his depredations, over-awed the quiet and defenceless to purchase their safety by frequent contributions. Yet his electors could have no idea of giving hereditary right to his descendants, because such a perpetual exclusion of themselves was incompatible with the free and unrestrained principles they professed to live by. Wherefore, hereditary succession in the early ages of monarchy could not take place as a matter of claim, but as something casual or complimental; but as few or no records were extant in those days, and traditionary history stuffed with fables, it was very easy after the lapse of a few generations, to trump up some superstitious tale conveniently timed, Mahomet like, to cram hereditary right down the throats of the vulgar. Perhaps the disorders which threatened, or seemed to threaten, on the decease of a leader and the choice of a new one (for elections among ruffians could not be very orderly) induced many at first to favour hereditary pretensions; by which means it happened, as it hath happened since, that what at first was submitted to as a convenience was afterwards claimed as a right.

England since the conquest hath known some few good monarchs, but groaned beneath a much larger number of bad ones: yet no man in his senses can say that their claim under William the Conqueror is a very honourable one. A French Bastard landing with an armed Banditti and establishing himself king of England against the consent of the natives, is in plain terms a very paltry rascally original. It certainly hath no divinity in it. However, it is needless to spend much time in exposing the folly of hereditary right, if there are any so weak as to believe it, let them promiscuously worship the Ass and Lion and welcome. I shall neither copy their humility nor disturb their devotion.

. . . But it is not so much the absurdity as the evil of hereditary succession which concerns mankind. Did it ensure a race of good and wise men it would have the seal of divine authority, but as it opens a door to the *foolish*, the *wicked*, and the *improper*, it hath in it the nature of oppression. Men who look upon themselves born to reign, and others to obey, soon grow insolent— selected from the rest of Mankind their minds are easily poisoned by importance; and the world they act in differs so materially from the world at large, that they have but little opportunity of knowing its true interests, and when they succeed to the governments are frequently the most ignorant and unfit of any throughout the dominions.

Another evil which attends hereditary succession, is, that the throne is subject to be possessed by a minor at any age; all which time the regency acting under the cover of a king have every opportunity and inducement to betray their trust. The same national misfortune happens when a king worn out with age and infirmity enters the last stage of human weakness. In both these cases the public becomes a prey to every miscreant who can tamper successfully with the follies either of age or infancy.

The most plausible plea which hath ever been offered in favour of hereditary succession, is, that it preserves a Nation from Civil wars; and were this true, it would be weighty; whereas it is the most barefaced falsity ever imposed upon mankind. The whole history of England disowns the fact. Thirty kings and two minors have reigned in that distracted kingdom since the conquest, in which time there has been (including the Revolution) no less than eight civil wars and nineteen Rebellions. Wherefore instead of making for peace, it makes against it, and destroys the very foundation it seems to stand upon.

. . . If we enquire into the business of a King we shall find that in some countries they have none; and after sauntering away their lives without pleasure to themselves or advantage to the nation, withdraw from the scene and leave their successors to tread the same idle round. In absolute monarchies the whole weight of business civil and military lies on the King; the children of Israel in their request for a King urged this plea "that he may judge us, and go out before us and fight our battles." But in countries where he is neither a judge nor a general as in England, a man would be puzzled to know what is his business.

. . . In England a king hath little more to do than to make war and give away places; which in plain terms, is to impoverish the nation and set it together by the ears. A pretty business indeed for a man to be allowed eight hundred thousand sterling a year for, and worshipped into the bargain! Of more worth is one honest man to society and in the sight of God, than all the crowned ruffians that ever lived.

THOUGHTS, on the present STATE of AMERICAN AFFAIRS.

In the following pages I offer nothing more than simple facts, plain arguments, and common sense: and have no other preliminaries to settle with the reader, than that he will divest himself of prejudice and prepossession, and suffer his reason and his feelings to determine for themselves: that he will put on or rather that he will not put off the true character of a man, and generously enlarge his views beyond the present day.

Volumes have been written on the subject of the struggle between England and America. Men of all ranks have embarked in the controversy, from different motives, and with various designs; but all have been ineffectual, and the period of debate is closed. Arms as the last resource decide the contest; the appeal was the choice of the King, and the Continent has accepted the challenge.

. . . By referring the matter from argument to arms, a new era for politics is struck — a new method of thinking hath arisen. All plans, proposals, etc. prior to the 19th of April, i.e. to the commencement of hostilities, are like the almanacks of the last year; which tho' proper then, are superceded and useless now. Whatever was advanced by the advocates on either side of the question then, terminated in one and the same point, viz. a union with Great Britain; the only difference between the parties, was the method of effecting it; the one proposing force the other friendship; but it hath so far happened that the first hath failed, and the second hath withdrawn her influence.

As much hath been said of the advantages of reconciliation, which like an agreeable dream, hath passed away and left us as we were, it is but right, that we should examine the contrary side of the argument, and enquire into some of the many material injuries which these Colonies sustain, and always will sustain, by being connected with and dependent on Great Britain. To examine that connection and dependence on the principles of nature and common sense, to see what we have to trust to if separated, and what we are to expect if dependent.

I have heard it asserted by some, that as America hath flourished under her former connection with Great Britain, that the same connection is necessary towards her future happiness and will always have the same effect. Nothing can be more fallacious than this kind of argument: — we may as well assert that because a child hath thrived upon milk, that it is never to have meat, or that the first twenty-years of our lives is to become a precedent for the next twenty. But even this is admitting more than is true, for I answer, roundly, that America would have flourished as much, and probably much more had no European power taken any notice of her. The commerce by which she hath enriched herself are the necessaries of life, and will always have a market while eating is the custom of Europe.

... It hath lately been asserted in parliament, that the Colonies have no relation to each other but through the Parent Country, i.e. that Pennsylvania and the Jerseys and so on for the rest, are sister Colonies by the way of England; this is certainly a very roundabout way of proving relationship, but it is the nearest and only true way of proving enmity (or enemyship, if I may so call it.) France and Spain never were, nor perhaps ever will be our enemies as *Americans* but as our being the *subjects of Great Britain*.

But Britain is the parent country say some. Then the more shame upon her conduct. Even brutes do not devour their young, nor savages make war upon their families; wherefore the assertion if true, turns to her reproach; but it happens not to be true, or only partly so, and the phrase, *parent* or *mother country*, hath been jesuitically adopted by the King and his parasites, with a low papistical design of gaining an unfair bias on the credulous weakness of our minds. Europe and not England is the parent country of America. This new World hath been the asylum for the persecuted lovers of civil and religious liberty from *every part* of Europe. Hither have they fled, not from the tender embraces of the mother, but from the cruelty of the monster; and it is so far true of England, that the same tyranny which drove the first emigrants from home, pursues their descendants still.

In this extensive quarter of the Globe, we forget the narrow limits of three hundred and sixty miles (the extent of England) and carry our friendship on a larger scale; we claim brotherhood with every European Christian, and triumph in the generosity of the sentiment.

... But admitting, that we were all of English descent, what does it amount to? Nothing. Britain being now an open enemy, extinguishes every other name and title: and to say that reconciliation is our duty, is truly farcical.

. . . I challenge the warmest advocate for reconciliation, to show, a single advantage that this Continent can reap, by being connected with Great Britain. I repeat the challenge, not a single advantage is derived. Our corn will fetch its price in any market in Europe and our imported goods must be paid for buy them where we will.

But the injuries and disadvantages we sustain by that connection, are without number, and our duty to mankind at large, as well as to ourselves, instruct us to renounce the alliance: because any submission to, or dependence on Great Britain, tends directly to involve this Continent in European wars and quarrels. As Europe is our market for trade, we ought to form no political connection with any part of it. 'Tis the true interest of America, to steer clear of European contentions, which she never can do, while by her dependence on Britain, she is made the make-weight in the scale of British politics.

Europe is to thickly planted with Kingdoms, to be long at peace, and whenever a war breaks out between England and any foreign power, the trade of America goes to ruin, *because of her connection with Britain*.

. . . Though I would carefully avoid giving unnecessary offence, yet I am inclined to believe, that all those who espouse the doctrine of reconciliation, may be included within the following descriptions. Interested men who are not to be trusted, weak men who cannot see, prejudiced men who will not see, and a certain set of moderate men who think better of the European world than it deserves; and this last class, by an ill-judged deliberation, will be the cause of more calamities to this Continent, than all the other three.

It is the good fortune of many to live distant from the scene of present sorrow; the evil is not sufficiently brought to their doors to make them feel the precariousness with which all American property is possessed. But let our imaginations transport us for a few moments to Boston; that feat of wretchedness will teach us wisdom, and instruct us for ever to renounce a power in whom we can have no trust. The inhabitants of that unfortunate city who but a few months ago were in ease and affluence, have now no other alternative than to stay and starve, or turn out to beg. Endangered by the fire of their friends if they continue within the city, and plundered by government if they leave it. In their present condition they are prisoners without the hope of redemption, and in a general attack for their relief, they would be exposed to the fury of both armies.

Men of passive tempers look somewhat lightly over the offences of Britain, and still hoping for the best, are apt to call out, *Come, come, we shall be friends again for all this*. But examine the passions and feelings of mankind: bring the doctrine of reconciliation to the touchstone of nature, and then tell me, whether you can hereafter love, honour, and faithfully serve the power that hath carried fire and sword into your land? If you cannot do all these, then are you only deceiving yourselves, and by your delay bringing ruin upon posterity. Your future connection with Britain whom you can neither love nor honour, will be forced and unnatural, and being formed only on the plan of present convenience, will in a little time, fall into a relapse more wretched than the first. But if you say, you can still pass the violations over, then I ask, hath your house been burnt? Hath your property been destroyed before your face? Are your wife and children destitute of a bed to lie on, or bread to live on? Have you lost a parent or a child by their hands, and yourself the ruined and wretched survivor? If you have not, then are you not a judge of those who have. But if you have and still can shake hands with the murderers, then are you unworthy the name of husband, father, friend, or lover, and whatever may be your rank or title in life, you have the heart of a coward, and the spirit of a sycophant.

This is not inflaming or exaggerating matters, but trying them by those feelings and affections which nature justifies, and without which, we should be incapable of discharging the social duties of life, or enjoying the felicities of it. I mean not to exhibit horrors for the purpose of provoking revenge, but to awaken us from fatal and unmanly slumbers, that we may pursue determinately some fixed object. 'Tis not in the power of England or of Europe to conquer America, if she doth not conquer herself by delay and timidity. The present winter is worth an age if rightly employed, but if lost or neglected, the whole Continent will partake of the misfortune; and there is no punishment which that man doth not deserve, be he who, or what, or where he will, that may be the means of sacrificing a season so precious and useful.

... Every quiet method for peace hath been ineffectual. Our prayers have been rejected with disdain; and hath tended to convince us that nothing flatters vanity or confirms obstinacy in Kings more than repeated petitioning — and nothing hath contributed more, than that very measure, to make the Kings of Europe absolute. Witness Denmark and Sweden. Wherefore, since nothing but blows will do, for God's sake let us come to a final separation, and not leave the next generation to be cutting throats under the violated unmeaning names of parent and child.

To say they will never attempt it again is idle and visionary, we thought so at the repeal of the stamp-act, yet a year or two undeceived us; as well may we suppose that nations which have been once defeated will never renew the quarrel.

As to government matters 'tis not in the power of Britain to do this Continent justice: the business of it will soon be too weighty and intricate to be managed with any tolerable degree of convenience, by a power so distant from us, and so very ignorant of us; for if they cannot conquer us, they cannot govern us. To be always running three or four thousand miles with a tale or a petition, waiting four or five months for an answer, which when obtained requires five or six more to explain it in, will in a few years be looked upon as folly and childishness —there was a time when it was proper, and there is a proper time for it to cease.

Small islands not capable of protecting themselves are the proper objects for governments to take under their care: but there is something very absurd, in supposing a Continent to be perpetually governed by an island. In no instance hath nature made the satellite larger than its primary planet, and as England and America with respect to each other reverse the common order of nature, it is evident they belong to different systems. England to Europe: America to itself.

I am not induced by motives of pride, party or resentment to espouse the doctrine of separation and independence; I am clearly positively, and conscientiously persuaded that 'tis the true interest of this Continent to be so; that every thing short of that is mere patchwork, that it can afford no lasting felicity— that it is leaving the sword to our children, and shrinking back at a time, when a little more, a little farther, would have rendered this Continent the glory of the earth.

. . . No man was a warmer wisher for reconciliation than myself, before the fatal 19th of April 1775, but the moment the event of that day was make known, I rejected the hardened, sullen tempered Pharoah of England for ever; and disdain the wretch, that with the pretended title of FATHER OF HIS PEOPLE can unfeelingly hear of their slaughter, and composedly sleep with their blood upon his soul.

. . . And in order to show that reconciliation *now* is a dangerous doctrine, I affirm, *that it would be policy in King at this time, to repeal the acts for the sake of reinstating himself in the government of the provinces*; in order that HE MAY ACCOMPLISH BY CRAFT AND SUBTILTY, IN THE LONG RUN, WHAT HE CANNOT DO BY FORCE AND VIOLENCE IN THE SHORT ONE. Reconciliation and ruin are nearly related.

. . . But the most powerful of all arguments is, that nothing but independence i.e. a continental form of government, can keep the peace of the continent and preserve it inviolate from civil wars. I dread the event of a reconciliation with Britain *now*, as it is more than probable, that it will be followed by a revolt some where or other, the consequences of which may be far more fatal than all the malice of Britain.

Thousands are already ruined by British barbarity; (thousands more will probably suffer the same fate;) Those men have other feelings than us who have nothing suffered. All they *now* possess is liberty, what they before enjoyed is sacrificed to its service, and having nothing more to lose, they disdain submission. Besides, the general temper of the colonies towards a British government, will be like that of a youth, who is nearly out of his time; they will care very little about her: And a government which cannot preserve the peace, is no government at all, and in that case we pay our money for nothing; and pray what is it that Britain can do, whose power will be wholly on paper, should a civil tumult break out the very day after reconciliation? I have heard some men say, many of whom I believe spoke without thinking, that they dreaded an independence, fearing that it would produce civil wars: It is but seldom that our first thoughts are truly correct, and that is the case here; for there are ten times more to dread from a patched up connection, than from independence. I make the sufferers case my own, and I protest, that were I driven from house and home, my property destroyed, and my circumstances ruined, that as a man sensible of injuries, I could never relish the doctrine of reconciliation, or consider myself bound thereby.

The colonies hath manifested such a spirit of good order and obedience to continental government, as is sufficient to make every reasonable person easy and happy on that head. No man can assign the least pretence for his fears, on any other grounds, than such as are truly childish and ridiculous, viz. that one colony will be striving for superiority over another.

Where there are no distinctions, there can be no superiority; perfect equality affords no temptations. The republics of Europe are all, (and we may say always) in peace. Holland and Swisserland, are without wars, foreign or domestic: Monarchical governments, it is true, are never long at rest; the crown itself is a temptation to enterprising ruffians at *home*; and that degree of pride and insolence ever attendant on regal authority, swells into a rupture with foreign powers, in instances, where a republican government by being formed on more natural principles, would negociate the mistake.

. . . But where say some is the King of America? I'll tell you friend, he reigns above; and doth not make havoc of mankind like the Royal Brute of Great Britain. Yet that we may not appear to be defective even in earthly honours, let a day be solemnly set a part for proclaiming the Charter; let it be brought forth placed on the Divine Law, the Word of God; let a crown be placed thereon, by which the world may know, that so far as we approve of monarchy, that in America THE LAW IS KING. For as in absolute governments the King is law, so in free countries the law ought to be king; and there ought to be no other. But lest any ill use should afterwards arise, let the Crown at the conclusion of the ceremony be demolished, and scattered among the people whose right it is.

... Ye that oppose independence now, ye know not what ye do: ye are opening a door to eternal tyranny, by keeping vacant the seat of government. There are thousands, and tens of thousands, who would think it glorious to expel from the Continent, that barbarous and hellish power, which have stirred up the Indians and the Negroes to destroy us, the cruelty hath a double guilt, it is dealing brutally by us, and treacherously by them.

... Ye that tell us of harmony and reconciliation, can ye restore to us the time that is past? can ye give to prostitution its former innocence? neither can ye reconcile Britain and America. The last cord now is broken, the people of England are presenting addresses against us. There are injuries which nature cannot forgive; she would cease to be nature if she did. As well can the lover forgive the ravisher of his mistress, as the Continent forgive the murders of Britain. The Almighty hath implanted in us these unextinguishable feelings for good and wise purposes. They are the Guardians of his Image in our hearts. They distinguish us from the herd of common animals. The social compact would dissolve, and justice be extirpated from the earth, or have only a casual existence were we callous to the touches of affection. The robber and the murderer would often escape unpunished, did not the injuries which our tempers sustain, provoke us into justice.

O ye that love mankind! Ye that dare oppose not only the tyranny but the tyrant, stand forth! Every spot of the old world is over-run with oppression. Freedom hath been hunted round the Globe. Asia and Africa have long expelled her. Europe regards her like a stranger, and England hath given her warning to depart. O! receive the fugitive, and prepare in time an asylum for mankind.

... Resolution is our inherent character, and courage hath never yet forsaken us. Wherefore, what is it that we want? why is it that we hesitate? From Britain, we can expect nothing but ruin. If she is once admitted to the government of America again, this Continent will not be worth living in. Jealousies will be always arising; insurrections will be constantly happening; and who will go forth to quell them? who will venture his life to reduce his own countrymen to a foreign obedience?

... The infant state of the Colonies, as it is called, so far from being against, is an argument in favour of independence. We are sufficiently numerous, and were we more so, we might be less united. 'Tis a matter worthy of observation, that the more a country is peopled, the smaller their armies are. In military numbers the ancients far exceeded the moderns: and the reason is evident, for trade being the consequence of population, men become too much absorbed thereby to attend to any thing else. Commerce diminishes the spirit both of Patriotism and military defence. And history sufficiently informs us that the bravest achievements were always accomplished in the non-age of a nation. With the increase of commerce England hath lost its spirit. The city of London, notwithstanding its numbers, submits to continued insults with the patience of a coward. The more men have to lose, the less willing are they to venture. The rich are in general slaves to fear, and submit to courtly power with the trembling duplicity of a spaniel.

Youth is the seed time of good habits as well in nations as in individuals. It might be difficult, if not impossible to form the Continent into one Government half a century hence. The vast variety of interests occasioned by an increase of trade and population would create confusion. Colony would be against Colony. Each being able would scorn each others assistance: and while the proud and foolish gloried in their little distinctions, the wise would lament that the union had not been formed before. Wherefore, the present time is the true time for establishing it. The intimacy which is contracted in infancy, and the friendship which is formed in misfortune, are of all others, the most lasting and unalterable. Our present union is marked with both these characters: we are young, and we have been distressed; but our concord hath withstood our troubles, and fixes a memorable Era for posterity to glory in.

. . . These proceedings may at first appear strange and difficult, but like all other steps which we have already passed over, will in a little time become familiar and agreeable: and until an independence is declared, the Continent will feel itself like a man who continues putting off some unpleasant business from day to day, yet knows it must be done, hates to set about it, wishes it over, and is continually haunted with the thoughts of its necessity.

thomas jefferson

The fever of independence which Thomas Paine had encouraged with his pamphlet *Common Sense* in January 1776 caught other American leaders, and they too demanded formal separation from England. Samuel Adams, John Adams, and John Hancock urged this course and during the spring such a resolution came to be expected. On June 7, a resolution was introduced by Richard Henry Lee and the Congress assigned the drafting of a declaration of independence to Thomas Jefferson, Benjamin Franklin, John Adams, Robert R. Livingston, and Roger Sherman. While Jefferson actually wrote the document, Franklin and Adams revised it before it was introduced into Congress, where it was revised again and finally adopted by Congress on July 4, 1776.

Its principal author, Thomas Jefferson, was born in Virginia in 1743. His mother, Jane Randolph, was a member of a distinguished Virginia family, and his father was a member of the House of Burgesses and a civil engineer. As a planter's son, Jefferson enjoyed the privileges of that class, especially private tutoring when very young. At the age of sixteen, he entered William and Mary College. Recognizing the value of law as a powerful social instrument, Jefferson excelled in this discipline. He was admitted to the bar in 1767 and practiced law for the next seven years, after which he turned his interests to political philosophy.

Jefferson proved very effective as a member of the House of Burgesses, and became, in 1775, a delegate from Virginia to the Continental Congress in Philadelphia, where he became one of its foremost leaders through his work on committees. As a public speaker, the tall sandy-haired representative never excelled. He preferred reflection and writing to public debate and argument.

Drafting the Declaration of Independence at the age of thirty-three, Jefferson relied heavily on the doctrines of John Locke and on the preamble to the Virginia Constitution of 1776, which he had prepared earlier. His careful emphasis upon consent of the governed, the equality of all men, and the inalienable rights of man made the Declaration one of the most famous and eloquent documents in the history of western civilization. A variety of patriots since that time to the present, including Ho Chi Minh, have turned to that document as a model for preparing their own.

In September 1776, Jefferson left Congress and returned to Virginia and the process of establishing a stable republican government in that state. He firmly believed that the laws of privilege, based upon the aristocracy of birth and wealth, must be eliminated in Virginia. Equally anxious to prevent a government from becoming tyrannical, he wanted the people to be liberally educated so that they would recognize selfish ambitions. Moreover, this liberal education at public expense could provide potential leaders with the knowledge necessary to administer a wise and honest government. His "Bill for the More General Diffusion of Knowledge" recognized the vital importance of education for the people.

A bill which Jefferson believed ranked with the Declaration of Independence was his proposal for establishing religious freedom. Convinced that freedom of conscience must be secured, he wanted no state church in Virginia. Passage of this bill in 1786, despite the storm of opposition by religious leaders, gave impetus to the separation of church and state doctrine in the United States.

The last selection included below is Jefferson's Report of Government for the Western Territory. It provided that the lands ceded by the states to the federal government would not be held as colonies by the United States. Rather, they would have the rights and responsibilities of the other states. Jefferson's provision regarding slavery was defeated by a vote of seven to six in the Congress.

Jefferson's brilliant mind recognized human needs and the principles necessary for reconstructing society. As American minister to France, Secretary of State, Vice President, and finally President of the United States, he continued to serve the new Republic. Jefferson realized the true objectives of a revolution, and the American society which he wrote about in the Declaration of Independence achieved unparalleled liberty and stability before his death in 1826. His writings and leadership helped to spread the fever of freedom.

Declaration of Independence

In Congress, July 4, 1776. The Unanimous Declaration of the thirteen United States of America.

When in the Course of human events, it becomes necessary for one people to dissolve the political bands which have connected them with another, and to assume among the powers of the earth, the separate and equal station to which the Laws of Nature and of Nature's God entitle them, a decent respect to the opinions of mankind requires that they should declare the causes which impel them to the separation.

We hold these truths to be self-evident, that all men are created equal, that they are endowed by their Creator with certain inalienable rights, that among these are Life, Liberty, and the pursuit of Happiness.—That to secure these rights, Governments are instituted among Men, deriving their just powers from the consent of the governed.—That whenever any Form of Government becomes destructive of these ends, it is the right of the People to alter or to abolish it, and to institute new Government, laying its foundation on such principles, and organizing its powers in such forms, as to them shall seem most likely to effect their Safety and Happiness. Prudence, indeed, will dictate that Governments long established should not be changed for light and transient causes; and accordingly all experience hath shown, that mankind are more disposed to suffer, while evils are sufferable, than to right themselves by abolishing the forms to which they are accustomed. But when a long train of abuses and usurpations pursuing invariably the same Object, evinces a design to reduce them under absolute Despotism, it is their right, it is their duty, to throw off such Government, and to provide new Guards for their future security. Such has been the patient sufferance of these Colonies; and such is now the necessity which constrains them to alter their former Systems of Government. The history of the present King of Great Britain is a history of repeated injuries and usurpations, all having in direct object the establishment of an absolute Tyranny over these States.

. . . In every stage of these Oppressions We have Petitioned for Redress in the most humble terms: Our repeated Petitions have been answered only by repeated injuries.

A Prince whose character is thus marked by every act which may define a Tyrant, is unfit to be the ruler of a free people.

From *The Writings of Thomas Jefferson,* edited by Paul Leicester Ford, G.P. Putnam's Sons, New York, II (1893), pp. 42-45, 53-58.

Nor have We been wanting in attentions to our British brethren. We have warned them from time to time of attempts by their legislature to extend an unwarrantable jurisdiction over us. We have reminded them of the circumstances of our emigration and settlement here. We have appealed to their native justice and magnanimity and we have conjured them by the ties of our common kindred to disavow these usurpations which would inevitably interrupt our connection and correspondence. They too have been deaf to the voice of justice and of consanguinity. We must therefore acquiesce in the necessity which denounces our separation and hold them, as we hold the rest of mankind, Enemies in War, in Peace Friends.

We, therefore, the Representatives of the United States of America, in General Congress Assembled, appealing to the Supreme Judge of the world for the rectitude of our intentions, do, in the Name, and by Authority of the good People of these Colonies, solemnly publish and declare, that these United Colonies are, and of Right ought to be Free and Independent States; that they are Absolved from all allegiance to the British Crown, and that all political connection between them and the State of Great Britain, is and ought to be totally dissolved; and that as Free and Independent states, they have full Power to levy War, conclude Peace, contract Alliances, establish Commerce, and to do all other Acts and Things which Independent States may of right do.

And for the support of this Declaration, with a firm reliance on the protection of divine Providence, we mutually pledge to each other our Lives, our Fortunes, and our sacred Honor.

A Bill for the More General Diffusion of Knowledge

Whereas it appeareth that however certain forms of government are better calculated than others to protect individuals in the free exercise of their natural rights, and are at the same time themselves better guarded against degeneracy, yet experience hath shewn, that even under the best forms, those entrusted with power have, in time, and by slow operations, perverted it into tyranny; and it is believed that the most effectual means of preventing this would be, to illuminate, as far as practicable, the minds of the people at large, and more especially to give them knowledge of those facts, which history exhibiteth, that, possessed thereby of the experience of other ages and countries, they may be enabled to

From *The Writings of Thomas Jefferson,* II, pp. 220-221. The bill was recommended in the Report of the Revisions to the Virginia Assembly in 1779 as a revision of state laws.

know ambition under all its shapes, and prompt to exert their natural powers to defeat its purposes; And whereas it is generally true that that people will be happiest whose laws are best, and are best administered, and that laws will be wisely formed, and honestly administered, in proportion as those who form and administer them are wise and honest; whence it becomes expedient for promoting the publick happiness that those persons, whom nature hath endowed with genius and virtue, should be rendered by liberal education worthy to receive, and able to guard the sacred deposit of the rights and liberties of their fellow citizens, and that they should be called to that charge without regard to wealth, birth or other accidental condition or circumstance; but the indigence of the greater number disabling them from so educating at their own expence, those of their children whom nature hath fitly formed and disposed to become useful instruments for the public, it is better that such should be sought for and educated at the common expence of all, than that the happiness of all should be confined to the weak or wicked: . . .

A Bill for Establishing Religious Freedom

SECTION I. Well aware that the opinions and belief of men depend not on their own will, but follow involuntarily the evidence proposed to their minds; that Almighty God hath created the mind free, and manifested his supreme will that free it shall remain by making it altogether insusceptible of restraint; that all attempts to influence it by temporal punishments, or burthens, or by civil incapacitations, tend only to beget habits of hypocrisy and meanness, and are a departure from the plan of the holy author of our religion, who being lord both of body and mind, yet choose not to propagate it by coercions on either, as was in his Almighty power to do, but to exalt it by its influence on reason alone; that the impious presumption of legislature and ruler, civil as well as ecclesiastical, who, being themselves but fallible and uninspired men, have assumed dominion over the faith of others, setting up their own opinions and modes of thinking as the only true and infallible, and as such endeavoring to impose them on others, hath established and maintained false religions over the greatest part of the world and through all time: That to compel a man to furnish contributions of money for the propagation of opinions which he disbelieves and abhors, is sinful and tyrannical; that even the forcing him to support this or that

From *The Writings of Thomas Jefferson*, II, pp. 237-239. The bill was also a part of the Report of the Revision.

teacher of his own religious persuasion, is depriving him of the comfortable liberty of giving his contributions to the particular pastor whose morals he would make his pattern, and whose powers he feels most persuasive to righteousness; and is withdrawing from the ministry those temporary rewards, which proceeding from an approbation of their personal conduct, are an additional incitement to earnest and unremitting labours for the instruction of mankind; that our civil rights have no dependance on our religious opinions, any more than our opinions in physics or geometry; and therefore the proscribing any citizen as unworthy the public confidence by laying upon him an incapacity of being called to offices of trust or emolument, unless he profess or renounce this or that religious opinion, is depriving him injudiciously of those privileges and advantages to which, in common with his fellow-citizens, he has a natural right; that it tends also to corrupt the principles of that very religion it is meant to encourage, by bribing with a monopoly of worldly honours and emoluments, those who will externally profess and conform to it; that though indeed these are criminals who do not withstand such temptation, yet neither are those innocent who lay the bait in their way; that the opinions of men are not the object of civil government, nor under its jurisdiction; that to suffer the civil magistrate to intrude his powers into the field of opinion and to restrain the profession or propagation of principles on supposition of their ill tendency is a dangerous fallacy, which at once destroys all religious liberty, because he being of course judge of that tendency will make his opinions the rule of judgment, and approve or condemn the sentiments of others only as they shall square with or suffer from his own; that it is time enough for the rightful purposes of civil government for its officers to interfere when principles break out into overt acts against peace and good order; and finally, that truth is great and will prevail if left to herself; that she is the proper and sufficient antagonist to error, and has nothing to fear from the conflict unless by human interposition disarmed of her natural weapons, free argument and debate; errors ceasing to be dangerous when it is permitted freely to contradict them.

SECT. II. We the General Assembly of Virginia do enact that no man shall be compelled to frequent or support any religious worship place, or ministry whatsoever, nor shall be enforced, restrained, molested, or burthened in his body or goods, or shall otherwise suffer, on account of his religious opinions or belief; but that all men shall be free to profess, and by argument to maintain their opinions in matters of religion, and that the same shall in no wise diminish, enlarge, or affect their civil capacities.

SECT. III. And though we well know that this Assembly, elected by the people for their ordinary purposes of legislation only, have no power to restrain the acts of succeeding Assemblies, constituted with powers equal to our own, and that therefore to declare this act to be irrevocable would be of no effect in law; yet we are free to declare, and do declare, that the rights hereby asserted are of the natural rights of mankind, and that if any act shall be hereafter passed to repeal the present or to narrow its operations, such act will be an infringement of natural right.

Report of Government For the Western Territory

... That the settlers on any territory so purchased & offered for sale shall, either on their own petition, or on the order of Congress, receive authority from them with appointments of time & place for their free males of full age, within the limits of their state to meet together for the purpose of establishing a temporary government, to adopt the constitution and laws of any one of the original states, so that such laws nevertheless shall be subject to alteration by their ordinary legislature; & to erect, subject to a like alteration, counties or townships for the election of members for their legislature.

That such temporary government shall only continue in force in any state until it shall have acquired 20,000 free inhabitants, when giving due proof thereof to Congress, they shall receive from them authority with appointment of time & place to call a convention of representatives to establish a permanent Constitution & Government for themselves. Provided that both the temporary & permanent governments be established on these principles as their basis. 1. That they shall forever remain a part of this confederacy of the United States of America. 2. That in their persons, property & territory they shall be subject to the Government of the United States in Congress assembled, & to the articles of Confederation in all those cases in which the original states shall be so subject. 3. That they shall be subject to pay a part of the federal debts contracted or to be contracted, to be apportioned on them by Congress, according to the same common rule & measure, by which apportionments thereof shall be made on the other states. 4. That their respective Governments shall be in republican forms and shall admit no person to be a citizen who holds any hereditary title. 5. That after the year 1800 of the Christian era, there shall be neither slavery nor involuntary servitude in any of the said states, otherwise than in punishment of crimes whereof the party shall have been convicted to have been personally guilty. . . .

From *The Writings of Thomas Jefferson*, III (1894), pp. 431-432.

simón bolívar

Born in Caracas, Venezuela, to aristocratic parents in 1783—the same year which marked the end of the American Revolution—Bolívar became acquainted at an early age, through the teachings of his tutors, with the ideas of Rousseau and other figures of the Enlightenment. Further education in Spain and France convinced him that Spanish America was ready for independence. When French armies invaded Spain in 1808 and Ferdinand VII was imprisoned, Bolívar and others began working for the independence of Venezuela.

In 1811, the Congress of Venezuela declared the nation independent, and Bolívar entered the Venezuelan army and took over Caracas. Hailed as *el Libertador*, he was forced to abandon the city less than a year later, and Venezuela became again a Spanish-controlled colony. Living in Jamaica, then Haiti, Bolívar gathered forces and supplies for a new invasion, but failed in two attempts. Rejecting further coastal invasions, he developed the strategy of building a stable base at Angostura (now called Ciudad Bolívar), an inland port on the Orinoco River which had been founded in 1764, and then carrying the battle into New Granada and invading Venezuela from the west.

Before carrying out this strategy, he called for the Congress of Angostura and presented his ideas on the political future of northern South America. His address on February 15, 1819, is considered a masterpiece on the principles for establishing a stable government. Careful to blend his plans for the future government with the heritage of the people, Bolívar presented an amazing plan of organization. He drew from the lessons of the past, warning against anarchy and tyranny and urging stability. The selections from that famous address indicate his aspirations and anxieties: they present the views of a thoughtful political theorist, hardened by the realities of intense political battle and defeat.

Victorious on the battlefield and chosen President of the Republic of Great Colombia (which incorporated New Granada, Venezuela, and Quito), Bolívar led the forces of independence to make his "paper" republic a political reality by 1822. Continuing to unite a continent, Bolívar led military expeditions in Peru, bringing independence to that area, which made Bolívar its president and named part of its lands Bolivia.

In the years after 1825, Bolívar's dream of a united continent shattered as different national leaders sought more power: Peru invaded Colombia, Venezuela seceded from her union with Colombia, and insurrections covered Bolívar's once proud union. He died in 1830 from tuberculosis in the midst of the anarchy he had feared when he spoke to the Congress at Angostura.

To the Congress of Angostura

... The epoch in the life of the Republic over which I have presided has not been a mere political storm; it has been neither a bloody war, nor yet one of popular anarchy. It has been indeed, the development of all disorganizing elements; it has been the flooding of an infernal torrent which has overwhelmed the land of Venezuela. A man, aye, such a man as I am, what check could he offer to the march of such devastation? In the midst of this sea of woes I have simply been a mere plaything of the revolutionary storm, which tossed me about like a frail straw. I could do neither good nor harm. Irresistible forces have directed the trend of our events. To attribute this to me would not be fair, it would be assuming an importance which I do not merit. Do you desire to know who are the authors of past events and the present order of things? Consult then the Annals of Spain, of America, of Venezuela; examine the Laws of the Indies, the rule of the old executives; the influence of religion and of foreign domination; observe the first acts of the Republican Government, the ferocity of our enemies and our national temperament. Do not ask me what are the effects of such mishaps, ever to be lamented. I can scarcely be accounted for but as a mere

From *An Address of Bolívar to the Congress of Angostura* (February 15, 1819), translated from Spanish by Francisco Javier Yanes, Washington, D.C., n.d.: pp. 17-35, 37-39.

instrument of the great forces which have been at work in Venezuela. However, my life, my conduct, all my acts, both public and private, are subject to censure by the people. Representatives! You are to judge them. I submit the history of my tenure of office to your impartial decision; I shall not add one thing more to excuse it; I have already said all that could be my apology. If I deserve your approval, I have attained the sublime title of a good citizen, to me preferable to that of *Liberator*, given me by Venezuela, that of *Pacificator*, which Cundinamarca accorded me, and all the titles that the whole world could bestow upon me.

Legislators! I deposit in your hands the supreme command of Venezuela. Yours is now the august duty of devoting yourselves to achieving the happiness of the Republic; you hold in your hands the scales of our destinies, the measure of our glory; your hands will seal the decrees insuring our Liberty. At this moment the Supreme Chief of the Republic is nothing but a plain citizen, and such he wishes to remain until death. I will serve, however, in the career of a soldier while there are enemies in Venezuela. The country has a multitude of most worthy sons capable of guiding her; talents, virtues, experience, and all that is required to direct free men, are the patrimony of many of those who are representing the people here; and outside of this Sovereign Body, there are citizens, who at all times have shown their courage in facing danger, prudence in avoiding it, and the art, in short, to govern themselves and of governing others. These illustrious men undoubtedly merit the vote of Congress, and they will be entrusted with the Government that I have just resigned so cordially and sincerely and forever.

The continuation of authority in the same person has frequently proved the undoing of democratic governments. Repeated elections are essential to the system of popular government, because there is nothing so dangerous as to suffer Power to be vested for a long time in one citizen. The people become accustomed to obeying him, and he becomes accustomed to commanding, hence the origin of usurpation and tyranny. A proper zeal is the guarantee of republican liberty, and our citizens must very justly fear that the same Magistrate who has governed them for a long time, may continue to rule them forever.

And, now that by this act of adherence to the Liberty of Venezuela, I can aspire to the glory of being counted among her most faithful lovers, permit me, Sirs, to state with the frankness of a true republican, my respectful opinion regarding the scope of this *Project of a Constitution*, which I take the liberty to submit, as a token of the sincerity and candor of my sentiments. As this is a question involving the welfare of all, I venture to believe that I have the right to be heard by the Representatives of the People.

. . . America, on becoming separated from the Spanish monarchy, found itself like the Roman Empire, when that enormous mass fell to pieces in the midst of the ancient world. Each dismembered portion formed then an independent nation in accordance with its situation or its interests, the difference being that those members established anew their former associations. We do not even preserve the vestiges of what once we were; we are not Europeans, we are not Indians, but an intermediate species between the aborigines and the Spaniards— Americans by birth and Europeans in right, we are placed in the dilemma of disputing with the natives our titles of possession and maintaining ourselves in the country where we were born, against the opposition of the invaders. Thus, ours is a most extraordinary and complicated case. Moreover, our part has always been a purely passive one; our political existence has always been null, and we find ourselves in greater difficulties in attaining our liberty than we ever had when we lived on a plane lower than servitude, because we had been robbed not only of liberty but also of active and domestic tyranny.

. . . Spain [did not permit] us to share in our own domestic affairs and interior administration. This deprivation had made it impossible for us to become acquainted with the course of public affairs; neither did we enjoy that personal consideration which the glamour of power inspires in the eyes of the multitude, so important in the great revolutions. I will say, in short, we were kept in estrangement, absent from the universe and all that relates to the science of government.

The people of America having been held under the triple yoke of ignorance, tyranny and vice, have not been in a position to acquire either knowledge, power or virtue. Disciples of such pernicious masters, the lessons we have received and the examples we have studied, are most destructive. We have been governed more by deception than by force, and we have been degraded more by vice than by superstition. Slavery is the offspring of Darkness; an ignorant people is a blind tool, turned to its own destruction; ambition and intrigue exploit the credulity and inexperience of men foreign to all political, economical or civil knowledge; mere illusions are accepted as reality, license is taken for liberty, treachery for patriotism, revenge for justice. Even as a sturdy blind man who, relying on the feeling of his own strength, walks along with the assurance of the most wideawake man and, striking against all kinds of obstacles, can not steady his steps.

A perverted people, should it attain its liberty, is bound to lose this very soon, because it would be useless to try to impress upon such people that happiness lies in the practice of righteousness; that the reign of law is more powerful than the reign of tyrants, who are more inflexible, and all ought to submit to the wholesome severity of the law; that good morals, and not force, are the pillars of the law and that the exercise of justice is the exercise of liberty. Thus, Legislators, your task is the more laborious because you are to deal with men misled by the illusions of error, and by civil incentives. Liberty, says Rousseau, is a succulent food, but difficult to digest. Our feeble fellow-citizens will have to strengthen their mind much before they will be ready to assimilate such wholesome nourishment. Their limbs made numb by their fetters, their eyesight weakened in the darkness of their dungeons and their forces wasted away through their foul servitude, will they be capable of marching with a firm step towards the august temple of Liberty? Will they be capable of coming close to it, and admiring the light it sheds, and of breathing freely its pure air?

. . . Nature, in truth, endows us at birth with the instinctive desire for liberty; but whether because of negligence, or because of an inclination inherent in humanity, it remains still under the bonds imposed on it. And as we see it in such a state of debasement we seem to have reason to be persuaded that the majority of men hold as a truth the humiliating principle that it is harder to maintain the balance of liberty than to endure the weight of tyranny. Would to God that this principle, contrary to the morals of Nature, were false! Would to God that this principle were not sanctioned by the indolence of man as regards his most sacred rights!

Many ancient and modern nations have cast off oppression; but those which have been able to enjoy a few precious moments of liberty are most rare, as they soon relapsed into their old political vices; because it is the people more often than the government, that bring on tyranny. The habit of suffering domination makes them insensible to the charms of honor and national prosperity, and leads them to look with indolence upon the bliss of living in the midst of liberty, under the protection of laws framed by their own free will. The history of the world proclaims this awful truth!

. . . I am filled with unbounded joy because of the great strides made by our republic since entering upon its noble career. Loving that which is most useful, animated by what is most just and aspiring to what is most perfect, Venezuela in separating from the Spanish Nation has recovered her independence, her freedom, her equality, her national sovereignty. In becoming a democratic republic, she proscribed monarchy, distinctions, nobility, franchises and privileges; she declared the rights of man, the liberty of action, of thought, of speech, of writing. These preeminently liberal acts will never be sufficiently admired for the sincerity by which they are inspired.

. . . The more I admire the excellence of the Federal Constitution of Venezuela, the more I am persuaded of the impossibility of its application in our State. And, in my opinion, it is a wonder that its model in North America may endure so successfully, and is not upset in the presence of the first trouble or danger. Notwithstanding the fact that that people is a unique model of political virtues and moral education; notwithstanding that it has been cradled in liberty, that it has been reared in freedom and lives on pure liberty, I will say more, although in many respects that people is unique in the history of humanity, it is a prodigy, I repeat, that a system so weak and complicated as the federal system should have served to govern that people in circumstances as difficult and delicate as those which have existed. But, whatever the case may be, as regards the American Nation, I must say that nothing is further from my mind than to try to assimilate the conditions and character of two nations as different as the Anglo-American and the Spanish-American. Would it not be extremely difficult to apply to Spain the Code of political, civil and religious liberty of England? It would be even more difficult to adapt to Venezuela the laws of North America. Does not the *Spirit of Laws* state that they must be suited to the people for whom they are made; that it is a great coincidence when the laws of one nation suit another; that laws must bear relation to the physical features of a country, its climate, its soil, its situation, extension and manner of living of the people; that they must have reference to the degree of liberty that their constitution may be able to provide for the religion of the inhabitants, their inclination, wealth, number, trade, customs and manners? Such is the Code that we should consult, not that of Washington!

... Representatives of the People! You have been called to confirm or suppress whatever you may deem worthy of being preserved, amended or rejected in our social compact. To your lot falls the correction of the work of our first legislators; I would fain say that it behooves you to cover a portion of the beauties found in our political code, because not every heart is so made as to love all beauties, nor can all eyes stand the heavenly light of perfection. The book of the Apostles, the doctrines of Jesus, the divine writings sent us by Providence to better mankind, so sublime, so holy, is a rain of fire in Constantinople, and Asia entire would be a fiery conflagration should such a book of peace be suddenly imposed as a code of religion, law and customs. Permit me to call the attention of Congress to a matter which may be of vital importance. We must bear in mind that our population is not the people of Europe, not of North America, that it is rather a composite of Africa and America, which is an offspring of Europe. Spain herself ceases to be European on account of her African blood, her institutions and her temperament. It is impossible to point out with preciseness to what human family we belong. The greater portion of the natives has been annihilated, the European has mixed with the native American and the African, and this has mixed again with the Indian and the European. All having been born of the same mother, our parents, of different origin and blood, are foreigners, and all differ visibly in color of skin. This dissimilarity is a hindrance of the greatest importance.

... The diversity of origin requires to be handled with infinite firmness, with infinite delicate tact in order to deal with an heterogeneous society whose complicated mechanism will become disjointed, divided, will dissolve at the slightest alteration. The most perfect system of government is that which produces the greatest sum of happiness possible, the greatest sum of social security and political stability. Through the laws enacted by the first Congress we have the right to expect that happiness be the lot of Venezuela, and through your laws we must hope that security and stability will perpetuate such happiness. It is for you to solve the problem. But how, after having broken all the chains of our former oppression, could we accomplish the marvelous task of preventing the remnants of our fetters from being turned into liberticide weapons? The relics of Spanish domination will last a long time before we succeed in annihilating them; contagion of despotism has vitiated our atmosphere, and neither the fire of war nor yet the remedy of our wholesome laws has succeeded in purifying the air we breathe. Our hands are now free, while our hearts still suffer the ills of servitude. Man in losing his liberty,—Homer has said,—loses one-half of his manhood.

A republican government has been, is and must be that of Venezuela, based on the sovereignty of the people, the division of power, civil liberty, proscription of slavery, abolition of monarchy and privileges. We need equality to recast, so to speak, in a single mass the classes of men, political beliefs and public customs.

... And passing now from ancient to modern times, we find England and France attracting attention of all nations, and teaching them eloquent lessons of all sorts in the matter of government. The revolution of these two great peoples, like a brilliant meteor, has flooded the world with such a profusion of political light that now all thinking men have learned what are the rights of men, what are their duties, what constitutes the excellency of a government and what its vices. All know how to appreciate the intrinsic value of the speculative theories of modern philosophers and lawmakers. In fine, that star, in its luminous career, has even inflamed the heart of the apathetic Spaniards, who have also entered the political whirlwind, have made ephemeral attempts at liberty, have acknowledged their incapacity to live under the gentle rule of law, and have gone back to their inmemorial dungeons and the stake.

... We must never forget that the superiority of a government does not consist in its theories, or in its form, or in its mechanism, but in its being appropriate to the nature and character of the nation for which it has been instituted.

Rome and Great Britain are the two nations which have excelled most among ancient and modern peoples. Both were born to rule and to be free, but both were constituted not with dazzling forms of liberty, but built on solid foundations. Hence, I recommend you, Representatives, to study the British Constitution, which is the one that seems destined to do the most possible good to the peoples that adopt it.

... Our fundamental laws would not be altered in the least should we adopt a legislative power similar to the British Parliament. We have divided, as Americans did, national representation into two Chambers, the Representatives and the Senate. The first is very wisely constituted, enjoys all the functions appertaining to it, and is not susceptible of a radical reform, because it is the Constitution which gave it origin, form and such faculties as the will of the people deemed necessary to be legally and properly represented. If the Senate, instead of being elective were hereditary, it would be, in my opinion, the foundation, the binding tie, the very soul of our republic. This body would arrest the lightning of government in our political storms, and would break the popular waves. Attached to the government, because of its natural interest of self-preservation, it will always oppose the invasions attempted by the people against the jurisdiction and the authority of its rulers. We must confess it: the generality of men fail to recognize what their real interests are and constantly endeavor to asail them in the hands of their trustees; and the individual struggles against the masses, and the masses against the authorities. It is necessary, therefore, that a neutral body should exist in every government, always siding with the aggrieved party to disarm the offender. This neutral body, to be such, must not owe its origin to the election of the government, nor to the election of the people, so as to enjoy a full measure of freedom, neither fearing nor expecting anything from either of these two sources of authority. The hereditary Senate, as a part of the people, shares in its interests, in its sentiments, in its spirit. For this reason it is not to be presumed that a hereditary Senate would disregard the popular interests or forget its legislative duties. The Roman Senators and the Lords of London have been the staunchest columns on which the structure of political and civil liberty has been erected.

These Senators would be elected by Congress the first time. The succession to the Senate should engage the first attention of the government, which would educate them in a college specially devoted to instructing these tutors, future legislators of the country. They should learn the arts, sciences and letters, the accomplishments of the mind of public men; from childhood they should know the career to which Providence has destined them, and from a tender age they should temper their soul to the dignity awaiting them.

The creation of a hereditary Senate would be in nowise a violation of political equality; I do not pretend to establish a nobility because, as a famous republican has said, it would be to destroy at the same time equality and liberty. It is a calling for which candidates must be prepared; it is an office requiring much knowledge and the proper means to become learned in it. Everything must not be left to chance and fortune in the elections; the people are more easily deceived than Nature perfected by art, and although it is true that these Senators would not spring from the womb of Perfection, it is also true that they would spring from the womb of a learned education.

. . . No matter how the nature of the Executive Power of England is examined nothing can be found to lead to the belief that it is not the most perfect model, whether for a kingdom, an aristocracy, or a democracy. Let us apply to Venezuela this sort of Executive Power in the person of a President appointed by the people or their representatives, and we would have taken a great step toward national happiness.

. . . However excessive the authority of the Executive Power of England may appear to be, it might not be excessive in the Republic of Venezuela. Here, Congress has bound the hands and even the head of the officials. This deliberative body has assumed a portion of the Executive functions, against the maxim of Montesquieu, that a representative body must not take any active resolution; it must make the laws and see whether the laws made are properly executed. Nothing is more contrary to harmony between powers than having them mix; nothing is more dangerous to the people than a weak Executive, and if in a Kingdom it has been deemed necessary to grant the Executive so many faculties, in a republic these faculties are much more indispensable.

Let us direct our attention to this difference, and we will find that the balance of power must be distributed in two ways. In republics the Executive must be the stronger, because everything conspires against it, while in monarchies the stronger must be the Legislative Power, because everything conspires in favor of the monarch. The veneration of peoples for Royalty is a fascination which has powerful influence in increasing the superstitious respect paid to its authority. The splendor of the throne, of the crown, of the purple, the formidable support of nobility, the immense wealth that whole generations accumulate under the same dynasty, the fraternal protection that kings mutually receive, are very considerable advantages in favor of royal authority, making it almost unlimited. These very advantages are, therefore, those which must confirm the necessity of granting a republican Executive a greater authority than that possessed by a constitutional prince.

A republican Executive is a man isolated in the midst of a community, to restrain the impulse of the people towards license, the inclination of judges and administrators towards the abuse of the law. He is responsible to the Legislative body, the Senate and the people; he is one single man resisting the combined attack of the opinions, the interests and the passions of the social state, which, as Carnot has said, does nothing but continually struggle between the desire to dominate and that of getting away from domination. He is, in short, an athlete pitted against a multitude of athletes.

... Let us not be presumptuous, Legislators, let us be moderate in our pretentions. It is not likely that we should attain that which humanity has not succeeded in attaining, what the greatest and wisest nations never attained. Indefinite liberty, absolute democracy are the rocks upon which all republican hopes have been wrecked. Cast your eye over the ancient republics, the modern republics, the rising republics; almost all have tried to establish themselves as absolute democracies, and almost all have failed in their just aspirations. They are praiseworthy, undoubtedly, who wish for legitimate institutions and social perfection! But, who has told men that they possess already all the wisdom, that they practice all the virtues uncompromisingly demanded by the union of power and justice. Only angels, not mere men, can exist free, peaceful, happy, while exercising all the sovereign power.

... Love of country, love of law, love of the authorities, are the noble passions which must have exclusive sway in a republican soul. The Venezuelans love their country, but do not love their laws, because these were noxious and the source of evil; nor could they love their authorities, because they were unjust, and the new authorities are scarcely known in their new calling. If there is not a holy respect for the country, the laws and the authorities, society becomes a disorder, an abyss; an individual conflict between man and man, and hand to hand.

In order to bring our rising republic out of this chaos, all our moral power will not be sufficient unless we cast the entire mass of the people in one single body, the composition of the government in one single body, legislation in one single body, and national spirit in one single body. Union, Union, Union, must be our motto. Our citizens are of different blood, let us mix it for the sake of union; our constitution has divided the powers, let us bind them together for the sake of union; our laws are sorry relics of all the ancient and modern despotisms; let us demolish such an awful structure. Let it fall, and discarding even its ruins let us create a temple to Justice, and under the auspices of its holy inspiration, let us frame a code of Venezuelan laws. If we wish to consult monuments and models of legislation, Great Britain, France, North America have admirable ones.

Popular education should be the paramount care of the paternal love of Congress. Morals and enlightenment are the poles of a republic; morals and enlightenment are our prime necessities. Let us take from Athens here Areopagus, and the guardians of customs and laws; let us take from Rome her censors and domestic tribunals, and forming a holy alliance of those useful institutions, let us revive on earth the idea of a people which is not contented with being free and strong, but wants also to be virtuous.

... I would not mention to you the most notable acts of my administration, did they not concern the majority of the Venezuelans. I refer, Gentlemen, to the most important resolutions taken in this last period. Atrocious, godless slavery covered with its sable mantle the land of Venezuela and our skies were overcast with storm clouds threatening a deluge of fire. I implored the protection of the God of Humanity, and Redemption scattered the storm. Slavery broke its chains and Venezuela has found herself surrounded by her new children, grateful children who have turned their instruments of captivity into arms of liberty. Yea, those who were slaves are now free; those who were the enemies of their foster mother are now the defenders of a country. To emphasize the justice, the necessity, the beneficent results of this measure, is superfluous, when you know the history of the Helots, Spartacus and Haiti; when you know that one can not be free and enslaved at the same time, unless in violation of the laws of nature and the civil and political laws. I leave to your sovereign decision the reform or abrogation of all my statutes and decrees; but I implore of you the confirmation of the absolute freedom of the slaves, as I would beg for my life and the life of the Republic.

. . . Now that after infinite victories we have succeeded in annihilating the Spanish hosts, the Court of Madrid in desperation has vainly endeavored to impose upon the mind of the magnanimous sovereigns who have just destroyed usurpation and tyranny in Europe, and must be the protectors of the legality and justice of the American cause. Being incapable of attaining our submission by force of arms, Spain has recourse to her insidious policy; being unable to conquer us, she has brought into play her devious artfulness. Ferdinand has humbled himself to the extent of confessing that he needs foreign protection to bring us back to his ignominious yoke, a yoke that there is no power which could impose on us! Venezuela, fully convinced of possessing sufficient strength to repel her oppressors, has made known by the voice of the government her final determination to fight to the death in defense of her political life, not only against Spain, but against all men, if all men had degraded themselves to the extent of espousing the defense of a devouring government whose only incentives are a death dealing sword and the flames of the inquisition. A government that wants not domains, but deserts, not cities but ruins, not vassals but graves.

. . . The merging of New Granada and Venezuela into one Great State has been the unanimous wish of the peoples and the government of both republics. The fortunes of war have effected this union so earnestly desired by all Colombians; in fact, we are incorporated. These sister countries have already entrusted to you their interests, their rights and their destinies. In contemplating the union of these countries my soul rises to the heights demanded by the colossal perspective of such a wonderful picture. Soaring among the coming ages my imagination rests on the future centuries, and seeing from afar with admiration and amazement the prosperity, the splendor and the life which have come to this vast region, I feel myself carried away, and I see her in the very heart of the universe, stretching along her lengthy shores between two oceans which Nature has separated, but which our country unites through long wide channels. I can see her as the bond, as the center, as the emporium of the human family. I can see her sending to all the corners of the globe the treasure hidden in her mountains of silver and gold; I see her sending broadcast, by means of her divine plants, health and life to the sufferers of the old world; I see her confiding her precious secrets to the learned who do not know how much her store of knowledge is superior to the store of wealth bestowed by Nature upon her; I can see her sitting on the throne of liberty, the scepter of justice in her hand, crowned by glory, showing the old world the majesty of the modern world.

Deign, Legislators, to accept with indulgence the profession of my political faith, the highest wishes of my heart and the fervent prayer which on behalf of the people I dare address you: Deign to grant to Venezuela a government preeminently popular, preeminently just, preeminently moral, which will hold in chains oppression, anarchy and guilt. A government which will allow righteousness, tolerance, peace to reign; a government which will cause equality and liberty to triumph under the protection of inexorable laws.

Gentlemen, commence your duties; I have finished mine.

william lloyd garrison

When Americans spoke of Revolution in the nineteenth century, many dwelled increasingly upon the excesses and horrors of the French Revolution. Recalling the Goddess of Reason, the guillotine, the brutality of the French mobs, they warned against revolution out of fear that America would become involved in similar brutality. On the other hand, a few observers recalled the causes of that Revolution, and the despotism and fury which preceded it. Thomas Jefferson did and understood: William Lloyd Garrison was another genius who placed that Revolution in proper perspective and hastened to warn Americans that their values must change or their society would be doomed. He thought that moral force rather than physical force must lead the march of justice across America. Immediate reform could prevent the otherwise ultimate destruction threatening the American nation.

Born in Newburyport, Massachusetts, in 1805, Garrison had only a few years of education before entering the printer's craft in 1818 as an apprentice. Completing his apprenticeship, he served as editor of two newspapers before joining Benjamin Lundy as co-editor of the Baltimore Quaker newspaper, *Genius of Universal Emancipation*. When he first accepted the position, he agreed with Lundy's view that slavery should be totally abolished, and the freed slaves be sent off to some distant area to begin a new society. However before he arrived in Baltimore, he had rejected this racist approach and believed slavery must be abolished immediately and the freed slaves had every right to stay in American society. To do less must be labelled sinful. Since Southern Quakers were numerous on the subscription lists of Lundy's newspaper, Garrison's columns alienated many of these readers. As the circulation declined, Garrison sought funds to support immediate abolition, and turned to his liberal religious mentor in Boston, the Reverend Lyman Beecher, a Presbyterian revivalist, for moral and financial support. However, he learned that Beecher also advocated a gradual emancipation and viewed Garrison's total dedication with alarm and hostility.

Instead of weakening Garrison's determination, the reception in Boston only strengthened his resolve, and on January 1, 1831, he published the first issue of his own weekly newspaper, *The Liberator*, and explained his objective as a crusade for the immediate emancipation of all slaves: "I *will be* as harsh as truth, and as uncompromising as justice. On this subject, I do not wish to think, or speak, or write, with moderation. No! no! Tell a man whose house is on fire, to give a moderate alarm; tell him to moderately rescue his wife from the hands of the ravisher; tell the mother to gradually extricate her babe from the fire into which it has fallen;—but urge me not to use moderation in a cause like the present. I am in earnest—I will not equivocate—I will not excuse—I will not retreat a single inch—AND I WILL BE HEARD."

Garrison, more than any other American reformer, believed in one race, the human race, and the pages of his newspaper reflected this outlook. Because of his radical perspective, *The Liberator*'s circulation numbered no more than 3,000 subscribers, one-fourth of them white. Despite the enforced poverty, he married Helen Benson in 1834, and had a family of seven children.

A Christian idealist, or simply a Christian, Garrison believed desperately that others would follow his doctrines. Often frustrated, Garrison in 1844 declared that sincere citizens could no longer give allegiance to a racist government. Increasingly, though Garrison urged non-violence, his followers supported violence and insurrections. When John Brown died in 1859, Garrison condoned a violent solution, and he supported the Civil War when Lincoln issued the Emancipation Proclamation. The passage of the Thirteenth Amendment to the Constitution in 1865 brought him national acclaim, and at the end of that year he published the last issue of *The Liberator*.

This remarkably sensitive man devoted the remainder of his years to other reforms such as women's suffrage, and better conditions for American Indians. Truly a liberating influence in the United States, Garrison and his superb rhetoric in the pages of *The Liberator* reminded Americans of the unity of mankind.

The Liberator and Slavery

The past has been a year more than ordinarily eventful to this country and the world. Henceforth there is to be no peace on the earth—no cessation of revolutionary movements—no exhausted imbecility—until unjust rule be at an end; until personal thraldom be broken; until thrones be scattered in ashes to the winds; until hereditary titles and distinctions be effaced; until knowledge be diffused as freely as sun-light, and be as readily inhaled by all classes of the people as the vital atmosphere; until landed monopolies be distributed in equitable shares; until all labor be voluntary, receive its just remuneration, be protected in its own earnings, be a crown of honor and not a mark of servitude; until every government be elective and republican; until the right to worship God, according to the dictates of every man's conscience, be secured; until, in short, freedom of thought and speech and writing—freedom of choice—freedom of action—be not only the inalienable right but the positive exercise of every rational creature. The Spirit of Liberty is no longer young and feeble—it is no longer to make an abortive struggle, and then be passive for years: it is abroad with power—thundering at castle-gates and prison doors: from revolutionizing neighborhoods, it is going on to revolutionize nations: instead of agitating a kingdom, as formerly, it is now shaking the world. When it once fairly gets the mastery over its enemy Oppression, will not its retaliation be terrible? We to those who dress in purple and fine linen, and fare sumptuously every day, having defrauded the laborer of his hire and oppressed the poor! Wo to those who entrench themselves behind hereditary privileges and conduct, and declare that for the crimes which they commit, their ancestors must be responsible! Wo to that policy or system which has no other foundation than injustice, tyranny and wrong! which consults expediency and not right! which expects to satisfy the hungry with a crumb of knowledge—to content the benighted wanderer with a few scattered rays of light—to comfort the naked with half a blanket, or a whole suit of rags! which mocks the remonstrances of prudence, repels the suggestions of wisdom, forgets all the lessons of history, discredits the uniform results of experience, defies the moral and physical power of its victims! Wo, wo, for all that is oppressive—for all that lives by usurpation—for those who hearken not to the voice of nature—for the persecutors of their fellow men, wherever they may be found! There will be no discrimination with God or man, in favor of any class of despots: they who tread, with iron heels, upon the necks of their slaves in this

From *The Liberator* (a weekly periodical published in Boston from 1831 through 1865), January 7, 1832.

country, will not be thought less blameworthy than the tyrants of Europe. Despotism in a republic is as sure of punishment, as in a monarchy.

Happy will it be for us, as a people, if, treasuring up these truths in our memories, we check the retributive thunders of justice 'in mid volley,' by a timely repentance. We are a nation of blind, unrelenting, haughty, cruel, heaven-daring oppressors. The chains which we rivet upon the bodies of two millions of our fellow-countrymen, are as galling and heavy as were ever forged for human limbs. Shall those chains be broken by physical or moral power? Infatuated as we may be, we are conscious that, at some period or other, in some way or other, our slaves must be free. Gigantic as may be our strength, we are too intelligent to believe that it will enable us always to oppress with impunity. Secure as we may feel, we tremble for posterity—for our children, and our children's children. . . .

On Lyman Beecher

. . . He oracularly asserts, in the style of our Fourth-of-July orators, that 'a great experiment is now making. It is the experiment of human liberty; and if it fails here, all hope will be taken from the earth. If we cannot succeed, no nation will try it again.'

The wonderful 'experiment' that we are now making is precisely this—to see how long we can plunder, with impunity, two millions and a half of our population; how much labor we can extort with the cartwhip; how near to a level with the brute creation we can reduce every sixth man, woman and child in the land; how large a commerce we may pursue as human flesh-mongers; how tyrannical we may be without endangering our safety! —By this 'experiment' we are attempting to perform impossibilities. 'If it fails here,' says Dr. B.; but IT HAS FAILED—we are not, we have never been, and while slavery exists we can never be, a free people—we have not, never have had, never can have, until slavery is abolished, a union of the States—and we are rushing down to destruction as fast as time will allow us. Our 'great experiment' is for the purpose of proving to an incredulous world, that liberty is best promoted by the establishment and extension of slavery! that knowledge and ignorance, purity and pollution, christianity and heathenism, light and darkness, oil and water, fire and gunpowder, God and Mammon, Christ and Belial, are perfectly reconcilable and of rare affinity! 'It is

From *The Liberator*, July 23, July 30, and August 6, 1836. Garrison attacked Beecher, a Presbyterian minister, for failing to emphasize the inhumanity of slavery.

the experiment of human liberty'—to forbid the circulation of the Bible, to annul the marriage covenant, to make merchandize of God's image, to crush the human intellect, to ruin the deathless soul, to crucify the Son of God afresh, and to dethrone the Almighty! 'If it fails'! as if it were yet, or could ever have been, problematical! The delusion belongs to fatuity, it approaches to impiety! From the commencement, this 'experiment' has been absurd, impracticable, insane, disastrous, diabolical! And yet Dr. Beecher dares to assert, that 'if it fails here, *all hope will be taken from the earth* (!) If we cannot succeed, *no nation will try it again*' (!!) False prediction—monstrous conclusion—preposterous declamation! As if God had suspended the fate of all nations, and hazarded the fulfilment of his glorious promises, upon the result of a wild and cruel 'experiment' by a land-stealing, blood-thirsty, man-slaying and slave-trading people in one corner of the globe! As if God could not easily dash this nation in pieces, as a potter's vessel is broken, and thereby vindicate his eternal justice, advance the cause of human liberty, promote his fear in the earth, and establish a kingdom of righteousness! And it seems probable that he will do so—that he will cause it to fall, as did Lucifer, like lightning from heaven—that he will make it a bye-word and an astonishment through all time! For what are the United States in the estimation of the Almighty? Do their dimensions excite his wonder? Is he awed by the array of their naval and military power? Is he impressed by their arts and sciences, their enterprise and opulence, their politics and religion, their high pretensions and solemn protestations? Does his throne tremble, is he himself alarmed for the safety of the universe, lest this nation should apostatize, and thus not only blot out that 'great sun of the moral world,' the Sabbath, but make creation a blank? It is as true and as certain now, as it ever was, that 'the nation and kingdom that will not serve him shall perish; yea, those nations shall be utterly wasted. For the day of vengeance is in his heart, and the year of his redeemed is come. . . .

. . . We have dwelt at some length upon this infidel prophecy, because the pride of this nation needs to be humbled; because it haughtily imagines that it has a charmed life, an immortal existence; because it ought to be made to realize, that, were it a thousand times more mighty and influential than it is, God can sink it as a millstone in the depths of oblivion, and it shall never be missed, nor shall its loss prevent the regeneration of the world, the complete enfranchisement of the human race; and because the 'experiment' we are now making is not such as is represented by Dr. Beecher, but heathenish and in-human. That our example must be widely felt, for good or for evil—that our responsibility is awful, our ability to do good to the whole world unequalled, our influence commanding and prevalent, our success of amazing consequence—these are self-evident truths. But, blessed be God! it is not in our power, by any excess of wickedness, or suicidal act of depravity, to prevent the coming of the millenial day.

The Dr. undertakes to 'glance at some of the perils which threaten us,' but the existence of slavery is not in the catalogue! He has no microscopic eye—he can behold mountains only—and therefore so minute an evil must necessarily escape his vision!. . . .

'Another alarming evil that threatens us,' he says, 'is *the breaking up of the family alliance*, and throwing all our property into common stock for infidels to handle. They, kind souls! will no doubt be honest, and give you the crumbs, and take *very good care of all the rest*.' It is marvelous to behold the anxiety and alarm of Dr. B. as he contemplates the possibility of the overthrow of the marriage institution, and the establishment of a system of robbery, among our *white* population; while he is unmoved, and as tranquil as a summer's twilight, in view of 'the breaking up of the family alliance' among two millions and a half of our *colored* population, and 'throwing all *their* property into common stock for *slaveholders* to handle—who, kind souls! give the *slaves* the crumbs, and take very good care of all the rest.' What is slavery but a legalized system of agrarianism and whoredom, incomparably worse than anything ever contemplated by Robert Owen, or Fanny Wright, or even the Jacobins of France? Why should not infidels have as much liberty to subsist by plunder, by taking property which does not belong to them, as professing christians and clerical robbers at the south? Why should there be a monopoly of lewdness and incest among church-going members and slave-holding believers, to the exclusion of those who deny the existence of a God, and the authenticity of the Bible?—Neither Robert Owen nor Fanny Wright is base enough to advocate the right to make merchandize of human beings. . . . We maintain, that the doctrines avowed by southern ecclesiastical conferences, synods, presbyteries and churches, in relation to the enslavement of almost one half of the southern population, and the utter destruction of the 'family alliance' among four hundred thousand colored families, are as ruinous and diabolical, and as radically subvert the foundations of God's moral government, as any which have ever been put forth in the Free Enquirer, or Kneeland's Investigator. It is not possible for human depravity to conceive or enforce a more hellish system than American slavery. It is a troop of wolves preying upon defenceless lambs. It is a burning, ever-generating, all-desolating Vesuvius of lust and impurity. It is a slaughter-house of souls. It is a visible exhibition of Pandemonium.

Referring to those who are called agrarians, Dr. B. says—'There are demagogues who seek to make our laboring population feel as if they were despised and wronged, and that there is oppression in the fact that others should be richer than they.' And is it not true that our laboring population are, to an alarming extent, despised and wronged? Is not honest labor becoming more and more servile and despicable in the eyes of a growing aristocracy, both at the north and at the south? To say nothing of the treatment of the southern laboring population, (who have little or no share in the thoughts either of Dr. Beecher or the agrarian party,) our northern working-men have every reason to be alarmed at the prospect before them. There is a conspiracy all over the land against them. There is a proud aristocracy at the north, sympathizing with and publicly approbating a still more haughty aristocracy at the south; and, together, it is their aim, if possible, to degrade and defraud working-men of all classes, irrespective of color. The attempt at the north to subjugate the laboring population, may never succeed so far as to make merchandize of their bodies; but, unless this class arises in its might for the extirpation of southern slavery, it will be ground more and more to the dust, its time will be more and more limited, its wages more and more inadequate, its means of intelligence more and more circumscribed. . . .

Again, 'When once the mass of our people,' says the Dr. 'shall come to feel that all property above them is held by oppression, the foundations of the nation are shaken, and nothing is before us but revolution and anarchy.' There is an insinuation in this extract, which amounts to wholesale slander. There is no danger, whatever, that 'the mass of our people' will ever be carried headlong into excesses by cherishing such an opinion. The real danger is, that *they* will not long be regarded as men and as brethren, but as a servile and distinct race; that, as it respects their time, labor, improvement, and political and social equality, they will be defrauded by grinding monopolies, and reduced by systematic processes; and, hence, that they will have cause for complaint, and may be driven ultimately to revolution. We do not believe that there is any class of working-men, however ignorant or depraved, who 'feel that *all* property above them is held by oppression'—but all classes *know*, and some *feel*, that there is a growing aristocracy in our land; that privileges are granted to the wealthy few, to the injury and impoverishment of the laborious many; that an equality of rights must beget an equality of conditions; that dissatisfaction arises, not because property is acquired, but on account of the manner of its acquisition; and that oppression, not wealth, excites to resistance, anarchy, and common plunder. How does it happen, that Dr. Beecher's sympathies and fears side only with the rich and the powerful? Is there no cause for anxiety, lest they may be tempted to keep back the hire of the laborers who reap down their fields, and regard the operative and mechanic as mere implements of industry? Shall they not be admonished at least as often as the poor and needy? If it is in the nature of destitution to be envious, is it not also in the nature of wealth to be extortionate? If the feeble covet strength, do not the strong incline to despotism? Our laboring population, whether white or colored, are not held in due estimation; they are generally overtasked; they are seldom adequately remunerated, according to the just rule, 'Thou shalt love thy neighbor as thyself,' and the other reasonable and disinterested requirement, 'Whatsoever ye would that men should do to you, do ye even so to them'; they are valued according to the strength of their bodies, rather than to the intelligence of their minds and the improvement of their hearts. The lower they are found in degradation, the nearer they approach to starvation, (even when owing to obscurity of birth or the fate of adversity!) the less sympathy is extended to them—the less aid do they find. Man is not regarded as man—his inherent and perfect equality is not understood—his princely and indestructible dignity is not recognised—even though to him is given dominion over the beasts of the field and the fowls of the air, and though he is created in the image of God, and though Jesus, the Lord of Glory, descended from heaven, and died that he might live! When the abolitionists inculcate the duty of remunerating the colored laborer for his work, the cry is raised against them of 'fanaticism!' and when the white laborer protests against unrighteous monopolies, the same proud conservatives clamor about 'agrarianism,' 'levellers,' etc. As an apology for keeping our colored population in chains, we are referred to 'the scenes of St. Domingo!' although the struggle in that island was between an army of French invaders and an emancipated people. It was the consequence of an attempt to enslave freemen, not of liberating bondmen. So, whenever the workingmen strive to effect a just reform, they are made hideous, and driven back, by a fresh delineation of the horrors of the 'French revolution.' What has that dire tragedy to do with justice between man and man, or with equality between the employer and the employed? And were there no causes which produced it? It is popular to speak of the Goddess of Reason, of Robespierre and his vindictive associates, of the guillotine, and of the reign of atheism. But who dwells upon the fact, that a despotic government, a false religion, and a wicked priesthood, had conspired to crush, ruin and enslave the people, so that human endurance could bear no more, and all that was associated with the name of christianity became hateful? To a kingly and priestly despotism, long imposed and borne as long, must the origin of that tragedy be ascribed. Knowing nothing either of the character or the fruits of true religion,—detesting that which the Man of Sin forced upon their observance,—perceiving that they were made the victims of superstition and tyranny,—catching some faint glimpses of the natural equality of mankind,—and maddened to desperation by the wrongs heaped upon them,—they rose to obtain not only redress, but revenge, and in their blind fury made a sacrifice of the true with the false, of liberty with despotism, of all that was virtuous with much that was vile. But they were not made prodigies of impiety and cruelty in a day. They were trained to be atheists in the school of a false christianity. Yet the French revolution has been a fine windfall for the priesthood and the aristocracy in all countries. The causes of it are almost wholly forgotten—its terrible effects only are remembered. Both the aristocracy and the priesthood, however, need to be instructed by it more than the people. . . .

A Short Catechism, Adapted to All Parts of the United States

1. Why is American slaveholding in all cases not sinful?
Because its victims are *black*.

2. Why is gradual emancipation right?
Because the slaves are *black*.

3. Why is immediate emancipation wrong and dangerous?
Because the slaves are *black*.

4. Why ought one-sixth portion of the American population to be exiled from their native soil?
Because they are *black*.

5. Why would the slaves, if emancipated, cut the throats of their masters?
Because they are *black*.

6. Why are our slaves not fit for freedom?
Because they are *black*.

7. Why are American slaveholders not thieves, tyrants and men-stealers?
Because their victims are *black*.

8. Why does the Bible justify American slavery?
Because its victims are *black*.

9. Why ought not the Priest and the Levite, 'passing by on the other side,' to be sternly rebuked?
Because the man who has fallen among thieves, and lies weltering in his blood, is *black*.

10. Why are abolitionists fanatics, madmen and incendiaries?
Because those for whom they plead are *black*.

11. Why are they wrong in their principles and measures?
Because the slaves are *black*.

12. Why is all the prudence, moderation, judiciousness, philanthropy and piety on the side of their opponents?
Because the slaves are *black*.

From *The Liberator*, November 17, 1837.

13. Why ought not the free discussion of slavery to be tolerated?
Because its victims are *black*.

14. Why is Lynch law, as applied to abolitionists, better than common law?
Because the slaves, whom they seek to emancipate, are *black*.

15. Why are the slaves contented and happy?
Because they are *black*!

16. Why don't they want to be free?
Because they are *black*!

17. Why are they not created in the image of God?
Because their skin is *black*.

18. Why are they not cruelly treated, but enjoy unusual comforts and privileges?
Because they are *black*!

19. Why are they not our brethren and countrymen?
Because they are *black*.

20. Why is it unconstitutional to pity and defend them?
Because they are *black*.

21. Why is it a violation of the national compact to rebuke their masters?
Because they are *black*.

22. Why will they be lazy, improvident, and worthless, if set free?
Because their skin is *black*.

23. Why will the whites not wish to amalgamate with them in a state of freedom?
Because they are *black*!!

24. Why must the Union be dissolved, should Congress abolish slavery in the District of Columbia?
Because the slaves in that District are *black*.

25. Why are abolitionists justly treated as outlaws in one half of the Union?
Because those whose cause they espouse are *black*.

26. Why is slavery 'the corner-stone of our republican edifice'?
Because its victims are *black*.

We have thus given twenty-six replies to those who assail our principles and measures—that is, one reply, unanswerable and all-comprehensive, to all the cavils, complaints, criticisms, objections and difficulties which swarm in each State in the Union, against our holy enterprize. The victims are BLACK! 'That alters the case!' There is not an individual in all this country, who is not conscious before God, that if the slaves at the South should be to-day miraculously transformed into men of white complexions, to-morrow the abolitionists would be recognised and cheered as the best friends of their race; their principles would be eulogised as sound and incontrovertible, and their measures as rational and indispensable! Then, indeed, immediate emancipation would be the right of the slaves, and the duty of the masters!

Is it not so? Who has ever heard any complaints made against those who have denounced Turkish oppression, Russian oppression, or the oppression of our northern country in the times that tried men's souls? Everything may be done and said against those who enslave white men, and it is all very proper. But wo to those, who, in relation to human rights, will imitate God, and be no respector of men's complexions and persons! What does all this prove, but that the men who are so furiously assailing abolitionists and their sacred cause, (making all due allowance for those who know not what they do,) are the basest of hypocrites—the shameless enemies of men on account of their color—the libellers of the wisdom and goodness of God in the creation of man? In the hands of a just God we must leave them—but, unless they repent, and bring forth fruits meet for repentance, it shall be more tolerable for Sodom and Gomorrah in the day of judgment than for them—it were good for them that they had never been born.

Declaration of Sentiments Adopted by the Peace Convention

... Our country is the world, our countrymen are all mankind. We love the land of our nativity, only as we love all other lands. The interests, rights, liberties of American citizens are no more dear to us, than are those of the whole human race. Hence, we can allow no appeal to patriotism, to revenge any national insult or injury. The PRINCE OF PEACE, under whose stainless banner we rally, came not to destroy, but to save, even the worst of enemies. He has left us an example, that we should follow his steps. GOD COMMENDETH HIS LOVE TOWARD US, IN THAT WHILE WE WERE YET SINNERS, CHRIST DIED FOR US.

We conceive, that if a nation has no right to defend itself against foreign enemies, or to punish its invaders, no individual possesses that right in his own case. The unit cannot be of greater importance than the aggregate. If one man

From *The Liberator*, September 28, 1838.

may take life, to obtain or defend his rights, the same license must necessarily be granted to communities, states, and nations. If *he* may use a dagger or a pistol, *they* may employ cannon, bomb-shells, land and naval forces. The means of self-preservation must be in proportion to the magnitude of interests at stake, and the number of lives exposed to destruction. But if a rapacious and blood-thirsty soldiery, thronging these shores from abroad, with intent to commit rapine and destroy life, may not be resisted by the people or magistracy, then ought no resistance to be offered to domestic troublers of the public peace, or of private security. No obligation can rest upon Americans to regard foreigners as more sacred in their persons than themselves, or to give them a monopoly of wrong-doing with impunity.

The dogma, that all the governments of the world are approvingly ordained of God, and that THE POWERS THAT BE in the United States, in Russia, in Turkey, are in accordance with his will, is not less absurd than impious. It makes the impartial Author of human freedom and equality, unequal and tyrannical. It cannot be affirmed, that THE POWERS THAT BE, in any nation, are actuated by the spirit, or guided by the example of Christ, in the treatment of enemies: therefore, they cannot be agreeable to the will of God: and, therefore, their overthrow, by a spiritual regeneration of their subjects, is inevitable.

We register our testimony, not only against all wars, whether offensive or defensive, but all preparations for war; against every naval ship, every arsenal, every fortification; against the militia system and a standing army; against all military chieftains and soldiers; against all monuments commemorative of victory over a foreign foe, all trophies won in battle, all celebrations in honor of military or naval exploits; against all appropriations for the defence of a nation by force and arms, on the part of any legislative body; against every edict of government, requiring of its subjects military service. Hence, we deem it unlawful to bear arms, or to hold a military office.

As every human government is upheld by physical strength, and its laws are enforced virtually at the point of the bayonet, we cannot hold any office which imposes upon its incumbent the obligation to compel men to do right, on pain of imprisonment or death. We therefore voluntarily exclude ourselves from every legislative and judicial body, and repudiate all human politics, worldly honors, and stations of authority. If *we* cannot occupy a seat in the legislature, or on the bench, neither can we elect *others* to act as our substitutes in any such capacity.

It follows, that we cannot sue any man at law, to compel him by force to restore any thing which he may have wrongfully taken from us or others; but, if he has seized our coat, we shall surrender up our cloak, rather than subject him to punishment.

We believe that the penal code of the old covenant, AN EYE FOR AN EYE, AND A TOOTH FOR A TOOTH, has been abrogated by Jesus Christ; and that, under the new covenant, the forgiveness, instead of the punishment of enemies, has been enjoined upon all his disciples, in all cases whatsoever. To extort money from enemies, or set them upon a pillory, or cast them into prison, or hang them upon a gallows, is obviously not to forgive, but to take retribution. VENGEANCE IS MINE—I WILL REPAY, SAITH THE LORD.

The history of mankind is crowded with evidences, proving that physical coercion is not adapted to moral regeneration; that the sinful dispositions of man can be subdued only by love; that evil can be exterminated from the earth only by goodness; that it is not safe to rely upon an arm of flesh, upon man whose breath is in his nostrils, to preserve us from harm; that there is great security in being gentle, harmless, long-suffering, and abundant in mercy; that it is only the meek who shall inherit the earth, for the violent who resort to the sword are destined to perish with the sword. Hence, as a measure of sound policy,—of safety to property, life and liberty,—of public quietude and private enjoyment,—as well as on the ground of allegiance to HIM who is KING OF KINGS, and LORD OF LORDS,—we cordially adopt the non-resistance principle; being confident that it provides for all possible consequences, will ensure all things needful to us, is armed with omnipotent power, and must ultimately triumph over every assailing force.

We advocate no jacobinical doctrines. The spirit of jacobinism is the spirit of retaliation, violence, and murder. It neither fears God, nor regards man. *We* would be filled with spirit of CHRIST. If we abide by our principles, it is impossible for us to be disorderly, or plot treason, or participate in any evil work: we shall submit to every ordinance of man, FOR THE LORD'S SAKE; obey all the requirements of government, except such as we deem contrary to the commands of the gospel; and in no case resist the operation of law, except by meekly submitting to the penalty of disobedience.

But, while we shall adhere to the doctrine of non-resistance, and passive submission to enemies, we purpose, in a moral and spiritual sense, to speak and act boldly in the cause of God; to assail iniquity, in high places and in low places; to apply our principles to all existing civil, political, legal, and ecclesiastical institutions; and to hasten the time, when the kingdoms of this world will have become the kingdoms of our LORD and of his CHRIST, and he shall reign for ever. . . .

A Farce in One Act*

... the *republican* character of the antislavery cause, which allows persons of both sexes, and of all classes and complexions—farmers, mechanics, workingmen, 'niggers,' women, and all—to stand on the same platform, and enjoy the same rights and privileges, to have the same freedom of speech and an equal amount of controlling power, has been from the beginning vulgar and odious in the eyes of chief priest, scribe and pharisee, those who are ever grasping for power, place, emolument. The true secret of the wonderful progress of our cause, aside from its intrinsic excellence, has been the entrusting of its management to THE PEOPLE—the bone and muscle of community—the unambitious, unaspiring, courageous, disinterested, true-hearted friends of bleeding humanity. . . .

On the Execution of John Brown**

... Was John Brown justified in his attempt? Yes, if Washington was in his; if Warren and Hancock were in theirs. If men are justified in striking a blow for freedom, when the question is one of a threepenny tax on tea, then, I say, they are a thousand times more justified, when it is to save fathers, mothers, wives and children from the slave-coffle and the auction-block, and to restore to them their God-given rights. (Loud applause.) Was John Brown justified in interfering in behalf of the slave population of Virginia, to secure their freedom and independence? Yes, if LaFayette was justified in interfering to help our revolutionary fathers If Kosciusko, if Pulaski, if Steuben, if De Kalb, if all who joined them from abroad were justified in that act, then John Brown was incomparably more so. If you believe in the right of assisting men to fight for freedom who are of your own color—(God knows nothing of color or complexion—human rights know nothing of these distinctions)—then you must cover, not only with a mantle of charity, but with the admiration of your hearts, the effort of John Brown at Harper's Ferry. I am trying him by the American standard; and I hesitate not to say, with all deliberation, that those who are attempting to decry him are dangerous members of the community; they are those in whom the love

*From *The Liberator,* June 21, 1839.

**From *The Liberator,* December 16, 1859. Garrison had delivered this speech at a meeting in Tremont Temple, Boston, on December 2.

of liberty has died out; they are the lineal descendants of the tories of the Revolution, only a great deal worse. (Applause.) If the spirit of '76 prevailed to-day, as it did at that period, it would make the soil of the Commonwealth too hot to hold them. . . .

. . . A word upon the subject of Peace. I am a non-resistant—a believer in the inviolability of human life, under all circumstances; I, therefore, in the name of God, disarm John Brown, and every slave at the South. But I do not stop there; if I did, I should be a monster. I also disarm, in the name of God, every slaveholder and tyrant in the world. (Loud applause.) For wherever that principle is adopted, all fetters must instantly melt, and there can be no oppressed, and no oppressor, in the nature of things. How many agree with me in regard to the doctrine of the inviolability of human life? How many non-resistants are there here to-night? (A single voice—'I.') There is *one*! (Laughter.) Well, then, you who are otherwise are not the men to point the finger at John Brown, and cry 'traitor'—judging you by your own standard. (Applause.) Nevertheless, I am a non-resistant, and I not only desire, but have labored unremittingly to effect the peaceful abolition of slavery, by an appeal to the reason and conscience of the slaveholder; yet, as a peace man—an 'ultra' peace man—I am prepared to say, 'Success to every slave insurrection at the South, and in every slave country.' (Enthusiastic applause.) And I do not see how I compromise or stain my peace profession in making that declaration. Whenever there is a contest between the oppressed and the oppressor,—the weapons being equal between the parties,— God knows that my heart must be with the oppressed, and always against the oppressor. Therefore, whenever commence, I cannot but wish success to all slave insurrections. (Loud applause.) I thank God when men who believe in the right and duty of wielding carnal weapons are so far advanced that they will take those weapons out of the scale of despotism, and throw them into the scale of freedom. It is an indication of progress, and a positive moral growth; it is one way to get up to the sublime platform of non-resistance; and it is God's method of dealing retribution upon the head of the tyrant. Rather than see men wearing their chains in a cowardly and servile spirit, I would, as an advocate of peace, much rather see them breaking the head of the tyrant with their chains. Give me, as a non-resistant, Bunker Hill, and Lexington, and Concord, rather than the cowardice and servility of a Southern slave plantation. . . .

eugene v debs

Among the famous activists in the history of the American labor movement, Eugene V. Debs stands as a unique and, in some ways, tragic figure. In an era when craft unions were developing power, he sought the organization of laboring men according to industry, rather than craft, thereby improving the economic conditions of the unskilled as well as the skilled workers. Beginning in the 1890's, when men such as Samuel Gompers won better wages, better working conditions, and collective bargaining for skilled craftsmen in the American Federation of Labor, Debs fought frustrating battles for the solidarity of all workingmen. Gompers, the pragmatist, cooperated with American capitalism; Debs, the socialist dreamer, raged against it.

Born in Terre Haute, Indiana, in 1855 to parents who had come to America from Alsace six years earlier, Debs spent his boyhood years in Indiana. He attended school until the age of fifteen, when he took a job with the railroad. First in the railroad shops, and later as a locomotive fireman, he observed the weakness of labor's power. At the age of nineteen he became a grocery store clerk, although his enthusiasm for organizing the railroad workers continued. Becoming secretary of Terre Haute's new lodge of the Brotherhood of Locomotive Firemen, he continued to focus his tremendous energies on improving their status: in 1878 he became associate editor of the *Firemen's Magazine* and, two years later, editor and secretary-treasurer for the national Brotherhood.

In the year 1885 he married Katherine Metzel and in the same year was elected to the Indiana legislature. Continuing to work for the Brotherhood, he urged the formation of the American Railway Union in 1893, and became its first president. When the Pullman Company workers in Chicago went on strike in 1894, they appealed to the Union for a sympathy strike, and, though Debs opposed the move, the Union in convention answered the appeal and ordered a boycott on moving Pullman cars. Federal authorities and troops were ordered into Chicago to keep the mail moving. The inevitable confrontation resulted in a federal charge of conspiracy to obstruct the mails, and Debs was arrested on July 10, and again one week later, for contempt of court in violating the injunction. Debs' appeal to Gompers and the Federation for support during the strike was turned down.

Convicted on the second charge, Debs was sentenced to six months in jail in 1895, the beginning of the four years he would spend in prison during his lifetime. Reading in his jail cell and reflecting on the plight of labor, especially the bitter experiences of the Pullman Strike, Debs became an avowed Socialist. In 1897 he merged the A.R.U. into the Social Democratic Party of America. Three years later, as the Socialist candidate for President, he campaigned on a platform of revolution—the overthrow of the capitalist system, replacing the wage system with cooperative sharing. Calling for the emancipation of the working class, Debs bent over the edge of the stage, thundered against the capitalist system, and shook his finger at the injustice in American society. His fame and oratory brought him almost 100,000 votes in the election of 1900.

During the years which followed, Debs vigorously described the injustices in American life which blacks and other members of the working class suffered. Demanding death to wage slavery, he campaigned for President again in 1904, and received 400,000 votes. As editor of the *Appeal to Reason*, a socialist weekly in Girard, Kansas, he wrote and lectured on the evils in American society including that of war, abuses in child labor, and the unfair treatment of women. Repeatedly he urged his audiences to develop self-reliance, and he warned them against becoming too dependent on leadership: as long as they could be led by an individual, they would be betrayed by an individual.

A presidential candidate in 1908 and 1912 for the Socialist Party, he gained popularity during these years of social ferment, and in the latter year he received 900,000 votes. He was opposed to American entry into World War I, and de-nounced the action. At the Socialist state convention in Canton, Ohio, on June 16, 1918, he attacked as oppressive the federal government's actions in finding certain Socialist critics of the war together with leaders of the Industrial Workers of the World guilty of sedition. Because of the speech, Debs was charged with violation of the Espionage Act, and was sentenced to ten years' imprisonment.

While in the penitentiary in Atlanta, he became for the fifth time the Socialist candidate for President and this time received more than 900,000 votes.

President Warren G. Harding granted him a pardon in December 1921, though his citizenship was withheld. In the following years, in poor health, he wrote on prison conditions, and became editor of *American Appeal*, a national Socialist weekly. His appeals to reason ended when he died in a sanitarium near Chicago in 1926.

Outlook For Socialism in the United States

... What the workingmen of the country are profoundly interested in is the private ownership of the means of production and distribution, the enslaving and degrading wage-system in which they toil for a pittance at the pleasure of their masters and are bludgeoned, jailed or shot when they protest—this is the central, controlling, vital issue of the hour, and neither of the old party platforms has a word or even a hint about it.

... The working class must get rid of the whole brood of masters and exploiters, and put themselves in possession and control of the means of production, that they may have steady employment without consulting a capitalist employer, large or small, and that they may get the wealth their labor produces, every bit of it, and enjoy with their families the fruits of their industry in comfortable and happy homes, abundant and wholesome food, proper clothing and all other things necessary to "life, liberty and the pursuit of happiness." It is therefore a question, not of "reform," the mask of fraud, but of revolution. The capitalist system must be overthrown, the class-rule abolished and wage-slavery supplanted by co-operative industry.

... The differences between the Republican and Democratic parties involve no issue, no principle in which the working class has any interest, and whether the spoils be distributed by Hanna and Platt, or by Croker and Tammany Hall is all the same to them.

Between these parties socialists have no choice, no preference. They are one in their opposition to socialism, that is to say, the emancipation of the working class from wage-slavery, and every workingman who has intelligence enough to understand the interest of his class and the nature of the struggle in which it is

From *The International Socialist Review*, I (September 1900), pp. 133, 134.

involved, will once and for all time sever his relations with them both; and recognizing the class-struggle which is being waged between producing workers and non-producing capitalists, cast his lot with the class-conscious, revolutionary, socialist party, which is pledged to abolish the capitalist system, class-rule, and wage-slavery—a party which does not compromise or fuse, but, preserving inviolate the principles which quickened it into life and now give it vitality and force, moves forward with dauntless determination to the goal of economic freedom. . . .

The Negro in the Class Struggle

. . . The history of the negro in the United States is a history of crime without a parallel.

Why should the white man hate him? Because he stole him from his native land and for two centuries and a half robbed him of the fruit of his labor, kept him in beastly ignorance and subjected him to the brutal domination of the lash? Because, he tore the black child from the breast of its mother and ravished the black man's daughter before her father's eyes?

There are thousands of negroes who bear testimony in their whitening skins that men who so furiously resent the suggestion of "social equality" are far less sensitive in respect to the sexual equality of the races.

But of all the senseless agitation in capitalist society, that in respect to "social equality" takes the palm. The very instant it is mentioned the old aristocratic plantation owner's shrill cry about the "buck nigger" marrying the "fair young daughter" of his master is heard from the tomb and echoed and re-echoed across the spaces and repeated by the "white trash" in proud vindication of their social superiority.

Social equality, forsooth! Is the black man pressing his claims for social recognition upon his white burden bearer? Is there any reason why he should? Is the white man's social recognition of his own white brother such as to excite the negro's ambition to covet the noble prize? Has the negro any greater desire, or is there any reason why he should have, for social intercourse with the white man than the white man has for social relations with the negro? This phase of the negro question is pure fraud and serves to mask the real issue, which is not *social equality*, BUT ECONOMIC FREEDOM.

From *The International Socialist Review*, IV (November 1903), pp. 258-259.

There never was any social inferiority that was not the shrivelled fruit of economic inequality.

The negro, given economic freedom, will not ask the white man any social favors; and the burning question of "social equality" will disappear like mist before the sunrise.

I have said and say again that, properly speaking, there is no negro question outside of the labor question—the working class struggle. Our position as socialists and as a party is perfectly plain. We have simply to say: "The class struggle is colorless." The capitalists, white, black and other shades, are on one side and the workers, white, black and all other colors, on the other side.

When Marx said: "Workingmen of all countries unite," he gave concrete expression to the socialist philosophy of the class struggle; unlike the framers of the declaration of independence who announced that "all men are created equal" and then basely repudiated their own doctrine, Marx issued the call to all the workers of the globe, regardless of race, sex, creed, or any other condition whatsoever.

As a socialist party we receive the negro and all other races upon absolutely equal terms. We are the party of the working class, the whole working class, and we will not suffer ourselves to be divided by any specious appeal to race prejudice; and if we should be coaxed or driven from the straight road we will be lost in the wilderness and ought to perish there, for we shall no longer be a socialist party.

Let the capitalist press and capitalist "public opinion" indulge themselves in alternate flattery and abuse of the negro; we as socialists will receive him in our party, treat him in our counsels and stand by him all around the same as if his skin were white instead of black; and this we do, not from any considerations of sentiment, but because it accords with the philosophy of the class struggle, and is eternally right and bound to triumph in the end. . . .

The Socialist Party and the Working Class

. . . There has never been a free people, a civilized nation, a real republic on this earth. Human society always consisted of masters and slaves, and the slaves have

From *The International Socialist Review*, V (September 1904), pp. 129-132, 140-142. Debs, as presidential candidate of the Socialist Party, delivered this opening address in Indianapolis, Indiana, September 1, 1904.

always been and are today, the foundation stones of the social fabric.

Wage-labor is but a name; wage-slavery is a fact.

The twenty-five millions of wage-workers in the United States are twenty-five millions of twentieth century slaves.

This is the plain meaning of what is known as

THE LABOR MARKET

And the labor market follows the capitalist flag.

The most barbarous fact in all christendom is the labor market. The mere term sufficiently expresses the animalism of commercial civilization.

They who buy and they who sell in the labor market are alike dehumanized by the inhuman traffic in the brains and blood and bones of human beings.

The labor market is the foundation of so-called civilized society. Without these shambles, without this commerce in human life, this sacrifice of manhood and womanhood, this barter of babes, this sale of souls, the capitalist civilizations of all lands and all climes would crumble to ruin and perish from the earth.

Twenty-five millions of wage-slaves are bought and sold daily at prevailing prices in the American Labor Market.

This is the

PARAMOUNT ISSUE

in the present national campaign.

Let me say at the very threshold of this discussion that the workers have but the one issue in this campaign, the overthrow of the capitalist system and the emancipation of the working class from wage-slavery.

The capitalists may have the tariff, finance, imperialism and other dust-covered and moth-eaten issues entirely to themselves.

The rattle of these relics no longer deceives workingmen whose heads are on their shoulders.

. . . The capitalist class is represented by the Republican, Democratic, Populist and Prohibition parties, all of which stand for private ownership of the means of production and the triumph of any one of which will mean continued wage-slavery to the working class.

As the Populist and Prohibition sections of the capitalist party represent minority elements which propose to reform the capitalist system without disturbing wage-slavery, a vain and impossible task, they will be omitted from this discussion with all the credit due the rank and file for their good intentions.

The Republican and Democratic parties, or, to be more exact, the Republican-Democratic party, represents the capitalist class in the class struggle. They are the political wings of the capitalist system and such differences as arise between them relate to spoils and not to principles.

With either of these parties in power one thing is always certain and that is that the capitalist class are in the saddle and the working class under the saddle.

Under the administration of both these parties the means of production are private property, production is carried forward for capitalist profit purely, markets are glutted and industry paralyzed, workingmen become tramps and criminals while injunctions, soldiers and riot guns are brought into action to preserve "law and order" in the chaotic carnival of capitalistic anarchy.

... The Socialist party stands squarely upon its proletarian principles and relies wholly upon the forces of industrial progress and the education of the working class.

The Socialist party buys no votes and promises no offices. Not a farthing is spent for whisky or cigars. Every penny in the campaign fund is the voluntary offering of workers and their sympathizers and every penny is used for education.

What other parties can say the same?

Ignorance alone stands in the way of socialist success. The capitalist parties understand this and use their resources to prevent the workers from seeing the light.

Intellectual darkness is essential to industrial slavery.

Capitalist parties stand for Slavery and Night.

The Socialist party is the herald of Freedom and Light.

Capitalist parties cunningly contrive to divide the workers upon dead issues.

The Socialist party is uniting them upon the living issues:

Death to Wage Slavery!

When industrial slavery is as dead as the issues of the Siamese capitalist parties the Socialist party will have fulfilled its mission and enriched history.

... The Socialist party is not, and does not pretend to be, a capitalist party. It does not ask, nor does it expect the votes of the capitalist class. Such capitalists as do support it do so seeing the approaching doom of the capitalist system and with a full understanding that the Socialist party is not a capitalist party, nor a middle class party, but a revolutionary working class party, whose historic mission is to conquer capitalism on the political battle-field, take control of the government and through the public powers take possession of the means of wealth production, abolish wage-slavery and emancipate all workers and all humanity.

The people are as capable of achieving their industrial freedom as they were to secure their political liberty and both are necessary to a free nation.

The capitalist system is no longer adapted to the needs of modern society. It is outgrown and fetters the forces of progress. Industrial and commercial competition are largely of the past. The handwriting blazes on the wall. Centralization and combination are the modern forces in industrial and commercial life. Competition is breaking down, and co-operation is supplanting it.

The hand tools of early times are used no more. Mammoth machines have taken their places. A few thousand capitalists own them and many millions of workingmen use them.

All the wealth the vast army of labor produces above its subsistence is taken by the machine owning capitalists, who also own the land and the mills, the factories, railroads and mines, the forests and fields and all other means of production and transportation.

Hence wealth and poverty, millionaires and beggars, castles and caves, luxury and squalor, painted parasites on the boulevard and painted poverty among the red lights.

Hence strikes, boycotts, riots, murder, suicide, insanity, prostitution on a fearful and increasing scale.

The capitalist parties can do nothing. They are a part, an iniquitous part of the foul and decaying system.

There is no remedy for the ravages of death.

Capitalism is dying and its extremities are already decomposing. The blotches upon the surface show that the blood no longer circulates. The time is near when the cadaver will have to be removed and the atmosphere purified.

In contrast with the Republican and Democratic conventions, where politicians were the puppets of plutocracy, the convention of the Socialist party consisted of working men and women fresh from their labors, strong, clean, wholesome, self-reliant, ready to do and dare for the cause of labor, the cause of humanity.

. . . These are stirring days for living men. The day of crisis is drawing near and socialists are exerting all their power to prepare the people for it.

The old order of society can survive but little longer. Socialism is next in order. The swelling minority sounds warning of the impending change. Soon that minority will be the majority and then will come the co-operative commonwealth.

Every workingman should rally to the standard of his class and hasten the full-orbed day of freedom.

Every progressive democrat must find his way in our direction and if he will but free himself from prejudice and study the principles of socialism he will soon be a sturdy supporter of our party.

Every sympathizer with labor, every friend of justice, every lover of humanity should support the Socialist party as the only party that is organized to abolish industrial slavery, the prolific source of the giant evils that afflict the people.

. . . The overthrow of capitalism is the object of the Socialist party. It will not fuse with any other party and it would rather die than compromise.

The Socialist party comprehends the magnitude of its task and has the patience of preliminary defeat and the faith of ultimate victory.

The working class must be emancipated by the working class.

Woman must be given her true place in society by the working class.

Child labor must be abolished by the working class.

Society must be reconstructed by the working class.

The working class must be employed by the working class.

The fruits of labor must be enjoyed by the working class.

War, bloody war, must be ended by the working class.

These are the principles and objects of the Socialist party and we fearlessly proclaim them to our fellowmen.

We know our cause is just and that it must prevail.

With faith and hope and courage we hold our heads erect and with dauntless spirit marshal the working class for the march from Capitalism to Socialism, from Slavery to Freedom, from Barbarism to Civilization.

Revolutionary Unionism

... The average workingman imagines that he must have a leader to look to; a guide to follow, right or wrong. He has been taught in the craft union that he is a very dependent creature; that without a leader the goblins would get him without a doubt, and he therefore instinctively looks to his leader. And even while he is looking at his leader there is someone else looking at the same leader from the other side.

You have depended too much on that leader and not enough on yourself. I don't want you to follow me. I want you to cultivate self-reliance.

If I have the slightest capacity for leadership I can only give evidence of it by leading you to rely on yourselves.

As long as you can be led by an individual you will be betrayed by an individual. That does not mean that all leaders are dishonest or corrupt. I make no such sweeping indictment. I know that many of them are honest. I know also that many of them are in darkness themselves, blind leaders of the blind. That is the worst that can be said of them. And let me say to you that the most dangerous leader is not the corrupt leader, but the honest, ignorant leader. That leader is just as fatal to your interests as the one who deliberately sells you out for a paltry consideration.

You are a workingman! Now, at your earliest leisure look yourself over and

From Eugene V. Debs, *Debs: His Life, Writings and Speeches*, Appeal to Reason, Girard, Kansas, 1908, pp. 433-434, 435-436, 439, 441-442. Debs made this speech in Chicago, November 25, 1905.

take an inventory of your resources. Invoice your mental stock; see what you have on hand.

You may be of limited mentality; and that is all you require in the capitalist system. You need only small brains, but huge hands.

Most of your hands are calloused and you are taught by the capitalist politician, who is the political mercenary of the capitalist who fleeces you, you are taught by him to be proud of your horny hands. If that is true he ought to be ashamed of his. He doesn't have any horns on his hands. He has them on his brain. He is as busy with his brain as you are with your hands, and because he is busy with his brain and you neglect yours, he gets a goodly share of what you produce with your hands. He is the gentleman who calls you the horny handed sons of toil. That fetches you every time. I tell you that the time has come for you to use your brains in your own interest, and until you do that you will have to use your hands in the interest of your masters.

Now, after you have looked yourself over; after you have satisfied yourself what you are, or rather, what you are not, you will arrive at the conclusion that as a wage worker in capitalist society you are not a man at all. You are simply a thing. And that thing is bought in the labor market, just as hair, hides and other forms of merchandise are bought.

When the capitalist requires the use of your hands, does he call for men? Why, certainly not. He doesn't want men, he only wants hands. And when he calls for hands, that is what he wants. Have you ever seen a placard posted: "Fifty hands wanted"? Did you ever know of a capitalist to respond to that kind of invitation?

. . . Observe that you are displaced by the surplus product of your own labor; that what you produce is of more value under capitalism than you who produce it; that the commodity which is the result of your labor is of greater value under capitalism than your own life. You consist of palpitating flesh; you have wants. You have necessities. You cannot satisfy them, and you suffer. But the product of your labor, the property of the capitalist, that is sacred; that must be protected at all hazards. After you have been displaced by the surplus product of your labor and you have been idle long enough, you become restive and you begin to speak out, and you become a menace. The unrest culminates in trouble. The capitalist presses a button and the police are called into action. Then the capitalist presses button No. 2 and injunctions are issued by the judges, and judicial allies and servants of the capitalist class. Then button No. 3 is pressed and the state troops fall into line; and if this is not sufficient button No. 4 is pressed and the regular soldiers come marching to the scene. That is what President Roosevelt meant when he said that back of the mayor is the governor, back of the governor the President; or, to use his own words, back of the city, the state, and back of the state the nation—the capitalist nation.

If you have been working in a steel mill and you have made more steel than your master can sell, and you are locked out and get hungry, and the soldiers are called out, it is to protect the steel and shoot you who made the steel—to guard the men who steal the steel and kill the men who made it.

. . . I have said and say again that no strike was ever lost; that it has always been worth all it cost. An essential part of a workingman's education is the defeats he encounters. The strikes he loses are after all the only ones he wins. I am heartily glad for myself that I lost the strike. It is the best thing that ever happened to me. I lost the strike of the past that I may win the strike of the future.

I am a discredited labor leader, but I have good staying qualities. The very moment the capitalist press credits me with being a wise labor leader, I will invite you to investigate me upon the charge of treason. I am discredited by the capitalist simply because I am true to his victim. I don't want his favors. I do not court his approbation. I would not have it. I can't afford it. If I had his respect it would be at the price of my own.

I don't care anything about what is called public opinion. I know precisely what that means. It is but the reflect of the interests of the capitalist class. As between the respect of the public and my own, I prefer my own; and I am going to keep it until I can have both.

When I pick up a capitalist newspaper and read a eulogy of some labor leader, I know that that leader has at least two afflictions; the one is mental weakness and the other is moral cowardice—and they go together. Put it down that when the capitalist who is exploiting you credits your leader with being safe and conservative and wise, that leader is not serving you.

. . . Whatever may be said of the ignorant, barbarous past, there is no excuse for poverty today. And yet it is the scourge of the race. It is the Nemesis of capitalist civilization. Ten millions, one-eighth of our whole population, are in a state of chronic poverty. Three millions of these have been sunk to unresisting pauperism. The whole working class is in a sadly dependent state, and even the most favored wage-worker is left suspended by a single thread. He does not know what hour a machine may be invented to make his trade useless, displace him and throw him into the increasing army of the unemployed.

. . . Prostitution is a part, a necessary part, of capitalist society. The department store empties in the slums.

I have been here enough to know that when the daughter of a workingman is obliged to go up the street to look for employment, when she is fourteen or fifteen years of age, and ought to be in the care and keeping of a loving mother, and have all of the advantages that our civilization makes possible for all—when she is forced to go to a department store, to one of those capitalist emporiums, and there find a place, if she can, and work for a wage of $3 a week, and have to obey a code of cast iron regulations, appear tidy and neatly dressed and be subject to a thousand temptations daily, and then takes a misstep, the first, as she is more than apt to do, especially is she has no home in any decent sense of that term—the very instant this is added to her poverty, she is doomed—damned. All the doors of capitalist society are closed in her face. The coals of contumely are poured upon her head. There is for her no redemption, and she takes the next step, and the next, until at last she ends a disgraceful career in a brothel hell.

This may be your child. And if you are a workingman, and this should fall to the lot of the innocent blue-eyed child that you love more than you do your own life—I want you to realize that if such a horror be written in the book of fate, that you are responsible for it, if you use or misuse your power to perpetuate the capitalist system and working class slavery.

You can change this condition—not tomorrow, not next week, nor next year; but in the meantime the next thing to changing it is making up your mind that it shall be changed. . . .

Revolution

This is the first and only International Labor Day. It belongs to the working class and is dedicated to the Revolution.

Today the slaves of all the world are taking a fresh breath in the long and weary march; pausing a moment to clear their lungs and shout for joy; celebrating in festal fellowship their coming Freedom.

. . . Slavery, even the most abject—dumb and despairing as it may seem—has yet its inspiration. Crushed it may be, but extinguished never. Chain the slave as you will, O Masters, brutalize him as you may, yet in his soul, though dead, he yearns for freedom still.

The great discovery the modern slaves have made is that they themselves their freedom must achieve. This is the secret of their solidarity; the heart of their hope; the inspiration that nerves them all with sinews of steel.

They are still in bondage, but no longer cower;

From Eugene V. Debs, *Debs: His Life, Writings and Speeches*, pp. 305-306. The essay was originally published in the *New Yorker*, April 27, 1907.

No longer grovel in the dust,

But stand erect like men.

Concious of their growing power the future holds out to them her out-stretched hands.

As the slavery of the working class is international, so the movement for its emancipation.

The salutation of slave to slave this day is repeated in every human tongue as it goes ringing round the world.

The many millions are at last awakening. For countless ages they have suffered; drained to the dregs the bitter cup of misery and woe.

At last, at last the historic limitation has been reached, and soon a new sun will light the world.

Red is the life-tide of our common humanity and red our symbol of universal kinship.

Tyrants deny it; fear it; tremble with rage and terror when they behold it.

We reaffirm it and on this day pledge anew our fidelity—come life or death—to the blood-red Banner of the Revolution.

Socialist greetings this day to all our fellow-workers! To the god-like souls in Russia marching grimly, sublimely into the jaws of hell with the Song of the Revolution in their death-rattle; to the Orient, the Occident and all the Isles of the Sea!

VIVE LA REVOLUTION!

The most heroic word in all languages is REVOLUTION.

It thrills and vibrates; cheers and inspires. Tyrants and time-servers fear it, but the oppressed hail it with joy.

The throne trembles when this throbbing word is lisped, but to the hovel it is food for the famishing and hope for the victims of despair.

Let us glorify today the revolutions of the past and hail the Greater Revolution yet to come before Emancipation shall make all the days of the year May Days of peace and plenty for the sons and daughters of toil. . . .

War and the Working Class

. . . They tell us we live in a great Republic; our institutions are Democratic; we are a free people (*laughter*). This is too much, even as a joke (*laughter*). It is not a subject for levity; it is an exceedingly serious matter.

From Eugene V. Debs, *The Debs White Book*, Girard, Kansas, (n.d.), pp. 11, 19-20, 22-23, 28, 30.

To whom do the Wall Street junkers in our country—to whom do they marry their daughters? After they have wrung the countless hundreds of millions from your sweat, your agony, your life-blood, in a time of war as well as a time of peace, they invest these billions and millions in the purchase of titles of broken-down aristocrats, and to buy counts of no-account (*laughter*). Are they satisfied to wed their daughters to honest working men? (*Shouts from the crowd: "No."*) to real democrats? Oh, no. They scour the markets of Europe for fellows who have titles and nothing else (*laughter*). And they swap their millions for the titles; so that matrimony, with them, becomes entirely a matter of money (*laughter*), literally so.

These very gentry, who are today wrapped up in the American flag, who make the claim that they are only patriots, who have their magnifying glasses in hand, who are scanning the country for some evidence of disloyalty, so eager, so ready to apply the brand to the men who dare to even whisper opposition to junker rule in the United States. No wonder Johnson said that "Patriotism is the last refuge of scoundrels." He had the Wall Street gentry in mind, or their proto-types, at least; for in every age it has been the tyrant who has wrapped himself in the cloak of patriotism, or religion, or both (*shouts of "good, good," from the crowd*) (*applause*).

They would have you believe that the Socialist party consists, in the main, of disloyalists and traitors. It is true, in a certain sense. We are disloyalists and traitors to the real traitors of this nation (*applause*).

. . . The master class has always declared the war; the subject class has always fought the battles; the master class has had all to gain, nothing to lose, and the subject class has had nothing to gain and all to lose including their lives (*applause*). They have always taught you that it is your patriotic duty to go to war and to have yourselves slaughtered at a command. But in all of the histories of the world you, the people, never had a voice in declaring war. You have never yet had! And here let me state a fact—and it cannot be repeated too often: the working class who fight the battles, the working class who make the sacrifices, the working class who shed the blood, the working class who furnish the corpses, the working class have never yet had a voice in declaring war. The working class have never yet had a voice in making peace. It is the ruling class that does both. They declare war; they make peace. *"Yours not to ask the question why; Yours but to do and die."*

That is the motto, and we object on the part of the awakened workers.

If war is right, let it be declared by the people—you, who have your lives to lose; you certainly ought to have the right to declare war, if you consider a war necessary (*applause*).

. . . I went to Warren [Ohio] some years ago. It happened to be at the time that President McKinley was assassinated. In common with all others, I deplored that tragic event. There is not a Socialist, who would have been guilty of that crime. We do not attack individuals. We don't wreak our vengence upon any individual opposed to our faith. We have no fight with individuals. We are capable of teaching those who hate us (*applause*). We do not hate them; we know better; we would hand them a cup of water, if they needed it (*applause*). There is not any room in our heart for hate, except for a system—a system in which it is possible for one man to achieve a tremendous fortune doing nothing, while millions upon millions suffer and struggle and agonize and die for the bare necessities of life (*applause*).

. . . You are in the crucible today, Mr. Socialist. You are going to be tried, to what extent no one knows. If you are weak-fibred, that weakness will be sought out, and located. And if, through that weakness, you are conquered, you may be driven out of the Socialist movement. We will have to bid good-bye to you. You are not the stuff of which Revolutionists are made. We are sorry for you (*applause*), unless you happen to be an intellectual. The intellectuals, a good many of them, are already gone. No—no loss on our side, nor any gain on theirs.

. . . They [capitalist leaders] are talking about your patriotic duty. Among other things, they are advising you to cultivate war gardens—cultivate a war garden. While they are doing this, a government war report shows that practically 52 percent of the arable tillable soil is held out of use by the profiteers, by the land manipulators—held out of use. They, themselves, do not cultivate it. They could not if they would. They don't allow others to cultivate it; they keep it idle to enrich themselves; to pocket the hundreds of dollars of unearned increment. Who is it that makes their land valuable while it is fenced in and kept out of use? It is the people. Who pockets this tremendous value? The landlords. Who is the patriot? And while we are upon the subject, I want you to think upon the term "landlord." Landlord. Lord of the land? This lord of the land is a great patriot. This lord, who professionally owns the earth, tells you that he is fighting to make the world safe for Democracy—he, who shuts all humanity out—and he who profiteers at the expense of the people who have been slain by multiplied thousands, under the pretense of being the great patriot he is—he, who is your arch-enemy; he it is that you need to wipe from power (*applause*). It is he, it is he that is a menace to your loyalty and your liberty far more than the Prussian junker on the other side of the Atlantic ocean (*applause*). Fifty-two percent, according to their own figures. They tell you that there is a shortage of flour, and that you need to produce. We have got to save wheat that we can export more wheat for the soldiers who fight on the other side, while half of your tillable soil is held out of use by the profiteers. What do you think of that?

emma goldman

A nervous young woman, twenty-four years old, addressed an audience of thousands of unemployed workers in New York City's Union Square in August 1893. Tensions ran very high because of the industrial crisis. She continued her bitter attack on the political and economic conditions in the United States. In harsh language she described the State as the pillar of capitalism; Fifth Avenue as an avenue of gold lined by vast mansions of power; and the people's potential as a powerful giant. Ending her emotional address with the exhortation that if they were denied work and bread, they should take the bread, she received a storm of applause. Within weeks she was charged and convicted by authorities for inciting to riot, and sentenced to one year in jail. Another in a series of unusual experiences began for the young woman, Emma Goldman, later known as the "mother of American anarchy" and "Red Emma," who had come to the United States almost eight years earlier.

She was born in 1869 in Kovno, Lithuania, then part of the Russian empire, to Jewish parents. Part of her childhood was spent in Kurland province, where her father had a minor government position, and she witnessed the power of the wealthy whose sons were spared military service, while the poor were conscripted. Moreover, she felt the prejudice attached to being Jewish and a woman. At the age of seven she went to Königsberg, Prussia, to live with her grandmother and to attend school. A short time later, her parents moved there, and

Emma continued on with her schooling and also received private lessons in French and music, benefits of her middle-class life.

1882 was a critical year for her because the family moved to St. Petersburg, where her father had earlier taken a job as manager of a cousin's dry-goods store; however, shortly before the family arrived, the business failed. Emma had to take a job knitting shawls to support the family, and later worked in a cousin's glove factory which employed six hundred workers. The dreary work days turned into weeks and months, and she felt the wrath of her father when she sought to continue her lessons in French literature. Eager to escape from her hostile home environment, she begged and received her parents' permission to join her half-sister, who had gone to Rochester, New York, several years earlier.

Arriving in New York in early 1886, the young idealist began working in a Rochester clothing factory, and joined a German socialist group. The beautiful visions of the America that she had imagined in Russia turned bitter as she witnessed the brutal working conditions in the factories. Moreover, Puritan America depressed and almost suffocated her spirits. The Haymarket Riot and the trial which followed angered and depressed her still further. A brief marriage to Jacob Kershner ended in divorce. Soon after, she moved to New York City to be near the anarchist group led by Johann Most, whose paper, *Die Freiheit*, she had read avidly and admired. Her friendship with anarchists such as Most and Alexander Berkman (who was later imprisoned for an attempt on the life on Henry Frick) thrust her deeply into radical activities. Most taught her how to give public lectures on anarchism and urged her to be bold and arrogant on the platform.

The anarchist Benjamin R. Tucker, in his book *Instead of a Book by a Man Too Busy to Write One* published in 1893, castigated Most for failing to disown certain persons who as pseudo-anarchists had preyed on innocent people. He charged that a large number of members of the Social Revolutionary Club and the German Group of the International Working People's Association in New York City were in effect criminals because they taught others to take wealth regardless of circumstances. These pseudo-anarchists urged their friends to " . . . use dynamite, the dagger, or the torch to take it; kill innocent people to take it; but, at all events, take it." Insuring tenement houses and then setting fire to them in order to collect insurance became fashionable among these men in the mid 1880's. Innocent people died in those fires. Though Most refused to repudiate these human scavengers, Justus Schwab did and earned Most's condemnation. Schwab, labeled disloyal, resigned from the staff of *Die Freiheit*. By 1893, Emma had abandoned her intense allegiance to Most and endorsed Schwab's view of responsible anarchy.

After her own prison sentence, noted above, ended in 1894, Emma continued to lecture in America and in Europe where she met Peter Kropotkin. Famous and infamous on the public platform, she shouted out against the evils of wage slavery and the brutality of the American government. She favored voluntary cooperation among all people, and agreed with Proudhon's view of liberty as "not the Daughter, but the Mother of Order." She founded a monthly anarchist journal, *Mother Earth*, in 1906, and published several books including *Anarchism and Other Essays* (1910). Also advocating birth control, pacifism, and prison reform, she heightened the social ferment and social consciousness in America in the years before World War I. Opposed to American entry into the war, she was arrested in 1917 on charges of conspiracy to obstruct the selective service act and sentenced to two years in prison. After her release in September 1919, she was deported to Russia when authorities ruled she had lost her American citizenship acquired through her marriage. Her close friend Berkman, who had been released from prison in 1906 and again jailed in 1917, was also ordered deported along with more than two hundred other anarchists.

With Berkman in Russia, she found the Soviet bureaucracy suffocating and distressing, especially since she had exalted the Russian revolution on her American lecture tours. Her books, *My Disillusionment in Russia* (1923) and *My Further Disillusionment in Russia* (1924) describe the failure of the revolution. Living in Latvia, then Estonia, Sweden, Germany, England, and France, she continued to write and lecture. Her marriage to James Colton in England gave her British citizenship. She visited the United States in 1934 for a brief lecture tour and emphasized that the Soviet government was " . . . not a dictatorship of the proletariat but over the proletariat." When the Spanish Civil War began, she spoke out against the Franco forces and other Fascist regimes during lecture tours in England and Canada. She died in Toronto in 1940 and was buried in Chicago near the graves of the four men who had been hanged in 1887 for their activities in the Haymarket Riot. The life of this restless woman revolutionary and idealist, who had sought to educate America and the western world to the evils of injustice, was a colorful story of dissent and propaganda.

On Being an Anarchist

The questions were asked by Assistant District Attorney McIntyre.

Question You do not believe in the laws of the State?
Answer I am an Anarchist, and against all laws. My theory is that the Legislature and the courts are of no use to the mass of the people. The laws passed help the rich and grind the poor.

Question You don't believe in living up to these laws, then!
Answer I do not believe in any laws except those of morality.

Question Do you believe in Most and his teachings?
Answer Most is an Anarchist and I am an Anarchist, but we do not agree in a great many particulars.

Question Is there any government on earth whose laws you approve?
Answer No, Sir; for they are all against the people.

Question Why don't you leave this country if you don't like its laws?
Answer Where shall I go? Everywhere on earth the laws are against the poor, and they tell me I cannot go to Heaven, nor do I want to go there.

Question Do you believe in the Constitution of the United States?
Answer I think it is excellent in theory but it is not lived up to. It is distorted for the benefit of the rich.

Question You speak of tyrants here! Whom do you mean by that?
Answer The Vanderbilts and the Jay Goulds and the representatives of the Government who deprive its working people of food.

Question Why is it that you do not believe in any religion?
Answer Because I do not think that any church has ever done a single thing to ameliorate the condition of the poor.

Question Didn't you tell your hearers to take bread by force if they couldn't get it peaceably?
Answer No. But I think the time will come, judging by what has happened, when they will be compelled to do so. That is what I told them on the night I spoke.

Question What do these Anarchists want with dynamite bombs, anyhow?
Answer Why, they want to use them in the great war if the social revolution ever comes.

From the *New York Times*, October 7, 1893, reporting some of Emma Goldman's testimony in her trial for inciting to riot (see introductory note above).

Question Would you use dynamite?
Answer I do not know what I would do. The time may not come when it may
be necessary to use it. . . .
[On October 16, Emma Goldman, termed a "yellow-haired evangel of disorder"
by *The New York Times'* reporter, was sentenced to one year in the women's
penitentiary on Blackwell's Island.]

Anarchism and Freedom

. . . The new social order rests, of course, on the materialistic basis of life; but
while all Anarchists agree that the main evil today is an economic one, they
maintain that the solution of that evil can be brought about only through the
consideration of *every phase* of life,—individual, as well as the collective; the
internal, as well as the external phases.

. . . Anarchism is the only philosophy which brings to man the consciousness
of himself; which maintains that God, the State, and society are non-existent,
that their promises are null and void, since they can be fulfilled only through
man's subordination. Anarchism is therefore the teacher of the unity of life; not
merely in nature, but in man. There is no conflict between the individual and the
social instincts, any more than there is between the heart and the lungs: the one
the receptacle of a precious life essence, the other the repository of the element
that keeps the essence pure and strong. The individual is the heart of society,
conserving the essence of social life; society is the lungs which are distributing
the element to keep the life essence—that is, the individual—pure and strong.
. . . Anarchism is the great liberator of man from the phantoms that have held
him captive; it is the arbiter and pacifier of the two forces for individual and
social harmony. To accomplish that unity, Anarchism has declared war on the
pernicious influences which have so far prevented the harmonious blending of
individual and social instincts, the individual and society.
Religion, the dominion of the human mind; Property, the dominion of human
needs; and Government, the dominion of human conduct, represent the strong-
hold of man's enslavement and all the horrors it entails. Religion! How it dominates man's mind, how it humiliates and degrades his soul. God is everything,

From Emma Goldman, *Anarchism and Other Essays*, Mother Earth Publishing Association,
New York, 1910, pp. 56, 58-62, 65-73.

man is nothing, says religion. But out of that nothing God has created a kingdom so despotic, so tyrannical, so cruel, so terribly exacting that naught but gloom and tears and blood have ruled the world since gods began. Anarchism rouses man to rebellion against this black monster. Break your mental fetters, says Anarchism to man, for not until you think and judge for yourself will you get rid of the dominion of darkness, the greatest obstacle to all progress.

Property, the dominion of man's needs, the denial of the right to satisfy his needs. Time was when property claimed a divine right, when it came to man with the same refrain, even as religion, "Sacrifice! Abnegate! Submit!" The spirit of Anarchism has lifted man from his prostrate position. He now stands erect, with his face toward the light. He has learned to see the insatiable, devouring, devastating nature of property, and he is preparing to strike the monster dead.

"Property is robbery," said the great French Anarchist, Proudhon. Yes, but without risk and danger to the robber. Monopolizing the accumulated efforts of man, property has robbed him of his birthright, and has turned him loose a pauper and an outcast. Property has not even the time-worn excuse that man does not create enough to satisfy all needs. The A B C student of economics knows that the productivity of labor within the last few decades far exceeds normal demand a hundredfold. But what are normal demands to an abnormal institution? The only demand that property recognizes is its own gluttonous appetite for greater wealth, because wealth means power: the power to subdue, to crush, to exploit, the power to enslave, to outrage, to degrade. America is particularly boastful of her great power, her enormous national wealth. Poor America, of what avail is all her wealth, if the individuals comprising the nation are wretchedly poor? If they live in squalor, in filth, in crime, with hope and joy gone, a homeless, soilless army of human prey.

It is generally conceded that unless the returns of any business venture exceed the cost, bankruptcy is inevitable. But those engaged in the business of producing wealth have not yet learned even this simple lesson. Every year the cost of production in human life is growing larger (50,000 killed, 100,000 wounded in America last year); the returns to the masses, who help to create wealth, are ever getting smaller. Yet America continues to be blind to the inevitable bankruptcy of our business of production. Nor is this the only crime of the latter. Still more fatal is the crime of turning the producer into a mere particle of a machine, with less will and decision than his master of steel and iron. Man is being robbed not merely of the products of his labor, but of the power of free initiative, of originality, and the interest in, or desire for, the things he is making.

Real wealth consists in things of utility and beauty, in things that help to create strong, beautiful bodies and surroundings inspiring to live in. But if man is doomed to wind cotton around a spool, or dig coal, or build roads for thirty years of his life, there can be no talk of wealth. What he gives to the world is only gray and hideous things, reflecting a dull and hideous existence,—too weak to live, too cowardly to die. Strange to say, there are people who extol this deadening method of centralized production as the proudest achievement of our age. They fail utterly to realize that if we are to continue in machine subserviency, our slavery is more complete than was our bondage to the King. They do not want to know that centralization is not only the death knell of liberty, but also of health and beauty, of art and science, all these being impossible in a clock-like, mechanical atmosphere.

Anarchism cannot but repudiate such a method of production: its goal is the freest possible expression of all the latent powers of the individual. Oscar Wilde defines a perfect personality as "one who develops under perfect conditions, who is not wounded, maimed, or in danger." A perfect personality, then, is only possible in a state of society where man is free to choose the mode of work, the conditions of work, and the freedom to work. One to whom the making of a table, the building of a house, or the tilling of the soil, is what the painting is to the artist and the discovery to the scientist,—the result of inspiration, of intense longing, and deep interest in work as a creative force. That being the ideal of Anarchism, its economic arrangements must consist of voluntary productive and distributive associations, gradually developing into free communism, as the best means of producing with the least waste of human energy. Anarchism, however, also recognizes the right of the individual, or numbers of individuals, to arrange at all times for other forms of work, in harmony with their tastes and desires.

Such free display of human energy being possible only under complete individual and social freedom, Anarchism directs its forces against the third and greatest foe of all social equality; namely, the State, organized authority, or statutory law,—the dominion of human conduct.

. . . Order derived through submission and maintained by terror is not much of a safe guaranty; yet that is the only "order" that governments have ever maintained. True social harmony grows naturally out of solidarity of interests. In a society where those who always work never have anything, while those who never work enjoy everything, solidarity of interests is non-existent; hence social harmony is but a myth. The only way organized authority meets this grave situation is by extending still greater privileges to those who have already monopolized the earth, and by still further enslaving the disenherited masses. Thus the entire arsenal of government—laws, police, soldiers, the courts, legislatures, prisons,—is strenuously engaged in "harmonizing" the most antagonistic elements in society.

The most absurd apology for authority and law is that they serve to diminish crime. Aside from the fact that the State is itself the greatest criminal, breaking every written and natural law, stealing in the form of taxes, killing in the form of war and capital punishment, it has come to an absolute standstill in coping with crime. It has failed utterly to destroy or even minimize the horrible scourge of its own creation.

Crime is naught but misdirected energy. So long as every institution of today, economic, political, social, and moral, conspires to misdirect human energy into wrong channels; so long as most people are out of place doing the things they hate to do, living a life they loathe to live, crime will be inevitable, and all the laws on the statutes can only increase, but never do away with, crime. What does society, as it exists today, know of the process of despair, the poverty, the horrors, the fearful struggle the human soul must pass on its way to crime and degradation.

... Anarchism aims to strip labor of its deadening, dulling aspect, of its gloom and compulsion. It aims to make work an instrument of joy, of strength, of color, of real harmony, so that the poorest sort of a man should find in work both recreation and hope.

To achieve such an arrangement of life, government, with its unjust, arbitrary, repressive measures, must be done away with. At best it has but imposed one single mode of life upon all, without regard to individual and social variations and needs. In destroying government and statutory laws, Anarchism proposes to rescue the self-respect and independence of the individual from all restraint and invasion by authority. Only in freedom can man grow to his full stature. Only in freedom will he learn to think and move, and give the very best in him. Only in freedom will he realize the true force of the social bonds which knit men together, and which are the true foundation of a normal social life.

But what about human nature? Can it be changed? And if not, will it endure under Anarchism?

Poor human nature, what horrible crimes have been committed in thy name! Every fool, from king to policeman, from the flatheaded parson to the visionless dabbler in science, presumes to speak authoritatively of human nature. The greater the mental charlatan, the more definite his insistence on the wickedness and weaknesses of human nature. Yet, how can any one speak of it today, with every soul in a prison, with every heart fettered, wounded, and maimed?

... Anarchism, then, really stands for the liberation of the human mind from the dominion of religion; the liberation of the human body from the dominion of property; liberation from the shackles and restraint of government. Anarchism stands for a social order based on the free grouping of individuals for the purpose of producing real social wealth; an order that will guarantee to every human being free access to the earth and full enjoyment of the necessities of life, according to individual desires, tastes, and inclinations.

This is not a wild fancy or an aberration of the mind. It is the conclusion arrived at by hosts of intellectual men and women the world over; a conclusion resulting from the close and studious observation of the tendencies of modern society: individual liberty and economic equality, the twin forces for the birth of what is fine and true in man.

As to methods. Anarchism is not, as some may suppose, a theory of the future to be realized through divine inspiration. It is a living force in the affairs of our life, constantly creating new conditions. The methods of Anarchism therefore do not comprise an iron-clad program to be carried out under all circumstances. Methods must grow out of the economic needs of each place and clime, and of the intellectual and temperamental requirements of the individual. The serene, calm character of a Tolstoy will wish different methods for social reconstruction than the intense, overflowing personality of a Michael Bakunin or a Peter Kropotkin. Equally so it must be apparent that the economic and political needs of Russia will dictate more drastic measures than would England or America. Anarchism does not stand for military drill and uniformity; it does, however, stand for the spirit of revolt, in whatever form, against everything that hinders human growth. All Anarchists agree in that, as they also agree in their opposition to the political machinery as a means of bringing about the great social change.

"All voting," says Thoreau, "is a sort of gaming, like checkers, or backgammon, a playing with right and wrong; its obligation never exceeds that of expediency. Even voting for the right thing is doing nothing for it. A wise man will not leave the right to the mercy of chance, nor wish it to prevail through the power of the majority." A close examination of the machinery of politics and its achievements will bear out the logic of Thoreau.

What does the history of parliamentarism show? Nothing but failure and defeat, not even a single reform to ameliorate the economic and social stress of the people. Laws have been passed and enactments made for the improvement and protection of labor. Thus it was proven only last year that Illinois, with the most rigid laws for mine protection, had the greatest mine disasters. In States where child labor laws prevail, child exploitation is at its highest, and though with us the workers enjoy full political opportunities, capitalism has reached the most brazen zenith.

Even were the workers able to have their own representatives, for which our good Socialist politicians are clamoring, what chances are there for their honesty and good faith? One has but to bear in mind the process of politics to realize that its path of good intentions is full of pitfalls: wire-pulling, intriguing, flattering, lying, cheating; in fact, chicanery of every description, whereby the political aspirant can achieve success. Added to that is a complete demoralization of character and conviction, until nothing is left that would make one hope for anything from such a human derelict. Time and time again the people were foolish enough to trust, believe, and support with their last farthing aspiring politicians, only to find themselves betrayed and cheated.

It may be claimed that men of integrity would not become corrupt in the political grinding mill. Perhaps not; but such men would be absolutely helpless to exert the slightest influence in behalf of labor, as indeed has been shown in numerous instances. The State is the economic master of its servants. Good men, if such there be, would either remain true to their political faith and lose their economic support, or they would cling to their economic master and be utterly unable to do the slightest good. The political arena leaves one no alternative, one must either be a dunce or a rogue.

The political superstition is still holding sway over the hearts and minds of the masses, but the true lovers of liberty will have no more to do with it. Instead, they believe with Stirner that man has as much liberty as he is willing to take. Anarchism therefore stands for direct action, the open defiance of, and resistance to, all laws and restrictions, economic, social, and moral. But defiance and resistance are illegal. Therein lies the salvation of man. Everything illegal necessitates integrity, self-reliance, and courage. In short, it calls for free, independent spirits, for "men who are men, and who have a bone in their backs which you cannot pass your hand through."

Universal suffrage itself owes its existence to direct action. If not for the spirit of rebellion, of the defiance on the part of the American revolutionary fathers, their posterity would still wear the King's coat. If not for the direct action of a John Brown and his comrades, American would still trade in the flesh of the black man. True, the trade in white flesh is still going on; but that, too, will have to be abolished by direct action. Trade unionism, the economic arena of the modern gladiator, owes its existence to direct action. It is but recently that law and government have attempted to crush the trade union movement, and condemned the exponents of man's right to organize to prison as conspirators. Had they sought to assert their cause through begging, pleading, and compromise, trade unionism would today be a negligible quantity. In France, in Spain, in Italy, in Russia, nay even in England (witness the growing rebellion of English labor unions) direct, revolutionary, economic action has become so strong a force in the battle for industrial liberty as to make the world realize the tremendous importance of labor's power. The General Strike, the supreme expression of the economic consciousness of the workers, was ridiculed in America but a short time ago. Today every great strike, in order to win, must realize the importance of the solidaric general protest.

Direct action, having proved effective along economic lines, is equally potent in the environment of the individual. There a hundred forces encroach upon his being, and only persistent resistence to them will finally set him free. Direct action against the authority in the shop, direct action against the authority of the law, direct action against the invasive, meddlesome authority of our moral code, is the logical, consistent method of Anarchism.

Will it not lead to a revolution? Indeed, it will. No real social change has ever come about without a revolution. People are either not familiar with their history, or they have not yet learned that revolution is but thought carried into action.

Anarchism, the great leaven of thought, is today permeating every phase of human endeavor. Science, art, literature, the drama, the effort for economic betterment, in fact every individual and social opposition to the existing disorder of things, is illumined by the spiritual light of Anarchism. It is the philosophy of the sovereignty of the individual. It is the theory of social harmony. It is the great, surging, living truth that is reconstructing the world, and that will usher in the Dawn.

Revolution and Values

... Revolution is indeed a violent process. But if it is to result only in a change of dictatorship, in a shifting of names and political personalities, then it is hardly worth while. It is surely not worth all the struggle and sacrifice, the stupendous loss in human life and cultural values that result from every revolution. If such a revolution were even to bring greater social well being (which has not been the case in Russia) then it would also not be worth the terrific price paid: mere improvement can be brought about without bloodly revolution. It is not palliatives or reforms that are the real aim and purpose of revolution, as I conceive it.

In my opinion—a thousandfold strengthened by the Russian experience—the great mission of revolution, of the SOCIAL REVOLUTION, is a *fundamental transvaluation of values*. A transvaluation not only of social, but also of human values. The latter are even preëminent, for they are the basis of all social values. Our institutions and conditions rest upon deep-seated ideas. To change those conditions and at the same time leave the underlying ideas and values intact means only a superficial transformation, one that cannot be permanent or bring betterment. It is a change of form only, not of substance, as so tragically proven by Russia.

It is at once the great failure and the great tragedy of the Russian Revolution that it attempted (in the leadership of the ruling political party) to change only institutions and conditions while ignoring entirely the human and social values involved in the Revolution. . . .

From Emma Goldman, *My Further Disillusionment in Russia*, Doubleday, Page & Company, 1924, pp. 170-171.

malcolm x

Malcolm was born in Omaha, Nebraska, in 1925 to Reverend Earl Little, a Baptist minister from Georgia, and Louise Little, who had been born in Grenada, British West Indies. He learned about violence and racial hatred at a young age. Klan attacks on the family resulted in a decision to move to Milwaukee. After a short time the family moved to Lansing, Michigan. Reverend Little believed very deeply in the teachings of Marcus Garvey, whose Harlem-based Universal Negro Improvement Association urged American Negroes to return to Africa because freedom and independence could never be achieved in America. As a result, Reverend Little's home, whether in Omaha or Lansing, was the target of fire-bombs and shootings by white racists. He was killed in Lansing when Malcolm was six years old.

Rebellious and aggressive as a youngster, Malcolm rejected Christianity and the "status-symbol-oriented, integration-seeking type of Negroes" in Lansing. Living on a farm two miles outside Lansing, he experienced the security of land and the feeling of independence. As he wrote in *Autobiography*, the Little family fared far better than the town Negroes because they could grow much of their own food. However, the strain of losing her husband and the serious economic problems in trying to care for her eight children caused Mrs. Little to suffer a complete breakdown in the mid-1930's. The children became wards of the court.

After being expelled from school at the age of thirteen, Malcolm entered a detention home and attended school in a small town near Lansing where he achieved excellent grades. When counseled in the eighth grade that his plans for entering a profession such as law were unrealistic because he was a Negro, he became bitter and withdrawn. He moved to Boston after eighth grade graduation and learned how to survive in the large urban ghetto, where crime, drugs, and hustling lasted twenty-four hours a day. As a shoeshine boy at the Roseland State Ballroom, a dishwasher and waiter on passenger trains, and later as a waiter in a Harlem bar, Malcolm turned into a ghetto hustler.

Back in Boston in 1946 and convicted as a burglar, Malcolm was sentenced to ten years in prison. He spent most of his first months in solitary confinement because he broke prison rules. Gradually, through letters and visits from his brothers, he learned about the Islamic religion as taught by Elijah Muhammad. Especially vivid to Malcolm was Elijah's teaching that all white men were devils. In the prison library, Malcolm began reading again. He read books on philosophy, political science, and history and they reinforced his growing belief in the Muslim religion. For the first time he began appreciating the great civilization which had existed among black people in Africa. He accepted the Muslim discipline and stopped smoking and eating pork. He became convinced that the Muslim religion as taught by Elijah Muhammad was the true faith.

Freed in 1952, Malcolm soon dedicated his total energies to spreading the Muslim religion. Mr. Muhammad changed Malcolm's last name from Little to "X"—the X being a symbol for the African name he had never known. In the years which followed, Malcolm X delivered lectures and established Muslim temples in Detroit and New York and won many black persons to the Muslim faith. His fiery oratory was making him a dynamic leader of the black revolution. In 1958, he married Betty X, a student nurse in New York. He continued a furious pace of travelling, preaching, and organizing the Nation of Islam. The expanding civil rights struggle in America began a new era of awareness among all people in America. Malcolm X focused on the ideas of building a separate black society rather than integrating blacks into a corrupt white American society.

In March 1964 he broke with Elijah Muhammad and initiated the Muslim Mosque, Inc. and later the Organization of Afro-American Unity. On a trip to Mecca in April and May 1964, he made a startling revelation: the Muslim religion and Muslim society were color-blind! As he wrote, in this birthplace of the Muslim religion he associated with fellow Muslims whose eyes were blue, whose hair was blond, and who were white! He began to believe that white Americans might be able to accept the oneness of man, though he fully realized that American racism contained the potential of self-destruction for all of America.

On his return to America his speeches became appeals to human beings to accept one another. He sought to have blacks in America accepted into the existing system. With the new name, El-Hajj Malik El-Shabazz, he began preaching on the Islamic religion. As he reflected on the new insights he had recently gained, he realized some of the mistakes he had made in his earlier preaching. He hoped, however, that he had helped to expose the malignant cancer of racism in America, and that it would be destroyed.

His differences with the Black Muslims and death threats from racists made him increasingly apprehensive and anxious. Repeatedly he announced he had been marked for murder. On February 21, 1965, assassins shot him as he was beginning a lecture in Harlem. The violence which had accompanied him from his birth in Omaha to his death in New York finally silenced his life; however, his rhetoric of revolt continues to live.

Messages to the Grass Roots

...I would like to make a few comments concerning the difference between the black revolution and the Negro revolution. Are they both the same? And if they're not, what is the difference? What is the difference between a black revolution and a Negro revolution? First, what is a revolution? Sometimes I'm inclined to believe that many of our people are using this word "revolution" loosely, without taking careful consideration of what this word actually means, and what its historic characteristics are. When you study the historic nature of revolutions, the motive of a revolution, the objective of a revolution, the result of a revolution, and the methods used in a revolution, you may change words. You may devise another program, you may change your goal and you may change your mind.

Look at the American Revolution in 1776. That revolution was for what? For land. Why did they want land? Independence. How was it carried out? Bloodshed. Number one, it was based on land, the basis of independence. And the only way they could get it was bloodshed. The French Revolution—what was it based on? The landless against the landlord. What was it for? Land. How did they get it? Bloodshed. Was no love lost, was no compromise, was no negotiation. I'm telling you—you don't know what a revolution is. Because when you find out what it is, you'll get back in the alley, you'll get out of the way.

From Malcolm X, *Malcolm X Speaks: Selected Speeches and Statements*, edited by George Breitman, Grove Press, New York, 1965, pp. 6-10, 12-13. Reprinted with permission of Merit Publishers and Betty Shabazz. This speech was delivered in November 1963 in Detroit.

The Russian Revolution—what was it based on? Land: the landless against the landlord. How did they bring it about? Bloodshed. You haven't got a revolution that doesn't involve bloodshed. And you're afraid to bleed. I said, you're afraid to bleed.

As long as the white man sent you to Korea, you bled. He sent you to Germany, you bled. He sent you to the South Pacific to fight the Japanese, you bled. You bleed for white people, but when it comes to seeing your own churches being bombed and little black girls murdered, you haven't got any blood. You bleed when the white man says bleed; you bite when the white man says bite; and you bark when the white man says bark. I hate to say this about us, but it's true. How are you going to be nonviolent in Mississippi, as violent as you were in Korea? How can you justify being nonviolent in Mississippi and Alabama, when your churches are being bombed, and your little girls are being murdered, and at the same time you are going to get violent with Hitler, and Tojo, and somebody else you don't even know?

If violence is wrong in America, violence is wrong abroad. If it is wrong to be violent defending black women and black children and black babies and black men, then it is wrong for America to draft us and make us violent abroad in defense of her. And if it is right for America to draft us, and teach us how to be violent in defense of her, then it is right for you and me to do whatever is necessary to defend our own people right here in this country.

The Chinese Revolution—they wanted land. They threw the British out, along with the Uncle Tom Chinese. Yes, they did. They set a good example. When I was in prison, I read an article—don't be shocked when I say that I was in prison. You're still in prison. That's what America means: prison. When I was in prison, I read an article in *Life* magazine showing a little Chinese girl, nine years old; her father was on his hands and knees and she was pulling the trigger because he was an Uncle Tom Chinaman. When they had the revolution over there, they took a whole generation of Uncle Toms and just wiped them out. And within ten years that little girl became a full-grown woman. No more Toms in China. And today it's one of the toughest, roughest, most feared countries on this earth—by the white man. Because there are no Uncle Toms over there.

Of all our studies, history is best qualified to reward our research. And when you see that you've got problems, all you have to do is examine the historic method used all over the world by others who have problems similar to yours. Once you see how they got theirs straight, then you know how you can get yours straight. There's been a revolution, a black revolution, going on in Africa. In Kenya, the Mau Mau were revolutionary; they were the ones who brought the word "Uhuru" to the fore. The Mau Mau, they were revolutionary, they believed in scorched earth, they knocked everything aside that got in their way, and their revolution also was based on land, a desire for land. In Algeria, the northern part of Africa, a revolution took place. The Algerians were revolutionists, they wanted land. France offered to let them be integrated into France. They told France, to hell with France, they wanted some land, not some France. And they engaged in a bloody battle.

So I cite these various revolutions, brothers and sisters, to show you that you don't have a peaceful revolution. You don't have a turn-the-other-cheek revolution. There's no such thing as a nonviolent revolution. The only kind of revolution that is nonviolent is the Negro revolution. The only revolution in which the goal is loving your enemy is the Negro revolution. It's the only revolution in which the goal is a desegregated lunch counter, a desegregated theater, a desegregated park, and a desegregated public toilet . . . That's no revolution. Revolution is based on land. Land is the basis of all independence. Land is the basis of freedom, justice, and equality.

The white man knows what a revolution is. He knows that the black revolution is world-wide in scope and in nature. The black revolution is sweeping Asia, is sweeping Africa, is rearing its head in Latin America. The Cuban Revolution—that's a revolution. They overturned the system. Revolution is in Asia, revolution is in Africa, and the white man is screaming because he sees revolution in Latin America. How do you think he'll react to you when you learn what a real revolution is? You don't know what a revolution is. If you did, you wouldn't use that word.

Revolution is bloody, revolution is hostile, revolution knows no compromise, revolution overturns and destroys everything that gets in its way. And you, sitting around here like a knot on the wall, saying, "I'm going to love these folks no matter how much they hate me." No, you need a revolution. Whoever heard of a revolution where they lock arms, as Rev. Cleage was pointing out beautifully, singing "We Shall Overcome"? You don't do that in a revolution. You don't do any singing, you're too busy swinging. It's based on land. A revolutionary wants land so he can set up his own nation, an independent nation. These Negroes aren't asking for any nation—they're trying to crawl back on the plantation.

When you want a nation, that's called nationalism. When the white man became involved in a revolution in this country against England, what was it for? He wanted this land so he could set up another white nation. That's white nationalism. The American Revolution was white nationalism. The French Revolution was white nationalism. The Russian Revolution too—yes, it was—white nationalism. You don't think so? Why do you think Khrushchev and Mao can't get their heads together? White nationalism. All the revolutions that are going on in Asia and Africa today are based on what?—black nationalism. A revolutionary is a black nationalist. He wants a nation.

. . . There is nothing in our book, the Koran, that teaches us to suffer peacefully. Our religion teaches us to be intelligent. Be peacefull, be courteous, obey the law, respect everyone; but if someone puts his hand on you, send him to the cemetery. That's a good religion. In fact, that's that old-time religion. That's the one that Ma and Pa used to talk about: an eye for an eye, and a tooth for a tooth, and a head for a head, and a life for a life. That's a good religion. And nobody resents that kind of religion being taught but a wolf, who intends to make you his meal.

This is the way it is with the white man in America. He's a wolf—and you're sheep. Any time a shepherd, a pastor, teaches you and me not to run from the white man, and, at the same time, teaches us not to fight the white man he's a traitor to you and me. Don't lay down a life all by itself. No, preserve your life, it's the best thing you've got. And if you've got to give it up, let it be even-steven. . . .

The Ballot or the Bullet

. . . I'm not a politician, not even a student of politics; in fact, I'm not a student of much of anything. I'm not a Democrat, I'm not a Republican, and I don't even consider myself an American. If you and I were Americans, there'd be no problem. Those Hunkies that just got off the boat, they're already Americans; Polacks are already Americans; the Italian refugees are already Americans. Everything that came out of Europe, every blue-eyed thing, is already an American. And as long as you and I have been over here, we aren't Americans yet.

Well, I am one who doesn't believe in deluding myself. I'm not going to sit at your table and watch you eat, with nothing on my plate, and call myself a diner. Sitting at the table doesn't make you a diner, unless you eat some of what's on that plate. Being here in America doesn't make you an American. Being born here in America doesn't make you an American. Why, if birth made you American, you wouldn't need any legislation, you wouldn't need any amendments to the Constitution, you wouldn't be faced with civil-rights filibustering in Washington, D.C., right now. They don't have to pass civil-rights legislation to make a Polack an American.

No, I'm not an American. I'm one of the 22 million black people who are the victims of Americanism. One of the 22 million black people who are the victims of democracy, nothing but disguised hypocrisy. So, I'm not standing here

From *Malcolm X Speaks*, pp. 25-26, 31-32. The speech was delivered April 3, 1964.

speaking to you as an American, or a patriot, or a flag-saluter, or a flag-waver—
no, not I. I'm speaking as a victim of this American system. And I see America
through the eyes of the victim. I don't see any American dream; I see an
American nightmare.

. . . So, where do we go from here? First, we need some friends. We need some
new allies. The entire civil-rights struggle needs a new interpretation, a broader
interpretation. We need to look at this civil-rights thing from another angle—
from the inside as well as from the outside. To those of us whose philosophy is
black nationalism, the only way you can get involved in the civil-rights struggle is
give it a new interpretation. That old interpretation excluded us. It kept us out.
So, we're giving a new interpretation to the civil-rights struggle, an interpretation
that will enable us to come into it, take part in it. And these handkerchief-heads
who have been dillydallying and pussyfooting and compromising—we don't
intend to let them pussyfoot and dillydally and compromise any longer.

How can you thank a man for giving you what's already yours? How then can
you thank him for giving you only a part of what's already yours? You haven't
even made progress, if that's being given to you, you should have had already.
That's not progress. And I love my Brother Lomax, the way he pointed out
we're right back where we were in 1954. We're not even as far up as we were in
1954. We're behind where we were in 1954. There's more racial animosity, more
racial hatred, more racial violence today in 1964, than there was in 1954. Where
is the progress?

And now you're facing a situation where the young Negro's coming up. They
don't want to hear that "turn-the-other cheek" stuff, no. In Jacksonville, those
were teenagers, they were throwing Molotov cocktails. Negroes have never done
that before. But it shows you there's a new deal coming in. There's new thinking
coming in. There's new strategy coming in. It'll be Molotov cocktails this month,
hand grenades next month, and something else next month. It'll be ballots, or
it'll be bullets. It'll be liberty, or it will be death. The only difference about this
kind of death—it'll be reciprocal. You know what is meant by "reciprocal"?
That's one of Brother Lomax's words, I stole it from him. I don't usually deal
with those big words because I don't usually deal with big people. I deal with
small people. I find you can get a whole lot of small people and whip hell out of
a whole lot of big people. They haven't got anything to lose, and they've got
everything to gain. And they'll let you know in a minute: "It takes two to tango;
when I go, you go.". . . .

The Black Revolution

... During recent years there has been much talk about a population explosion. Whenever they are speaking of the population explosion, in my opinion they are referring primarily to the people in Asia or in Africa—the black, brown, red, and yellow people. It is seen by people of the West that, as soon as the standard of living is raised in Africa and Asia, automatically the people begin to reproduce abundantly. And there has been a great deal of fear engendered by this in the midst of the people of the West, who happen to be, on this earth, a very small minority.

In fact, in most of the thinking and planning of whites in the West today, it's easy to see the fear in their minds, conscious minds and subconscious minds, that the masses of dark people in the East, who already outnumber them, will continue to increase and multiply and grow until they eventually overrun the people of the West like a human sea, a human tide, a human flood. And the fear of this can be seen in the minds, in the actions, of most of the people here in the West in practically everything that they do. It governs their political views and it governs their economic views and it governs most of their attitudes toward the present society.

... If George Washington didn't get independence for this country nonviolently, and if Patrick Henry didn't come up with a nonviolent statement, and you taught me to look upon them as patriots and heroes, then it's time for you to realize that I have studied your books well. . . .

1964 will see the Negro revolt evolve and merge into the world-wide black revolution that has been taking place on this earth since 1945. The so-called revolt will become a real black revolution. Now the black revolution has been taking place in Africa and Asia and Latin America; when I say black, I mean non-white—black, brown, red or yellow. Our brothers and sisters in Asia, who were colonized by the Europeans, our brothers and sisters in Africa, who were colonized by the Europeans, and in Latin America, the peasants, who were colonized by the Europeans, have been involved in a struggle since 1945 to get the colonialists, or the colonizing powers, the Europeans, off their land, out of their country.

This is a real revolution. Revolution is always based on land. Revolution is never based on begging somebody for an integrated cup of coffee. Revolutions are never fought by turning the other cheek. Revolutions are never based upon

From *Malcolm X Speaks*, pp. 45-46, 49-51, 56-57. The speech was delivered in New York on April 8, 1964.

love-your-enemy and pray-for-those-who-spitefully-use-you. And revolutions are never waged singing "We Shall Overcome." Revolutions are based upon bloodshed. Revolutions are never compromising. Revolutions are never based upon negotiations. Revolutions are never based upon any kind of tokenism whatsoever. Revolutions are never even based upon that which is begging a corrupt society or a corrupt system to accept us into it. Revolutions overturn systems. And there is no system on this earth which has proven itself more corrupt, more criminal than this system that in 1964 still colonizes 22 million African-Americans, still enslaves 22 million Afro-Americans.

There is no system more corrupt than a system that represents itself as the example of freedom, the example of democracy, and can go all over this earth telling other people how to straighten out their house, when you have citizens of this country who have to use bullets if they want to cast a ballot.

The greatest weapon the colonial powers have used in the past against our poeple has always been divide-and-conquer. America is a colonial power. She has colonized 22 million Afro-Americans by depriving us of first-class citizenship, by depriving us of civil rights, actually by depriving us of human rights. She has not only deprived us of the right to be a citizen, she has deprived us of the right to be human beings, the right to be recognized and respected as men and women. In this country the black can be fifty years old and he is still a "boy."

I grew up with white people. I was integrated before they even invented the word and I have never met white people who—if you are around them long enough—refer to you as a "boy" or a "gal," no matter how old you are or what school you came out of, no matter what your intellectual or professional level is. In this society we remain "boys."

So America's strategy is the same strategy as that which was used in the past by the colonial powers: divide and conquer. She plays one Negro leader against the other. She plays one Negro organization against the other. She makes us think we have different objectives, different goals. As soon as one Negro says something, she runs to this Negro and asks him, "What do you think about what he said?" Why, anybody can see through that today—except some of the Negro leaders.

All of our people have the same goals, the same objective. That objective is freedom, justice, equality. All of us want recognition and respect as human beings. We don't want to be integrationists. Nor do we want to be separationists. We want to be human beings. Integration is only a method that is used by some groups to obtain freedom, justice, equality and respect as human beings. Separation is only a method that is used by other groups to obtain freedom, justice, equality or human dignity.

... You have whites in the community who express sincerity when they say they want to help. Well, how can they help? How can a white person help the black man solve his problem? Number one, you can't solve it for him. You can help him solve it, but you can't solve it for him today. One of the best ways that you can help him solve it is to let the so-called Negro, who has been involved in the civil-rights struggle, see that the civil-rights struggle must be expanded beyond the level of civil rights to human rights. Once it is expanded beyond the level of civil rights to the level of human rights, it opens the door for all of our brothers and sisters in Africa and Asia, who have their independence, to come to our rescue.

. . . So, in my conclusion, in speaking about the black revolution, America today is at a time or in a day or at an hour where she is the first country on this earth that can actually have a bloodless revolution. In the past, revolutions have been bloody. Historically you just don't have a peaceful revolution. Revolutions are bloody, revolutions are violent, revolutions cause bloodshed and death follows in their paths. America is the only country in history in a position to bring about a revolution without violence and bloodshed. But America is not morally equipped to do so.

Why is America in a position to bring about a bloodless revolution? Because the Negro in this country holds the balance of power, and if the Negro in this country were given what the Constitution says he is supposed to have, the added power of the Negro in this country would sweep all of the racists and the segregationists out of office. It would change the entire political structure of the country. It would wipe out the Southern segregationism that now controls America's foreign policy, as well as America's domestic policy.

And the only way without bloodshed that this can be brought about is that the black man has to be given full use of the ballot in every one of the fifty states. But if the black man doesn't get the ballot, then you are going to be faced with another man who forgets the ballot and starts using the bullet.

Revolutions are fought to get control of land, to remove the absentee landlord and gain control of the land and the institutions that flow from that land. The black man has been in a very low condition because he has had no control whatsoever over any land. He has been a beggar economically, a beggar politically, a beggar socially, a beggar even when it comes to trying to get some education. The past type of mentality, that was developed in this colonial system among our people, today is being overcome. And as the young ones come up, they know what they want. And as they listen to your beautiful preaching about democracy and all those flowery words, they know what they're supposed to have.

So you have a people today who not only know what they want, but also know what they are supposed to have. And they themselves are creating another generation that is coming up that not only will know what it wants and know what it should have, but also will be ready and willing to do whatever is necessary to see that what they should have materializes immediately. Thank you.

Letter from Saudi Arabia

... America needs to understand Islam, because this is the one religion that erases the race problem from its society. Throughout my travels in the Muslim world, I have met, talked to, and even eaten with, people who would have been considered "white" in America, but the religion of Islam in their hearts has removed the "white" from their minds. They practice sincere and true brotherhood with other people irrespective of their color.

Before America allows herself to be destroyed by the "cancer of racism" she should become better acquainted with the religious philosophy of Islam, a religion that has already molded people of all colors into one vast family, a nation or brotherhood of Islam that leaps over all "obstacles" and stretches itself into almost all the Eastern countries of this earth.

The whites as well as the non-whites who accept true Islam become a changed people. I have eaten from the same plate with people whose eyes were the bluest of blue, whose hair was the blondest of blond, and whose skin was the whitest of white—all the way from Cairo to Jedda and even in the Holy City of Mecca itself—and I felt the same sincerity in the words and deeds of these "white" Muslims that I felt among the African Muslims of Nigeria, Sudan and Ghana.

True Islam removes racism, because people of all colors and races who accept its religious principles and bow down to the one God, Allah, also automatically accept each other as brothers and sisters, regardless of difference in complexion.

You may be shocked by these words coming from me, but I have always been a man who tries to face facts, and to accept the reality of life as new experiences and knowledge unfold it. The experiences of this pilgrimage have taught me much, and each hour here in the Holy Land opens my eyes even more. If Islam can place the spirit of true brotherhood in the hearts of the "whites" whom I have met here in the Land of the Prophets, then surely it can also remove the "cancer of racism" from the heart of the white American, and perhaps in time to save America from imminent racial disaster, the same destruction brought upon Hitler by his racism that eventually destroyed the Germans themselves. . . .

From *Malcolm X Speaks*, pp. 59-60. The letter is dated April 20, 1964.

Liberty versus Racism*

... In the past, I have permitted myself to be used to make sweeping indictments of all white people, and these generalizations have caused injuries to some white people who did not deserve them. Because of the spiritual rebirth which I was blessed to undergo as a result of my pilgrimage to the Holy City of Mecca, I no longer subscribe to sweeping indictments of one race. My pilgrimage to Mecca ... served to convince me that perhaps American whites can be cured of the rampant racism which is consuming them and about to destroy this country. In the future, I intend to be careful not to sentence anyone who has not been proven guilty. I am not a racist and do not subscribe to any of the tenets of racism. In all honesty and sincerity it can be stated that I wish nothing but freedom, justice and equality: life, liberty and the pursuit of happiness—for all people. My first concern is with the group of people to which I belong, the Afro-Americans, for we, more than any other people, are deprived of these inalienable rights.

What's behind the "Hate-Gang" Scare?**

... *Question:* What political and economic system does Malcolm X want?

Answer: I don't know. But I'm flexible.... As was stated earlier, all of the countries that are emerging today from under the shackles of colonialism are turning toward socialism. I don't think it's an accident. Most of the countries that were colonial powers were capitalist countries, and the last bulwark of capitalism today is America. It's impossible for a white person to believe in capitalism and not believe in racism. You can't have capitalism without racism. And if you find one and you happen to get that person into a conversation and they have a philosophy that makes you sure they don't have this racism in their outlook, usually they're socialists or their political philosophy is socialism....

*From *Malcolm X Speaks,* pp. 58-59. The speech from which this excerpt is taken was delivered in Chicago, May 23, 1964.

**From *Malcolm X Speaks,* p. 69. Malcolm's comment was made at a symposium in New York, May 29, 1964.

On Not Turning the Other Cheek

... When I was in Africa, I noticed some of the Africans got their freedom faster than others. Some areas of the African continent became independent faster than other areas. I noticed that in the areas where independence had been gotten, someone got angry. And in the areas where independence had not been achieved yet, no one was angry. They were sad—they'd sit around and talk about their plight, but they weren't mad. And usually, when people are sad, they don't do anything. They just cry over their condition.

But when they get angry, they bring about a change. When they get angry, they aren't interested in logic, they aren't interested in odds, they aren't interterested in consequences. When they get angry, they realize the condition that they're in—that their suffering is unjust, immoral, illegal, and that anything they do to correct it, or eliminate it, they're justified. When you and I develop that type of anger and speak in that voice, then we'll get some kind of respect and recognition, and some changes from these people who have been promising us falsely already for far too long.

... They've always said that I'm anti-white. I'm for anybody who's for freedom. I'm for anybody who's for justice. I'm for anybody who's for equality. I'm not for anybody who tells me to sit around and wait for mine. I'm not for anybody who tells me to turn the other cheek when a cracker is busting up my jaw. I'm not for anybody who tells black people to be non-violent while nobody is telling white people to be non-violent. I know I'm in the church, I probably shouldn't be talking like this—but Jesus himself was ready to turn the synagogue inside out and upside down when things weren't going right. In fact, in the Book of Revelations, they've got Jesus sitting on a horse with a sword in his hand, getting ready to go into action. But they don't tell you or me about that Jesus. They only tell you and me about that peaceful Jesus. They never let you get down to the end of the book. They keep you up there where everything is, you know, non-violent. No, go and read the whole book, and when you get to Revelations, you'll find that even Jesus' patience ran out. And when his patience ran out, he got the whole situation straightened out. He picked up the sword. ...

From *Malcolm X Speaks*, pp. 107-108, 112. Malcolm gave this speech at a rally on December 20, 1964, in Harlem, in support of Mrs. Fannie Lou Hamer, Mississippi Freedom Democratic Party candidate for Congress.

Hatred of Africa and Self-hatred

... Now what effect does [the struggle over Africa] have on us? Why should the
black man in America concern himself since he's been away from the African
continent for three or four hundred years? Why should we concern ourselves?
What impact does what happens to them have upon us? Number one, you have
to realize that up until 1959 Africa was dominated by the colonial powers.
Having complete control over Africa, the colonial powers of Europe projected
the image of Africa negatively. They always project Africa in a negative light:
jungle savages, cannibals, nothing civilized. Why then naturally it was so negative
that it was negative to you and me, and you and I began to hate it. We didn't
want anybody telling us anything about Africa, much less calling us Africans. In
hating Africa and in hating the Africans, we ended up hating ourselves, without
even realizing it. Because you can't hate the roots of a tree, and not hate the
tree. You can't hate your origin and not end up hating yourself. You can't hate
Africa and not hate yourself.

You show me one of these people over here who has been thoroughly brain-
washed and has a negative attitude toward Africa, and I'll show you one who has
a negative attitude toward himself. You can't have a positive attitude toward
yourself and a negative attitude toward Africa at the same time. To the same
degree that your understanding of and attitude toward Africa become positive,
you'll find that your understanding of and your attitude toward yourself will
also become positive. And this is what the white man knows. So they very
skillfully make you and me hate our African identity, our African characteristics.

You know yourself that we have been a people who hated our African characteristics. We hated our heads, we hated the shape of our nose, we wanted one of
those long dog-like noses, you know; we hated the color of our skin, hated the
blood of Africa that was in our veins. And in hating our features and our skin
and our blood, why, we had to end up hating ourselves. And we hated ourselves.
Our color became to us a chain—we felt that it was holding us back; our color
became to us like a prison which we felt was keeping us confined, not letting us
go this way or that way. We felt that all of these restrictions were based solely
upon our color, and the psychological reaction to that would have to be that as
long as we felt imprisoned or chained or trapped by black skin, black features
and black blood, that skin and those features and blood, holding us back automatically had to become hateful to us. And it became hateful to us.

From *Malcolm X Speaks*, pp. 168-169. This speech was made in Detroit on February 14,
1965, several hours after Malcolm X, his wife, and four young children escaped from their
home in Queens which had been fire-bombed.

It made us feel inferior; it made us feel inadequate; it made us feel helpless. And when we fell victims to this feeling of inadequacy or inferiority or helplessness, we turned to somebody else to show us the way. We didn't have confidence in another black man to show us the way, or black people to show us the way. In those days we didn't. We didn't think a black man could do anything except play some horns—you know, make some sound and make you happy, with some songs and in that way. But in serious things, where food, clothing, shelter and education were concerned, we turned to the white man. We never thought in terms of bringing these things into existence for ourselves, we never thought in terms of doing things for ourselves. Because we felt helpless. What made us feel helpless was our hatred for ourselves. And our hatred for ourselves stemmed from our hatred for things African. . . .

Oppression and Hypocrisy

. . . *Bernard*: Are you suggesting revolution?

Malcolm: No, I'm saying this: that when you respect the intelligence of black people in this country as being equal to that of whites, then you will realize that the reaction of the black man to oppression will be the same as the reaction of the white man to oppression. The white man will not turn the other cheek when he's being oppressed. He will not practice any kind of love of a Klan or a Citizens Council or anyone else. But at the same time the white man is asking the black man to do this. So all I'm saying is, I absolutely believe the situation can be changed. But I don't think it can be changed by white people taking a hypocritical approach, pretending that it is not as bad as it is, and by black leaders, so-called responsible leaders, taking a hypocritical approach, trying to make white people think that black people are patient and long-suffering and are willing to sit around here a long time, or a great deal of time longer, until the problem is made better. . . .

From *Malcolm X Speaks*, p. 183. Malcolm X's last radio appearance occurred on February 18, 1965, as a guest on a panel program hosted by Stan Bernard on station WINS in New York.

part three third world

thomas paine
thomas jefferson
simon bolivar
william lloyd garrison
eugene v debs
emma goldman
malcolm x

apolinario mabini

Revolutionary nationalism erupted again in the Philippine Islands in 1898 when the soldier activist Emilio Aguinaldo, and the frail visionary and philosopher Apolinario Mabini, together sought modern nationalism for the Islands. Together they established a new nation, subservient neither to Spain nor to the United States; together, in the language of Mabini, they called for sacrifice, devotion, and national honor.

Born in Talaga, south of Manila, in 1864 to Inocencio Mabini and Dionisia Maranan, Apolinario studied in Tanawan and later under the famous Philippine teacher Father Valerio Malabanan. Further schooling at San Juan de Letran and the University of Santo Tomás in Manila led to a law degree. In January 1896, a serious illness resulted in paralysis of Mabini's legs for the remainder of his life. Soon afterwards, because of his nationalist sentiments, he was arrested by Spanish authorities when a revolt broke out, but was later released.

Shortly after the United States declared war on Spain in April 1898, the conflict spread to the Philippine Islands, where Aguinaldo had been induced by the Americans to return from Hong Kong and join in the war against Spain. Mabini viewed the war as presenting new opportunities for independence and cautioned revolutionary leaders against committing their forces too soon. On June 12, Aguinaldo proclaimed the Independence of the Philippine Islands at Cavite el Viejo. Not long before, Aguinaldo had read Mabini's shrewd suggestions advising caution in the revolution and had requested that Mabini serve as his personal advisor. Mabini had accepted and was spirited through Spanish lines in early June to join Aguinaldo at Cavite, where he became the "Brains of the Revolution."

A cautious man, Mabini believed Aguinaldo's unilateral declaration of independence for the Philippines a precipitous move, since warfare with Spain continued and the Americans had not decided the future status of the Islands. Mabini urged Aguinaldo to establish a stable government and thus impress foreign nations with the stability of the revolutionary forces. By June 23, with Mabini's guidance, Aguinaldo initiated a revolutionary government which had as its objective a working democratic government for the Philippines and the eventual establishment of a full-fledged republic. Several weeks later Mabini became president of the cabinet, appointed by Aguinaldo, and, later, Secretary of Foreign Affairs.

Tensions with the American forces and government increased as Filipino leaders grew suspicious of American intentions. During late summer and fall, American negotiators met with Spanish diplomats, and in the Treaty of Paris, signed in December 1898, the Philippines were transferred to the United States. Nevertheless, Filipino revolutionaries called for the proclamation of the Constitution of the Philippine Republic, based on the sovereignty of the Filipino people, on January 20, 1899. Aguinaldo became President of the Republic and chose Mabini as the Premier. The formation of a Republic drew strong reactions from the United States.

During the months which followed, warfare raged between the two republics. Finally, an American committee, the Shurman Commission, made its recommendations in May for a new Philippine government which did not include recognition of Philippine independence. Mabini rejected the recommendations, and resigned from the cabinet when the Philippine Congress (with only 20 members out of 110 present) demanded an "understanding" with the Americans. A new cabinet lessened the emphasis on nationalism, and Mabini remained, in the words of William Howard Taft, the Civil Governor of the Islands, the "most prominent irreconcilable among the Filipinos." He posed such an obstacle that the American government had him deported to Guam in January 1900. Remaining the most stubborn of the Filipino leaders, he refused to take an oath of allegiance until 1903, and then he was permitted to return to the Islands, where he died a short time later. Forty-three years later, his homeland achieved the independence he had sought.

To the Revolutionary Leaders

Colleagues:

The war between Spain and the United States of North America having been declared, it is very probable that within a few days a North American squadron would land on our shores and would, by force, take possession, as an act of offensive hostility towards Spain, of one or various seaboard points that it may consider necessary to the execution of the plans and instructions of its Government.

Although the real cause of the war is not and cannot be other than the helplessness of Spain to crush the revolution in Cuba, where the North Americans have big interests to protect, should the outcome of the war be unfavorable to Spain as it is to be expected, given the relative strength of the two combatants, and if because of this the Spanish Government should find itself having the necessity of asking the North American Government for peace, it is very probable that the latter would impose as a condition the independence of Cuba, and, as an indemnification of war, some portion of the Spanish peninsula or of this beautiful Archipelago.

Should the last contingency take place, our situation would be extremely difficult because, bound by duty and by our own honor and advantage to watch over the independence of our country, we should never consent to the dismemberment of this part and parcel of our own lives.

But, not having enough means or strength to oppose formal resistance to either one of the warring parties, we should have recourse to skill and astuteness, restraining the impetuosity of our hearts and subordinating our actions to cool reasoning.

. . . It is not convenient for the revolutionary forces to start hostilities against the forces of the Spanish government before the outcome of the combat is known, because the Spaniards may win; in which case they will earn respect in the eyes of the Filipino soldiers, and then they will have the necessary supremacy over the former and use the same in attacking the towns which have declared themselves independent.

It may be said that attacking the Spaniards and weakening them would make the triumph of the North Americans certain; but as we do not know what these people have in mind, should they happen to covet the possession of these

From Apolinario Mabini, *The Letters of Apolinario Mabini,* with a Preface by Carlos Quirino, compiled and translated by the National Heroes Commission, Manila, 1965, pp. 39, 41-42. Reprinted with the permission of the Commission. The letter is dated April 1898.

Islands, then, we shall have unwittingly helped them, as if we had voluntarily opened to them the doors of our house to let them rule over it.

And do not deceive yourself. The North Americans, like the Spaniards and all other European powers, covet this most beautiful pearl of the Orient Seas. But we prize it more ourselves, not only because God has given it to us as a present, but also because we have already shed so much blood for it.

But when those colossi of ambition and of power shall be convinced that there exists here a strong and organized people who know how to defend the laws of justice and their honor, they shall be forced to restrain themselves and to seek just settlements in order to get the best terms possible.

We, on our part, shall take care that they do not deceive us and that they should realize that we know how to live on our own, so that they will lend themselves to aid us at the cost of some sacrifices.

I am taking the liberty, dear colleagues, to propose these measures to you so that, should you not find any inconvenience, you would deign to adopt them for our common good. But, even if there should be any drawback, if it is but a matter of little importance, you should still adopt them for the sake of the unity that should guide all our acts, until such time as you should have designated the person whom you want to obey.

To Archbishop Bernardino Nozaleda

I have the satisfaction to acknowledge receipt of your letter of August 21st, last, and of the one which the Most Eminent Cardinal Rampolla addressed to you in behalf of the freedom of the Spanish prisoners. Before going further, I have to beg you that, in answering the letter of the above-mentioned Cardinal, you should make clear to him that the clergy and the Catholic people of the Philippines are imbued with the most irrevocable attachment to the Holy See.

You are so right when you say in retaining the Spanish prisoners, especially the religious ones, we are neither prompted by the repugnant spirit of commercialism nor by the memory of affronts that we keep in our minds. Our only aim is that it should serve us as a beneficial lesson for the future, and never for purposes of wreaking vengeance, which is incompatible with the valor and charity of which we hope to give some proofs to the cultured world.

In retaining the Spanish members of the religious orders of whom Monsignor

From *The Letters of Apolinario Mabini*, pp. 215-216. The letter is undated.

Rampolla speaks, we have been moved by the highest spirit of justice and by the sacred interests of the Catholic religion in the Philippines.

When Pope Alexander VI granted on May 4, 1493, to the Catholic Kings of Spain the authority to extend the Christian Gospel to the East Indies, he did not authorize them in such a manner that after the discovered people shall have been preached the Gospel they shall be given over and sold like merchandise to the pagan nations. I may be permitted to call the North American nation pagan, because the Constitution of the same has not declared the Catholic religion as official religion in the way that the Spanish Constitution does.

We know that the Vatican, before looking after the welfare of a few members of the religious orders, should be more interested in the fate of eight millions of Catholic Filipinos, who are channeled into slavery by the deed and virtue of that immoral sale. The Filipino people, in opposing that sale, sacrificing their lives and their interests, labor not only for their freedom but also for their religion and their fidelity to the Holy See. That is why I, who, as a Filipino, have to fight for the independence of my country and, as a Catholic, have to look after the integrity of the Catholic religion, consider myself duty-bound to temporarily deprive of freedom those persons whose brothers are working tirelessly for the consummation of the above-mentioned sale, until I can have the certainty that they cannot harm us any more.

. . . You should not worry regarding the moral effect that the retention of the Spanish prisoners will produce on public opinion. When public conscience, which is said to be cultured and the sole repository of civilization, will consider the sale of countries as licit and ordinary just because they are classified as colonies, even if this sale be the continuation in grand scale of the old slave trade, we know that we are excused for flattering that opinion. The Vatican dares not raise its authoritative voice against that inveterate custom, which is so opposed to Christian morals but regarded as lawful in the positive international law, because it does not find itself convenient to be in open controversy with the interests of many world powers. For this very reason, I do not doubt that it will also respect the interests of the Filipino people, interests that would advise the temporary retention of some Spanish members of the religious orders. Besides, I believe said religious prisoners would prefer to live in the midst of a Catholic country to being turned over to another which is pagan or which practices free cult. . . .

Self-government and the Filipino People

1. Q. Is it possible that there may not be a Revolution?
   A. It is.
   Q. How?
   A. By satisfying the aspirations of the people.
2. Q. What were the causes of the Revolution?
   A. The causes of the Revolution can be condensed as follows:
   The popular desire of the people to have a government that would assure to the Filipinos freedom of thought, conscience and association; immunity in their persons, homes and correspondence; popular representation in the drafting of laws and imposition of taxes; equality of participation in public offices and public benefits; respect for laws and property; and the progressive development of public welfare with the help of means offered by modern progress.
3. Q. Would all the Tagalog people be satisfied should Aguinaldo stay as President?
   A. All the Filipinos, not the Tagalogs alone, will be happy with a President that they themselves would elect in a way that may be stipulated in the United States Congress. Today, they acknowledge General Aguinaldo as President because he personifies their aspirations. But the moment they observe that his acts are prompted only by personal ambitions, they will withdraw their support and acknowledge another who proves to be most worthy of their trust.
4. Q. Will all the people be happy?
   A. This has been included in the previous question.
5. Q. Does Mr. Aguinaldo possess enough strength to bring the Islands to order?
   A. He has, as long as he counts with the support of the people.
6. Q. Where will the money for running the Government come from?
   A. For the expenses that are absolutely necessary in the installation of a permanent Government a foreign loan in sufficient amount with the guarantees and conditions previously stipulated with the Congress of the United States shall be negotiated. For the amortization of this debt and for the ordinary expenses of public administration, taxes voted by the representatives of the people shall be imposed with the greatest equity.
7. Q. And the Southern Islands?
   A. They follow by the decisions made in Luzon as they have always shown. Those who assure that there is no national aspiration in these Islands and that the Revolution is purely Tagalog in nature show gross ignorance of the Filipinos.

From *The Letters of Apolinario Mabini*, pp. 234-236. Mabini is answering questions posed by General Joseph Wheeler of the United States Army in the Philippines, December 25, 1899.

From the year 1872, in which the Spaniards unjustly decapitated three Filipino priests—among whom was Father Burgos—the people began to reflect on their sad plight and showed their discontent, although nobody as yet dared to show it outside the inner circle and intimacy of the home. Later on, Rizal, Marcelo H. del Pilar, and others who went to Europe to obtain higher learning, started a resolute and energetic campaign to instruct their countrymen in their rights and in the freedoms that are enjoyed in other countries. With this, the unanimous aspiration of the Filipinos, which was vague at the beginning, acquired definite form, with the persecution organized by the Spanish Government against reformist and secret societies greatly contributing to this development. It is true that the less-educated classes, and the more numerous at that, could not translate into clear words their aspirations and wishes, a fact which also happens in the more progressive countries; but the popular and unanimous aspiration exists. The Revolution of 1896 started from this class, and later, it was taken up by the whole social strata, all fused together in a single ideal, in 1898. When Aguinaldo returned from Hong Kong, the people, by spontaneous inspiration, rose up in a mass and fought against the Spaniards without orders nor instructions nor help from the said General, as is proven by the swift surrender of the Spaniards. All the Filipinos acknowledged Aguinaldo as their leader in order to avoid internal struggles and rivalries. The Revolution is not the work of Aguinaldo, but of the circumstances, and he will maintain his popularity as long as he remains worthy of the confidence of the people.

8. Q. Do the people of these Islands like war?

A. No; so much so, that during the 300 years of Spanish domination, not one has been registered except the one that broke out in 1896, of which the present one is but a continuation, and which the Filipinos are sustaining in the assurance [*sic*] that they are defending sacred rights that are inherent to all peoples.

9. Q. Do the people want a good government by the United States?

A. The Filipinos, like all other peoples, believe that the best Government is their own. Hence, when they are convinced that it is not possible for them now to obtain a government from the United States without other limitations than those that are determined in an agreement or a written Constitutional Charter drafted by their representatives, it is probable that the government which the United States will impose on the Filipinos by force would serve to exemplify the attainment of a government more to their own liking inasmuch as progress, which is the law of all people, so demands it. Should the American people oppose this law, the time of their decadence and ruin will not be far away.

10. Q. Do the Filipino people like progress, railroads, etc., very much?

A. One of the causes of the Revolution is the aspiration to a life of progress that the greater facility of communication with other countries nowadays has awakened in the hearts of the Filipinos notwithstanding the efforts of the Spanish Government to neutralize this influence.

11. Q. Is it the manner that Spain governs that the Filipinos want?

A. The sensible opinion is the country detests the Spanish administration for the deep-rooted vices it carries with it. That was why when Aguinaldo chose as advisers some persons who wanted to revive the Spanish system of government and showed little energy to repress the old abuses, the honest Filipinos began to withdraw and disillusionment among the people became evident.

To American Correspondents

Distinguished Gentlemen:

Convinced that you treat the Filipino question with impartiality in order that the public opinion of the U.S. may not be misled and may be worthy of a great, free and cultured nation, I take the liberty of requesting you to consider and make known the following points:

1st. The Filipino nation does not encourage any hatred against foreigners; but on the contrary, she welcomes with pleasure and gratitude whoever wishes to cooperate with her to attain her liberties and prosperity.

2nd. The Filipinos maintain the fight against American forces not because of hatred, but to demonstrate to the American nation that, far from looking with indifference to the country's political situation, they know, on the contrary, to sacrifice for a government that will assure her of individual liberties in accordance with the wishes and necessities of the nation. They have not been able to avoid such a fight because so far they have not obtained any clear or formal promise from the government of the U.S. for the establishment of such a kind of government.

3rd. The present state of war does not permit the nation to manifest sincerely her aspirations. The Filipinos ardently wish that the American Congress find a means of hearing them before adopting any resolution which will decide definitely her future.

4th. For this end, the Filipino people are asking Congress for the following: that it either appoint an American Commission that will come in contact with Filipinos who are influential with both the peaceful civilians and those engaged

From *The Letters of Apolinario Mabini*, pp. 239–240. The letter is dated January 22, 1900.

in battle, or accept a Commission of this group of people in order that it may be informed about the wishes of our nation.

5th. In order that the information can be complete and the work of the Commission, in one way or another, can give results for the coming of peace, it is necessary that the American forces of occupation refrain from curtailing the open manifestations of public opinion in the press and in peaceful reunions; suspend temporarily the attacks against Filipino barracks, whenever Filipinos do not intentionally attack the Americans; and give the Commissioners the utmost in facility of communication with the revolutionists.

6th. The Filipinos, without much reflection upon seeing the triumph of American forces, will not be able to think less than that all concessions in favor of the Philippines in these moments proceed exclusively from the liberality of the North American nation, which is one more reason for Congress to show more benevolence and indulgence.

I ardently hope and trust that when both the American people and the Filipino people will know each other better, the present conflict will not only cease but will avoid future ones. The sensible opinion of the U.S. seems to be more inclined not to draw away from their traditions and form their spirit of Justice and Humanity which, at the present, constitutes the only hope of an honest Filipino nation. . . .

mohandas gandhi

As twentieth century colonies sought their independence from western colonial rule, an atmosphere of bitterness, hatred, and envy covered the colonial environment. Most of the colonial revolutionary leaders turned to violence in order to achieve their national objectives. They employed force in the shape of insurrections and guerrilla warfare; their colonial masters initiated or adopted similar tactics, and the worst kinds of human passions were inflamed. One man, however, Mohandas Gandhi, the most revolutionary of them all, dedicated his life to non-violence during these years. He awakened a new self-awareness and dignity among the people of India, especially during their attempts to gain independence from Great Britain.

Born in Porbandar, Kathiawar, in 1869, Gandhi came from a trading caste. His father and grandfather served as chief minister in the local government; his mother's religious influence on him was tremendous. After schooling in Rajkot and in London he was admitted to the bar in 1889, and practiced law in Bombay and Rajkot before going to Durban, South Africa. Racial discrimination against him caused a personal crisis in 1893, and after serious reflection, he decided to oppose racial and religious discrimination by active non-violence. During the next ten years he founded the Natal Indian Congress party, organized an ambulance corps during the South African War, and gradually turned to writing.

In 1904, he became the publisher of *Indian Opinion*, a weekly journal with eight hundred subscribers, published in South Africa for the Indian settlers. In its columns, Gandhi urged passive resistance as a reply to injustice. During this time, he read the essay, *Unto This Last*, written in 1860 by the English social theorist and critic, John Ruskin. This critique, which questioned the values in English bourgeois society and industrialism, profoundly impressed Gandhi and he came away with a deeper awareness that the good of the individual was to be found in the good of the community. Certain ideas contained in several books by Alekscy Tolstoy, Henry Thoreau, the Bible, and the Koran also became part of his life style as he reevaluated Indian and western European civilizations.

His first major work, *Hind Swaraj* or *Indian Home Rule*, was first published serially in the columns of *Indian Opinion* in late 1909 in the Gujarati language, spoken in western India. Issued in book form in January 1910, Gandhi's study preached the gospel of love rather than hate. Nevertheless, it was proscribed in India by the government of Bombay in March. That same month, spurred on by the impending censorship, Gandhi authorized publication of an English translation, and subsequent editions circulated throughout the world. *Indian Home Rule* gave Gandhi's answer to the growing Indian violence.

Written in the question-answer style, with Gandhi being the "Editor," this dissertation on the destructiveness of western industrial civilization remains a classic, and its emphasis on non-violence had a profound influence on other leaders such as Martin Luther King, Jr. Gandhi's continued reliance on *Satyagraha*, which means a "force which is born of truth and love or non-violence," and his belief that India would advance by discarding modern civilization appealed to the Indian people. His protests against British rule and his mass campaigns of civil disobedience in India led to mass arrests in India during the four decades after 1909. Before his death by assassination in 1948, Gandhi had introduced a new self-awareness among Indians, and, though he opposed the partition of India, he prayed and fasted so that the Hindus, Muslims, and Sikhs would become nonviolent. His life and, indeed, his death portrayed the many emotional and violent problems surrounding Indian home rule.

Indian Home Rule

READER: Now you will have to explain what you mean by civilization.
EDITOR: It is not a question of what I mean. Several English writers refuse to call that civilization which passes under that name. Many books have been

From *Indian Home Rule (Hind Swaraj)*, reprinted in *The Selected Works of Mahatma Gandhi,* IV, edited by Shriman Narayan, Navajivan Publishing House, Ahmedabad, 1968, pp. 118-122, 149-153, 169-181. Reprinted with permission of the Navajivan Trust.

written upon that subject. Societies have been formed to cure the nation of the evils of civilization. A great English writer has written a work called *Civilization: Its Cause and Cure*. Therein he has called it a disease.

READER: Why do we not know this generally?

EDITOR: The answer is very simple. We rarely find people arguing against themselves. Those who are intoxicated by modern civilization are not likely to write against it. Their care will be to find out facts and arguments in support of it, and this they do unconsciously, believing it to be true. A man whilst he is dreaming, believes in his dream; he is undeceived only when he is awakened from his sleep. A man labouring under the bane of civilization is like a dreaming man. What we usually read are the works of defenders of modern civilization, which undoubtedly claims among its votaries very brilliant and even some very good men. Their writings hypnotize us. And so, one by one, we are drawn into the vortex.

READER: This seems to be very plausible. Now will you tell me something of what you have read and thought of this civilization?

EDITOR: Let us first consider what state of things is described by the word "civilization." Its true test lies in the fact that people living in it make bodily welfare the object of life. We will take some examples. The people of Europe today live in better-built houses than they did a hundred years ago. This is considered an emblem of civilization, and this is also a matter to promote bodily happiness. Formerly, they wore skins, and used spears as their weapons. Now, they wear long trousers, and, for embelishing their bodies, they wear a variety of clothing, and, instead of spears, they carry with them revolvers containing five or more chambers. If people of a certain country, who have hitherto not been in the habit of wearing much clothing, boots, etc., adopt European clothing, they are supposed to have become civilized out of savagery. Formerly, in Europe, people ploughed their lands mainly by manual labour. Now, one man can plough a vast tract by means of steam engines and can thus amass great wealth. This is called a sign of civilization. Formerly, only a few men wrote valuable books. Now, anybody writes and prints anything he likes and poisons people's minds. Formerly, men travelled in wagons. Now, they fly through the air in trains at the rate of four hundred and more miles per day. This is considered the height of civilization. It has been stated that, as men progress, they shall be able to travel in airships and reach any part of the world in a few hours. Men will not need the use of their hands and feet. They will press a button, and they will have their clothing by their side. They will press another button, and they will have their newspaper. A third, and a motor-car will be in waiting for them. They will have a variety of delicately dished up food. Everything will be done by machinery. Formerly, when people wanted to fight with one another, they measured between them their bodily strength; now it is possible to take away thousands of lives by one man working behind a gun from a hill. This is civilization. Formerly, men worked in the open air only as much as they liked. Now thousands of workmen meet together and for the sake of maintenance work in factories or mines. Their condition is worse than that of beasts. They are obliged to work, at the risk of their lives, at most dangerous occupations, for the sake of million-aires. Formerly, men were made slaves under physical compulsion. Now they are enslaved by temptation of money and of the luxuries that money can buy. There are now diseases of which people never dreamt before, and an army of doctors is engaged in finding out their cures, and so hospitals have increased. This is a test of civilization. Formerly, special messengers were required and much expense was incurred in order to send letters; today, anyone can abuse his fellow by means of a letter for one penny. True, at the same cost, one can send one's thanks also. Formerly, people had two or three meals consisting of home-made bread and vegetables; now, they require something to eat every two hours so that they have hardly leisure for anything else. What more need I say? All this you can ascertain from several authoritative books. These are all true tests of civilization. And if anyone speaks to the contrary, know that he is ignorant. This civilization takes note neither of morality nor of religion. Its votaries calmly state that their business is not to teach religion. Some even consider it to be a superstitious growth. Others put on the cloak of religion, and prate about morality. But, after twenty years' experience, I have come to the conclusion that immorality is often taught in the name of morality. Even a child can understand that in all I have described above there can be no inducement to morality. Civilization seeks to increase bodily comforts, and it fails miserably even in doing so.

This civilization is irreligion, and it has taken such a hold on the people in Europe that those who are in it appear to be half mad. They lack real physical strength or courage. They keep up their energy by intoxication. They can hardly be happy in solitude. Women, who should be the queens of households, wander in the streets or they slave away in factories. For the sake of a pittance, half a million women in England alone are labouring under trying circumstances in factories or similar institutions. This awful fact is one of the causes of the daily growing suffragette movement.

This civilization is such that one has only to be patient and it will be self-destroyed. According to the teaching of Mahomed this would be considered a Satanic Civilization. Hinduism calls it the Black Age. I cannot give you an adequate conception of it. It is eating into the vitals of the English nation. It must be shunned. Parliaments are really emblems of slavery. If you will suffi-ciently think over this, you will entertain the same opinion and cease to blame the English. They rather deserve our sympathy. They are a shrewd nation and I therefore believe that they will cast off the evil. They are enterprising and industrious, and their mode of thought is not inherently immoral. Neither are they bad at heart. I therefore respect them. Civilization is not an incurable disease, but it should never be forgotten that the English people are at present afflicted by it.

READER: You have denounced railways, lawyers and doctors. I can see that you will discard all machinery. What then is civilization?

EDITOR: The answer to that question is not difficult. I believe that the civilization India has evolved is not to be beaten in the world. Nothing can equal the seeds sown by our ancestors. Rome went, Greece shared the same fate; the might of the Pharaohs was broken; Japan has become Westernized; of China nothing can be said; but India is still, somehow or other, sound at the foundation. The people of Europe learn their lessons from the writings of the men of Greece or Rome, which exist no longer in their former glory. In trying to learn from them, the Europeans imagine that they will avoid the mistakes of Greece and Rome. Such is their pitiable condition. In the midst of all this India remains immovable and that is her glory. It is a charge against India that her people are so uncivilized, ignorant and stolid, that it is not possible to induce them to adopt any changes. It is a charge really against our merit. What we have tested and found true on the anvil of experience, we dare not change. Many thrust their advice upon India, and she remains steady. This is her beauty: it is the sheet-anchor of our hope.

Civilization is that mode of conduct which points out to man the path of duty. Performance of duty and observance of morality are convertible terms. To observe morality is to attain mastery over our mind and our passions. So doing, we know ourselves. The Gujarati equivalent for civilization means "good conduct."

If this definition be correct, then India, as so many writers have shown, has nothing to learn from anybody else, and this is as it should be. We notice that the mind is a restless bird; the more it gets the more it wants, and still remains unsatisfied. The more we indulge our passions the more unbridled they become. Our ancestors, therefore, set a limit to our indulgences. They saw that happiness was largely a mental condition. A man is not necessarily happy because he is rich, or unhappy because he is poor. The rich are often seen to be unhappy, the poor to be happy. Millions will always remain poor. Observing all this, our ancestors dissuaded us from luxuries and pleasures. We have managed with the same kind of plough as existed thousands of years ago. We have retained the same kind of cottages that we had in former times and our indigenous education remains the same as before. We have had no system of life-corroding competition. Each followed his own occupation or trade and charged a regulation wage. It was not that we did not know how to invent machinery, but our forefathers knew that, if we set our hearts after such things, we would become slaves and lose our moral fibre. They, therefore, after due deliberation decided that we should only do what we could with our hands and feet. They saw that our real happiness and health consisted in a proper use of our hands and feet. They further reasoned that large cities were a snare and a useless encumbrance and that people would not be happy in them, that there would be gangs of thieves and robbers, prostitution and vice flourishing in them and that poor men would be robbed by rich men. They were, therefore, satisfied with small villages. They saw that kings and their swords were inferior to the sword of ethics, and they, therefore, held the sovereigns of the earth to be inferior to the Rishis and Fakirs. A nation with a constitution like this is fitter to teach others than to learn from others. This nation had courts, lawyers and doctors, but they were all within bounds. Everybody knew that these professions were not particularly superior; moreover, these vakils and vaids did not rob the people; they were considered people's dependents, not their masters. Justice was tolerably fair. The ordinary rule was to avoid courts. There were no touts to lure people into them. This evil, too, was noticeable only in and around capitals. The common people lived independently and followed their agricultural occupation. They enjoyed true Home Rule.

And where this cursed modern civilization has not reached, India remains as it was before. The inhabitants of that part of India will very properly laugh at your newfangled notions. The English do not rule over them, nor will you ever rule over them. Those in whose name we speak we do not know, nor do they know us. I would certainly advise you and those like you who love the motherland to go into the interior that has yet been not polluted by the railways and to live there for six months; you might then be patriotic and speak of Home Rule.

Now you see what I consider to be real civilization. Those who want to change conditions such as I have described are the enemies of the country and are sinners.

READER: It would be all right if India were exactly as you have described it, but it is also India where there are hundreds of child widows, where two year old babies are married, where twelve year old girls are mothers and housewives, where women practise polandry, where the practice of Niyoga obtains, where, in the name of religion, girls dedicate themselves to prostitution, and in the name of religion sheep and goats are killed. Do you consider these also symbols of the civilization that you have described?

EDITOR: You make a mistake. The defects that you have shown are defects. Nobody mistakes them for ancient civilization. They remain in spite of it.

Attempts have always been made and will be made to remove them. We may utilize the new spirit that is born in us for purging ourselves of these evils. But what I have described to you as emblems of modern civilization are accepted as such by its votaries. The Indian civilization, as described by me, has been so described by its votaries. In no part of the world, and under no civilization, have all men attained perfection. The tendency of the Indian civilization is to elevate the moral being, that of the Western civilization is to propagate immorality. The latter is godless, the former is based on a belief in God. So understanding and so believing, it behoves every lover of India to cling to the old Indian civilization even as a child clings to the mother's breast.

READER: Is there any historical evidence as to the success of what you have called soul-force or truth-force? No instance seems to have happened of any nation having risen through soul-force. I still think that the evildoers will not cease doing evil without physical punishment.

EDITOR: The poet Tulsidas has said: "Of religion, pity, or love, is the root, as egotism of the body. Therefore, we should not abandon pity so long as we are alive." This appears to me to be a scientific truth. I believe in it as much as I believe in two and two being four. The force of love is the same as the force of the soul or truth. We have evidence of its working at every step. The universe would disappear without the existence of that force. But you ask for historical evidence. It is, therefore, necessary to know what history means. The Gujarati equivalent means: "It so happened." If that is the meaning of history, it is possible to give copious evidence. But, if it means the doings of kings and emperors, there can be no evidence of soul-force or passive resistance in such history. You cannot expect silver ore in a tin mine. History, as we know it, is a record of the wars of the world, and so there is a proverb among Englishmen that a nation which has no history, that is, no wars, is a happy nation. How kings played, how they became enemies of one another, how they murdered one another, is found accurately recorded in history, and if this were all that had happened in the world, it would have been ended long ago. If the story of the universe had commenced with wars, not a man would have been found alive today. Those people who have been warred against have disappeared as, for instance, the natives of Australia of whom hardly a man was left alive by the intruders. Mark, please, that these natives did not use soul-force in self-defense, and it does not require much foresight to know that the Australians will share the same fate as their victims. "Those that take the sword shall perish by the sword." With us the proverb is that professional swimmers will find a watery grave.

The fact that there are so many men still alive in the world shows that it is based not on the force of arms but on the force of truth or love. Therefore, the greatest and most unimpeachable evidence of the success of this force is to be found in the fact that, in spite of the wars of the world, it still lives on.

Thousands, indeed tens of thousands, depend for their existence on a very active working of this force. Little quarrels of millions of families in their daily lives disappear before the exercise of this force. Hundreds of nations live in peace. History does not and cannot take note of this fact. History is really a record of every interruption of the even working of the force of love or of the soul. Two brothers quarrel; one of them repents and re-awakens the love that was lying dormant in him; and the two again begin to live in peace; nobody takes note of this. But if the two brothers, through the intervention of solicitors or some other reason take up arms or go to law—which is another form of the exhibition of brute force—their doings would be immediately noticed in the press, they would be the talk of their neighbours and would probably go down to history. And what is true of families and communities is true of nations. History, then, is a record of an interruption of the course of nature. Soul-force, being natural, is not noted in history.

READER: According to what you say, it is plain that instances of this kind of passive resistance are not to be found in history. It is necessary to understand this passive resistance more fully. It will be better, therefore, if you enlarge upon it.

EDITOR: Passive resistance is a method of securing rights by personal suffering; it is the reverse of resistance by arms. When I refuse to do a thing that is repugnant to my conscience, I use soul-force. For instance, the Government of the day has passed a law which is applicable to me. I do not like it. If by using violence I force the Government to repeal the law, I am employing what may be termed body-force. If I do not obey the law and accept the penalty for its breach, I use soul-force. It involves sacrifice of self.

Everybody admits that sacrifice of self is infinitely superior to sacrifice of others. Moreover, if this kind of force is used in a cause that is unjust, only the person using it suffers. He does not make others suffer for his mistakes. Men have before now done many things which were subsequently found to have been wrong. No man can claim that he is absolutely in the right or that a particular thing is wrong because he thinks so, but it is wrong for him so long as that is his deliberate judgement. It is therefore meet that he should not do that which he knows to be wrong, and suffer the consequence whatever it may be. This is the key to the use of soul-force.

READER: You would then disregard laws—this is rank disloyalty. We have always been considered a law-abiding nation. You seem to be going even beyond the extremists. They say that we must obey the laws that have been passed, but that if the laws be bad, we must drive out the law-givers even by force.

EDITOR: Whether I go beyond them or whether I do not is a matter of no consequence to either of us. We simply want to find out what is right and to act accordingly. The real meaning of the statement that we are a law-abiding nation is that we are passive resisters. When we do not like certain laws, we do not break the heads of law-givers but we suffer and do not submit to the laws. That we should obey laws whether good or bad is a newfangled notion. There was no such thing in former days. The people disregarded those laws they did not like and suffered the penalties for their breach. It is contrary to our manhood if we obey laws repugnant to our conscience. Such teaching is opposed to religion and means slavery. If the Government were to ask us to go about without any clothing, should we do so? If I were a passive resister, I would say to them that I would have nothing to do with their law. But we have so forgotten ourselves and become so compliant that we do not mind any degrading law.

A man who has realized his manhood, who fears only God, will fear no one else. Man-made laws are not necessarily binding on him. Even the Government does not expect any such thing from us. They do not say: "You must do such and such a thing," but they say "If you do not do it, we will punish you." We are sunk so low that we fancy that it is our duty and our religion to do what the law lays down. If man will only realize that it is unmanly to obey laws that are unjust, no man's tyranny will enslave him. This is the key to self-rule or home-rule.

It is a superstition and ungodly thing to believe that an act of a majority bends a minority. Many examples can be given in which acts of majorities will be found to have been wrong and those of minorities to have been right. All reforms owe their origin to the initiation of minorities in opposition to majorities. If among a band of robbers a knowledge of robbing is obligatory, is a pious man to accept the obligation? So long as the superstition that men should obey unjust laws exists, so long will their slavery exist. And a passive resister alone can remove such a superstition.

To use brute force, to use gunpowder, is contrary to passive resistance, for it means that we want our opponent to do by force that which we desire but he does not. And if such a use of force is justifiable, surely he is entitled to do likewise by us. And so we should never come to an agreement. We may simply fancy, like the blind horse moving in a circle round a mill, that we are making progress. Those who believe that they are not bound to obey laws which are repugnant to their conscience have only the remedy of passive resistance open to them. Any other must lead to disaster.

READER: From what you say I deduce that passive resistance is a splendid weapon of the weak, but that when they are strong they may take up arms.

EDITOR: This is gross ignorance. Passive resistance, that is, soul-force, is matchless. It is superior to the force of arms. How, then, can it be considered only a weapon of the weak? Physical-force men are strangers to the courage that is requisite in a passive resister. Do you believe that a coward can ever disobey a law that he dislikes? Extremists are considered to be advocates of brute force. Why do they, then, talk about obeying laws? I do not blame them. The can say nothing else. When they succeed in driving out the English and they themselves become governors, they will want you and me to obey their laws. And that is a fitting thing for their constitution. But a passive resister will say he will not obey a law that is against his conscience, even though he may be blown to pieces at the mouth of a cannon.

What do you think? Wherein is courage required—in blowing others to pieces from behind a cannon, or with a smiling face to approach a cannon and be blown to pieces? Who is the true warrior—he who keeps death always as a bosom-friend, or he who controls the death of others? Believe me that a man devoid of courage and manhood can never be a passive resister.

This however, I will admit: that even a man weak in body is capable of offering this resistance. One man can offer it just as well as millions. Both men and women can indulge in it. It does not require the training of an army; it needs no jiu-jitsu. Control over the mind is alone necessary, and when that is attained man is free like the king of the forest and his very glance withers the enemy.

Passive resistance is an all-sided sword, it can be used anyhow; it blesses him who uses it and him against whom it is used. Without drawing a drop of blood it produces far-reaching results. It never rusts and cannot be stolen. Competition between passive resisters does not exhaust. The sword of passive resistance does not require a scabbard. It is strange indeed that you should consider such a weapon to be a weapon merely of the weak.

READER: You have said that passive resistance is a speciality of India. Have cannons never been used in India?

EDITOR: Evidently, in your opinion, India means its few princes. To me it means its teeming millions on whom depends the existence of its princes and our own.

Kings will always use their kingly weapons. To use force is bred in them. They want to command, but those who have to obey commands do not want guns: and these are in a majority throughout the world. They have to learn either body-force or soul-force. Where they learn the former, both the rulers and the ruled become like so many madmen; but where they learn soul-force, the commands of the rulers do not go beyond the point of their swords, for true men disregard unjust commands. Peasants have never been subdued by the sword, and never will be. They do not know the use of the sword, and they are not frightened by the use of it by others. That nation is great which rests its head upon death as its pillow. Those who defy death are free from all fear. For those who are labouring under the delusive charms of brute-force, this picture is not overdrawn. The fact is that, in India, the nation at large has generally used passive resistance in all departments of life. We cease to co-operate with our rulers when they displease us. This is passive resistance.

I remember an instance when, in a small principality, the villagers were offended by some command issued by the prince. The former immediately, began vacating the village. The prince became nervous, apologized to his subjects and withdrew his command. Many such instances can be found in India. Real Home Rule is possible only where passive resistance is the guiding force of the people. Any other rule is foreign rule.

READER: Then you will say that it is not at all necessary for us to train the body?

EDITOR: I will certainly not say any such thing. It is difficult to become a passive resister unless the body is trained. As a rule, the mind, residing in a body that has become weakened by pampering, is also weak, and where there is no strength of mind there can be no strength of soul. We shall have to improve our physique by getting rid of infant marriages and luxurious living. If I were to ask a man with a shattered body to face a cannon's mouth I should make a laughing-stock of myself.

READER: From what you say, then, it would appear that it is not a small thing to become a passive resister, and, if that is so, I should like you to explain how a man may become one.

EDITOR: To become a passive resister is easy enough but it is also equally difficult. I have known a lad of fourteen years become a passive resister; I have known also sick people do likewise; and I have also known physically strong and otherwise happy people unable to take up passive resistance. After a great deal of experience it seems to me that those who want to become passive resisters for the service of the country have to observe perfect chastity, adopt poverty, follow truth, and cultivate fearlessness.

Chastity is one of the greatest disciplines without which the mind cannot attain requisite firmness. A man who is unchaste loses stamina, becomes emasculated and cowardly. He whose mind is given over to animal passions is not capable of any great effort. This can be proved by innumerable instances. What, then, is a married person to do is the question that arises naturally; and yet it need not. When a husband and wife gratify the passions, it is no less an animal indulgence on that account. Such an indulgence, except for perpetuating the race, is strictly prohibited. But a passive resister has to avoid even that very limited indulgence because he can have no desire for progeny. A married man, therefore, can observe perfect chastity. This subject is not capable of being treated at greater length. Several questions arise: How is one to carry one's wife with one, what are her rights, and other similar questions. Yet those who wish to take part in a great work are bound to solve these puzzles.

Just as there is necessity for chastity, so is there for poverty. Pecuniary ambition and passive resistance cannot well go together. Those who have money are not expected to throw it away, but they *are* expected to be indifferent about it. They must be prepared to lose every penny rather than give up passive resistance.

Passive resistance has been described in the course of our discussion as truth-force. Truth, therefore, has necessarily to be followed and that at any cost. In this connection, academic questions such as whether a man may not lie in order to save a life, etc., arise, but these questions occur only to those who wish to justify lying. Those who want to follow truth every time are not placed in such a quandary; and if they are, they are still saved from a false position.

Passive resistance cannot proceed a step without fearlessness. Those alone can follow the path of passive resistance who are free from fear, whether as to their possessions, false honour, their relatives, the government, bodily injuries or death.

These observances are not to be abandoned in the belief that they are difficult. Nature has implanted in the human breast ability to cope with any difficulty or suffering that may come to man unprovoked. These qualities are worth having, even for those who do not wish to serve the country. Let there be no mistake, as those who want to train themselves in the use of arms are also obliged to have these qualities more or less. Everybody does not become a warrior for the wish. A would-be warrior will have to observe chastity and to be satsified with poverty as his lot. A warrior without fearlessness cannot be conceived of. It may be thought that he would not need to be exactly truthful, but that quality follows real fearlessness. When a man abandons truth, he does so owing to fear in some shape or form. The above four attributes, then, need not frighten anyone. It may be as well here to note that a physical-force man has to have many other useless qualities which a passive resister never needs. And you will find that whatever extra effort a swordsman needs is due to lack of fearlessness. If he is an embodiment of the latter, the sword will drop from his hand that very moment. He does not need its support. One who is free from hatred requires no sword. A man with a stick suddenly came face to face with a lion and instinctively raised his weapon in self-defense. The man saw that he had only prated about fearlessness when there was none in him. That moment he dropped the stick and found himself free from all fear.

ho chi minh

As a guerrilla leader, Ho Chi Minh had few moments for serious reflection on the issues and objectives of revolution. Indeed from early childhood his life style grew increasingly mobile as he rejected the French colonial environment of Vietnam and worked for a better society outside the land of his birth. After several decades of exile he returned to his native land and fought for its independence.

Born as Nguyen That Thanh in 1890 to a peasant family in the village of Kim Lien in central Vietnam, he became aware at an early age of the discontent, particularly in his province (Nghé An), caused by absentee landlords. His schooling at the French *lycée* at Vinh ended abruptly with dismissal because he protested the colonial character of the academic classes and textbooks. Without funds he sought other avenues of education in Saigon but eventually became a galleyhand on a French liner and travelled to France, Great Britain, the United States, and Africa. These years convinced him that colonialism was an evil, and whether the geographic area was labelled Africa, Middle East, or Vietnam, colored people as colonials were exploited and considered as less than human. His bitterness intensified as he observed the biased practices of western colonial officials. He believed that all the victims of colonization must unite and throw off imperialism.

When World War I began in 1914, Ho took a kitchen job in London, and also became active in the Chinese Overseas Workers' Association. In 1917 he moved to Paris, joined the French Socialist Party, and vigorously pushed forward Vietnamese nationalist aims, while at the same time becoming more powerful in the Socialist hierarchy. Thus, even among those Socialists who urged an international outlook, Ho emphasized the plight of Vietnam first. The name he used most often during the 1920's, "Nguyen Ai Quoc," pointed up his hunger for an independent nation because Ai Quoc means "the Patriot." Often during the succeeding years Communist leaders sought his energies for the world revolution while he made the independence of his homeland and anticolonialism his major objectives. At the Versailles Peace Conference in 1919, Ho appealed to the great powers with a one page printed statement urging greater rights for Vietnam such as better laws, more schools, and equality between the people and colonial officials. A practical man, he did not appeal for independence, probably believing it completely beyond reach at that time.

At the Eighteenth National Congress of the French Socialist Party in December 1920, Ho joined other left-wing members, urged the establishment of a French Communist Party, and called for joining the Third International. He became one of the French Party's first members, and during the next few years wrote numerous articles on the evils of colonialism for the French journals, *Le paria*, *l'Humanité*, and *La Vie ouvrière*. In the mid-twenties, he attended the Fifth Congress of the Communist International in Moscow. He then went on to Canton, China, to organize young Vietnamese revolutionaries who then returned to Vietnam and established units of the Revolutionary Youth League. Marxism spread through the country, and Communist groups from the three areas of Vietnam (north, center, and south) merged into the Communist Party of Indo-China under the guidance of Ho, who had been selected by the Communist International for this role.

During the 1930's he lived in Hong Kong, Shanghai, Moscow, and Berlin, and continued to send articles on colonialism and Communism to the Indo-China Communist Party. Returning to Vietnam in 1941, he organized a number of nationalist groups into the Vietnam League for Independence, called the "Vietminh," which became popular in the areas of Tonkin, Annam, and Cochin China. He also became known during these years as Ho Chi Minh. The League began preparations for destroying the Japanese occupation forces which had teamed up with Vichy-appointed French officials and army. As the power of the Japanese empire fragmented, French officials were interned by Japan in March 1945. With the Allied victory over Japan through the use of the A-bomb in mid-August 1945, Ho and the League sought independence for Vietnam.

On September 2, 1945, the Declaration of Independence of the Democratic Republic of Vietnam was issued in Hanoi, and in March 1946 the National

Assembly approved the Constitution. Also in this month, the French government recognized the Republic as being a free state within the French Union; however, South Vietnam, called Cochin China, was not included in the Republic. The agreement with France broke down in December 1946, and a civil war erupted with the Vietminh controlling the countryside, and the French army, the cities. France brought back the former emperor, Bao Dai, to head up an opposition government in Saigon in mid-1949, the same year that Russia and the People's Republic of China granted recognition to Ho's republic. In 1954, at the Geneva Conference, Vietnam was partitioned along the seventeenth parallel between the government at Hanoi in the north, and the Saigon government in the south. Moreover, with a view to Vietnamese unity, elections were promised for 1956, although never held.

In 1956, farmers in Ho's native province rebelled because of an unjust land reform bill. Admitting the Party's errors, Ho assumed the secretary-general post in the Vietnam Worker's Party, which had been the Communist Party in Vietnam since 1951. In the years which followed, Ho, still taking the pragmatic approach, avoided involvement in the Sino-Soviet rivalry and received support from both powers during his struggle with South Vietnam and the United States.

On September 3, 1969, Ho died and was buried in Hanoi in Badinh Square, where he had proclaimed Independence in 1945. After his death, his personal testament, written May 10, 1969, was released. It told of his conviction that victory against United States aggression would be secured, and that he would then tour Socialist countries and extend his personal gratitude. Uncertain as to how much longer it would be before he went to join Karl Marx, Vladimir Lenin, and other elder revolutionaries, Ho praised the unity of the people. Moreover, he told of his hopes that unity would return to world Communism on the basis of Marxism-Leninism. Finally, as he had been saying most of his life, he wrote that his greatest desire was for a unified, independent, peaceful, and democratic Vietnam. In effect, this would be his contribution to the world revolution.

Some Considerations on the Colonial Question

... In his theses on the colonial question, Lenin clearly stated that 'the workers of colonizing countries are bound to give the most active assistance to the

From Ho Chi Minh, *Selected Works,* I, Hanoi, Foreign Languages Publishing House, 1961, pp. 10-12. Originally published in *l'Humanite,* May 25, 1922.

liberation movements in subject countries.' To this end, the workers of the mother country must know what a colony really is, they must be acquainted with what is going on there, and with the suffering—a thousand times more acute than theirs—endured by their brothers, the proletarians in the colonies. In a word, they must take an interest in this question.

Unfortunately, there are many militants who still think that a colony is nothing but a country with plenty of sand underfoot and of sun overhead, a few green coconut palms and coloured folk, that is all. And they take not the slightest interest in the matter.

In colonized countries—in old Indo-China as well as in new Dahomey—[the people do not know what class struggle and proletarian strength are] for the simple reason that there are neither big commercial and industrial enterprises, nor workers' organization. In the eyes of the natives, Bolshevism—a word which is the more vivid and expressive because frequently used by the bourgeoisie—means either the destruction of everything or emancipation from the foreign yoke. The first sense given to the word drives the ignorant and timorous masses away from us; the second leads them to nationalism. Both senses are equally dangerous. Only a tiny section of the intelligentsia knows what is meant by Communism. But these gentry, belonging to the native bourgeoisie and supporting the bourgeois colonialists, have no interest in the Communist doctrine being understood and propagated. On the contrary, like the dog in the fable, they prefer to bear the mark of the collar and to have their piece of bone. Generally speaking, the masses are thoroughly rebellious, but completely ignorant. They want to free themselves, but do not know how to go about doing so.

The mutual ignorance of two proletariats gives rise to prejudices. The French workers look upon the native as an inferior and negligible human being incapable of understanding and still less of taking action. The natives regard all the French as wicked exploiters. Imperialism and capitalism do not fail to take advantage of this mutual suspicion and this artificial racial hierarchy to frustrate propaganda and divide forces which ought to unite.

If the French colonialists are unskillful in developing colonial economy, they are masters in the art of savage repression and the manufacture of loyalty made to measure. The Gandhis and the de Valeras would have long since entered heaven had they been born in one of the French colonies. Surrounded by all the refinements of courts martial and special courts, a native militant cannot educate his oppressed and ignorant brothers without the risk of falling into the clutches of his civilizers.

Faced with these difficulties, what must the Party do?

Intensify propaganda to overcome them.

Injustice in Indo-China*

... Today, instead of contributing, together with you, to world revolution, I come here with deep sadness to speak as a member of the Socialist Party, against the imperialists who have committed abhorent crimes on my native land. (*Very good!*) You all have known that French imperialism entered Indo-China half a century ago. In its selfish interests, it conquered our country with bayonets. Since then we have not only been oppressed and exploited shamelessly, but also tortured and poisoned pitilessly. Plainly speaking, we have been poisoned with opium, alcohol, etc. I cannot, in some minutes, reveal all the atrocities that the predatory capitalists have inflicted on Indo-China. Prisons outnumber schools and are always overcrowded with detainees. Any natives having socialist ideas are arrested and sometimes murdered without trial. Such is the so-called justice in Indo-China. In that country the Vietnamese are discriminated against, they do not enjoy safety like Europeans or those having European citizenship. We have neither freedom of press nor freedom of speech. Even freedom of assembly and freedom of association do not exist. We have no right to live in other countries or to go abroad as tourists. We are forced to live in utter ignorance and obscurity because we have no right to study. In Indo-China the colonialists find all ways and means to force us to smoke opium and drink alcohol to poison and beset us. Thousands of Vietnamese have been led to a slow death or massacred to protect other people's interests.

Comrades, such is the treatment inflicted upon more than twenty million Vietnamese, that is more than half the population of France. And they are said to be under French protection (*applause*)! The Socialist Party must act practically to support the oppressed natives (*ovation*). . . .

On the Founding of the Communist Party of Indo-China**

Workers, peasants, soldiers, youth and pupils!
Oppressed and exploited compatriots!
Sisters and brothers! Comrades!

*From Ho Chi Minh, *Selected Works*, II, pp. 11-12. Ho gave this speech at the Eighteenth National Congress of the French Socialist Party, December 25-30, 1920.

**From Ho Chi Minh, *Selected Works*, II, pp. 145-148. The speech was made February 18, 1930.

Imperialist contradictions were the cause of the 1914-1918 World War. After this horrible slaughter, the world was divided into two camps: One is the revolutionary camp including the oppressed colonies and the exploited working class throughout the world. The vanguard force of this camp is the Soviet Union. The other is the counter-revolutionary camp of international capitalism and imperialism whose general staff is the League of Nations.

During this World War, various nations suffered untold losses in property and human lives. The French imperialists were the hardest hit. Therefore, in order to restore the capitalist forces in France, the French imperialists have resorted to every underhand scheme to intensify their capitalist exploitation in Indo-China. They set up new factories to exploit the workers with low wages. They plundered the peasants' land to establish plantations and drive them to utter poverty. They levied many heavy taxes. They imposed public loans upon our people. In short, they reduced us to wretchedness. They increased their military forces, firstly to strangle the Vietnamese revolution, secondly to prepare for a new imperialist war in the Pacific aimed at capturing new colonies, thirdly to suppress the Chinese revolution, fourthly to attack the Soviet Union because the latter helps the revolution of the oppressed nations and the exploited working class. World War Two will break out. When it breaks the French imperialists will certainly drive our people to a more horrible slaughter. If we give them a free hand to prepare for this war, suppress the Chinese revolution and attack the Soviet Union, if we give them a free hand to stifle the Vietnamese revolution, it is tantamount to giving them a free hand to wipe our race off the earth and drown our nation in the Pacific.

However the French imperialists' barbarous oppression and ruthless exploitation have awakened our compatriots who have all realised that revolution is the only road to life, without it they will die out piecemeal.

This is the reason why the Vietnamese revolutionary movement has grown ever stronger with each passing day: The workers refuse to work, the peasants demand land, the pupils strike, the traders boycott. Everywhere the masses have risen to oppose the French imperialists.

The Vietnamese revolution has made the French imperialists tremble with fear. On the one hand, they utilise the feudalists and comprador bourgeois in our country to oppress and exploit our people. On the other, they terrorise, arrest, jail, deport and kill a great number of Vietnamese revolutionaries. If the French imperialists think that they can suppress the Vietnamese revolution by means of terrorist acts, they are utterly mistaken. Firstly, it is because the Vietnamese revolution is not isolated but enjoys the assistance of the world proletarian class in general and of the French working class in particular. Secondly, while the French imperialists are frenziedly carrying out terrorist acts, the Vietnamese

Communists, formerly working separately, have now united into a single party, the Communist Party of Indo-China, to lead our entire people in their revolution.

Workers, peasants, soldiers, youth, pupils!
Oppressed and exploited compatriots!

The Communist Party of Indo-China is founded. It is the Party of the working class. It will help the proletarian class to lead the revolution in order to struggle for all the oppressed and exploited people. From now on we must join the Party, help it and follow it in order to implement the following slogans:

1. To overthrow French imperialism, feudalism and the reactionary Vietnamese capitalist class.

2. To make Indo-China completely independent.

3. To establish a worker-peasant and soldier government.

4. To confiscate the banks and other enterprises belonging to the imperialists and put them under the control of the worker-peasant and soldier government.

5. To confiscate the whole of the plantations and property belonging to the imperialists and the Vietnamese reactionary capitalist class and distribute them to poor peasants.

6. To implement the 8 hours working day.

7. To abolish public loans and poll-tax. To waive unjust taxes hitting the poor people.

8. To bring back all freedoms to the masses.

9. To carry out universal education.

10. To implement equality between man and woman.

Declaration of Independence of the Democratic Republic of Viet Nam

All men are created equal. They are endowed by their Creator with certain inalienable rights, among these are Life, Liberty and the pursuit of Happiness.

This immortal statement was made in the Declaration of Independence of the United States of America in 1776. In a broader sense, this means: All the peoples on the earth are equal from birth, all the peoples have a right to live, to be happy and free.

From Ho Chi Minh, *Selected Works,* III, pp. 17-21. The declaration is dated September 2, 1945.

The Declaration of the French Revolution made in 1791 on the Rights of Man and the Citizen also states:

"All men are born free and with equal rights, and must always remain free and have equal rights."

Those are undeniable truths.

Nevertheless, for more than eighty years, the French imperialists, abusing the standard of Liberty, Equality and Fraternity, have violated our Fatherland and oppressed our fellow-citizens. They have acted contrary to the ideals of humanity and justice.

In the field of politics, they have deprived our people of every democratic liberty.

They have enforced inhuman laws; they have set up three distinct political regimes in the North, the Centre and the South of Viet Nam in order to wreck our national unity and prevent our people from being united.

They have built more prisons than schools. They have mercilessly slain our patriots; they have drowned our uprisings in rivers of blood.

They have fettered public opinion; they have practised obscurantism against our people.

To weaken our race they have forced us to use opium and alcohol.

In the field of economics, they have fleeced us to the backbone, impoverished our people and devastated our land.

They have robbed us of our ricefields, our mines, our forests and our raw materials. They have monopolized the issuing of bank-notes and the export trade.

They have invented numerous unjustifiable taxes and reduced our people, especially our peasantry, to a state of extreme poverty.

They have hampered the prospering of our national bourgeoisie; they have mercilessly exploited our workers.

In the autumn of 1940, when the Japanese fascists violated Indo-China's territory to establish new bases in their fight against the Allies, the French imperialists went down on their bended knees and handed over our country to them.

Thus, from that date, our people were subjected to the double yoke of the French and the Japanese. Their sufferings and miseries increased. The result was that from the end of last year to the beginning of this year, from Quang Tri province to the North of Viet Nam, more than two millions of our fellow-citizens died from starvation. On the 9th of March, the French troops were disarmed by the Japanese. The French colonialists either fled or surrendered, showing that not only were they incapable of "protecting" us, but that, in the span of five years, they had twice sold our country to the Japanese.

... From the autumn of 1940, our country had in fact ceased to be a French colony and had become a Japanese possession.

After the Japanese had surrendered to the Allies, our whole people rose to regain our national sovereignty and to found the Democratic Republic of Viet Nam.

The truth is that we have wrested our independence from the Japanese and not from the French.

The French have fled, the Japanese have capitulated, Emperor Bao Dai has abdicated. Our people have broken the chains which for nearly a century have fettered them and have won independence for the Fatherland. Our people at the same time have overthrown the monarchic regime that has reigned supreme for dozens of centuries. In its place has been established the present Democratic Republic.

For these reasons, we, members of the Provisional Government, representing the whole Vietnamese people, declare that from now on we break off all relations of a colonial character with France; we repeal all the international obligation that France has so far subscribed to on behalf of Viet Nam and we abolish all the special rights the French have unlawfully acquired in our Fatherland.

The whole Vietnamese people, animated by a common purpose, are determined to fight to the bitter end against any attempt by the French colonialists to reconquer their country.

We are convinced that the Allied nations which at Teheran and San Francisco have acknowledged the principles of self-determination and equality of nations, will not refuse to acknowledge the independence of Viet Nam.

A people who have courageously opposed French domination for more than eighty years, a people who have fought side by side with the Allies against the fascists during these last years, such a people must be free and independent.

For these reasons, we, members of the Provisional Government of the Democratic Republic of Viet Nam, solemnly declare to the world that Viet Nam has the right to be a free and independent country—and in fact it is so already. The entire Vietnamese people are determined to mobilize all their physical and mental strength, to sacrifice their lives and property in order to safeguard their independence and liberty.

Letter to Comrades in North Viet Nam

... we must resolutely get rid of the following shortcomings. . . .:

c — Militarism and bureaucracy

To behave like a small king when in charge of a region. To be arrogant and high-handed. To belittle one's superiors and abuse one's authority and weigh heavily upon one's subalterns. To frighten the people by a haughty bearing. This despotic state of mind has brought about much ill-feeling and discord, and dug the gap between the higher and lower levels, the organizations and the people.

d — Narrow-mindedness

We must bear in mind that: everyone has his strong and weak points. We must make use of his strong points and help him correct his shortcomings. To use people is like using wood. A skilled worker can make use of all kinds of wood whether it is big or small, straight or curved.

Narrow-mindedness leads to petty deeds and it results in many enemies and few friends. A narrow-minded man receives little assistance from the others. And a narrow-minded organization cannot thrive.

e — Formalism

Questions are not considered for their practical results or urgency, but only for showing off. For example, at present, military training aims only at handling guns, daggers, hand-grenades, turning to account topographical conditions, cleverly moving in the dark and reconnoitering, in a word: to train everybody for guerrilla warfare. But in many localities time is devoted only to training on parade. This is like practising music for putting out a fire. . . .

f — Paper-work

Love for red-tape. To sit in one's office and send out orders without going to the spot to check the carrying out of the work and to map out plans for the good implementation of the instructions and resolutions of the organization. They are not aware whether the instructions and resolutions sent by the higher levels to the localities can be carried out or not. This style of work is very harmful. It

From Ho Chi Minh, *Selected Works*, III, pp. 99-102. The letter is dated March 1, 1947.

prevents us from closely following the movement and from grasping the real situation. Therefore many of our policies are not carried out thoroughly. . . .

h — Selfishness, debauchery

There are comrades who still suffer from megalomania. They are out for a position in some committee or a chairmanship. Others indluge in good food and fine clothing, try to turn public property into their own, abuse their authority or job to indulge in trading transactions and get rich, think more of their private business than public affairs. Revolutionary virtues and public opinion are of no significance to them. . . .

Twelve Recommendations

The nation has its root in the people.

In the Resistance war and national reconstruction, the main force lies in the people. Therefore all the people in the army, administration and mass organizations who are in contact or live with the people, must remember and carry out the following twelve recommendations:

Six forbiddances:

1. Not to do what is likely to damage the land and crops or spoil the houses and belongings of the people.

2. Not to insist on buying or borrowing what the people are not willing to sell or lend.

3. Not to bring living hens into mountainous people's houses.

4. Never break our word.

5. Not to give offence to people's faith and customs (such as to lie down before the altar, to raise feet over the hearth, to play music in the house, etc.).

6. Not to do or speak what is likely to make people believe that we hold them in contempt.

Six permissibles:

1. To help the people in their daily work (harvesting, fetching fire-wood, carrying water, sewing, etc.).

2. Whenever possible to buy commodities for those who live far from markets (knife, salt, needle, thread, pen, paper, etc.).

From Ho Chi Minh, *Selected Works*, III, pp. 146-147. The piece is dated April 5, 1948.

3. In spare time, to tell amusing simple and short stories useful to the Resistance, but not betraying secrets.

4. To teach the population the national script and elementary hygiene.

5. To study the customs of each region so as to be acquainted with them in order to create an atmosphere of sympathy first, then gradually to explain to the people to abate their superstitions.

6. To show to the people that you are correct, diligent and disciplined.

Stimulating poem

The above-mentioned twelve recommendations
Are feasible to all
He who loves his country,
Will never forget them.
When the people have a habit,
All are like one man,
With good armymen and good people,
Everything will be crowned with success.
Only when the root is firm, can the tree live long,
And victory is built with the people as foundation.

Independence Day Speech

Compatriots,
Fighters and officers,

Today, we are jubilantly commemorating our August Revolution and Independence Day.

This independence was won as a result of 80 years of heroic struggle by our people.

This independence has been maintained as a result of 8 years of valiant resistance of our nation.

Throughout nearly a century, the imperialists and feudalists kept our people in the hell of slavery. They thought they had stamped out our people's patriotism. But they were grossly mistaken. Internally, thanks to the close solidarity and valiant struggle of our people; internationally, thanks to the victory of the Soviet

From Ho Chi Minh, *Selected Works*, III, pp. 397-399. The speech was made on the August Revolution Day and National Day, 1953.

Union over Japanese imperialism, our August Revolution was victorious, our country has been unified and has become independent.

But the aggressive imperialists and the die-hard Vietnamese traitors have provoked war in an attempt to reimpose their domination upon our country. In the face of this aggressive action, our Party and Government are determined to lead and unite the people to fight to the end, thereby continuing the glorious cause of the August Revolution and maintaining the unity and independence of our Fatherland.

... On the occasion of National Day, on behalf of our people, army and Government, I express thanks for the support of the people of friendly countries, of the French people and people all over the world who are struggling for peace.

I bow respectfully before the memories of the martyrs who have sacrificed themselves for the Fatherland.

I convey my heartfelt consolations to disabled and sick armymen and families of martyrs;

Congratulations to all fighters of the National Defence Army, local armies, militia, guerrilla and public security forces,

War servicemen and women,

Model workers and farmers,

Cadres of the army, people's organizations, administration and Party,

Elderly people, my nephews and nieces, the youth and children,

Compatriots living in temporarily-occupied zones and abroad.

On this occasion, I call on those who have strayed from the right path by following the enemy to think over their error and return to the Fatherland. Our Government and people are always lenient towards those who have returned to the right path.

Though we have won many great successes, we absolutely must not be complacent and underestimate the enemy. To win real independence and unity, our resistance must still be long and hard, our army and people must be determined to overcome all difficulties, and to carry out the following tasks:

— The army must strive in political and military training, heighten its fighting spirit, annihilate more enemy forces and smash all enemy attempts at offensive.

— The people must emulate with each other in increasing production and practising economy and taking part in the resistance.

— The people living in the enemy's rear must strive to support the resistance, struggle against enemy raids, pressganging and destruction of production, and defend their lives and property.

— Let everybody actively take part in and support the mobilisation of the masses to carry out the agrarian policy.

— Our cadres must strive in political study, develop their qualities and correct their shortcomings, wholeheartedly serve the people, correctly carry out the Party and Government's policies, and correctly follow the mass line. To fulfil these tasks, our army, people and cadres must:

— Strengthen their conviction that our resistance must be long and self-reliant, clearly realize who are ourselves, who are our friends and who are our enemies; always remain coolheaded and strive to smash all deceitful and offensive attempts of the enemy, and smash the policy of "using Vietnamese to fight Vietnamese, using war to feed war."

Let the entire people unite, overcome all difficulties, fulfil their tasks, push forward the resistance, and firmly maintain our independence.

Our long resistance will certainly be victorious!

Independence and unity will certainly be achieved! *Greetings of affection and determination to win.*

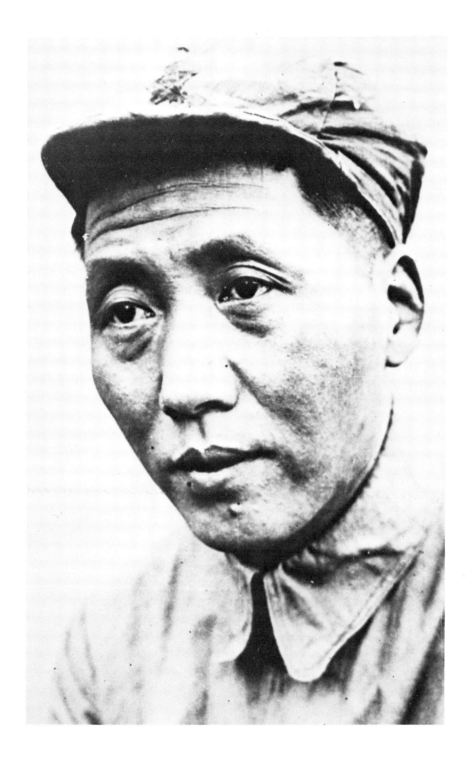

mao tse-tung

Born in the central Chinese province of Hunan in 1893, Mao Tse-Tung, the son
of fairly prosperous peasant parents, became very sensitive to the society surrounding him, as well as to the chaotic Chinese government. Reading widely and
attending several schools, he evaluated various forms of western government and,
for a time, anarchism. In 1918, while working at the Peking University Library,
he came under the powerful influence of Professors Li Ta-chao and Ch'en Tu-
hsiu, and their ideas on Communism. Returning to Hunan, he taught school and
then assisted in the establishment of the Chinese Communist Party in 1921.
Rising rapidly in the Communist ranks, Mao served the Party in Shanghai and
Canton, and also began organizing the Hunan peasants on his visits to that
province.

The Kuomintang or Nationalist Party of China worked alongside the Communists during these years, and Mao served a brief term as propagandist for the
coalition. In 1927, when Nationalist armies sought to destroy the peasant rebellions, Mao fled and established small Communist groups in Southeastern China
during the next few years. Eager to identify with the Soviet Union, Mao became
Chairman of the newly proclaimed Soviet Republic of China in 1931, although
he shared the power with other Chinese leaders. Intensive military campaigns by
the Kuomintang armies under Chiang Kai-shek forced him to lead his Red army
in 1935-1936 over six thousand tortuous miles from Kiangsi province north to

Yenan in Shensi province. This spectacular expedition, called The Long March, not only gave evidence of his endurance but also enhanced his power, and by 1938 Mao had become recognized as the leader of the Communist Party in China. Moreover, during these years he had the opportunity for reflection, and developed his philosophy of revolution. Thus he became famous not only as a guerrilla leader but also as a philosopher of revolution.

Japanese expansionist designs and military operations against China brought another tenuous alliance between Communist and Kuomintang forces, especially as Mao became more publicly flexible, and lessened his emphasis upon dogma. After the surrender of Japan in 1945, civil war returned to China as Mao's armies challenged Kuomintang forces for the control of China. Relentless in his dedication to victory, and assisted by the Soviet Union, Mao forced Chiang's armies off the mainland, and established a People's Republic in 1949. As Chairman of the People's Republic, Mao greatly admired Stalin, and concluded an economic assistance plan with him in the first months of his new government. When Stalin died in 1953, Mao's theories and leadership among Communist countries became more prominent, and within ten years, the rivalry between Moscow and Peking for world leadership became public and hostile.

Though he resigned his position as President of the Republic in 1959, he continued on as party Chairman and, during the decade of the 1960's, sought to instill a greater revolutionary fervor among the government officials. He remained thoroughly dedicated to the view he had expressed in 1935, which is reprinted in his book, *Quotations From Chairman Mao Tse-Tung*: "We the Chinese nation have the spirit to fight the enemy to the last drop of our blood, the determination to recover our lost territory by our own efforts, and the ability to stand on our own feet in the family of nations."

Mao believed in two major kinds of revolution: bourgeois and proletarian. The former kind is over while the latter may be divided into those which occur in highly industrial societies on the one hand, and those which are led by the peasants in colonial or semi-colonial societies. Revolution in the industrial society occurs in one stage and is violent. Revolution in colonial societies develops, he maintained, in two stages, bourgeois-democratic, and proletariat-socialist: the first stage, led by proletariat and other revolutionary groups, such as the peasants and national bourgeoisie, seeks political independence and nationalizes certain areas of public wealth, thus securing the independence of the nation. The second stage, proletariat-socialist, takes the nation along a thoroughly socialist development with the establishment of communes and is a continuation of the first step.

Thus, in China, Mao sought to remove the contradictions and enmity between the proletariat and the national bourgeoisie rather than simply eliminating the latter. Mao tried to persuade the national bourgeoisie to accept a peaceful revolution and thus departed from communist orthodoxy which rejected a non-violent revolution. Later, the cultural revolution in China weakened Mao's theory, and national bourgeoisie were eliminated as counter-revolutionaries. Nevertheless, Mao's faith in the peasants and the two stage revolution continued, and though somewhat doubtful, he believed the young generation would continue the enthusiasm of the revolution.

Fatalistic, Mao explained in a major speech in China in 1957, "On the Correct Handling of Contradictions among the People," that many persons were speculating about the eventuality of a third world war. Though opposed to war, he said he did not fear one, because the birth of the Soviet Union had followed World War I; a socialist camp of nine hundred million people had followed World War II; and, if imperialist powers launched a third world war, several hundred million more persons would turn to socialism and probably bring on the total collapse of imperialism. Clearly, the future society, Mao believed, would belong to the final product of revolution—socialism.

Combat Liberalism

We stand for active ideological struggle because it is the weapon for ensuring unity within the Party and the revolutionary organizations in the interest of our fight; Every Communist and revolutionary should take up this weapon.

But liberalism rejects ideological struggle and stands for unprincipled peace, thus giving rise to a decadent, philistine attitude and bringing about political degeneration in certain units and individuals in the Party and the revolutionary organizations.

Liberalism manifests itself in various ways.

To let things slide for the sake of peace and friendship when a person has clearly gone wrong, and refrain from principled argument because he is an old acquaintance, a fellow townsman, a schoolmate, a close friend, a loved one, an old colleague or old subordinate. Or to touch on the matter lightly instead of going into it thoroughly, so as to keep on good terms. The result is that both the organization and the individual are harmed. This is one type of liberalism.

To indulge in irresponsible criticism in private instead of actively putting

From *Selected Works of Mao Tse-tung*, Foreign Language Press, Peking, 1967, II, pp. 31-33. This essay is dated September 7, 1937.

forward one's suggestions to the organization. To say nothing to people to their faces but to gossip behind their backs, or to say nothing at a meeting but to gossip afterwards. To show no regard at all for the principles of collective life but to follow one's own inclination. This is a second type.

To let things drift if they do not affect one personally; to say as little as possible while knowing perfectly well what is wrong, to be worldly wise and play safe and seek only to avoid blame. This is a third type.

Not to obey orders but to give pride of place to one's own opinions. To demand special consideration from the organization but to reject its discipline. This is a fourth type.

To indulge in personal attacks, pick quarrels, vent personal spite or seek revenge instead of entering into an argument and struggling against incorrect views for the sake of unity or progress or getting the work done properly. This is a fifth type.

To hear incorrect views without rebutting them and even to hear counter-revolutionary remarks without reporting them, but instead to take them calmly as if nothing had happened. This is a sixth type.

To be among the masses and fail to conduct propaganda and agitation or speak at meetings or conduct investigations and inquiries among them, and instead to be indifferent to them and show no concern for their well-being, forgetting that one is a Communist and behaving as if one were an ordinary non-Communist. This is a seventh type.

To see someone harming the interests of the masses and yet not feel indignant, or dissuade or stop him or reason with him, but to allow him to continue. This is an eighth type.

To work half-heartedly without a definite plan or direction; to work perfunctorily and muddle along—"So long as one remains a monk, one goes on tolling the bell." This is a ninth type.

To regard oneself as having rendered great service to the revolution, to pride oneself on being a veteran, to disdain minor assignments while being quite unequal to major tasks, to be slipshod in work and slack in study. This is a tenth type.

To be aware of one's own mistakes and yet make no attempt to correct them, taking a liberal attitude towards oneself. This is an eleventh type.

We could name more. But these eleven are the principal types.

They are all manifestations of liberalism.

Liberalism is extremely harmful in a revolutionary collective. It is a corrosive which eats away unity, undermines cohesion, causes apathy and creates dissension. It robs the revolutionary ranks of compact organization and strict discipline, prevents policies from being carried through and alienates the Party organizations from the masses which the Party leads. It is an extremely bad tendency.

Liberalism stems from petty-bourgeois selfishness, it places personal interests first and the interests of the revolution second, and this gives rise to ideological, political and organizational liberalism.

People who are liberals look upon the principles of Marxism as abstract dogma. They approve of Marxism, but are not prepared to practise it or to practise it in full; they are not prepared to replace their liberalism by Marxism. These people have their Marxism, but they have their liberalism as well—they talk Marxism but practise liberalism; they apply Marxism to others but liberalism to themselves. They keep both kinds of goods in stock and find a use for each. This is how the minds of certain people work.

Liberalism is a manifestation of opportunism and conflicts fundamentally with Marxism. It is negative and objectively has the effect of helping the enemy; that is why the enemy welcomes its perseveration in our midst. Such being its nature, there should be no place for it in the ranks of the revolution.

We must use Marxism, which is positive in spirit, to overcome liberalism, which is negative. A Communist should have largeness of mind and he should be staunch and active, looking upon the interests of the revolution as his very life and subordinating his personal interests to those of the revolution; always and everywhere he should adhere to principle and wage a tireless struggle against all incorrect ideas and actions, so as to consolidate the collective life of the Party and strengthen the ties between the Party and the masses; he should be more concerned about the Party and the masses than about any private person, and more concerned about others than about himself. Only thus can he be considered a Communist.

All loyal, honest, active and upright Communists must unite to oppose the liberal tendencies shown by certain people among us, and set them on the right path. This is one of the tasks on our ideological front.

The Chinese Revolution and the Chinese Communist Party

... we know that present-day Chinese society is a colonial, semi-colonial and semi-feudal society. Only when we grasp the nature of Chinese society will we be able clearly to understand the targets, tasks, motive forces and character of the

From *Selected Works of Mao Tse-tung,* II, pp. 315, 316-318. The book from which this excerpt is taken was published as a textbook in 1939.

Chinese revolution and its perspectives and future transition. A clear understanding of the nature of Chinese society, that is, of Chinese conditions, is therefore the key to a clear understanding of all the problems of the revolution.

Since the nature of present-day Chinese society is colonial, semi-colonial and semi-feudal, what are the chief targets or enemies at this stage of the Chinese revolution?

They are imperialism and feudalism, the bourgeoisie of the imperialist countries and the landlord class of our country. For it is these two that are the chief oppressors, the chief obstacles to the progress of Chinese society at the present stage. The two collude with each other in oppressing the Chinese people, and imperialism is the foremost and most ferocious enemy of the Chinese people, because national oppression by imperialism is the more onerous.

... the enemies of the Chinese revolution are very powerful. They include not only powerful imperialists and powerful feudal forces, but also, at times, the bourgeois reactionaries who collaborate with the imperialist and feudal forces to oppose the people. Therefore, it is wrong to underestimate the strength of the enemies of the revolutionary Chinese people.

In the face of such enemies, the Chinese revolution cannot be other than protracted and ruthless. With such powerful enemies, the revolutionary forces cannot be built up and tempered into a power capable of crushing them except over a long period of time. With enemies who so ruthlessly suppress the Chinese revolution, the revolutionary forces cannot hold their own positions, let alone capture those of the enemy, unless they steel themselves and display their tenacity to the full. It is therefore wrong to think that the forces of the Chinese revolution can be built up in the twinkling of an eye, or that China's revolutionary struggle can triumph overnight.

In the face of such enemies, the principal means or form of the Chinese revolution must be armed struggle, not peaceful struggle. For our enemies have made peaceful activity impossible for the Chinese people and have deprived them of all political freedom and democratic rights. . . .

In the face of such enemies, there arises the question of revolutionary base areas. Since China's key cities have long been occupied by powerful imperialists and their reactionary Chinese allies, it is imperative for the revolutionary ranks to turn the backward villages into advanced, consolidated base areas, into great military, political, economic and cultural bastions of the revolution from which to fight their vicious enemies who are using the cities for attacks on the rural districts, and in this way gradually to achieve the complete victory of the revolution through protracted fighting; it is imperative for them to do so if they do not wish to compromise with imperialism and its lackeys but are determined to fight on, and if they intend to build up and temper their forces, and avoid decisive battles with a powerful enemy while their own strength is inadequate. Such being the case, victory in the Chinese revolution can be won first in the rural areas, and this is possible because China's economic development is uneven (her economy not being a unified capitalist economy), because her territory is extensive (which gives the revolutionary forces room to manoeuvre), because the counter-revolutionary camp is disunited and full of contradictions, and because the struggle of the peasants who are the main force in the revolution is led by the Communist Party, the party of the proletariat; but on the other hand, these very circumstances make the revolution uneven and render the task of winning complete victory protracted and arduous. Clearly then the protracted revolutionary struggle in the revolutionary base areas consists mainly in peasant guerrilla warfare led by the Chinese Communist Party. Therefore, it is wrong to ignore the necessity of using rural districts as revolutionary base areas, to neglect painstaking work among the peasants, and to neglect guerrilla warfare.

However, stressing armed struggle does not mean abandoning other forms of struggle; on the contrary, armed struggle cannot succeed unless co-ordinated with other forms of struggle. And stressing the work in the rural base areas does not mean abandoning our work in the cities and in the other vast rural areas which are still under the enemy's rule; on the contrary, without the work in the cities and in these other rural areas, our own rural base areas would be isolated and the revolution would suffer defeat. Moreover, the final objective of the revolution is the capture of the cities, the enemy's main bases, and this objective cannot be achieved without adequate work in the cities.

It is thus clear that the revolution cannot triumph either in the rural areas or in the cities without the destruction of the enemy's army, his chief weapon against the people. Therefore, besides annihilating the enemy's troops in battle, there is the important task of disintegrating them.

It is also clear that the Communist Party must not be impetuous and adventurist in its propaganda and organizational work in the urban and rural areas which have been occupied by the enemy and dominated by the forces of reaction and darkness for a long time, but that it must have well-selected cadres working underground, must accumulate strength and bide its time there. In leading the people in struggle against the enemy, the Party must adopt the tactics of advancing step by step slowly and surely, keeping to the principle of waging struggles on just grounds, to our advantage, and with restraint, and making use of such open forms of activity as are permitted by law, decree and social custom; empty clamour and reckless action can never lead to success. . . .

On New Democracy

... In China, it is perfectly clear that whoever can lead the people in over-throwing imperialism and the forces of feudalism can win the people's confidence, because these two, and especially imperialism, are the mortal enemies of the people. Today, (January 1940) whoever can lead the people in driving out Japanese imperialism and introducing the democratic government will be the saviours of the people. History has proved that the Chinese bourgeoisie cannot fulfil this responsibility, which inevitably falls upon the shoulders of the pro-letariat.

Therefore, the proletariat, the peasantry, the intelligentsia and the other sections of the petty bourgeoisie undoubtedly constitute the basic forces deter-mining China's fate. These classes, some already awakened and others in the process of awakening, will necessarily become the basic components of the state and governmental structure in the democratic republic of China, with the prole-tariat as the leading force. The Chinese democratic republic which we desire to establish now must be a democratic republic under the joint dictatorship of all anti-imperialist and anti-feudal people led by the proletariat, that is, a new-democratic republic, a republic of the genuinely revolutionary new Three People's Principles with their Three Great Policies.

This new-democratic republic will be different from the old European-American form of capitalist republic under bourgeois dictatorship, which is the old democratic form and already out of date. On the other hand, it will also be different from the socialist republic of the Soviet type under the dictatorship of the proletariat which is already flourishing in the U.S.S.R., and which, moreover, will be established in all the capitalist countries and will undoubtedly become the dominant form of state and governmental structure in all the industrially advanced countries. However, for a certain historical period, this form is not suitable for the revolutions in the colonial and semi-colonial countries. During this period, therefore, a third form of state must be adopted in the revolutions of all colonial and semi-colonial countries, namely, the new-democratic republic. This form suits a certain historical period and is therefore transitional; never-theless, it is a form which is necessary and cannot be dispensed with.

Thus the numerous types of state system in the world can be reduced to three basic kinds according to the class character of their political power: (1) republics under bourgeois dictatorship; (2) republics under the dictatorship of the prole-tariat; and (3) republics under the joint dictatorship of several revolutionary classes.

From *Selected Works of Mao Tse-tung*, II, pp. 349-351, 353-354, 380-382. This essay is dated January 1940.

The first kind comprises the old democratic states. Today, after the outbreak of the second imperialist war, there is hardly a trace of democracy in many of the capitalist countries, which have come or are coming under the bloody militarist dictatorship of the bourgeoisie. Certain countries under the joint dictatorship of the landlords and the bourgeoisie can be grouped with this kind.

The second kind exists in the Soviet Union, and the conditions for its birth are ripening in capitalist countries. In the future, it will be the dominant form throughout the world for a certain period.

The third kind is the transitional form of state to be adopted in the revolutions of the colonial and semi-colonial countries. Each of these revolutions will necessarily have specific characteristics of its own, but these will be minor variations on a general theme. So long as they are revolutions in colonial or semi-colonial countries, their state and governmental structure will of necessity be basically the same, i.e., a new-democratic state under the joint dictatorship of several anti-imperialist classes. . . .

. . . The republic will take certain necessary steps to confiscate the land of the landlords and distribute it to those peasants having little or no land, carry out Dr. Sun Yat-sen's slogan of "land to the tiller," abolish feudal relations in the rural areas, and turn the land over to the private ownership of the peasants. A rich peasant economy will be allowed in the rural areas. Such is the policy of "equalization of land ownership." "Land to the tiller" is the correct slogan for this policy. In general, socialist agriculture will not be established at this stage, though various types of co-operative enterprises developed on the basis of "land to the tiller" will contain elements of socialism.

China's economy must develop along the path of the "regulation of capital" and the "equalization of landownership", and must never be "privately owned by the few"; we must never permit the few capitalists and landlords to "dominate the livelihood of the people"; we must never establish a capitalist society of the European-American type or allow the old semi-feudal society to survive. Whoever dares to go counter to this line of advance will certainly not succeed but will run into a brick wall.

Such are the internal economic relations which a revolutionary China, a China fighting Japanese aggression, must and necessarily will establish.

Such is the internal economy of New Democracy.

And the politics of New Democracy are the concentrated expression of the economy of the New Democracy.

. . . New-democratic culture is national. It opposes imperialist oppression and upholds the dignity and independence of the Chinese nation. It belongs to our own nation and bears our own national characteristics. It links up with the socialist and new-democratic cultures of all other nations and they are related in such a way that they can absorb something from each other and help each other to develop, together forming a new world culture; but as a revolutionary national culture it can never link up with any reactionary imperialist culture of whatever nation. To nourish her own culture China needs to assimilate a good deal of foreign progressive culture, not enough of which was done in the past. We should assimilate whatever is useful to us today not only from the present-day socialist and new-democratic cultures but also from the earlier cultures of other nations, for example, from the culture of the various capitalist countries of the Age of Enlightenment. However, we should not gulp any of this foreign material down uncritically, but must treat it as we do our food—first chewing it, then submitting it to the working of the stomach and intestines with their juices and secretions, and separating it into nutriment to be absorbed and waste matter to be discarded—before it can nourish us. To advocate "wholesale westernization" (Wholesale westernization was the view held by a number of westernized Chinese bourgeois intellectuals who unconditionally praised the outmoded individualist bourgeois culture of the West and advocated the servile imitation of capitalist Europe and America.) is wrong. China has suffered a great deal from the mechanical absorption of foreign material. Similarly, in applying Marxism to China, Chinese communists must fully and properly integrate the universal truth of Marxism with the concrete practice of the Chinese revolution, or in other words, the universal truth of Marxism must be combined with specific national characteristics and acquire a definite national form if it is to be useful, and in no circumstances can it be applied subjectively as a mere formula. Marxists who make a fetish of formulas are simply playing the fool with Marxism and the Chinese revolution, and there is no room for them in the ranks of the Chinese revolution. Chinese culture should have its own form, its own national form. National in form and new-democratic in content—such is our new culture today. . . . New-democratic culture belongs to the broad masses and is therefore democratic. It should serve the toiling masses of workers and peasants who make up more than 90 percent of the nation's population and should gradually become their very own. There is a difference of degree, as well as a close link, between the knowledge imparted to the revolutionary cadres and the knowledge imparted to the revolutionary masses, between the raising of cultural standards and popularization. Revolutionary culture is a powerful revolutionary weapon for the broad masses of the people. It prepares the ground ideologically before the revolution comes and is an important, indeed essential, fighting front in the general revolutionary front during the revolution. . . A revolutionary cultural worker who is not close to the people is a commander without an army, whose fire-power cannot bring the enemy down. To attain this objective, written Chinese must be reformed, given the requisite conditions, and our spoken language brought closer to that of the people, for the people, it must be stressed, are the inexhaustible source of our revolutionary culture.

A national, scientific and mass culture—such is the anti-imperialist and anti-feudal culture of the people, the culture of New Democracy, the new culture of the Chinese nation.

Combine the politics, the economy and the culture of New Democracy, and you have the new-democratic republic, the Republic of China both in name and reality, the new China we want to create.

Behold, New China is within sight. Let us all hail her!

Her masts have already risen above the horizon. Let us all cheer in welcome!

Raise both your hands. New China is ours!

On the Correct Handling of Contradictions among the People

... To form a correct evaluation of our work in suppressing counter-revolutionaries, let us see what effect the Hungarian events (the Hungarian Revolution in 1956) have had in China. After their occurrence there was some unrest among a section of our intellectuals, but there were no squalls. Why? One reason, it must be said, is that we had succeeded in suppressing the counter-revolutionaries quite thoroughly.

Of course, the consolidation of our state is not primarily due to the suppression of counter-revolution. It is due primarily to the fact that we have a Communist Party, a Liberation Army and a working people tempered in decades of revolutionary struggle. Our Party and our armed forces are rooted in the masses; they have been tempered in the flames of a protracted revolution; they have the capacity to fight. Our People's Republic was not built overnight, but developed step by step out of the revolutionary base areas. Some democratic personages have also been tempered in the struggle in varying degrees, and they have gone through troubled times together with us. Some intellectuals were tempered in the struggles against imperialism and reaction; since liberation many of them have gone through a process of ideological remoulding aimed at enabling them to distinguish clearly between ourselves and the enemy. In addition, the consolidation of our state is due to the fact that our economic measures are basically sound, that the people's livelihood is secure and is steadily improving, that our policies towards the national bourgeoisie and other classes are correct, and so on.

From Mao Tse-tung, *Four Essays on Philosophy*, Foreign Language Press, Peking, 1968, pp. 97-99, 100, 113-116, 117-118, 119-121, 126-127. This essay is dated February 27, 1957.

Nevertheless, our success in suppressing counter-revolutionaries is undoubtedly an important reason for the consolidation of our state. For all these reasons, with few exceptions our college students are patriotic and support socialism, although many of them come from other than working class families; they did not give way to unrest during the Hungarian events. The same was true of the national bourgeoisie, to say nothing of the basic masses—the workers and peasants.

After liberation, we rooted out a number of counter-revolutionaries. Some were sentenced to death for major crimes. This was absolutely necessary, it was the demand of the people, it was done to free the masses from long years of oppression by the counter-revolutionaries and all kinds of local tyrants; in other words, it was done to release the productive forces. If we had not done so, the masses would not have been able to lift their heads. Since 1956, however, there has been a radical change in the situation. In the country as a whole, the bulk of the counter-revolutionaries have been cleared out. Our basic task has changed from unfettering the productive forces to protecting and expanding them in the context of the new relations of production. Because of their failure to understand that our present policy fits the present situation and our past policy fitted the past situation, some people want to make use of the present policy to reverse decisions on past cases and to deny the great success we achieved in suppressing counter-revolution. This is quite wrong, and the masses will not permit it.

Successes were the main thing in our work of suppressing counter-revolutionaries, but there were also mistakes. In some cases there were excesses and in others counter-revolutionaries slipped through our net. Our policy is: "Counter-revolutionaries must be suppressed wherever found, mistakes must be corrected whenever discovered." Our line in the work of suppressing counter-revolution is the mass line. Of course, even with the mass line mistakes may still occur in our work, but they will be fewer and easier to correct. The masses gain experience through struggle. From what is done correctly they learn how things should be done. From what is done wrong they learn useful lessons as to how mistakes should be avoided.

. . . The present situation with regard to counter-revolutionaries can be described in these words: There still are counter-revolutionaries, but not many. In the first place, there are still counter-revolutionaries. Some people say that there aren't any more and all is at peace and that we can therefore lay our heads on our pillows and just drop off to sleep. But this is not the way things are. The fact is, there still are counter-revolutionaries (of course, that is not to say you'll find them everywhere and in every organization), and we must continue to fight them. It must be understood that the hidden counter-revolutionaries still at large will not take things lying down, but will certainly seize every opportunity to make trouble. The U.S. imperialists and the Chiang Kai-shek clique are constantly sending in secret agents to carry on disruptive activities. Even after all the existing counter-revolutionaries have been combed out, new ones may emerge. If we drop our guard, we shall be badly fooled and shall suffer severely. Counter-revolutionaries must be rooted out with a firm hand wherever they are found making trouble. But, taking the country as a whole, there are certainly not many counter-revolutionaries. It would be wrong to say that there are still large numbers of counter-revolutionaries in China. Acceptance of that view would also end up in a mess. . . .

. . . "Let a hundred flowers blossom, let a hundred schools of thought contend" and "long-term coexistence and mutual supervision"—how did these slogans come to be put forward? They were put forward in the light of China's specific conditions on the basis of the recognition that various kinds of contradictions still exist in socialist society, and in response to the country's urgent need to speed up its economic and cultural development. Letting a hundred flowers blossom and a hundred schools of thought contend is the policy for promoting the progress of the arts and sciences and a flourishing socialist culture in our land. Different forms and styles in art should develop freely and different schools in science should contend freely. We think that it is harmful to the growth of art and science if administrative measures are used to impose one particular style of art or school of thought and to ban another. Questions of right and wrong in the arts and sciences should be settled through free discussion in artistic and scientific circles and through practical work in these fields. They should not be settled in summary fashion. A period of trial is often needed to determine whether something is right or wrong. Throughout history, new and correct things have often failed at the outset to win recognition from the majority of people and have had to develop by twists and turns in struggle. Often correct and good things have first been regarded not as fragrant flowers but as poisonous weeds. Copernicus' theory of the solar system and Darwin's theory of evolution were once dismissed as erroneous and had to win through over bitter opposition. Chinese history offers many similar examples. In a socialist society, conditions for the growth of the new are radically different from and far superior to those in the old society. Nevertheless, it still often happens that new, rising forces are held back and rational proposals constricted. Moreover, the growth of new things may be hindered in the absence of deliberate suppression simply through the lack of discernment. It is therefore necessary to be careful about questions of right and wrong in the arts and sciences, to encourage free discussion and avoid hasty conclusions. We believe that such an attitude can help to ensure a relatively smooth development of the arts and sciences.

Marxism, too, has developed through struggle. At the beginning, Marxism was subjected to all kinds of attack and regarded as a poisonous weed. It is still being attacked and is still regarded as a poisonous weed in many parts of the world. In the socialist countries, it enjoys a different position. But non-Marxist and, moreover, anti-Marxist ideologies exist even in these countries. In China, although in the main socialist transformation has been completed with respect to the system of ownership, and although the large-scale and turbulent class struggles of the masses characteristic of the previous revolutionary periods have in the main come to an end, there are still remnants of the overthrown landlord and comprador classes, there is still a bourgeoisie, and the remoulding of the petty bourgeoisie has only just started. The class struggle is by no means over. The class struggle between the proletariat and the bourgeoisie, the class struggle between the different political forces, and the class struggle in the ideological field between the proletariat and the bourgeoisie will continue to be long and tortuous and at times will even become very acute. The proletariat seeks to transform the world according to its own world outlook, and so does the bourgeoisie. In this respect, the question of which will win out, socialism or capitalism, is still not really settled. Marxists are still a minority among the entire population as well as among the intellectuals. Therefore, Marxism must still develop through struggle. Marxism can develop only through struggle, and not only is this true of the past and the present, it is necessarily true of the future as well. What is correct invariably develops in the course of struggle with what is wrong. The true, the good and the beautiful always exist by contrast with the false, the evil and the ugly, and grow in struggle with the latter. As soon as a wrong thing is rejected and a particular truth accepted by mankind, new truths begin their struggle with new errors. Such struggles will never end. This is the law of development of truth and, naturally, of Marxism as well.

It will take a fairly long period of time to decide the issue in the ideological struggle between socialism and capitalism in our country. The reason is that the influence of the bourgeoisie and of the intellectuals who come from the old society will remain in our country for a long time to come, and so will their class ideology. If this is not understood, or is not sufficiently understood, the gravest mistakes will be made and the necessity of waging the struggle in the ideological field will be ignored. Ideological struggle is not like other forms of struggle. The only method to be used in this struggle is that of painstaking reasoning and not crude coercion. Today, socialism is in an advantageous position in the ideological struggle. The main power of the state is in the hands of the working people led by the proletariat. The Communist Party is strong and its prestige stands high. . . .

. . . What should our policy be towards non-Marxist ideas? As far as unmistakable counter-revolutionaries and saboteurs of the socialist cause are concerned, the matter is easy: we simply deprive them of their freedom of speech. But incorrect ideas among the people are quite a different matter. Will it do to ban such ideas and deny them any opportunity for expression? Certainly not. It is not only futile but very harmful to use summary methods in dealing with ideological questions among the people, with questions concerned with man's mental world. You may ban the expression of wrong ideas, but the ideas will still be there. On the other hand, if correct ideas are pampered in hot-houses without being exposed to the elements or immunized from disease, they will not win out against erroneous ones. Therefore, it is only be employing the method of discussion, criticism and reasoning that we can really foster correct ideas and overcome wrong ones, and that we can really settle issues.

... At first glance, the two slogans—let a hundred flowers blossom and let a hundred schools of thought contend—have no class character; the proletariat can turn them to account, and so can the bourgeoisie or other people. But different classes, strata and social groups each have their own views on what are fragrant flowers and what are poisonous weeds. What then, from the point of view of the broad masses of the people, should be the criteria today for distinguishing fragrant flowers from poisonous weeds? In the political life of our people, how should right be distinguished from wrong in one's words and actions? On the basis of the principles of our Constitution, the will of the overwhelming majority of our people and the common political positions which have been proclaimed on various occasions by our political parties and groups, we consider that, broadly speaking, the criteria should be as follows:

(1) Words and actions should help to unite, and not divide, the people of our various nationalities.

(2) They should be beneficial, and not harmful, to socialist transformation and socialist construction.

(3) They should help to consolidate, and not undermine or weaken, the people's democratic dictatorship.

(4) They should help to consolidate, and not undermine or weaken, democratic centralism.

(5) They should help to strengthen, and not discard or weaken, the leadership of the Communist Party.

(6) They should be beneficial, and not harmful, to international socialist unity and the unity of the peace-loving people of the world.

Of these six criteria, the most important are the socialist path and the leadership of the Party. These criteria are put forward not to hinder but to foster the free discussion of questions among the people. Those who disapprove of these criteria can still put forward their own views and argue their case. However, since the majority of the people have clear-cut criteria to go by, criticism and self-criticism can be conducted along proper lines, and the criteria can be applied to the people's words and actions to determine whether they are right or wrong, whether they are fragrant flowers or poisonous weeds. These are political criteria. Naturally, in judging the validity of scientific theories or assessing the aesthetic value of works of art, additional pertinent criteria are needed. But these six political criteria are applicable to all activities in the arts and the sciences. In a socialist country like ours, can there possibly be any useful scientific or artistic activity which runs counter to these political criteria?

The views set out above are based on China's specific historical conditions. Conditions vary in different socialist countries and with different Communist Parties. Therefore, we do not maintain that other countries and Parties should or must follow the Chinese way. . . .

. . . People all over the world are now discussing whether or not a third world war will break out. On this question, too, we must be mentally prepared and do some analysis. We stand firmly for peace and against war. But if the imperialists insist on unleashing another war, we should not be afraid of it. Out attitude on this question is the same as our attitude towards any disturbance: first, we are against it; second, we are not afraid of it. The First World War was followed by the birth of the Soviet Union with a population of 200 million. The Second World War was followed by the emergence of the socialist camp with a combined population of 900 million. If the imperialists insist on launching a third world war, it is certain that several hundred million more will turn to socialism, and then there will not be much room left on earth for imperialists; it is also likely that the whole structure of imperialism will utterly collapse.

In given conditions, each of the two opposing aspects of a contradiction invariably transforms itself into its opposite as a result of the struggle between them. Here, the conditions are essential. Without the given conditions, neither of the two contradictory aspects can transform itself into its opposite. Of all the classes in the world the proletariat is the one which is most eager to change its position, and next comes the semi-proletariat, for the former possesses nothing at all while the latter is hardly better off. The present situation in which the United States controls a majority in the United Nations and dominates many parts of the world is a temporary one, which will eventually be changed. China's position as a poor country denied her rights in international affairs will also be changed—the poor country will change into a rich one, the country denied its rights into one enjoying its rights—a transformation of things into their opposites. Here, the decisive conditions are the socialist system and the concerted efforts of a united people. . . .

fidel castro

During the 1950's, protests grew in Cuba as diverse groups pointed out the grave abuses of the government of Fulgencio Batista. These organizations were comprised of various elements: nationalists who desired a more representative government, economic theorists who sought to eliminate colonialism, social activists who opposed the Cuban aristocracy, and humanists who hungered for the elimination of poverty, together with the political instability common to Latin American nations. Active in the attempts at reform, Fidel Castro believed that Cubans, in fact, all Americans, wanted neither freedom with famine, nor plenty without freedom. Under his leadership and that of Che Guevara, Cuba became a model, especially for other Latin American revolutionaries, of a national liberation movement.

Castro was born in Oriente province in 1926. His father, Spanish-born, was a wealthy planter, and his mother, a native Cuban. Educated in Santiago and Havana, he received his law degree from the University of Havana in 1950. His education during those years extended beyond the classroom, because as a student activist he was involved in attempts to overthrow the Dominican Republic President, Rafael Trujillo, and, also with others, his protests in Colombia led to rioting in Bogotá. His dedication to reform and revolution surfaced again in 1953 when he led 160 other young dissidents against an army post in Santiago de Cuba on July 26, 1953, hoping to overthrow the regime of Batista who had seized power a year earlier. Captured in the attack, he was tried, found guilty, and sentenced to fifteen years in prison. Granted political amnesty a short time later, he went to Mexico, and with his brother, Rául, began training Cuban exiles in the tactics of guerrilla warfare. Joined by Che Guevara in Mexico, the group of eighty-two men invaded Cuba on December 2, 1956, and, after disastrous losses, made its way to the Sierra Maestra Mountains and continued guerrilla warfare under the name of the "26th of July Movement."

As military defeats by his government forces multiplied, Batista fled into exile on January 1, 1959, and a new government with Manuel Urrutia as president and Castro as prime minister took over. During these months, Castro shaped the government. Increasingly, those assistants who had supported the new independence movement came to realize the Marxist-Leninist orientation of Castro and resigned from the government, fearful that a Communist tyranny was being established on the island. Other persons, inside and outside Cuba, while unsure of Castro's ultimate intentions, believed he was simply seeking the development of Latin American resources for the benefit of the people within those countries.

While Castro's intense dislike for earlier foreign exploitation in Cuba was evident in 1959 and early 1960, his May Day speech of 1960 displayed the depth of his bitterness, and the direction the Cuban revolution would take. With exuberant rhetoric, he described the remarkable unity and spirit of the Cuban people. With effective oratory, he reminded his large audience of the cruel sufferings caused by colonialism, and the future rewards promised by a revolutionary Cuban society.

In January 1961, the United States broke off diplomatic relations with Cuba, and, before the year ended, Castro announced that he had been a Marxist-Leninist for many years and had hidden this relationship in order to advance the revolution. That same year the Soviet Union awarded him the Lenin Peace Prize; Cuba's friendship with the Soviet Union deepened during the 1960's. Castro continued to emphasize "*Patria o muerte*," which his followers translated as "Give me liberty or give me death." The tremendous charismatic appeal of Castro to Cubans and to other Latin Americans continues, and the island on the perimeter of the United States pursues the process of revolution.

The Destiny of Cuba

. . . Many things we have had to learn, many things we have all learned, all of us without exception. Today, for example, as the organized units of people filed back and forth in endless numbers to march for seven consecutive hours, today while we have had an opportunity to see the tremendous strength of the people, while we have had the opportunity to see the incomparable and invincible strength of the people, we asked: But is this people today the same as the people of yesterday?

How is it possible that a people with such tremendous and extraordinary strength should have had to endure what our people have had to endure? How was it possible, with the tremendous strength of hundreds of thousands of Cuban farmers, and the tremendous strength of more than a million Cuban workers, and the tremendous strength of hundreds of thousands of young people like those who paraded today in the ranks of the patrols and the student militias? How was it possible? How can they be the same men and women as yesterday?

Since these citizens who paraded here today are the same citizens that made up our people just a few years ago, how is it possible then that we should have had to suffer such extreme abuse? How is it possible that so many hundreds of thousands of families in our rural areas lived in conditions of starvation without land and were so exploited, as victims of the most heartless exploitation by foreign companies that lorded over our land, while those almighty who gave orders were those who in most cases not only had never planted a seed on our land but furthermore had never even seen our land?

While so much courage was in the hearts of our people, how was it possible to abuse our workers so? How was so much exploitation possible? How was so much crookedness, so much theft, so much plundering of our people possible? While we had so much strength, how was so much crime possible? How was it possible for a handful of men, a band of mercenaries, or a plague of petty politicians to dominate our people and direct the destiny of our people during half a century?

How was it possible for our people to have to pay a price so high that to give us a clear notion of it we would need to see united together here in a square many times bigger than this the millions of Cubans who were left unable to read or write, the hundreds of thousands of children who died without seeing a doctor, the ocean of suffering and anguish, of hunger and misery, of abuse and humiliation that the sons and daughters of this land had to endure because of

From Fidel Castro, *Labor Day Address about the Destiny of Cuba* (May 1, 1960), Havana, (n.d.): pp. 6-14, 16-17, 20-21.

poverty, or because of illiteracy, or because of their color, or because of their sex.

Ah, our people had reserves of extraordinary energy and extraordinary strength, but we did not know it, or we had not been permitted to draw that strength together, to organize it. And therefore, the privileged and educated minorities were able to do more with the help of alien interests than our people were able to do with their tremendous reserves of strength.

That has been the great lesson of this day, because never so much as today have Cubans had the opportunity to see our own strength. Never so much as today could the Cuban people have an exact idea of their own strength. The endless stream of columns marching for seven hours has been necessary so that our people should have a concrete idea of their own strength. And this great lesson should be an unforgettable lesson for us.

... Before, the tactics of those who used to rule over our destiny consisted of dividing us and of setting one force against another.

They set the soldier against the farmer. They set the interests of the farmer against the interests of the worker. They set every faction of the people against the other factions as part of an international strategy of the big reactionary interests of the world. They set sister nations against each other and they set the various sectors of each nation against each other to serve the privileged classes.

They set one group of the lower classes against another group of the lower classes. They took a poor farmer and made him a soldier. Then they corrupted this soldier and made him an enemy of the worker and an enemy of the farmer.

They weakened the people by their practice of setting one humble sector against others. They divided the people into petty political parties that brought no guidance to the nation. They divided the ignorant and misled people into factions supporting unscrupulous and greedy politicians. Thus they weakened the people. Thus they confused the people and thus the apparatus of the government with its rigid and reactionary institutions destroyed all hope, all possibility of progress for our society. Every means to teach ideas—the movie, the majority of the press, the centers of learning, and all the administrative apparatus of the state—were at the service of this policy of oppressing and weakening the people.

That was what used to happen. What was the First of May in those days? The workers used to be almost unable to walk under the weight of all the posters that they carried on their shoulders every First of May. Today, the workers have not brought a single demand.

The First of May was an opportunity for the workers to parade carrying posters, in the hope of satisfying those demands or some of those demands. The First of May used to be, actually, a mockery for the workers. The next year they had to return once again carrying the same posters with the same demands.

Nothing that they attained was granted to them graciously. Anything they attained was granted to them only after a grueling fight, after strikes and organized movements demanding wage increases. The worker knew that he had to fight. The worker had to keep up a constant fight in order to obtain some small benefit in the economic order. He had to fight so that his most elemental rights would be respected.

Therefore, every First of May they had to come carrying their demands. What else could they do? The worker knew that what he did not do for himself nobody else would do for him. The worker knew that what he did not win by his own work nobody would win for him. You, worker, you, farmer, always worked for others. You did your own work and the work of others. You—worker, farmer, doctor, intellectual worker, and all the rest of you workers—did your own work and the work of others.

But nobody ever worked for you, farmer, nor for you, laborer. You gave everything with generosity, you gave your sweat and your energy. You gave your life. Many times you denied yourselves your hours of rest. You gave to everybody, but to you nobody ever gave anything. What you did not do for yourselves, nobody would ever do for you. You were the majority of the people. You, the farmers, the workers, the youth, were the majority of the people. You who produce, you who made sacrifices, you who work, you were always and you are today and will be tomorrow, the majority of the people. But you did not govern. You were the majority, but others governed in your stead and governed against you.

They invented a democracy for you—a strange, a very strange democracy, in which you, who were the majority, did not count for anything. Although you, farmer and worker, were the ones who produced the majority of the wealth and—together with the intellectual workers—produced the total of the wealth, many of those of you who produced everything did not even have the opportunity to learn to sign your name.

They invented a strange democracy for you—a democracy in which you who were the majority did not even exist politically within society. They spoke to you of civil rights. In that situation of civil rights your child could die of hunger before the unconcerned glance of the government. Your child could be left without learning to read or write a single letter and you yourself had to go sell your work at the price that they wanted to pay you for it and whenever anybody was interested in buying it from you.

They spoke to you of rights that never existed for you. Your children could not be sure even of the right to a school. Your children could not be guaranteed even the right to a doctor. Your children did not have the guaranteed right even to a piece of bread, and you yourself did not have the guarantee even of the right to work.

They invented for you a democracy that meant that you, you who were the majority, did not count for anything. And thus, despite your tremendous force, despite your sacrifices, despite your work for others in our national life, despite the fact that you were the majority, you neither governed nor counted for anything. You were not taken into account.

And that they called democracy! Democracy is (a form of government) in which the majority governs. Democracy is that form of government in which the majority is taken into account. Democracy is that form of government in which the interests of the majority are defended. Democracy is that form of government that guarantees to man not just the right to think freely but the right to know how to think, the right to know how to write what he thinks, the right to know how to read what is thought by others. Democracy guarantees not only the right to bread and the right to work but also the right to culture and the right to be taken into account within society. Therefore, this is democracy. The Cuban Revolution is democracy.

This is democracy, where you, farmer, are given the land that we have recovered from usurious foreign hands that used to exploit it. Democracy is *this*, where you, the sugar plantation workers, receive 80,000 *caballerias* [each caballeria is approximately 33½ acres] of land in order that you shall not have to live in *guardarrayas* [shacks on a strip of land, termed, "guardarraya" adjacent to a country road].

This is democracy, where you, worker, are guaranteed the right to work, so that you cannot be thrown out on the streets to go hungry.

Democracy is *this*, where you, students, have the opportunity to win a university degree if you are intelligent, even though you may not be rich.

Democracy is *this*, where you, whether you are the son of a worker, the son of a farmer, or the son of any other humble family, have a teacher to educate you and a school where you can be taught.

Democracy is *this*, where you, old man, have your sustenance guaranteed after you can no longer depend on your own effort.

Democracy is *this*, where you, Cuban negro, have the right to work without anybody being able to deprive you of that right because of stupid prejudice.

Democracy is *this*, where the women acquire rights equal to those of all other citizens and have a right even to bear arms alongside the men to defend their country.

Democracy is *this*, in which a government converts its fortresses into schools, and in which a government wants to build a house for every family so that every family can have a roof of their own over their heads.

Democracy is *this*—a government that wants every invalid to have a doctor's care.

Democracy is *this*, that which does not recruit a farmer to make a soldier out of him, corrupt him and convert him into an enemy of the worker or into an enemy of his own farmer-brother, but, rather, converts the soldier into a defender of the rights of his brothers, the farmers and the workers, instead of converting him into a defender of the privileged classes.

Democracy is *this*, that which does not divide the humble people into factions by setting some against others.

Democracy is *this*, in which a government finds the force of the people and unites it. Democracy is *this*, that which makes a people strong by uniting them.

Democracy is *this*, that which gives a gun to the farmers, gives a gun to the workers, gives a gun to the students, gives a gun to the women, gives a gun to the Negroes, gives a gun to the poor, and gives a gun to any other citizen who is willing to defend a just cause.

Democracy is *this*, that which not only takes the rights of the majority into account, but also gives arms to this majority. Only a government truly democratic can do this. This can be done only by a government truly democratic, a government where the majority governs.

... But (all) this does not mean that the rights of others are not taken into account. The rights of others count just as the rights of the majority count, in proportion to the extent to which the rights of the majority count, but the *rights* of the majority should prevail above the *privileges* of minorities.

This true democracy, this democracy to which no one can object, this sincere and honest democracy, is the democracy that has existed in our country since the first of January, 1959. This democracy has been expressed directly in the close union and identification of the government and the people, in this direct relationship, in this working and fighting in favor of the majority of the country and in the interests of the great majority of the country. This direct democracy we have exercised here has more purity, a thousand times more purity, than that false democracy that uses all the means of corruption and fraud to falsify the true will of the people.

Our democracy today has prevailed in this direct way, because we are in a revolutionary process. Tomorrow will be as the people desire, tomorrow will be as the necessities of the people demand, as the aspirations of our people demand, as the interests of our people demand. Today there is a direct relation between the people and the government.

When the revolutionary process has gone far enough and the people understand that we are approaching new procedures—and the revolutionary government will always understand this just as the people understand it—then the people and the government will adopt whatever procedure the circumstances of a consolidated and victorious revolution demand of you and of us.

... Our enemies, our detractors, ask about elections. Even one Latin American leader, the chief of state of one Latin American nation, has declared recently that the Organization of American States should be made up of only those countries whose leaders are chosen by electoral processes. As if a true Revolution like this in Cuba could come into power disregarding the will of the people! As if the only democratic procedure for taking over power were the electoral processes so often prostituted to falsify the will and the interests of the people and so many times used to put into office the most inept and most shrewd, rather than the most competent and the most honest.

As if after so many fraudulent elections, as if after so much false and treacherous politicking, as if after so much corruption, the people could be made to believe that the only democratic procedure for a people to choose their leaders were the electoral procedure. And as if *this* procedure were not democratic—this procedure through which a people choose their leaders not with a pencil, but with the blood and the lives of 20,000 fellow patriots, struggling without arms against a professional and well-armed army, trained and outfitted by a powerful foreign country.

The people of Cuba broke their chains and, by breaking the chains that enslaved them, they put an end to the (unfair) privileges, they put an end to the injustices, and they put an end forever, to the practice of criminal abuse (of the citizens by the government).

The people of Cuba have begun a true democratic phase of progress, of liberty, of justice. If there is any process in which the incompetent fall behind, if there is any process in which the crooked fail, that is the revolutionary process.

In the revolutionary process, virtue opens a way for itself, merit prospers, and conniving, greed, and cheating fail. In a process of revolutionary struggle, as in no other struggle, only the strong men—those with true convictions and absolute loyalty—can stay in the ranks.

And a revolutionary process does not mean only the insurrectional phase of the war. The real revolution comes later. The rebellion of our people brought about the war. The creative spirit of our people has brought about the revolution.

For this reason we said that in Cuba a true democracy is very much at work, despite the allegations of the enemies of our revolution.

At this time what is the principal job we Cubans have ahead of us? What is it that every Cuban should know today? Why is our job fundamental now? What are the reasons for which our country sees itself threatened by aggression? What has the revolution done but good to its people? What has the revolution done but justice? What has the revolution done but defend the interests of the large majority of our people, of the most humble classes of our country—those who constitute the immense majority and who not only make up the majority with a right of their own to count in the destinies of our country, but who, furthermore, are also the part of our country that has suffered most? What has the revolution done but defend those who are not only the majority but are furthermore the exploited part of our country?

Where is the crime in fighting for the people? Where is the crime in wanting the farmer to have land? Where is the crime in giving land to the farmers? How is it a crime to fight for the people, to do what the revolution has done for the people? What the revolution has done for the people is given testimony by the presence here of this crowd, a crowd of flesh and bone, real men and women of the people, who came here spontaneously, who came here paying their own expenses, who came here from different places by travelling all night long and marching for a whole day, standing on foot during an entire day, under the sun, without drinking water, without eating. The presence of such a great crowd is the best proof that the revolution has fought for the people.

. . . That is the reality of our revolution. And why? What do they [the enemies of the revolution] want to punish in our revolution? They want to punish the example. Why do they want to defeat the Cuban Revolution at all costs? By any chance is it because we take anything away from them or because we represent any danger to any other country or because we want to exploit any other country? Is it because we want to make decisions about matters that are not our own? No.

They want to destroy the Cuban Revolution so that the example of the Cuban Revolution can not be followed by the sister nations of Latin America.

What everybody knows is that they want at all costs to destroy our revolution. They have sentenced our revolution to death simply so that the farmers of Latin America, the workers of Latin America, the students of Latin America, the intellectuals of Latin America, and the very peoples of Latin America should not follow the example of Cuba and should not someday carry out a Land Reform in all those countries and make a revolution in all those countries. They want, simply, to destroy our revolution in order to continue exploiting the other nations of Latin America.

In that way they want our Cuban people to "pay the freight" on the crimes that are being committed against other peoples. They want us to pay the price for them to be able to exploit other peoples. That is to say, they want to destroy us, because we have had the desire to liberate ourselves economically. They want to destroy us because we have desired to do justice. They want to destroy us because we have concerned ourselves with the humble of our land, because we have cast our lot with the poor of our country, because we have remembered the *guajiro* who had no land, because we have remembered the child who had no school, because we have remembered the worker who had no job, because we have remembered the family who lived in a hut, because we have remembered the sick who had no doctor, because we have remembered the student who had no books and no resources. Because we have remembered justice.

As though certain people of the world were obliged to live in wretchedness, backwardness, and exploitation! As though certain nations were obliged to wear a yoke over their shoulders and around their necks! As though certain nations were obliged to be slaves of others!

They want to destroy us because our people have desired to break the chains; because our people desire to progress; because our men, our women, our young people, and our old people want justice; because (we all) want to enjoy our work and want to live happily and in peace on land which is our own. We had the misfortune that one day foreign hands took possession of our lands, foreign hands took possession of our mines, foreign hands took possession of our natural resources and of our public utilities.

We had the misfortune that foreign hands took possession of our economy, of our politics, and of our destiny. They want to destroy us because this generation of Cubans has set for itself the great and honorable task of liberating our country from these bonds, of liberating our country from this exploitation.

Only for this, which is fair and which is a right about which nobody—neither Cubans nor any other people—can argue with us, they want to destroy us.

They want to destroy us because we want to make our own decisions, because we want to live our own lives, because we want to plan our own future, and because we want to attain our own happiness, without doing any harm to any other people. What we want is to live in peace and friendship with all the other peoples of the world.

No matter what sacrifice we have to face, we will do it happily, because that will be the greatness of this generation of Cubans and that is what *Patria o Muerte* means. It means that to take our country away from us, it is necessary first to take our lives away from us.

We are determined to have a worthy country and to leave a worthy country to the coming generations. Those three words, *"Patria o Muerte"* express the will of a people. Those three words say everything we have to say.

... It is not possible to destroy a revolution like this—a revolution with such extraordinary support from the people, a revolution that defends a cause so just, a cause that has the solidarity of all the men of revolutionary thinking of the American continent.

The most reasonable, the most sane, the most intelligent thing that could be done by those who do not want to resign themselves to this revolution would be exactly to resign themselves, because this revolution is a reality. It would be intelligent for them to leave us in peace. Otherwise, in the senseless attempt to destroy the revolution, they will lose much more than they have already lost.

Realities do not arise in the world through someone's whim. Revolutions, real revolutions, do not arise by the will of one man or one group. Revolutions are realities that obey other realities. Revolutions are remedies—bitter remedies, yes. But at times revolution is the only remedy that can be applied to evils even more bitter. The Cuban revolution is a reality in the world. The Cuban revolution is already a reality for the history of the world.

The Cuban revolution is a reality just as the people's support of it is a reality, just as the guns that can defend it are realities, just as the men who are willing to die for it inside Cuba and outside Cuba are realities.

Revolution and Solidarity

... And we believe it is necessary that revolutionary ideas prevail. If revolutionary ideas should be defeated, the Revolution in Latin America would be lost or would be indefinitely delayed. Ideas can hasten a process—or they can considerably delay it. And we believe that this triumph of revolutionary ideas among the masses—not all the masses, but a sufficiently vast part of them is absolutely necessary. This does not mean that action must wait for the triumph of ideas, and this is one of the essential points of the matter. There are those who believe that it is necessary for ideas to triumph among the masses before initiating action, and there are others who understand that action is one of the most efficient instruments for bringing about the triumph of ideas among the masses.

Whoever stops to wait for ideas to triumph among the majority of the masses before initiating revolutionary action will never be a revolutionary. For, what is the difference between such a revolutionary and a latifundium-owner, a wealthy bourgeois? Nothing!

Humanity will, of course, change; human society will, of course, continue to develop—in spite of human beings and the errors of human beings. But that is not a revolutionary attitude.

If that had been our way of thinking, we would never have initiated a revolu-

From Fidel Castro, *Revolucion Solidaridad,* (n.p.), (n.d.)—a speech delivered by Castro at the First Conference of the Organization of Latin American Solidarity, on August 10, 1967, pp. 19-21.

tionary process. It was enough for the ideas to take root in a sufficient number of men for the revolutionary action to be initiated, and, through this action, the masses started to acquire these ideas; the masses acquired that consciousness.

It is obvious that in Latin America there are already in many places a number of men who are convinced of such ideas, and that have started revolutionary action. And what distinguished the true revolutionary from the false revolutionary is precisely this: one acts to move the masses, the other waits for the masses to have a conscience already before starting to act.

... This does not mean that one has to go out and grab a rifle, and start fighting tomorrow, anywhere. That is not the question. It is a question of ideological conflict between those who want to make revolution and those who do not want to make it. It is the conflict between those who want to make it and those who want to curb it. Because, essentially, anybody can realize if it is possible, or if conditions are ripe, to take up arms or not.

No one can be so sectarian, so dogmatic, as to say that one has to go out and grab a rifle tomorrow, anywhere. And we ourselves do not doubt that there are some countries in which this task is not an immediate task, but we are convinced that it will be their task in the long run.

There are some who have put forward even more radical theses than those of Cuba; that we Cubans believe that in such and such a country are no conditions for armed struggle, but they claim that it is not so. But the funny thing is that it has been claimed in some cases, by representatives who are not quite in favor of the theses for armed struggle. We will not be angered by this. We prefer them to make mistakes trying to make revolution without the right conditions than to have them make the mistake of never making revolution. I hope no one will make a mistake! But nobody who really wants to fight will ever have discrepancies with us, and those who do not want to fight, ever, will always have discrepancies with us.

ernesto che guevara

The twentieth century American *condottiere*, Ernesto Guevara, was born in 1928 in Rosario, Argentina. He was the oldest of the five children of Celia de la Serna, of an aristocratic family, and Ernesto Guevara, then in the maté-growing business in Misiones Province. A sickly child who suffered from asthma, Ernesto moved to Buenos Aires, where his father entered the ship construction business, and then, at the age of four, to the resort town of Alta Gracia, a move prescribed by the doctor. The senior Ernesto dedicated the following years to improving his son's health and stamina and, as well, to discussing the current social and political issues. His mother also made known her strong feelings about Yankee exploitation and oppression of the poor.

A bright young man, Che led his class in primary school, although frequently absent because of ill health. The Guevara family moved to Cordoba in 1941, and Che entered high school, already an activist and adventurer, eager to discuss Marx and organize his fellow students and denounce the Church. In 1947 he entered premedical studies at the University of Buenos Aires and through his mother met many leading Argentine Marxists. Also during these years, strongly interested in the Argentine nation, he participated in anti-Perón riots. During his travels through Argentina and Chile, he became further embittered by the exploitation of the Indians by mining companies. Receiving his M.D. degree in 1953, Che hitchhiked through Ecuador and Panama, up to Nicaragua, and became increasingly enraged over the poverty, hunger, and exploitation along the highways. Cursing God and the United Fruit company, Che moved on to Guatemala City and sold encyclopedias. The next year he met members of the 26th of July Movement, a Cuban group which had attacked government forces in Cuba in 1953, and became an admirer of Fidel Castro.

At this time, Che was probably not a Communist; in fact, when he applied to the Ministry of Health in Guatemala for permission to join the hospital staff in Totonicapán, he was told he must first join the Communist Party and he refused. Nevertheless when the Arbenz regime was overthrown in Guatemala in 1954, Che expressed his admiration for that government. Moving on to Mexico, he continued his discussions with young revolutionary exiles, including Fidel Castro, and his brother Raul; soon he became the guerrilla group's doctor. Because he called his friends "Che," which means "buddy" in Argentine, Guevara was given the nickname "Che." In 1955 Che married Hilda Gadea, a Peruvian exile who had been active in Peru's Aprista Youth Movement and whom he had met in Guatemala City in 1954; she too had gone to Mexico soon after the Arbenz regime fell.

On December 2, 1956, the guerrilla group invaded Cuba, and fought their way to the Sierra Maestra, where twenty of the original eighty-two men survived. Continuing the struggle, the Cuban revolutionaries broke out of the Sierra Maestra area in the summer of 1958 into the Escambray Hills. In January 1959 they took Havana, where the new Cuban Council of Ministers made Che Guevara a Cuban citizen. Several months later, he divorced Hilda and married Aleida March, a member of the revolutionary expedition. He journeyed through Africa, Asia, and Europe during the summer of 1959. Soon after his return, he was appointed to head the Industrial Department of the National Institute of Agrarian Reform (INRA), and also became president of the National Bank of Cuba.

During the years which followed, Che's philosophical influences on the revolutionary movement grew as he argued that leaders must change man before they can build a socialist economy: they must emphasize that workers should find personal satisfaction in working for the goal of the community. Eager to abolish the discrimination of the past, he sought a classless society while recognizing that the emergence from a society based upon material rewards would take much time and effort. Soon, however, the new society would be achieved through love and sacrifice, and the twenty-first century man would arrive.

In 1965, Che's whereabouts became a matter of public speculation. In fact, he travelled to Vietnam, the Congo, and, in 1966 to several Latin American countries including Guatemala, Venezuela, and Peru. He also visited Argentina in 1967 before going on to Bolivia, where he entered another revolution. He was captured by Bolivian troops in October, and apparently was executed or died of wounds the next day. Thus ended the life of a unique American theoretician of the Marxist-Leninist school. Violence silenced another restless revolutionary.

On Sacrifice and Dedication*

A REVOLUTION like ours, a people's revolution, made by the will of the people, for the people, cannot advance unless each conquest, each step forward, is taken by the full mass of the public, by the entire mass of the people. And to take those steps, and take them enthusiastically, you must know the revolutionary process, you must know that those steps must be taken, and that they must be taken gladly. And you also have to know, whenever you make a sacrifice, why you are making it, because the road to industrialization, which is the road to collective well-being in this age of economic empires, isn't an easy one. On the contrary, it is an exceedingly difficult road.

And I would like to say still more. As all the rebellions and popular movements in all the underdeveloped regions of the world challenge the most aggressive exponent of economic imperialism, the United States of America, that power is going to turn with even more force on its nearest and most rigidly dominated territory, which is, obviously, America; and within America, that *mare nostrum* of theirs, which is the Caribbean. . . .

The Sin of the Revolution**

REVOLUTIONS, accelerated radical social changes, are made of circumstances; not always, almost never, or perhaps never can science predict their mature form in all its detail. They are made of passions, of man's fight for social vindication, and are never perfect. Neither was ours. It committed errors and some of these were paid for dearly. Today we know of another error, which did not have

*From Ernesto Che Guevara, *Venceremos! The Speeches and Writings of Ernesto Che Guevara,* edited by John Gerassi, Simon and Schuster, New York, 1968, p. 92. Reprinted with permission of The Macmillan Company (Copyright 1968 by John Gerassi). The speech was delivered on June 18, 1960 in Havana.

**From *Venceremos!* pp. 127, 129-130. The speech was delivered on February 12, 1961.

repercussions, but which demonstrates how true are the popular sayings, "water seeks its own level," and "birds of a feather flock together."

... From the first days serious differences arose which at times culminated in an exchange of violent words; but always our proper revolutionary wisdom prevailed, and we gave way for the sake of unity. We maintained the principle. We did not allow any stealing, nor did we give key posts to those who we knew had treachery on their minds. However, we did not eliminate them; we temporized—all for the benefit of a unity which was not properly understood. This was a *sin of the Revolution.*

This was the same sin that paid off very well for the Barquíns, Felipe Pazos, Teté Casuso, and so many more sinecure holders whom the Revolution kept on to avoid confrontation, trying to buy their cooperation with a tacit understanding between those who were paid off and a government which they were waiting for the right moment to betray. But the enemy had more money and more methods of subverting the people. After all, what could we offer to people like Fleitas and Menoyo, except a job demanding work and sacrifice?

Those men, who lived off the legend of a struggle, in which they did not participate, deceiving the people, looking out for jobs, trying always to be where money was, pushing into all the ministerial cabinets, deprecated by all true revolutionaries, these men were an insult to our revolutionary consciences. Constantly, by their presence, they showed us our sin—the sin of compromise in the face of the lack of revolutionary spirit, in the face of the actual or potential traitor, in the face of those weak in spirit, in the face of the coward, in the face of the bully.

Our conscience has been cleansed now because they have gone in boats to Miami. Thank you, "bully boys" of the second front. Many thanks for relieving us of the execrable presence of makeshift comandantes; of captains of jest; of heroes ignorant of the rigors of campaigns but not of the easy shelter of peasants' houses. Thanks for giving us this lesson, for showing us that one cannot buy consciences with favors from the revolution. This lesson is strict and exacting for all. Thanks for showing us that we must be inflexible in the face of error, weakness, deceit, bad faith; that we must stand up to denounce and punish wherever we find any vice which sullies the high principles of the Revolution. . . .

On Party Militancy

. . . A few months ago—just a few—we had to transfer a capable female official at the Ministry of Industry. Why? Because she had a position that often required her to go out into the provinces with inspectors or with the head, the director-general. This comrade, who was married (I believe to a member of the Rebel Army), could not go out alone; her husband would not consent to it. She had to make all her trips subject to her husband's being able to leave his job and accompany her to whatever place she had to go.

This is a boorish example of discrimination against women. Does a woman perchance have to accompany her husband each time he has to go into the interior or any other place so that she can watch him, lest he succumb to temptation or something of that sort?

What does this indicate? Well, simply that the past continues to weigh upon us and that the liberation of women should consist of the achievement of their total freedom—their *inner* freedom. It is not a matter of a physical restriction which is placed on them to hold them back from certain activities. It is also the weight of a previous tradition.

We are living in a new era, an era in which a socialist society is being created. All forms of discrimination are being swept away, and the only remaining dictatorship that counts is the dictatorship of the working class—the class organized on top of the classes that have been defeated. There is still a long way ahead of us that will be full of struggle and unpleasantness until we achieve the perfect society, which is the classless society—the society in which all differences will disappear. At our present stage no other dictatorship but the dictatorship of the proletariat as a class is acceptable.

The proletariat has no sex: It is all men and women taken together, who at all places of work in the nation, struggle consistently to reach a common goal.

This is an example of all there is to do. But naturally, it is only one example among many. Many things remain to be done. Without our going back to the time before the triumph of the Revolution, there are still many traditions belonging to the later past, that is, the past that pertains to our prerevolutionary history.

Whoever aspires to be a leader has to be able to face or, rather, expose himself to the verdict of the masses. He must be confident that he has been chosen or proposed as a leader because he is the best of the good—on account of his work, his spirit of sacrifice, and his constant sense of belonging to the vanguard in all

From *Venceremos!* pp. 241-243. The speech was delivered on March 24, 1963.

the struggles the proletariat must carry on daily in order to create a socialist society.

This still weighs us down. Our organizations are not totally free of this sin that has become part of our very young revolutionary traditions and has begun to do harm. We must banish totally everything that means thinking that being elected a member of some organization of the masses or of the ruling party of the Revolution—being chosen a leader in one of the Revolution's different activities—permits a comrade to enjoy the slightest opportunity to get something more than the rest of the people. We refer, in other words, to the policy of rewarding excellence with material things, to rewarding with material things the one who has shown greater conscientiousness and spirit of sacrifice.

There are two things that are constantly conflicting and dialectically becoming part of the process of creating a socialist society. On the one hand, material incentives are made necessary by our having emerged from a society that thought of only material incentives, and we are creating a new society on the foundation of that old society through a series of transformations in the minds of the people of that old society. On the other hand we still do not have enough to give each individual what he needs. For these reasons, interest in material things will be with us for a time during the process of creating a socialist society.

But precisely for this reason the function of the vanguard party is to raise the opposite banner as high as possible—the banner of interest in nonmaterial things, the banner of nonmaterial incentives, the banner of men who sacrifice and hope for nothing but recognition by their comrades. Such is the approval you have shown today to the comrades you have chosen to become part of the Partido Unido de la Revolución.

Material incentives are something left over from the past. They are something that we must accept but whose hold on the minds of the people we must gradually break as the revolutionary process goes forward. One type of incentive is definitely on the rise; the other must definitely be on the way to extinction. Material incentives will not play a part in the new society being created; they will die out as we advance. We must establish the conditions under which this type of motivation that is operative today will increasingly lose its importance and be replaced by nonmaterial incentives such as the sense of duty and the new revolutionary way of thinking. . . .

Man and Socialism in Cuba

DEAR COMRADE:

I am finishing these notes while traveling through Africa, moved by the desire to keep my promise, although after some delay. I should like to do so by dealing with the topic that appears in the title. I believe it might be of interest to Uruguayan readers.

It is common to hear how capitalist spokesmen use as an argument in the ideological struggle against socialism the assertion that such a social system, or the period of building socialism upon which we have embarked, is characterized by the extinction of the individual for the sake of the state. I will make no attempt to refute this assertion on a merely theoretical basis, but will instead establish the facts of the Cuban experience and add commentaries of a general nature. I shall first broadly sketch the history of our revolutionary struggle both before and after taking of power.

As we know, the exact date of the beginning of the revolutionary actions which were to culminate on January 1, 1959, was July 26, 1953. A group of men led by Fidel Castro attacked the Moncada military garrison in the province of Oriente, in the early hours of the morning of that day. The attack was a failure. The failure became a disaster and the survivors were imprisoned, only to begin the revolutionary struggle all over again, once they were amnestied.

During this process, which contained only the first seeds of socialism, man was a basic factor. Man—individualized, specific, named—was trusted and the triumph or failure of the task entrusted to him depended on his capacity for action.

Then came the stage of guerrilla warfare. It was carried out in two different environments: the people, an as yet unawakened mass that had to be mobilized, and its vanguard, the guerrilla, the thrusting engine of mobilization, the generator of revolutionary awareness and militant enthusiasm. This vanguard was the catalyst which created the subjective condition necessary for victory. The individual was also the basic factor in the guerrilla, in the framework of the gradual proletarianization of our thinking, in the revolution taking place in our habits and in our minds. Each and every one of the Sierra Maestra fighters who achieved a high rank in the revolutionary forces has to his credit a list of noteworthy deeds. It was on the basis of such deeds that they earned their rank.

It was the first heroic period in which men strove to earn posts of greater responsibility, of greater danger, with the fulfillment of their duty as the only

From *Venceremos!* pp. 387-388, 397-400. This letter to Carlos Quijano was written in early 1965.

satisfaction. In our revolutionary education work we often return to this instructive topic. The man of the future could be glimpsed in the attitude of our fighters.

At other times of our history there have been repetitions of this utter devotion to the revolutionary cause. During the October Crisis and at the time of the hurricane Flora, we witnessed deeds of exceptional valor and self-sacrifice carried out by an entire people. One of our fundamental tasks from the ideological standpoint is to find the way to perpetuate such heroic attitudes in everyday life.

The revolutionary government was established in 1959 with the participation of several members of the "sell-out" bourgeoisie. The presence of the rebel army constituted the guarantee of power as the fundamental factor of strength.

Serious contradictions arose which were solved in the first instance in February 1959, when Fidel Castro assumed the leadership of the government in the post of Prime Minister. This process culminated in July of the same year with the resignation of President Urrutia in the face of mass pressure.

With clearly defined features, there now appeared in the history of the Cuban Revolution a personage which will systematically repeat itself: the masses.

This multifacetic being is not, as it is claimed, the sum total of elements of the same category (and moreover, reduced to the same category by the system imposed upon them) and which acts as a tame herd. It is true that the mass follows its leaders, especially Fidel Castro, without hesitation, but the degree to which he has earned such confidence is due precisely to the consummate interpretation of the people's desires and aspirations, and to the sincere struggle to keep the promises made.

The mass participated in the agrarian reform and in the difficult undertaking of the management of the state enterprises; it underwent the heroic experience of Playa Girón; it was tempered in the struggle against the groups of bandits armed by the CIA; during the October Crisis it lived one of the most important definitions of modern times, and today it continues to work to build socialism.

. . . The large multitudes of people are developing themselves, the new ideas are acquiring an adequate impetus within society, the material possibilities of the integral development of each and every one of its members make the task ever more fruitful. The present is one of struggle; the future is ours.

To sum up, the fault of many of our intellectuals and artists is to be found in their "original sin": They are not authentically revolutionary. We can attempt to graft elm trees so they bear pears, but at the same time we must plant pear trees. The new generations will arrive free of "original sin." The likelihood that exceptional artists will arise will be that much greater because of the enlargement of the cultural field and the possibilities for expression. Our job is to keep the present generation, maladjusted by its conflicts, from becoming perverted and perverting the new generations. We do not want to create salaried workers docile to official thinking or "fellows" who live under the wing of the budget, exercising freedom in quotation marks. Revolutionaries will come to sing the song of the new man with the authentic voice of the people. It is a process that requires time.

In our society the youth and the party play a big role. The former is particularly important because it is the malleable clay with which the new man, without any of the previous defects, can be formed.

Youth receives treatment in consonance with our aspirations. Education is increasingly integral, and we do not neglect the incorporation of the students into work from the very beginning. Our scholarship students do physical work during vacation or together with their studies. In some cases work is a prize, while in others it is an educational tool; it is never a punishment. A new generation is being born.

The party is a vanguard organization. The best workers are proposed by their comrades for membership. The party is a minority, but the quality of its cadres gives it great authority. Our aspiration is that the party become a mass one, but only when the masses reach the level of development of the vanguard, that is, when they are educated for communism. Our work is aimed at providing that education. The party is the living example; its cadres must be full professors of assiduity and sacrifice; with their acts they must lead the masses to the end of the revolutionary task, which means years of struggle against the difficulties of construction, the class enemies, the defects of the past, imperialism.

I should now like to explain the role played by the personality, the man as the individual who leads the masses that make history. This is our experience, and not a recipe.

Fidel gave impulse to the Revolution in its first years, he has always given it leadership and set the tone, but there is a good group of revolutionaries developing in the same direction as Fidel and a large mass that follows its leaders because it has faith in them. It has faith in them because these leaders have known how to interpret the longings of the masses.

It is not a question of how many kilograms of meat are eaten or how many times a year someone may go on holiday to the seashore or how many pretty imported things can be bought with present wages. It is rather that the individual feels greater fulfillment, that he has greater inner wealth and many more responsibilities. In our country the individual knows that the glorious period in which it has fallen to him to live is one of sacrifice; he is familiar with sacrifice.

We first came to know it in the Sierra Maestra and wherever there was fighting;

later we have known it in all Cuba. Cuba is the vanguard of America and must make sacrifices because it occupies the advance position, because it points out to the Latin American masses the road to full freedom.

Within the country, the leaders have to fulfill their vanguard role; and it must be said with complete sincerity that in a true revolution, to which you give yourself completely without any thought for material retribution, the task of the vanguard revolutionary is both magnificent and anguishing.

Let me say, with the risk of appearing ridiculous, that the true revolutionary is guided by strong feelings of love. It is impossible to think of an authentic revolutionary without this quality. This is perhaps one of the great dramas of a leader; he must combine an impassioned spirit with a cold mind and make painful decisions without flinching. Our vanguard revolutionaries must idealize their love for the people, for the most hallowed causes, and make it one and indivisible. They cannot descend, with small doses of daily affection, to the terrain where ordinary men put their love into practice.

The leaders of the Revolution have children who do not learn to call their father with their first faltering words; they have wives who must be part of the general sacrifice of their lives to carry the Revolution to its destination; their friends are strictly limited to their comrades in revolution. There is no life outside the Revolution.

In these conditions the revolutionary leaders must have a large dose of humanity, a large dose of a sense of justice and truth, to avoid falling into dogmatic extremes, into cold scholasticism, into isolation from the masses. They must struggle every day so that their love of living humanity is transformed into concrete deeds, into acts that will serve as an example, as a mobilizing factor.

The revolutionary, ideological motor of the Revolution within his party, is consumed by this uninterrupted activity that ends only with death, unless construction be achieved on a worldwide scale. If his revolutionary eagerness becomes dulled when the most urgent tasks are carried on a local scale, and if he forgets about proletarian internationalism, the revolution that he leads ceases to be a driving force and it sinks into a comfortable drowsiness which is taken advantage of by imperialism, our irreconcilable enemy, to gain ground. Proletarian internationalism is a duty, but it is also a revolutionary need. This is how we educate our people.

It is evident that there are dangers in the present circumstances. Not only that of dogmatism, not only that of the freezing up of relations with the masses in the midst of the great task; there also exists the danger of weaknesses in which it is possible to incur. If a man thinks that in order to devote his entire life to the Revolution, he cannot be distracted by the worry that one of his children lacks a certain article, that the children's shoes are in poor condition, that his family lacks some necessary item; with this reasoning, the seeds of future corruption are allowed to filter through.

In our case we have maintained that our children must have, or lack, what the children of the ordinary citizen have or lack; our family must understand this and struggle for it. The Revolution is made by man, but man must forge his revolutionary spirit from day to day.

Thus we go forward. Fidel is at the head of the immense column—we are neither ashamed nor afraid to say so—followed by the best party cadres, and right after them, so close that their great strength is felt, come the people as a whole, a solid bulk of individualities moving toward a common aim; individuals who have achieved the awareness of what must be done; men who struggle to leave the domain of necessity and enter that of freedom.

That immense multitude is ordering itself; its order responds to an awareness of the need for order; it is no longer a dispersed force, divisible in thousands of fractions shot into space like the fragments of a grenade, trying by any and all means, in a fierce struggle with their equals, to achieve a position that would give them support in the face of an uncertain future.

We know that we have sacrifices ahead of us and that we must pay a price for the heroic fact of constituting a vanguard as a nation. We, the leaders, know that we must pay a price for having the right to say that we are at the head of the people that is at the head of America.

Each and every one of us punctually pays his share of sacrifice, aware of being rewarded by the satisfaction of fulfilling our duty, aware of advancing with everyone toward the new human being who is to be glimpsed on the horizon.

Allow me to attempt to come to some conclusions:

We socialists are more free because we are more fulfilled: We are more fulfilled because we are more free.

The skeleton of our complete freedom is formed, but it lacks the protein substance and the draperies. We will create them.

Our freedom and its daily sustenance are the color of blood and swollen with sacrifice.

Our sacrifice is a conscious one: It is in payment for the freedom we are building.

The road is long and in part unknown; we are aware of our limitations. We will make the twenty-first-century man; we ourselves.

We will be tempered in daily actions, creating a new human being with a new technology.

The personality plays the role of mobilization and leadership in so far as it incarnates the highest virtues and aspirations of the people and does not become detoured.

The road is opened up by the vanguard group, the best among the good, the party.

The basic raw material of our work is the youth: In it we place our hopes and we are preparing it to take the banner from our hands.

If this faltering letter has made some things clear, it will have fulfilled my purpose in sending it.

Accept our ritual greetings, as a handshake or an "Ave María Purísima."

Patria o muertes

camilo torres

Camilo Torres Restrepo was born in Bogotá in 1929 to Isabel Restrepo Gavira, a descendant of one of Colombia's oldest aristocratic families, and Calixto Torres Umava, a pediatrician. Sickly, and the youngest of four children, Camilo lived for a time in Belgium and Spain before returning to Colombia. He received private tutoring until the age of eight, and then began his studies in a German school in Bogotá. Rebellious, restless, and energetic, he established a school newspaper before he was ten years old. When the school closed because of World War II, he transferred several times before earning his bachelor's degree. After a brief career in journalism, he entered the diocesan seminary in Bogotá.

Camilo was eager to continue further studies in the social teaching of Roman Catholicism, and entered Louvain University in 1954 shortly after his ordination to the priesthood. After receiving a master's degree, he remained at Louvain and guided other Latin-American students enrolled there. Strongly influenced by his association with Abbé Pierre, the European priest of the homeless, he sought to comfort the lonely and suffering people in France. In 1958 he returned to Colombia and enrolled in doctoral studies in sociology. His research covered contemporary social and economic problems in Bogotá. Although he did not complete his dissertation, he was appointed lecturer and chaplain at the National University of Bogotá and continued to probe the bases of Colombian society.

Sympathetic to the work of student activists at the National University,

Camilo complained vehemently when the government halted a student strike and expelled ten students. His growing popularity and the tension of the situation caused the archbishop to ask for his resignation from the University. Camilo then began establishing cooperative farm community centers while serving as dean of the Institute of Social Administration. Moreover, he continued to produce scholarly sociological articles, and presented one at the Second International Congress of Pro Mundi Vita in Louvain in 1964. He was convinced that Christians must take the lead in bringing about significant changes in poor countries, and became willing to collaborate with Marxists if necessary in order to improve society.

Back in Colombia he became increasingly certain that a revolutionary movement was necessary to bring about political and social reforms. By the end of February 1964 he had designed a platform for all those dedicated to reforming Colombia. He urged the unions, peasant leagues, Indians, and middle-class youth to join a United Front of Popular Movements and labor for greater social and economic equality. In May his archbishop, Cardinal Concha Córdoba, pointed out the differences between Church doctrine and Camilo's platform. And, during June, Camilo moved toward confrontation as he leveled charges against the wealth and power of twenty-four Colombian families, Yankee imperialists. He called for power for the people, and proclaimed, "Long live the revolution." After his exhortation that Church properties be expropriated, he finally requested laicization, which was promptly granted.

During July he met Fabio Vásquez Castaño, who commanded guerrilla armies called the Army of National Liberation (ELN) in central Colombia. Together they sought means to insure the success of the United Front. Camilo edited a weekly newspaper, *Freñte Unido*, and served as well on picket lines and in strikes. Serious factions split the Front and increased his mounting frustration. Finally Camilo joined the ELN as a soldier in mid-October and fought to remove the injustices he had studied as a student and priest. Four months later, in February 1965, he was killed during a skirmish with a government patrol. His death unified the Front for a time as he became a popular symbol of the revolution against imperialism not only in Latin America but throughout the Third World.

Christianity, Communism, and Revolution

. . . Because of the traditional relationship between Christians and Marxists, between the Church and the Communist Party, suspicions and erroneous suppositions could arise with respect to the relationship established in the United Front between Christians and Marxists and between a priest and the Communist Party. For this reason, I think it necessary that my relationship with the Communist Party and its position within the United Front remian quite clear to the Colombian people.

I have said that, as a Colombian, as a sociologist, as a Christian, and as a priest, I am a revolutionary. I feel that the Communist Party has elements that are authentically revolutionary and because of that I cannot, either as a Colombian, or as a sociologist, or as a Christian, or as a priest, be anti-Communist. I am not anti-Communist as a Colombian because anti-Communism is oriented towards persecuting non-conformist compatriots, Communist or not, of whom the majority are the poor. I am not anti-Communist as a sociologist because in the Communist plan of fighting poverty, hunger, illiteracy, lack of housing and services for the people, effective and scientific solutions are to be found. I am not anti-Communist as a Christian because I believe that anti-Communism makes a blanket condemnation of everything Communists defend, and there are both just and unjust things in what they defend. In condemning them all we are condemning the just and the unjust equally, and this is anti-Christian. I am not anti-Communist as a priest because even though the Communists themselves do not know it, there are many among them who are truly Christian. If they are of good faith, they can have sanctifying grace; and if they have sanctifying grace and love their neighbor, they will be saved. My role as a priest, even though I do not exercise the external rite, is to try to lead men to God, and the most effective way to do this is to lead men to serve their neighbors according to their consciences,

I have no intention of proselytizing my Communist brothers, trying to get them to accept the dogma and to practice the cult of the Church. But this I am certainly working towards, that all men act according to their conscience, sincerely seek the truth, and love their neighbor in an effective way. The Communists must well know that I will not join their ranks, that I am not, nor will I be a Communist, either as a Colombian, or as a sociologist, or as a Christian, or as a priest. However, I am ready to fight alongside them for common goals: opposing the oligarchy and the domination of the United States, in order to take power for the popular class.

From Camilo Torres, *Revolutionary Writings*, New York, 1969, pp. 173-174, 189-191, 201-203. Reprinted with permission of Herder and Herder, Inc.

... The grass-roots union of the popular class is a simple matter. The hungry, the unemployed, the insecure, the poor, the uneducated identify themselves easily with concrete political objectives and especially with the main objective which is the seizing of power for the Colombian popular class.

The organization of the popular class has come about much more easily and quickly than it was thought. The organizational precedents left by the union, the cooperative, communal action, and so forth have helped. But the basic thing is the desire of the people to organize themselves. "Necessity is the mother of invention." The people have realized that organization is the basis of the revolutionary movement. For this reason they have succeeded in overcoming the feelings of inferiority, timidity, and apathy. The farmers and workers have begun to feel directly responsible for the Revolution and have therefore begun, without awaiting orders from above, to organize themselves into groups of three, five, ten, or more.

The organization of the grass-roots is a fact, and more and more of a fact each day. Among the leaders and intellectuals it is a different story. They are being cautious and thoughtful. But fortunately, while the "revolutionary intellectuals" are cudgeling their brains seeking "the exact formula" for the Colombian Revolution on the shelves of the libraries, the people have found this formula through their suffering and their awareness of being exploited, persecuted, and humiliated.

The United Front of the People is composed of the organized political movements that have approved the platform for struggle and of all Colombians (Liberals, Conservatives, Anapists, Lopists, the M.R.L., hard-liners, Communists expelled or not, organized or not, Christian Democrats, Nationalists, Independents, and so forth) who approve of this platform.

We need to unite the oppressed against the oppressors. But in Colombia the majority of the oppressed do not belong to organized political groups. They are the non-aligned, who on the whole want the Revolution but are not organized.

What then is the principal duty of the revolutionaries who are much more conscientious, more organized, and more aligned, not so much with their group but with the Colombian Revolution? It is to organize the non-aligned, to make them align themselves. And this must be the primary concern of the United Front. Is it necessary for them to become Christian Democrats, Communists, Emerrelists, or Anapists? Is not the main objective to have them align themselves with the Colombian Revolution? If they do not wish to join an already existent opposition group, are we going to prohibit them from taking part in the Revolution? By what right? By right of the majority? Not at all, because they are the majority. By right of being better prepared? This can only be judged on the basis of facts, not identification cards or declarations. History will be the judge. For now, let us have mutual respect, and rather than seek honor and high position in the revolutionary hierarchy, let us dedicate ourselves to the Revolution. Let us dedicate ourselves to organizing those who are not organized. Let us call them whatever they wish to be called: "Non-aligned," "Aligned with the United Front," "Revolutionaries." Although I do not approve of personality sway over and above all considerations of organization, if this is subordinated to the ideal of the organization, we can accept it for now. If the people wish to be called "Camilists," then let them, on the condition that they organize. It is not a question of forming a new party or a new movement, but rather a new organization of the unorganized to get them to align themselves with the United Front and the Revolution. But let us not oblige them to adopt new titles if they do not wish to.

It is logical that "at high levels" differences arise. Let us not get too worked up over this; let us just get on with the Revolution. The people will be the ones to decide on the name of the non-aligned. The people will decide if, in the future, they will form another party. For now the task is to convince them to form a new organization that will become part of the United Front. In the task of forming this organization all true revolutionaries and all members of the United Front of the People must join forces.

. . . For many years the poor of our country have awaited the battle cry to throw themselves into the final struggle against the oligarchy.

At those moments when the desperation of the people was extreme, the ruling class always found a way to fool the people, to distract them, pacifying them with new formulas which always had the same end: the suffering of the people and the well-being of the privileged caste. When the people sought a leader and found one in Jorge Eliecer Gaitan, the oligarchy murdered him. When the people sought peace, the oligarchy sowed violence in the country. When the people could no longer tolerate this violence and organized guerrillas to take power, the oligarchy staged a military operation so that the misled guerrillas would become involved. When the people called for democracy, they were again fooled by a plebiscite and a National Front which imposed the dictatorship of the oligarchy.

Now the people will no longer believe. The people do not believe in the elections. The people know that the legal means have been exhausted and that no means remain but to arm. The people are desperate and resolved to risk their lives so that the next generation of Colombians will not be enslaved. So that the sons of those who are willing to give their lives may have an education, a roof over their heads, clothing, food, and above all *dignity*. So that future Colombians will have a country of their own, free of North American jurisdiction.

Any sincere revolutionary must realize that armed struggle is the only means that remains. However, the people are waiting for the leaders to give, by their example and their presence, the battle cry.

I wish to tell the Colombian people that the moment has come. That I have not betrayed you. That I have gone from city to town campaigning for the unity and organization of the popular class for the take-over of power. That I have asked that we all devote ourselves to these objectives, even at the risk of death.

Now everything is ready. The oligarchy wants to stage another farce of an election: with candidates whom they renounced and now accept, with bipartisan committees, with a renovation movement based on ideas and personalities who are not only old but who have betrayed the people. What more are we waiting for, Colombians?

I have joined the armed struggle. I plan to continue the struggle from the Colombian mountains with a weapon in my hand until power has been won for the people. I have joined the Army of National Liberation because in it I found the same ideals as those of the United Front. Because I found the desire for and realization of a unity within the grass roots, without regard to party or religious differences, without any spirit of antagonism among the various revolutionary elements, without bossism. Because I found that it seeks to liberate the people from the exploitation of the oligarchy and of imperialism. That it will not lay down its arms while the power is not wholly in the hands of the people. That in its objectives it accepts the platform of the United Front.

All patriotic Colombians ought to place themselves on a war footing. Little by little experienced guerrillas will appear all over the country. Meanwhile, we must be alert. We must gather arms and ammunition, seek guerrilla training, confer with one another, gather clothing, drugs, and provisions, and prepare ourselves for a prolonged struggle.

Let us make small strikes against the enemy wherever victory seems assured. Let us test all those who call themselves revolutionaries and weed out the traitors. Let us not hesitate to act, but let us not be impatient. In a prolonged war everyone will have to take part in the action at some point. The important thing is that at that precise point everyone will be equipped and ready. There is no need for everyone to do everything; we must divide the work. The militants of the United Front must be the vanguard of initiative and action. Let us have patience in the confidence and expectation of final victory.

The people's struggle must be a national struggle. We have already begun, for the march is long.

Colombians: we must not hesitate to respond to the call of the people and of the Revolution.

Militants of the United Front: let us make our assignments realities:

For the unity of the popular class, unto death!

For the organization of the popular class, unto death!

For the seizure of power for the popular class, unto death!

Unto death because we have decided to continue to the end.

Unto victory because a people that is devoted unto death always obtains its victory.

Unto final victory with the assignments of the Army of National Liberation:

Not one step in retreat!

Liberation or death!